THE PASSPORT IN AMERICA

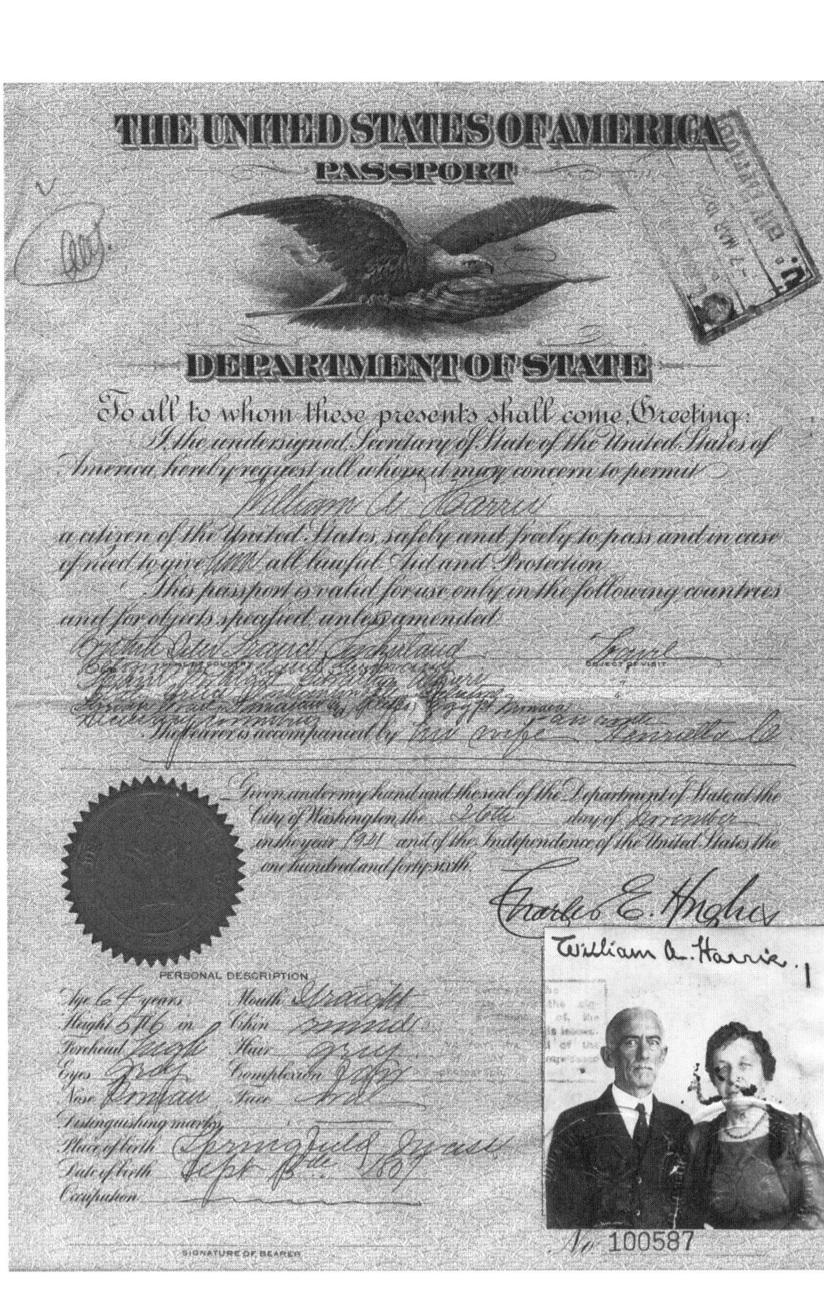

THE UNITED STATES OF AMERICA

PASSPORT

DEPARTMENT OF STATE

To all to whom these presents shall come, Greeting:

I, the undersigned, Secretary of State of the United States of America, hereby request all whom it may concern to permit

William A. Harris

a citizen of the United States, safely and freely to pass and in case of need to give him all lawful Aid and Protection.

This passport is valid for use only in the following countries and for objects specified, unless amended.

NAME OF COUNTRY | OBJECT OF VISIT

The bearer is accompanied by his wife

Given under my hand and the seal of the Department of State at the City of Washington, the 26th day of November in the year 1921 and of the Independence of the United States the one hundred and forty-sixth.

Charles E. Hughes

William A. Harris

PERSONAL DESCRIPTION

Age 64 years | Mouth Straight
Height 5 ft 6 in | Chin round
Forehead | Hair gray
Eyes gray | Complexion fair
Nose | Face oval
Distinguishing marks
Place of birth Springfield Mass
Date of birth Sept 8th
Occupation

SIGNATURE OF BEARER

No 100587

THE PASSPORT IN AMERICA

THE HISTORY OF A DOCUMENT

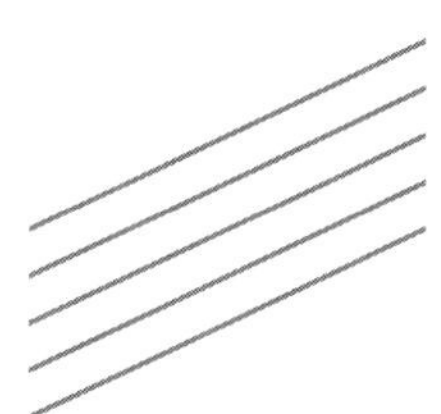

Craig Robertson

OXFORD
UNIVERSITY PRESS
2010

OXFORD
UNIVERSITY PRESS

Oxford University Press, Inc., publishes works that further
Oxford University's objective of excellence
in research, scholarship, and education.

Oxford New York
Auckland Cape Town Dar es Salaam Hong Kong Karachi
Kuala Lumpur Madrid Melbourne Mexico City Nairobi
New Delhi Shanghai Taipei Toronto

With offices in
Argentina Austria Brazil Chile Czech Republic France Greece
Guatemala Hungary Italy Japan Poland Portugal Singapore
South Korea Switzerland Thailand Turkey Ukraine Vietnam

Published by Oxford University Press, Inc.
198 Madison Avenue, New York, New York 10016

www.oup.com

Some of the material within appeared previously in
Craig Robertson, "Four Documents, a Non-Citizen, and Diplomatic Controversy:
The Documentation of Identity in the Mid-Nineteenth Century."
Journal of Historical Sociology 22 (2009): 476–496. Permission obtained.

Craig Robertson, "A Documentary Regime of Verification: The Emergence of the U.S.
Passport and the Archival Problematization of Identity."
Cultural Studies 23 (2009): 329–354. Permission obtained. ISSN 0950-2386

Library of Congress Cataloging-in-Publication Data
Robertson, Craig.
The passport in America : the history of a document / Craig Robertson.
p. cm.
Includes bibliographical references and index.
ISBN 978-0-19-973342-2
1. Passports—United States—History.
2. Citizenship—United States—History. I. Title.
KF4794.R63 2010
342.7308'2—dc22 2009049008

1 3 5 7 9 8 6 4 2

Printed in the United States of America
on acid-free paper

Acknowledgments

Numerous people have helped me along the way with the thinking and writing that has become this book. Its early life took place at the University of Illinois, Urbana-Champaign. While I have little fondness for those towns I have a great deal of affection for the people I met when I lived there as a graduate student, many of whom continue to challenge me intellectually. I am privileged to be able to thank Cameron McCarthy, John Nerone, James Hay, Antoinette Burton, and Toby Miller for their enthusiasm for the project and for giving me the intellectual freedom to initially pursue it. The arguments and ideas in this book simply could not have come to exist without another group of five people—Ted Bailey, Jack Bratich, Mary Coffey, Sammi King, and Jeremy Packer—who while technically fellow graduate students also took on the role of teachers and mentors to me, especially when I returned to graduate school after a two-year break.

During my time in Urbana-Champaign and subsequently in Boston the support of other friends and colleagues has been invaluable: Tony Ballantyne, Marcus Breen, Kevin Bruyneel, Alexis Burson, Murray Forman, Kelly Gates, Jullily Kohler-Hausmann, Marie Leger, Marina Levina, David Marshall, Dan McGee, Mark Nimkoff, Mary O'Donaghue, Joanne Morreale, Victor Pickard, Vincent Rocchio, Ben Scott, Simone Sidwell, Rob Sloane, Gretchen Soderlund, Beth Starr, Alan Zaremba, and especially Rachel Dubrofsky. I am also fortunate to have as current department colleagues two people who also somehow managed to make it from the University of Illinois to Northeastern University; David Monje and Kumi Silva continue to give me the support and understanding that only close friends can.

At different stages of the writing of what became this book some colleagues and friends provided particular assistance that I am very happy to acknowledge. At the very beginning Tony Ballantyne, Charis Thompson, and especially Lacey Torge helped me to figure out what history of the passport I wanted to write. Kelly Gates, Marie Leger, and Rob Sloane read the first hesitant attempts at putting thoughts on paper in that ugliest of genres, the draft dissertation chapter. Mark Andrejevic, Rachel Hall, Josh Lauer, and Chris Russill, through conversation and their own writings, sharpened my ideas as dissertation became book manuscript. I am grateful to Laura Frader and Carla Kaplan for their insightful suggestions on how to translate my arguments into an effective book proposal.

Research assistance in the form of financial support came from the Institute of Communications Research and the Graduate College of the University of Illinois at Urbana-Champaign, the Babson College Board of Research, and the Office of the Provost, the College of Arts and Sciences, and the Department of Communication Studies at Northeastern University. I received fantastic support from the Interlibrary Loan departments at Babson College, Northeastern University, and especially the University of Illinois. Other critical research support came in the form of the generous hospitality of Rob and Robin Wilder, who let me stay for many months in their house while I researched at National Archives in Washington, D.C., and Maryland. Ben Scott and Jenny Wustenberg also provided hospitality and accommodation during a brief mopping up visit to National Archives. Elizabeth Pryor was generous enough to give me access to her dissertation. The friendly staff at Caffe Paradiso in Urbana, Victrola on Capitol Hill in Seattle, and especially 1369 Coffee House in Inman Square in Cambridge indirectly provided writing support by letting a non–coffee drinker sit and write for long hours—I should add I have cultivated a tea-drinking habit, and I like to think I tip well.

I am very grateful to Susan Ferber at Oxford University Press for initially seeing the value of an interdisciplinary history of the passport in the United States. Most importantly, I appreciate her understanding during a very difficult time in my life. Jessica Ryan and Ben Sadock ensured the manuscript made it through the production process in better shape than it went in. I am also grateful to Jane Caplan and Adam McKeown for their generous and insightful reviews (and for identifying themselves, in what I take to be the spirit of this project).

My thanks and gratitude also go to my friends far away in New Zealand who, while they have never read a word of this, have provided their support in numerous ways: Sally Aitken, Bridget Byers, Paula Cody, Donald Reid, and Judith Holloway. Also far away are my family, who have provided a constant source of generosity, love, and confidence: Yvonne, Lisa, and Campbell; Grant and Alf; Stephen, Delwyn, and Cleo. As I was revising this book my father, Doug, died unexpectedly. Like all my family he fully supported everything I did but it is fair to say that he definitely championed me in his own unique way. That he will never get to hold this book nor be around to see what my future holds is something I continue to struggle with.

During this difficult time, and more frequently in happier times, I have also been fortunate enough to have the support of another family, the Shackelfords: Sarah, Dwayne, Jack, Ryan, Rhiana, and especially Jim and Janet.

Two people deserve somewhat more detailed thanks. I cannot thank my brother, Stephen, enough. On a practical level his expertise as a twentieth century U.S. historian meant he always had a book or journal article to point me to when I had written myself into a corner, and he was a steady source of strategic advice on how to develop this project. But more importantly his support and enthusiasm for this book have known no limits. I simply can't imagine how I would have completed this book without him.

Finally, but adhering to the conventions of academic acknowledgments by no means least, is Erin Shackelford. She is the person who shows me what matters in life, from her tireless efforts to help the underpaid and overworked get the respect their labor deserves to her unbelievable ability to know exactly what to say, or when to walk away, regardless of the situation. In terms of this project through conversation and probing questions she continually convinced me that a history of the passport could actually be interesting. More importantly Erin was there for the emotional roller coaster that was the backdrop as I completed this book. As well as experiencing the death of my father we have also experienced the joy of the birth of our daughter, Edie, and the wonderful first two years of her life. For all these things and more I thank you Erin, my best beloved and best friend.

Contents

THE PASSPORT IN AMERICA

Introduction

> The paradigmatic scene, perhaps of the modern era . . . is that of the immigration officer examining a passport. This is a scene which is both obvious and fathomless. Obvious is the enforced obligation of having an identity as this or that person; fathomless, and therefore insidious, is the method of proving, that—which?—identity.
>
> —Dieter Hoffmann-Axthelm, "Identity and Reality: The End of the Philosophical Immigration Officer"

In 1923 the *New York Times* published a brief Associated Press article about a Danish man who had recently visited Germany. He had arrived sporting a large up-turned moustache, which he soon shaved off upon discovering that "the Kaiser Wilhelm brand of upper lip decoration is not popular in the very modern commercial city of Hamburg." However, the Dane encountered a problem when, at the completion of his visit, he attempted to leave Germany. According to the article, "The heavily mustached chap on his passport photograph did not in the least resemble the smooth-faced modern appearing Dane. Passport officials turned him back and detectives gave him the third degree. In his changed appearance they found resemblance to a famous international swindler." Apparently "ashamed" of his failure to resemble himself, the unnamed Dane did not seek the assistance of Danish officials. Instead he chose to grow a new moustache, which the article confidently predicted "[would] enable him to measure up to his passport photograph." This article, one of a handful from the period that recounts the problems shaving purportedly created for male passport bearers, reads today as somewhat bizarre, if not perhaps a little preposterous.[1] While it may indeed be out of step with our contemporary understanding of official identification practices, and even if the events did not occur exactly as reported, the article accurately captures some of the cultural and social tensions that existed around the documentation of individual identity in the early decades of the twentieth century when travelers and immigrants first encountered universal demands for a passport. This book explores these tensions to offer a history of the emergence of the passport as an identification document in the United States. The informal introduction of official attempts to systematically use documents to verify identity pushes the beginnings of this history back to the mid-nineteenth century; the apparent general acceptance of the necessity and accuracy of the passport as an identification document a decade after the story of the clean-shaven Dane and his passport photograph brings this history to an end in the 1930s.

The article on the Dane requires thinking about the passport as having a history distinct from immigration, travel, and state formation. This article was one among a number of articles in newspapers and magazines in the 1920s that illustrated the "passport nuisance" or "passport question," a label given to the shock and complaints from the "better classes" when they encountered passport requirements for the first time. A passport required by all travelers challenged the popular association of identification practices with marginal and suspect populations—the criminal, the insane, the poor, and, to a lesser extent, immigrants. These were populations whose behavior and appearance were believed to indicate insufficient self-control to warrant trust, populations who therefore required the state to keep track of them. In contrast, travel was not considered a behavior that demanded similar attention. Collectively, the "passport nuisance" articles located the passport within an apparent anxiety about documentation and identification. They included complaints about red tape and cost, but often these complaints were simultaneously about the apparent disregard for a person's word perceived in the demand to prove identity through documents. For the vocal opponents of the passport such a requirement implied that their government did not trust them and that the government was actually telling them who they were. The story of the Dane shows how the passport nuisance encompassed an uncertainty over identity, or more specifically the struggle to grasp a new relationship between identity and identification. How was it that a person could no longer resemble himself in the eyes of the government?

Encountering these concerns in newspapers, magazines, and later in government documents led me to think about how exactly it is that a passport identifies someone and how a passport communicates identity. For the passport to be important to immigration, for it to be a way to manage international mobility, it had to successfully function as a communication medium, as an identification document.[2] Aspects of the passport nuisance indicate that the passport did not always successfully serve as an identification document, especially when it was first encountered. Not only members of the public but officials too contested the emergence of the passport. The assumption that identity could be documented was not a given; it had to develop. As the history of the passport shows, it did so in a somewhat ad hoc fashion. From the 1840s until the 1930s a series of social, political, and cultural shifts in the United States were necessary for an acceptance of both the accuracy of and need for the documentation of individual identity that we take for granted today. How was it that a piece of paper twelve inches by eighteen inches came to be accepted as a reliable answer to the question "Who are you?"

It is impossible to locate a precise moment of origin that definitively explains why a piece of paper came to be thought of as an identification document, and, equally importantly, a document that was considered reliable and accurate enough to secure the border of a nation-state. However, it is important to recognize that the history of the "modern" passport begins when technologies and techniques were gradually added to the document in an attempt to clearly identify the bearer as a specific individual. While "passports" existed prior to the nineteenth century, they tended to be documents issued outside of any system intended to identify someone unambiguously. These documents have been traced back as far as biblical times through passages of the book of Nehemiah (Neh. 2:7–9). More frequently, the origin of such "passports" is seen in two types of documents that began to appear in the eleventh century: "safe conducts," which evolved from the requirement for visiting negotiators to be given the promise of a safe passage, and a "kings license," a document that granted permission to leave a territory. The relationship between these "passports" and a contemporary passport provides a useful continuity in a history of sovereignty and the policing of territory, or a history of state formation.[3] But there is no such easy continuity if an attempt is made to place these documents in a history of the documentation of individual identity. The premodern "passport" seemed to carry with it the *assumption* that the person presenting it was the person named in the document (if indeed they were named). Although some "passports" were issued with more detailed personal information, it was only from the end of the eighteenth century that the passport began to consistently take on a more modern role as an identification document. Two important developments in this period were particularly critical to the passport: the emergence of the nation-state as an important geopolitical entity and the appearance throughout the nineteenth century of claims to objectivity in the production of knowledge, particularly via the contested emergence of scientific and bureaucratic practices. These developments not only helped provide the context in which the passport emerged, they also contributed to the process through which identity and identification became a problem for which the passport was seen as a solution.

In the United States the modern passport developed in an ad hoc fashion in a period in which the scale of social structures dramatically changed. The nineteenth-century emergence of the United States as a modern nation-state was marked by a rapid increase in scale of territory, population, and industry. One response to this was a centralization and standardization of governing and cultural practices. Modern management and bureaucratic practices emerged, first in railroad and telegraph corporations and then more gradually in the federal government.[4] Practices of centralization and standardization are evident in developments as diverse as the introduction of time zones in 1883 and the establishment of mass-circulation magazines in the 1890s, developments in which local communities came to be increasingly defined in relation to a national community.[5] Another response to changes in scale can be seen in the questioning of the terms through which the nation had previously been collectively understood, especially the racial identity that had been used to bind "we the people." Two significant flash points for this concern and anxiety were the granting of citizenship to African Americans and the sharp increase in the arrival of immigrant labor. Concerns over the latter structured early federal interest in policing U.S. borders, which culminated in immigration restriction laws in the 1920s. In both cases the challenge to perceptions of a national identity prompted debates about how to define "whiteness" that contributed to a perception that official identification practices had to be changed. While others have written eloquently on these debates around national and individual identity, what has yet to be addressed in a sustained manner are the changing ways in which identity was recast as an object of identification in this period—specifically, the ways in which the problem of identification can illuminate understandings of individual identity and national identity in a period of racial instability, class transformation, and national volatility.

From the middle of the nineteenth century social and cultural changes caused uncertainty over how much the government actually knew about United States society.[6] Although doubt over knowledge about population and industry was never at the center of national political or cultural debates, officials did occasionally raise issues such as how the census was enacted or the need to collect statistics about the production of goods. On occasion this interest in knowing more about the country involved the problem of how to identify individuals. These moments of concern included the federal government's attempts to challenge the practice of individual states' granting U.S. citizenship, the need to identify Chinese laborers to prevent them from entering the country, and the need to identify nationalities in response to immigration restrictions. Official identification, on the rare occasion when it was addressed by officials, increasingly came to be thought of as a problem of information, specifically the need to centralize and standardize the collection of information about individuals, particularly through the use of standardized forms, designated officials, and filing systems that would assist in the retrieval of files.

For much of the nineteenth century personal knowledge continued to be privileged in official identification over documents or scientific expertise. As a result there were limited attempts to centralize the collection and storage of information in a uniform way, such as by using standardized categories and forms. Across the Atlantic Charles Dickens in *Pickwick Papers* provides a useful (albeit fictional) example of the ongoing use of localized knowledge and personal experience, rather than a system of centralized documents in the construction of an institutional memory. Dickens describes a scene in a London prison, in which a new prisoner was seated in a chair as one guard "inspected him narrowly, while two others... studied his features with most intent and thoughtful faces."[7] The prison staff referred to this procedure as "sitting for your portrait." In this example officials developed a process to produce an individual memory by which they could personally recognize a specific prisoner. While this points to the need for an identity that might have to be remembered or retrieved, it suggests that personal and "local" solutions were considered the most practicable ones for identification problems. The scale of territory and population and the increased belief that the government needed to know its population would eventually disrupt these "local" practices of identification, especially when bureaucracy emerged as a viable mechanism to collect and store knowledge.[8] But even in the closing decades of the nineteenth century, when this bureaucratic apparatus came to be used within the federal government, it encountered a mode of governing where knowledge of industry and the population was still not a universal object of concern. Occasionally departments introduced specialized divisions to collect information more systematically.[9] The attitude to the registration of births is perhaps more indicative of the dominant approach to collecting information about the objects and subjects of government. While some states had birth registration laws their enforcement was inconsistent at best. If nineteenth-century births were recorded, it was more frequently through local practices such as baptismal certificates or in family Bibles. While the early twentieth century saw more states introduce birth registration, the federal government could not claim universal birth registration in the United States until 1933.[10]

The application of official identification practices in the nineteenth century was so limited in scope that most citizens remained largely unknown to the federal government aside from possibly having their name recorded in the census; for example, federal income tax was not introduced until 1913.[11] Identification practices that did exist tended to be circumscribed by local needs and local knowledge.[12] The limited sphere in which people traveled, and significantly in which business occurred, meant that it was rare that the need for identification could not be satisfied by personal knowledge or reputation.[13] The challenge and changes to these practices likewise occurred in the form of uneven responses to specific events. When business started to become an increasingly national practice, credit reporting emerged to supplement the limitations of personal knowledge and reputation. By the last decades of the nineteenth century the nationwide demand to know an individual merchant's credit risk created one of the first nationally based bureaucratic surveillance systems.[14] Outside of the immediate demands of business the need to abandon a local mode of identification for a centralized one was seemingly less urgent. In federal elections the identity of voters and their right to vote tended to be verified through community knowledge. In rural areas the three main sources of evidence were physical appearance, the collective memory of the community, and the word of the would-be voter. Voter registration first appeared in urban areas but encountered numerous problems, including the difficulty of reading handwritten lists and of locating names on lists that were rarely alphabetized. Voter registration also did not offer an immediate solution to the verification of residence, as most cities lacked systematic criteria for identifying individual houses.[15] In courtrooms most U.S. states relied on knowledge of a person's character to authenticate handwriting. Following an English legal tradition, courts banned the comparison of two sets of writing. Disputes over the genuineness of writing were instead resolved by bringing in an acquaintance of the writer who, with knowledge of the person and a claim to having seen him/her write at least once, could testify to the authenticity of the disputed text or signature.[16] In all of these examples personal knowledge as the basis of identification eventually came to be replaced by practices based in claims to textual objectivity underwritten by the authority of "experts" and/or the rationalized collection and storage of information. This move toward objectivity and rationalization constitutes the centralization and standardization of identification in which the passport took on its modern form.

However, the emergence of the passport involves more than the development of "modern" technologies and techniques to document individual identity; it also requires a critical rethinking of identification and identity. This rethinking is part of the novelty people experienced through the passport requirements of the 1920s—an identity that allowed a person not to resemble him- or herself. Instead of an identity drawn from personal knowledge of character, reputation, or general experience, bureaucratic or objective identification practices were used to produce identity as a specific set of information. For passport applicants this information was collected in a preprinted application form, and through an array of supporting documents signed by designated officials or witnesses who had satisfied a list of criteria to verify the claims a person made in his or her application. In a critical change in identification practice, evidence had to come not from the applicant but someone who was specifically designated by a centralized authority. From the perspective of government officials this standardized procedure ensured they received the information they wanted in a format that made it easiest to process; equally importantly, it adhered to the increasingly pervasive standards of truth, accuracy, and objectivity by which officials came to measure the reliability of information.

While these new practices were intended to create more certainty in official identification, they also introduced new elements of uncertainty. The documentation of individual identity entailed skills that had to be learned. The lack of trust read into the demands to verify identity and statements with documents framed the dominant frustration many citizens had with a passport application. This occurred in a world where people actively sought to grasp how to use documents, especially those which recorded facts about their lives. Into the 1920s passport applicants struggled to understand when an individual's opinion was acceptable as evidence and which individuals were granted authority to verify the facts of identity. The initial hesitant and awkward official attempts to adequately use documents to identify individuals undoubtedly accentuated this. As the Dane's encounter with German border guards in 1923 makes clear, the documentation of individual identity was a skill that had to be learned both by the public and officials. This is further revealed in an examination of the relationship of state officials and policies to three groups: (1) citizens at home and abroad in the second half of the nineteenth century, (2) immigrants at Ellis Island and along the land borders from the 1890s through the 1920s, and (3) Americans traveling in the 1920s. This analysis originates in four previously unasked questions in U.S. history: How were identities documented? What identities did people document? Who could document identity? For what social or institutional purposes did people document identities?[17]

In response to these questions, this book produces a history of the passport as an identification document that links it to debates over both individual identity and national identity.[18] These debates reveal the historically specific reasons that official identification became a problem, and how documentation emerged as a viable and practical solution. While this history makes explicit the consequences of shifts in the way individual identity is known and measured (read from a document, not a body; verified by an outside "expert," not through self-identification), an understanding of these shifts requires an engagement with the distinct stakes raised by the equally important questions of national identity and citizenship.[19] The book divides the history of the passport into two parts to address both these developments. The first part focuses on individual identity, while the second part prioritizes national identity. Collectively the book uses the modern passport to examine what made the documentation of identity possible and what the documentation of identity made possible.

Part one provides an examination of the various technologies and techniques officials used in the attempt to "reliably" translate identity into a document: personal name, signature, physical description, photograph, application form, and seal. While the seal and the secretary of state's signature were intended to establish the authenticity of the issuing authority, the other technologies were introduced in an attempt to accurately identify the correct bearer of the document. During the nineteenth century and early decades of the twentieth century the development of each of these technologies as a viable and useful way to determine identity was contested. Documentation required a complicated rethinking of ideas of authenticity and the self, and the relationship of individual identity to the body, particularly how class, gender and race were articulated to embody privilege.

Applicants and officials alike did not initially comprehend that practices of documentation and standardization did more than merely record on paper personal or local conceptions of truth. Precision, standardization, unity, and impersonal written rules redefined reliability as the eradication of individual "bias."[20] The authority that came to underwrite the documentation of individual identity derived in part from the contested group of techniques and procedures that we now think of as bureaucratic, along with a loose borrowing of the scientific objectivity used to justify other modern identification practices such as fingerprinting. The acceptance of the authority of modern identification technologies often occurred in other realms than the passport, but some debates were a result of their application to the passport. For example, into the last quarter of the nineteenth century some passport applicants did not recognize that a personal name had to be spelled consistently to ensure that it could be used to identify a person over a period of time and via a number of documents. Those who were frustrated with the State Department's request for a standardized spelling of a personal name appeared to still understand identification primarily in terms of face-to-face interactions—a "local" logic where extradocumentary knowledge of a person and his or her identity would always trump something like the misspelling of a name in a dispute because those involved would know who was being referred to in the document. The challenge standardization posed to understandings of self and identity was made even more explicit with the introduction of a passport photograph. Photography as an identification technology had to develop a unique standardized pose distinct from the repertoire of poses photographers had borrowed from portrait painting. Many applicants thought this standardized image distorted a person's appearance.

The oft-cited comparison between a passport photograph and a criminal "mug shot" made visible the cultural association of official identification with suspect populations. This association tended to provide the most effective way for citizens to articulate their indignation at having their word and reputation challenged in the demand to provide documentary evidence that they were who they said they were. For many of these disgruntled applicants, the seemingly incongruous use of these impersonal techniques to establish something as personal as identity made them feel not like trustworthy and responsible people but rather like dehumanized "objects of inquiry." This perceived challenge both to an individual's sense of self and to the authority of a local community to know its people drove the "passport nuisance" of the 1920s. This fits with a characterization of the 1920s as a decade in which individuals experienced the sense of alienation and disenchantment understood to characterize "modernity."[21]

This anxiety and uncertainty frequently took the form of complaints that the federal government was telling someone who they were. In fact, the demands of modern documentation meant this was precisely what government officials were doing. In limiting or rationalizing the information and individuals involved in identification, officials intended to stabilize the identity required for a document. Thus it can be argued that the documentation of individual identity produced a new identity, one distinct from how people usually thought about themselves, an identity that a passport holder had to attempt to compare him- or herself to. The novelty of documentation meant that it became readily apparent to many people that to document identity meant to create a new identity—recall the clean-shaven Dane who changed his appearance as it had been fixed on his passport and was therefore declared not to be the person represented in his passport. Thus, the claim that a document could objectively and accurately verify identity resulted in practice in the confirmation of a very specific identity, one that did not exist prior to the act of documentation and was in fact created in the very act of documentation.[22]

The significance of the articulation of a new official identity through documentation, bureaucracy, and objectivity is made apparent if these practices are understood in retrospect to constitute the emergence of a "documentary regime of verification."[23] To think of identification practices constituting a regime is to recognize that the appearance of an accurate identity depends on a process of exclusion and marginalization.[24] The first part of *The Passport in America* reveals that the assumption that identity could be documented required acceptance of official documentation over more personal or local forms of identification based on different understandings of authenticity, self, and status. It necessitated the acceptance of individual identity as a bureaucratic expression and therefore the nature of the evidence used to produce/verify that identity, and of the authorities and experts who could demand and evaluate that evidence. Only with the acceptance of these three aspects of documentation would it be possible to accept that identity could be accurately documented.

The early history of the modern passport makes it evident that the relationship between identity and identification is subject to a variety of logical and historical factors. To trace the emergence of a documentary regime of verification highlights the way in which historically distinctive practices were assimilated into the identification document in the process of its elaboration. These are made even more visible when the focus moves away from how the passport was assembled to identify an individual to how the initial documentation of individual identity was deployed in the name of national identity—the focus of the second part of the book. The increased use of the passport from the mid-nineteenth century on illustrates that the documentation of individual identity was understood to serve the purpose of enforcing and policing new policies and laws intended to secure and protect the nation. From this perspective national identity is analyzed in terms of the articulation of the nation (as a cultural idea) and the state (as an administrative entity). The contested development of documentation can also be attributed to the ultimately successful attempt of the federal government to claim the authority to document individual identity as both an official identity and a nationality. This latter aspect, the documentation of citizens and aliens, underlines the increasing importance of a new complex understanding of whiteness, race, and citizenship that emerged in the name of nationality, and the need to "know" and "remember" people on these terms. The second half of the book takes episodes from the passport's development in which official interactions with certain groups revealed the stakes involved in the contested emergence of the documentation of identity. Rather than a comprehensive history of the passport in the United States, this book provides a loose chronology that follows the passport from the nineteenth century into the early twentieth century, through its critical transition from something like a letter of introduction to a certificate of citizenship to an identification document.

Part two begins in the mid-nineteenth century when the State Department sought to use the passport more effectively as a certificate of citizenship in the midst of a period of racial and national instability. These early attempts to accurately record citizenship represented both a challenge to individual states' rights to grant U.S. citizenship and an example of how in the name of objectivity the ideal of a citizen as a white (and frequently Anglo-Saxon) male property holder affected the documentation of citizenship. For example, naturalized citizens were held to more rigorous application standards than native-born citizens, and women were rarely issued passports and were instead appended to their husband's passport through the phrase "and wife." On some occasions Mormons were not issued passports on the assumption they were traveling to recruit polygamists. This use of the passport to manage difference did not go unchallenged. Free African Americans and naturalized citizens sought to exploit both the new status given to the passport as a certificate of citizenship and the hesitant if not inefficient implementation of bureaucratic techniques in its issuance. In the 1840s and 1850s, prior to the Fourteenth Amendment, free African Americans who had been granted citizenship from specific states used passport applications as part of their campaign for U.S. citizenship. Until the 1907 Citizenship Act clarified repatriation, some naturalized citizens who returned to their former homelands regularly renewed U.S. passports in order to avoid that country's demand for military duty for themselves and their sons.

The use of the passport at the U.S. border was also contested. These debates reveal the complex understanding of identity and the body that supported the conception of whiteness that underwrote U.S. national identity in this period. Until the outbreak of World War I immigration and customs officials saw little value in documents, as they believed they could adequately identify a person standing in front of them. Officials identified people by articulating them into groups—rarely were they required to identify them as individuals. Therefore, identification at the U.S. border made use of dominant understandings of the body, personal appearance, and identity that were supported by scientific and popular claims for the reliability of exterior signs to ascertain an individual's "true," essential identity; depending on the circumstances, that identity could be an individual's race, class, gender, or character. Immigration policy meant that officials only needed to become astute observers of prostitutes, "imbeciles," and potentially unproductive immigrants, either diseased or lazy. In the case of the last category immigration officials and public health officials made use of racial and ethnic stereotypes to determine potentially suspect bodies, namely "new immigrants" from southern and eastern Europe, and nonwhite immigrants, especially from Asia. Even in the early decades of the enforcement of the 1882 Chinese Exclusion Act, which employed a system of documents, officials tended to rely on bodily evidence, such as the condition of hands, to determine whether an individual was an excluded laborer or an exempt merchant. However, the prioritizing of the body over a document changed when, for security reasons, it was determined that the government needed to know the *individual* identity of the people who crossed its borders. In World War I passports and visas became necessary as officials hoped these documents would assist in identifying German spies and Bolsheviks and controlling the movement of citizens abroad. In the 1920s the aim was to secure the racial identity of the nation through enforcement of the 1921 and 1924 Immigration Acts, which restricted immigration through nationality quotas. Nationality, introduced as a response to new understandings of a hierarchy of whiteness, was determined to be an identity that was more reliably read off a document than a body. Further, it was necessary to classify specific individuals as nationals to ensure a nation's annual quota was not exceeded.

From one perspective identity had slipped off the body. Identification had become the collection of documented information about individuals. In the larger context of a bureaucratic drive to gain knowledge about society and the economy, begun in earnest during World War I, the federal government actively sought to know and remember its population as individuals. While identities had been documented in some form prior to the early twentieth century, the passport provides an object through which to understand the contested acceptance of the reliability of these documents as a move away from the excessive documentation of "the other" to the documentation of the native born, the middle class, the respectable—the more pervasive and rigorous documentation critical to the modern nation-state. While the passport was not required by all citizens, it came to represent the anxieties and uncertainties associated with the increased "paperization" of life from the 1850s into the 1920s. It was the first required identification document that many people encountered. It therefore illuminates the cultural, social, and political negotiations involved in the acceptance of the necessity for, and accuracy of, the documentation of individual identity. The passport emerged as a "reliable" identification document in the United States as an accommodation to a variety of disputes over its authority and function—from officials who viewed documents in general as a challenge to their authority, to the various groups who read the application process and the requirement to carry a passport as a questioning of their privilege, honesty, and privacy. The history of the passport as an identification document allows us to understand what was at stake in the development of the documentation of individual identity that has become so critical to modern society; the historicization of identification documents forces us to consider how it is that we have come to believe that identity can be documented.

This book offers a particular history of the passport and the documentation of identity. More generally, the modern passport, both inside and outside of the United States, has a history that parallels and follows *The Passport in America*. The introduction of a passport system in France immediately after the French Revolution is usually cited as the point of origin for the modern passport.[25] Passports were systematically issued with the intention of establishing the bearer's personal and legal identity through the use of a standardized document produced within a centralized structure. Earlier attempts to introduce a passport system occurred in some regions in the fifteenth and sixteenth centuries, but the demand for these identification documents was rarely enforced.[26] The privilege and reputation of the limited number of people who traveled frequently trumped these early passport systems, or there was no official inclination to enforce them. This is not to deny that the ideal of unambiguous documentation of individuals and complete knowledge of the population existed in certain states in early modern Europe, notably under the Spanish King Philip II. However, these remained isolated cases that existed more as aspirations. This became apparent when the authority of the document and the practice of documentation had to be negotiated anew in the nineteenth and early twentieth century before they could become ubiquitous.

Despite its limited success, the French passport system offered a model that most European states adopted at some point during the nineteenth century. These states issued identification documents during specific periods as part of regulations that separated citizens and aliens or sought to control mobility, criminality, and military desertion.[27] This arose particularly as paupers and vagabonds became the target of passport regulations introduced in the 1830s and 1840s in response to the perceived danger of unemployment and the possibility of revolution. These documents had moderate success controlling more marginal populations but this was more limited further up the social hierarchy. An 1854 travel guide, anticipating the bemusement of the English traveler at German regulations, stated that ' "to a German the passport is the proof of his existence,' whereas in England 'it was a larger kind of turnpike ticket.' "[28] Many travelers went abroad without passports, either in ignorance of regulations or with the confidence that the social and class bias in identification practices would work to their benefit. The result of the increased use of passports was, therefore, a system in which officials inspected documents with varying degrees of interest and competence.[29] This ad hoc development of the passport—sometimes a document had a physical description, sometimes it did not, frequently it functioned not as a modern passport but as a visa issued to noncitizens as an entry permit—complicates any claim for a useful continuity between medieval passports and the development of the modern passport in the nineteenth century. What emerges in the increased scale of identification documentation in the nineteenth century is a cultural negotiation over the impersonal mode of trust considered necessary to achieve this goal, which needs to be understood as part of the broader mediation of public interactions that occurred during the nineteenth century.[30] This is critical to modern identification and something that still had to be bargained for at a time when "respectability" in the form of class, race, and gender could still be relied upon to trump documents. Only once respectability could no longer be expected to better documents can significance be attributed to required passports—and this only began to occur at the turn of the twentieth century.

The United States is an important site for understanding the discontinuities between the "passports" of early modern Europe and the passports of today. Lacking Europe's history of more rigorous attempts at systematic registration and identification, the United States provides an even clearer picture of the specific problems and novelties of modern identification practices. The United States was not exempt from attempts to use documents to manage internal mobility.[31] However, these documents were not part of a system of registration nor were they the product of an application process to verify the identity of the bearer; they lacked the attempt at centralization and standardization evident in some European states. "Passports" that were permits to travel through "Indian territory" were required by treaties and occasionally issued.[32] The closest the United States had to some European systems were the documents slaveholders and states issued to police the movement of African Americans. However, while slave passes were legislated in some state slave codes these documents lacked a standardized format and were not issued in a particularly systematic manner; it was important for African

Americans to carry "passes" or "free papers" but they were not often accepted.[33] Within the federal government a slightly more rigorous system existed to issue what were known as "Mediterranean Passports" or ship passports. These did not identify individuals but, following a European tradition, they were issued with the intention of ensuring U.S. ships could sail and conduct business in the Mediterranean without interference.[34] In the context of this limited documentation of movement, the federal government issued the regular passports that are the focus of this history. While passports were not centralized in the sense of present-day databases or record keeping, officials did record the issuance of these passports; for example the State Department issued 21,792 passports from April 2, 1801, to July 22, 1850.[35] But these documents were not issued to unambiguously identify an individual, nor did they signify citizenship, as these documents could legally be issued to non-U.S. citizens. No passports were required at U.S. borders. As with many foreign states the exception was during times of war—the Civil War in the case of the United States—when passports were seen as important for policing desertion. This centrally issued passport began to change in the United States (and other countries) in the decades from the middle of the nineteenth century to the 1930s when a document for managing movement and mobility through the identification of an individual in terms of nationality was deemed necessary and the documentation of identity was ultimately made viable and practical.

The belief that identity could, and equally importantly, should be documented became a general assumption in the 1930s. The passport in the United States obviously has a history beyond the 1930s. Debates about the right to travel (notably a 1950s controversy over the refusal to give passports to accused communist sympathizers) or the need to improve border security during the so-called war on terror are two key moments in this later history.[36] By arguing for an analysis of the passport as an identification document I intend to highlight the process through which the passport acquired this authority; that is, the process through which one particular identity became accepted as the identity that individuals have to prove. For the documentation of identity to make sense and be useful, it had to be rethought within the "archival problematization of identity."[37] This was the rethinking of identity and identification that produced the identity documented in a passport, a historically specific and not inevitable response to the need to have a distinct identity. In this process identity came to be thought of as a problem of documented information intentionally collected in anticipation of future use. This "modern" understanding of an official identity, which came to be accepted by the 1930s, continues to determine the ongoing conditions for responses to the problem of identification. This is not citizenship or nationality but identity as information that can be collected, classified, and circulated, and when necessary verified through the presentation of a document.

While in the early years of the twenty-first century biometrics is presented as a more reliable set of identification practices, the claims to reliability are still understood within an archival problematization of identity. Biometrics uses computer technology to identify individuals by matching people to records through patterns derived from the measurement of facial features, iris structures, fingerprints, and voice characteristics; identity is still thought of as a problem of information and of linking that information both to a body and a file. The digitalization of identity is purported to provide a more "accurate" set of identification practices as it continues the retreat from subjectivity begun with documents. The use of computers to verify identity speaks to the fundamental problem to which identification has had to respond since the beginning of the twentieth century—the perceived need to lessen the role of individuals in the verification of identity. The authority of the documentary regime vested in the hands of bureaucratic officials has been supplanted by the more disembodied objectivity of the digital regime. The debates around the REAL ID Act of 2005 made clear the establishment of the technical and scientific authority granted to "smart cards" relative to the now apparently "dumb documents" of the twentieth century. REAL ID mandated improved security for drivers' licenses and personal identity cards through a variety of methods including the use of digital photography, secure machine-readable technology, and information-sharing practices using interlinked databases of states' departments of motor vehicles.[38] The resultant new drivers' licenses and ID cards would embed both the archive and the body into a card, thus making it "smart."

The "dumb" twentieth century passport developed within a documentary regime of verification that emerged when fallibility in identification practices was increasingly attributed to the use of local practices of self-verification or personal knowledge. The development of technologies of verification such as "smart cards," digital fingerprinting, or retina scans represents attempts to produce increasingly less fallible forms of identification in the form of a digital regime of verification. From this perspective identification is understood as a process of comparison at the level of technologies as well as usage, such that verification procedures tend to be added to preexisting practice. But whether documents or biometrics are used, the identity that experts claim these technologies verify remains an official identity made conceivable and practicable within an archival problematization of identity. This rethinking of identity was, and is still, considered to return certainty to identification by stabilizing identity as a fixed object—or more precisely, stabilizing the parameters of a new form of identity that continues to define what constitutes "accuracy" in official identification practices. With the history of the passport not well known our contemporary acceptance of the claim that identity can be documented naturalizes the passport's function as an identification document. Investigating the production, recording and usages of identity and identification by American officials and the public challenges this naturalization. This particular history illustrates that "identity" and "identification" in the sense embodied by the passport are not pre-existing facts, but were developed through specific historical processes.

Part One: Assembling the Passport

Document

In 1911 the American Jewish Committee orchestrated a campaign against the Russian policy not to accept U.S. passports presented by Jews, thus denying them entry to Russia. More precisely, the campaign was the culmination of dissatisfaction with a 1907 State Department decision not to issue passports to Jews to travel to Russia unless they had written assurance from Russian authorities that they would receive a visa. In response to this campaign at the end of 1911 the U.S. government decided to formally and publicly annul the treaty Russia had used to justify its actions.[1] The campaign had focused on the argument that adherence to the Russian policy dishonored the equality that organizers considered grounded U.S. citizenship. But due to its success the efforts of the American Jewish Committee granted the passport an unprecedented degree of public recognition as a certificate of citizenship and a national symbol. Newspapers labeled the controversy "the passport question." During the campaign, newspaper mogul William Randolph Hearst told a public meeting at Carnegie Hall,

> The point at issue, plainly stated, is simply whether the seal and signature of the United States upon a certificate of citizenship render it valid and acceptable at its face value or subject to discount in [any]...country that chooses to depreciate it. This is a point vital to the honor and integrity of this Nation. It brings up the question of whether the United States is politically solvent, whether its guarantee is good.

At the same meeting another speaker proclaimed,

> The great seal of our country affixed to that passport is represented by an American eagle holding in one outstretched talon an olive branch, denoting peace and friendship, and in the other a quiver of arrows, denoting majesty and power and implying that every resource of the Nation will be employed for the protection of the citizen who holds and rightfully uses that passport.[2]

In outlining a perceived threat to U.S. authority, the rhetorical flourishes both speakers employed indicate how a particular kind of authority can be represented in a document. To their eyes, in agreeing to the Russian practice the State Department was in fact turning a blind eye to the symbols it placed on its passport. Therefore, the speakers isolated the techniques used to imbue a piece of paper with authority to express the message they believed a passport communicated. Officials had long used signatures and seals, along with dates and artistic ornamentation, to legitimate claims on paper.[3] However, the early history of the passport in the United States indicates that the application of these techniques to a new kind of document initiated a renegotiation of their acceptance as signs of authority. As with the almost parallel development of paper money and national currency, this was largely because these symbols of authority appeared on a document intended for mass communication, not on documents intended for the records or archives of a governing institution.[4] With both paper money and the passport the authority read into these symbols had to be read anew, as standardization and the mass production of documents became critical to the transmission of a centralized authority.

In 1911 the passport became a "question" within the diplomatic realm. It was understood as a document written by an official from one country to an official from another country. The passport identified the bearer as a U.S. citizen through the authority of the secretary of state in the form of a request for safe passage addressed to whomever the bearer presented the document to. While the declaration that the bearer was a citizen led not only Hearst, but also the State Department, to label a passport a certificate of citizenship, the format of a passport reflected an often awkward articulation of citizenship, protection, reciprocity, and trust. Its early history will reveal that at different moments and places the passport functioned not only as a certificate but also as a letter, and less frequently as an identification document. The format of the passport drew its elements from these three functions. While it did have a list of physical features used to describe the bearer, a greater portion of it was devoted to establishing the authority of the document. This was achieved through identifying the author of the document—the State Department and the secretary of state, as representative of the United States of America. This identification occurred through a combination of seal, ornamentation, and signature. The personification of the United States government in the secretary of state was critical to the passport, as the text was written in the form of a request. By the twentieth century the text of the passport had taken on a standardized form, subject only to very slight tweaking (figure 1.1). Usually underneath a large eagle and the words "United States of America" was the document's salutation, "To all to whom these Presents shall come, Greeting." Beneath this the following message appeared in smaller text: "The undersigned Secretary of State of the United States of America hereby request all whom it may concern to permit safely and fairly to pass [name of bearer] a Citizen of the United States and in case of need to give him all lawful Aid and Protection." Under this a separate paragraph indented to the right further stated and explained the authority of the document: "Given under my hand and the impression of the Seal of the Department of State at the City of Washington the [date] and in the [x] year of the Independence of these United States."

The passport written as a letter acknowledged its origins in diplomatic correspondence as a request, not as a document to identify someone.[5] The form of the passport as an official open letter from the secretary of state to other state officials meant that a citizen carried the passport as a messenger, not as the owner of the document. The State Department believed a passport's authority rested on the issuing government maintaining a "paramount right over it." In response to a query as to whether a passport could be used as security for the payment of personal debt, it was clarified that the fee passport applicants paid needed to be thought of as "a tax rather than a purchase price."[6] While this comment was made in the 1930s, in a world of required passports it still locates the passport in the tradition of diplomatic letters, within the realm of courtesy that had produced letters of introduction. Although the State Department claimed ultimate ownership of the U.S. passport this did not mean that only a U.S. official could alter or change the passport. The passport was designed to accommodate additions; the international system in which the passport functioned allowed the foreign officials to whom it was addressed to record their reading of it through the stamping of a visa accompanied by their

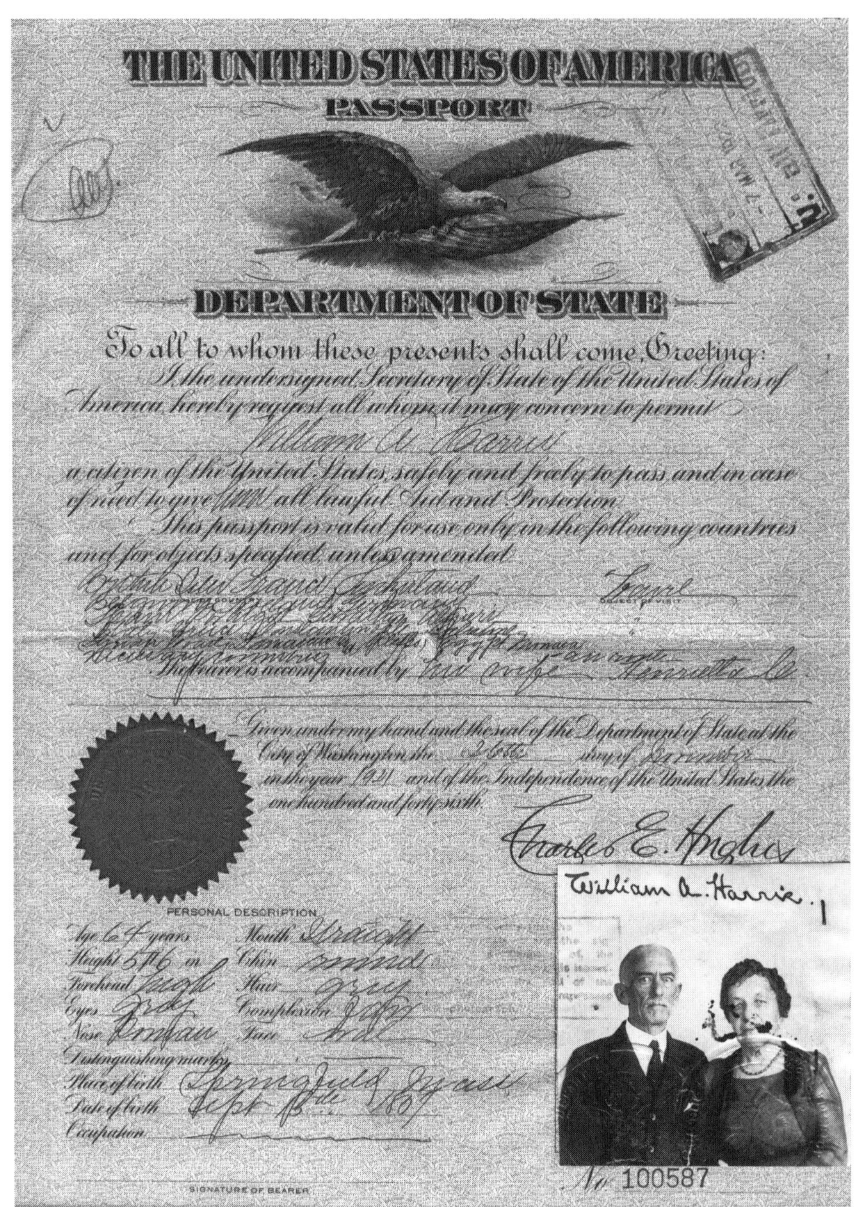

THE UNITED STATES OF AMERICA

PASSPORT

DEPARTMENT OF STATE

To all to whom these presents shall come, Greeting:

I, the undersigned Secretary of State of the United States of America, hereby request all whom it may concern to permit

William A. Harris

a citizen of the United States, safely and freely to pass and in case of need to give him all lawful Aid and Protection.

This passport is valid for use only in the following countries and for objects specified, unless amended

The bearer is accompanied by his wife

Given under my hand and the seal of the Department of State at the City of Washington the 26th day of [illegible] in the year 1921 and of the Independence of the United States the one hundred and forty-sixth.

Charles E. Hughes

William A. Harris.

PERSONAL DESCRIPTION

Age 64 years
Height 5 ft 6 in
Forehead high
Eyes gray
Nose Roman
Distinguishing marks
Place of birth Springfield Mass
Date of birth Sept [illegible]
Occupation

Mouth straight
Chin round
Hair gray
Complexion [illegible]
Face oval

SIGNATURE OF BEARER

No. 100587

Figure 1.1. Front sheet of passport issued in 1921 (collection of author).

signature, a certification that allowed a person to enter a country, as the passport itself does not perform the function of an entry document. However, the bearer of a passport could not mark the document in any way. One frustrated citizen discovered that officials considered the "one or two notes regarding foreign exchange" he had made on his passport an act of "mutilation" that made the document invalid.[7]

The passport as a letter between foreign officials was a letter making a request for protection to officials of like mind and status. In the nineteenth century officials differentiated between the passport and protection papers, which were used to communicate with "barbarous or semi-civilized states" over the principle of asylum.[8] That is, the passport as a letter of recognition needed to be "delivered" to a government that not only recognized the United States but was also recognized by the United States as a civilized state. By the twentieth century the State Department did not issue protection papers; nationalization of territory had become the marker of civilization. This created a problem when these unrecognized states increasingly required aliens to have passports. A dispute with Lithuania in the early 1920s illustrated how the State Department accommodated its understanding of the passport as an official letter to the requirements of the developing international passport system. After a complaint from Lithuanian representatives, the State Department agreed to issue U.S. passports for travel there without official recognition of Lithuania's independence from Russia on the grounds that it had always issued passports to colonies of empires without "intending to recognize them as independent states."[9]

In the context of the passport as correspondence between officials, the identity of the person making the request on behalf of the bearer was more important than the identity of the bearer. However, it is important not to overstate the extent to which a passport verified the identity of the authority that issued it. Officials issued early passports within a context of trust. At least that is the assumption that can be drawn from the lack of a standardized format through which to show that a document was indeed a passport issued by the appropriate authority, along with the limited information used to identify the bearer. Created within the realm of diplomatic correspondence, these early passports were requests issued to specific travelers usually known to the writer. Therefore, when documents called passports became more widely issued, they were limited in many cases to very brief requests related to travel. In the United States this was the case with so-called passports that authorized travel through Native American or foreign-held territory in the years immediately before and after the declaration of independence.[10] Outside of slave passes these appear to be the only documents formally required for travel in the United States. As with similar documents in Europe, there was not a sufficient infrastructure to enforce regulations. Although treaties required them to be issued by military agents or "Indian agents," governors also issued them, though people frequently traveled through the designated territories without them. Handwritten documents, they usually announced permission to enter and/or pass through territory. While these documents sometimes explained the point of the visit, the piece of paper offered no declaration of identity or citizenship. In contrast, the passports issued by the State Department at the same time did contain more information, and this difference, along with the changes in format through the nineteenth and early twentieth century, provides one insight into the contested transformation of the passport from a travel pass into an identification document.

By 1782 the passport, although not a required document, was sufficiently recognized that the Continental Congress gave the recently created Department of Foreign Affairs the responsibility to issue passports in the name of the United States. They became the subject of legislation for the first time in 1790 when Congress passed a law that provided punishment for "the violation of safe-conducts or passports issued by the U.S."[11] In the intervening eight years the adoption of the Constitution resulted in the Department of Foreign Affairs being renamed the Department of State. The earliest surviving passports issued in Washington, D.C., state the bearer is a citizen of the United States and request that he be allowed to enter foreign territories, freely move about as his "lawful pursuits may call him," and subsequently be granted, if necessary, the aid and protection that the United States would give its citizens. There is no description of the bearer, nor is "his" signature on the document. It is instead signed by the secretary of state, for it is in form and intention a letter from the secretary to support a person in his travels (figure 1.2).[12]

There are in fact extant U.S. passports that predate the ones issued in Washington, D.C. These were issued outside of the United States by representatives whom the fledging U.S. government had posted abroad from 1777. Notable among these are passports Benjamin Franklin issued while U.S. minister in France. Franklin printed these on his own press (figure 1.3). Not only did he use the text of passports the French government issued to its ambassadors, he kept the text in French. The passport requested free and safe passage for the bearer in his journey, acknowledging that any aid and assistance would be "as we would do in like circumstances for all those recommended to us."[13] The issuing of U.S. passports abroad according to the practices of the host country was not unique

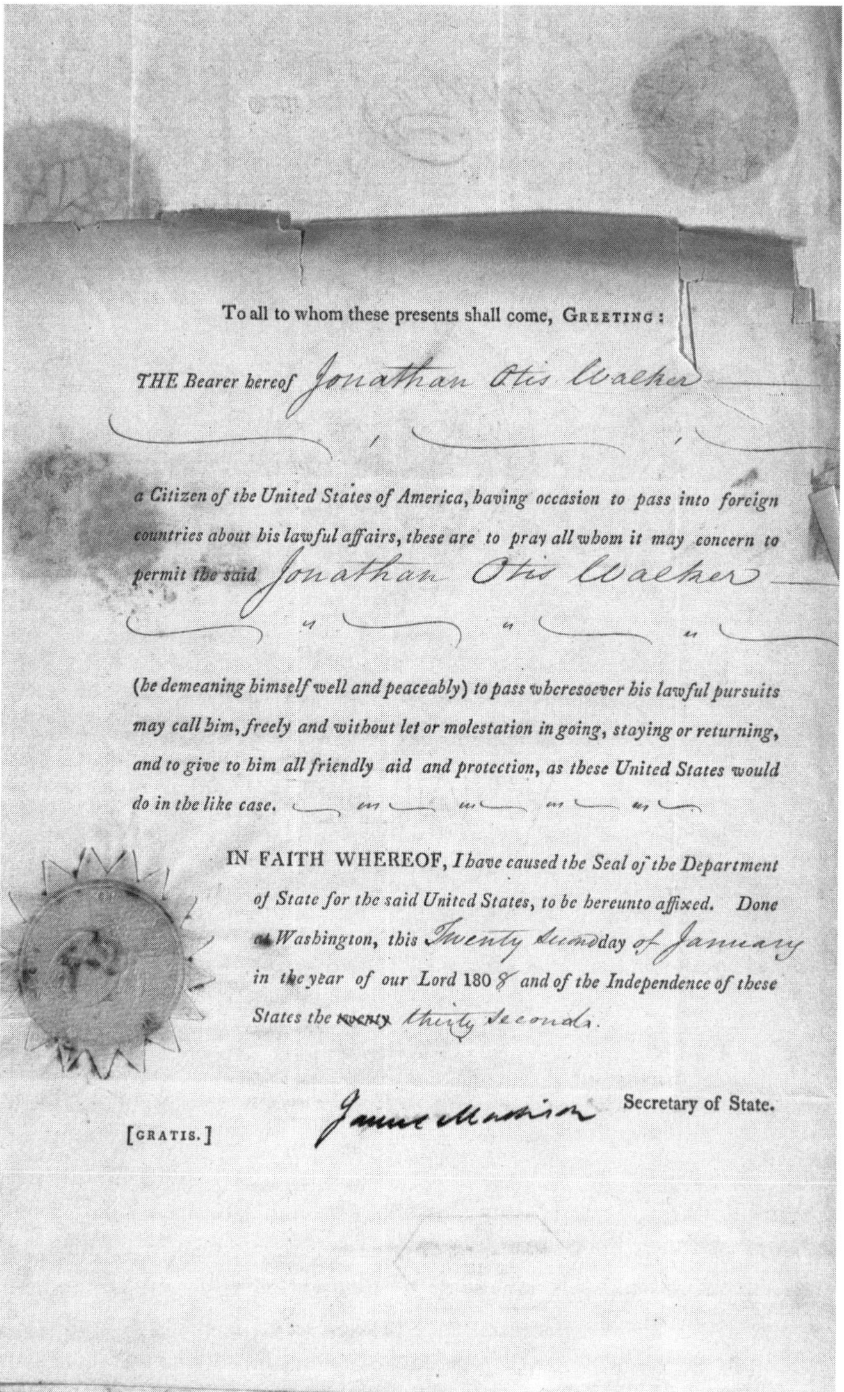
To all to whom these presents shall come, Greeting:

THE Bearer hereof Jonathan Otis Walker

a Citizen of the United States of America, having occasion to pass into foreign countries about his lawful affairs, these are to pray all whom it may concern to permit the said Jonathan Otis Walker

(he demeaning himself well and peaceably) to pass wheresoever his lawful pursuits may call him, freely and without let or molestation in going, staying or returning, and to give to him all friendly aid and protection, as these United States would do in the like case.

IN FAITH WHEREOF, I have caused the Seal of the Department of State for the said United States, to be hereunto affixed. Done at Washington, this Twenty second day of January in the year of our Lord 1808 and of the Independence of these States the ~~twenty~~ thirty second.

James Madison Secretary of State.

[GRATIS.]

Figure 1.2. Passport issued in 1808 (National Archives, College Park, MD).

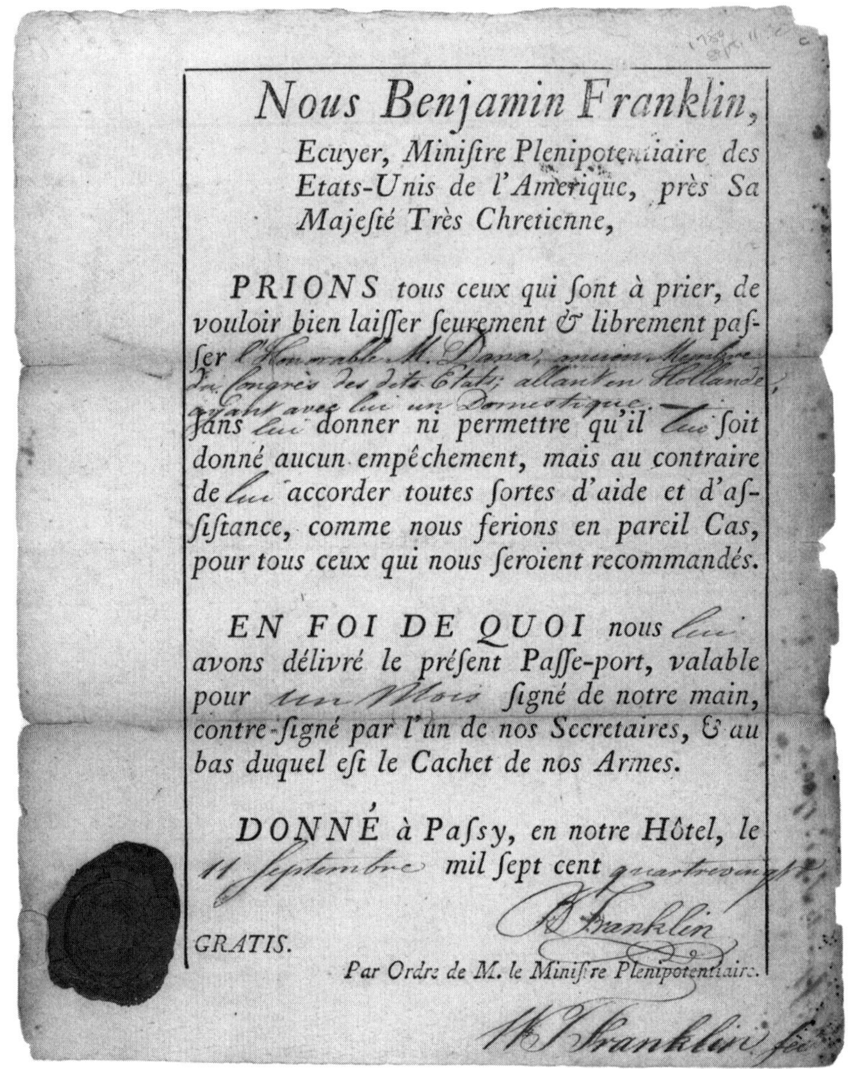

Nous Benjamin Franklin,

Ecuyer, Miniſtre Plenipotentiaire des Etats-Unis de l'Amérique, près Sa Majeſté Très Chretienne,

PRIONS tous ceux qui ſont à prier, de vouloir bien laiſſer ſeurement & librement paſſer l'Honnorable M. Dana, ancien Membre du Congrès des dits Etats; allant en Hollande, ayant avec lui un Domestique, ſans lui donner ni permettre qu'il lui ſoit donné aucun empêchement, mais au contraire de lui accorder toutes ſortes d'aide et d'aſſiſtance, comme nous ferions en pareil Cas, pour tous ceux qui nous ſeroient recommandés.

EN FOI DE QUOI nous lui avons délivré le préſent Paſſe-port, valable pour un Mois ſigné de notre main, contre-ſigné par l'un de nos Secretaires, & au bas duquel eſt le Cachet de nos Armes.

DONNÉ à Paſsy, en notre Hôtel, le 11 Septembre mil ſept cent quatrevingt,

B Franklin

GRATIS.

Par Ordre de M. le Miniſtre Plenipotentiaire.

W T Franklin sec

Figure 1.3. Passport issued by Benjamin Franklin in French in 1780 (Courtesy of the Massachusetts Historical Society).

to Franklin. Into the early decades of the nineteenth century U.S. officials abroad issued travel documents to U.S. citizens in a variety of forms; while some were technically what were then called visas, most were colloquially called passports (figure 1.4; figure 1.5).

In spite of the usefulness of bilingual documents for foreign travel the State Department only issued its passport in English. There was no law dictating that this be the case; by the twentieth century officials justified this action on the grounds that the passport as the official statement of nationality had to be issued in what they considered the national language of the United States, though an exception was made for passports issued by U.S. consuls in China.[14] In the case of travelers in Turkey the department also acknowledged the limited usefulness of the U.S. passport. It sanctioned the validity of the travel document required by local law on the grounds of its familiarity over a passport: "It is probable that in Turkey the variety of languages and races to be found in her dominions renders a foreign passport, which is in a language utterly unintelligible to local officials in districts remote from Constantinople, much less efficient and useful in protecting travelers than a Turkish teskereh, with familiar languages, seals and signatures."[15] Because many of the officials outside of China and Turkey that the secretary of state formally greeted also could not read English, the passport had to be both a document of recognition and a recognizable document. From at least the middle of the nineteenth century some State Department officials were apparently aware that, when presented with a passport in English, many foreign officials "simply look[ed] at the face of the passport" to "form an opinion of the character of the document by the emblems on the vignette and the seal."[16] Thus the importance of the appearance of the passport to the establishment of its authority provided a challenge to the sole authority of the State Department to issue U.S. passports. To the casual observer, the mere presence of a seal or ornamentation made the document official, not the specific seal or ornamentation. This became a problem when most countries continued their wartime passport requirements into the 1920s. As one U.S. consul complained "any big official looking paper written in English and bearing a pretentious seal will pass with many foreign officials for a passport."[17] Often such official looking papers were naturalization certificates or passports illegally issued by governors or mayors, but the document that caused the consul to make this comment was a membership card for the Philadelphia-based International Society for Collectors (figure 1.6). Although labeled a passport, this document bore little resemblance to a U.S. passport, yet a number of foreign officials had nonetheless affixed a visa to it during one member's 1923 vacation in Europe; other documents purportedly accepted by "ignorant sentries" included a baggage transfer check from New York's Grand Central Station and a ticket to the Polo Grounds.[18]

The passport consistently remained a "big official looking paper written in English." Its twelve-by-eighteen-inch size was not necessarily an asset to

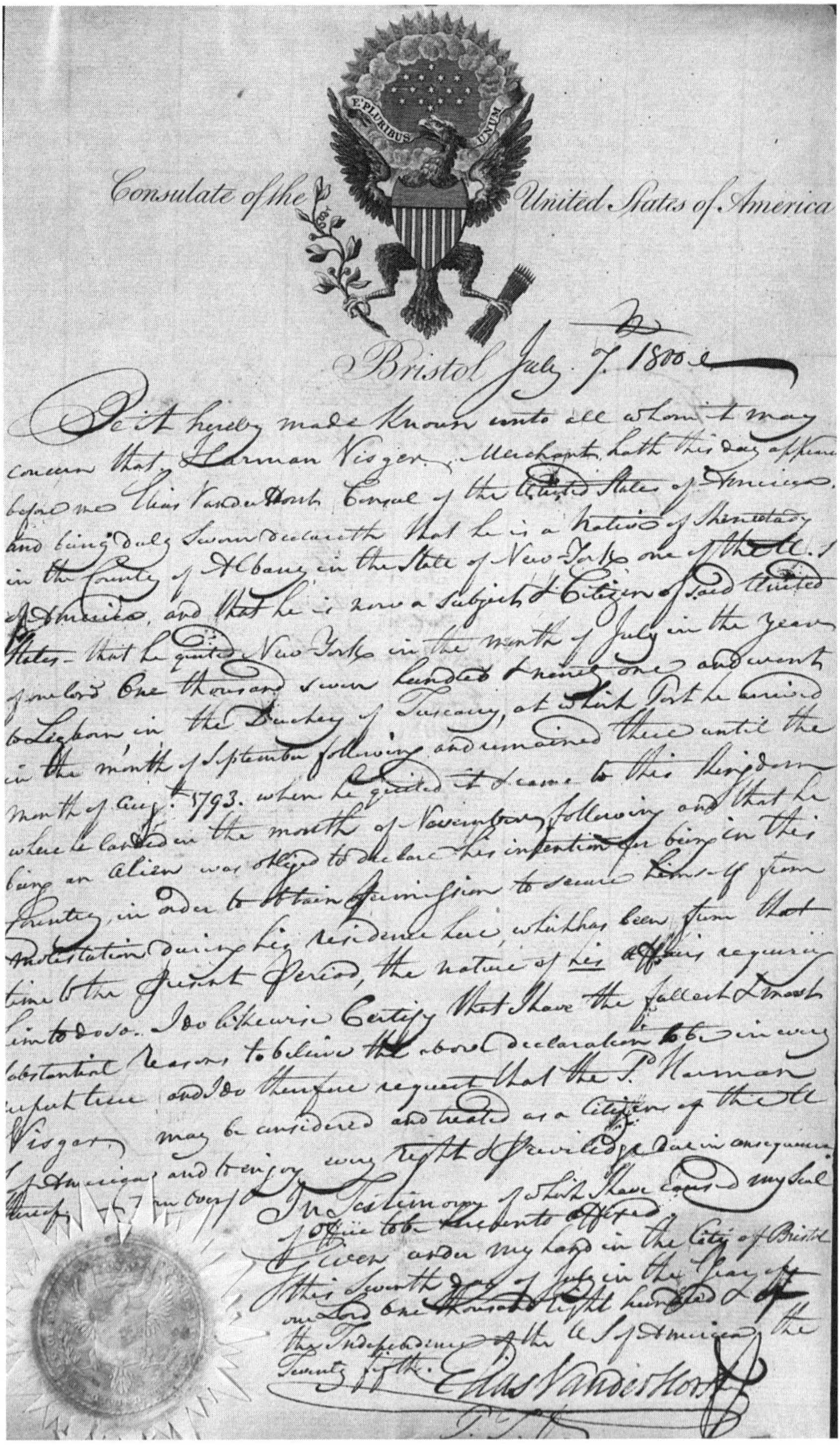

E PLURIBUS UNUM

Consulate of the United States of America

Bristol July 7. 1800

Be it hereby made known unto all whom it may concern that Harman Visger, Merchant, hath this day appeared before me Elias Vanderhorst, Consul of the United States of America, and being duly sworn declareth that he is a Native of Schenectady in the County of Albany in the State of New York one of the U. S. of America, and that he is now a subject & Citizen of said United States – that he quitted New York in the month of July in the year of our Lord One thousand seven hundred & ninety one and went to Leghorn in the Duchy of Tuscany, at which Port he arrived in the month of September following and remained there until the month of Aug.t 1793. when he quitted it & came to this Kingdom where he landed in the month of November following and that he being an alien was obliged to declare his intention for being in this Country, in order to obtain permission to secure himself from molestation during his residence here, which has been from that time to the present Period, the nature of his affairs requiring him to do so. I do likewise Certify that I have the fullest & most substantial reasons to believe the above declaration to be in every respect true and I do therefore request that the s.d Harman Visger may be considered and treated as a Citizen of the U. S. of America and to enjoy every right & privilege due in consequence thereof – Turn over

In Testimony of which I have caused my Seal of Office to be hereunto affixed

Given under my hand in the City of Bristol this Seventh day of July in the Year of our Lord One thousand eight hundred & of the Independence of the U S of America the Twenty fifth.

Elias Vanderhorst

Figure 1.4. Visa issued to U.S. citizen by U.S. consul, Bristol, England, 1800 (National Archives, College Park, MD).

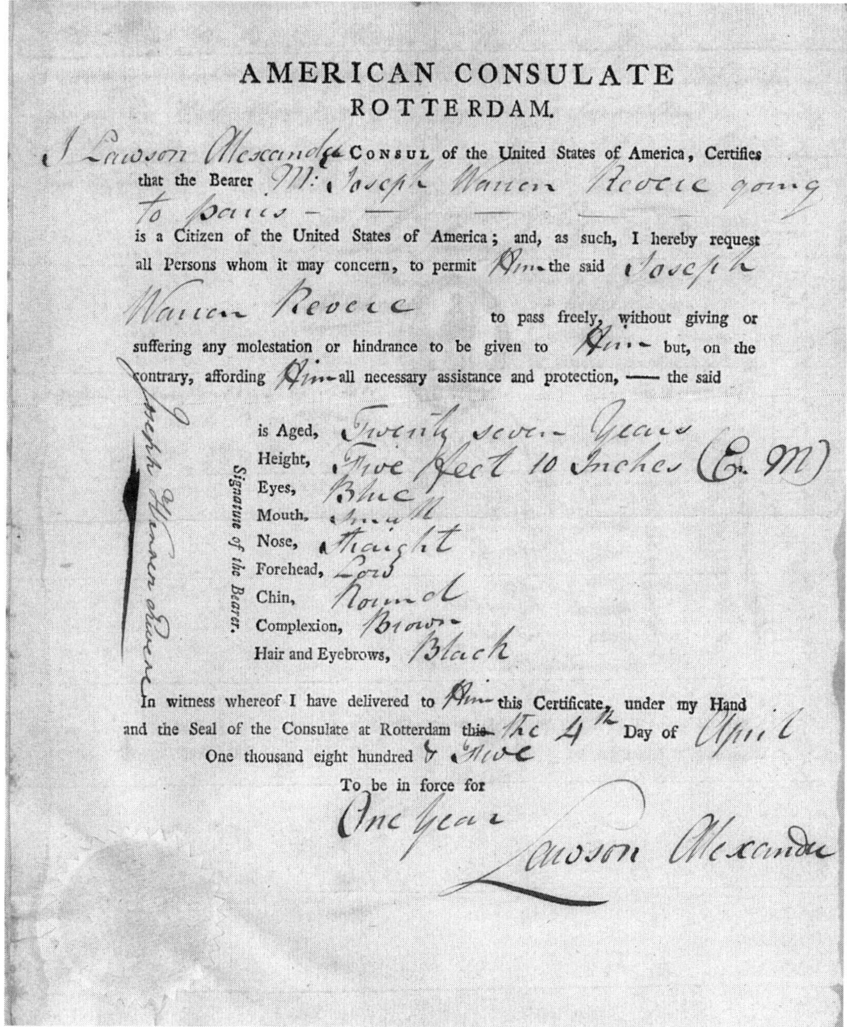
AMERICAN CONSULATE
ROTTERDAM.

J Lawson Alexander CONSUL of the United States of America, Certifies that the Bearer Mr. Joseph Warren Revere going to Paris — is a Citizen of the United States of America; and, as such, I hereby request all Persons whom it may concern, to permit him the said Joseph Warren Revere to pass freely, without giving or suffering any molestation or hindrance to be given to him but, on the contrary, affording him all necessary assistance and protection, — the said

is Aged, Twenty seven Years
Height, Five Feet 10 Inches (E. M)
Eyes, Blue
Mouth, Small
Nose, Straight
Forehead, Low
Chin, Round
Complexion, Brown
Hair and Eyebrows, Black

Signature of the Bearer. Joseph Warren Revere

In witness whereof I have delivered to him this Certificate, under my Hand and the Seal of the Consulate at Rotterdam ~~this~~ the 4th Day of April One thousand eight hundred & Five

To be in force for One Year

Lawson Alexander

Figure 1.5. Visa issued to U.S. citizen by U.S. consul, Rotterdam, 1805. The document also included a version in French (Courtesy of the Massachusetts Historical Society).

travelers. Carrying it around Russia, Isabel Hapgood, who would later compile and translate the *Service Book of the Holy Orthodox-Catholic (Greco-Russian) Church*, complained, that "no pocket of any sex would tolerate them," leading her to suggest that a traveler could "wear them as breastplates (folded) or as garments (full-size)."[19] However, while the passport remained a large document, its appearance did change through the nineteenth century. There were regular changes to the two techniques used to establish that

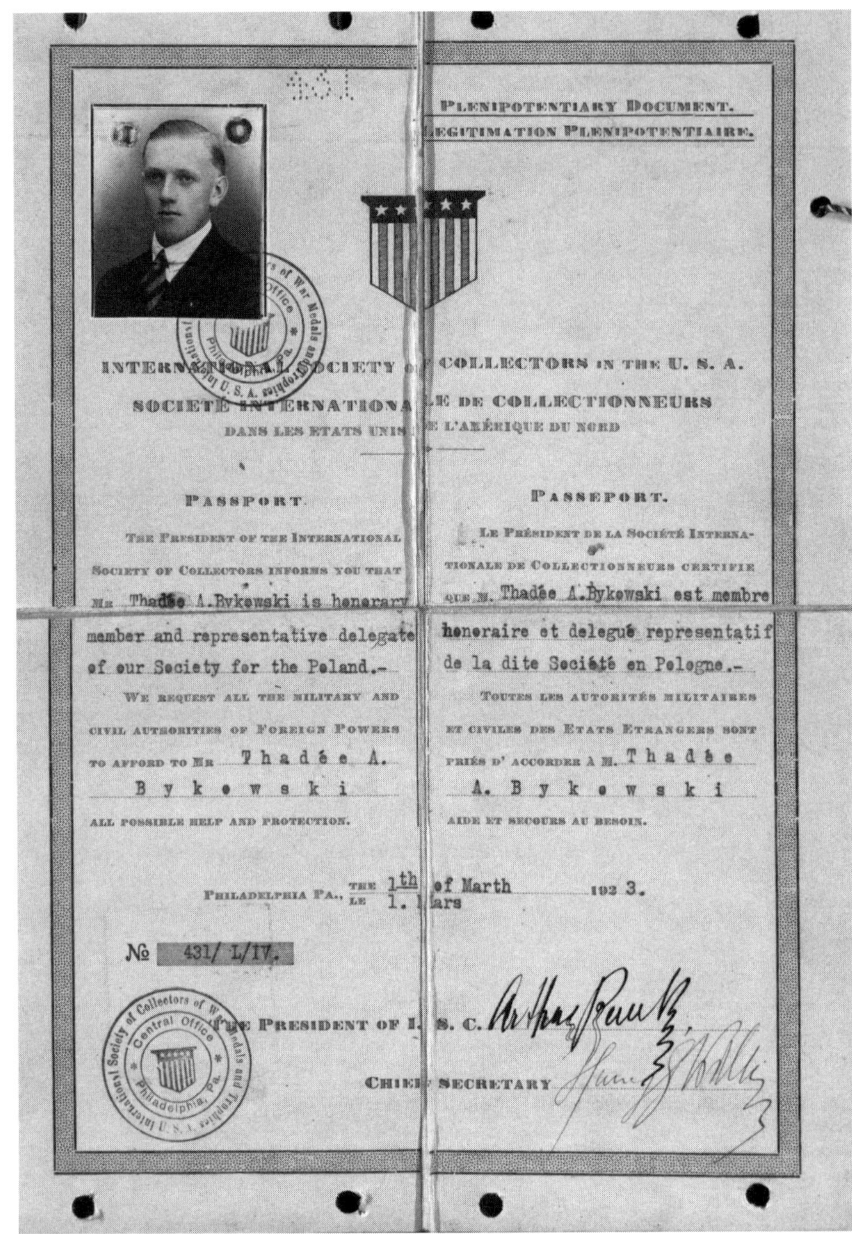

431

PLENIPOTENTIARY DOCUMENT.
LEGITIMATION PLENIPOTENTIAIRE.

INTERNATIONAL SOCIETY OF COLLECTORS IN THE U. S. A.
SOCIETE INTERNATIONALE DE COLLECTIONNEURS
DANS LES ETATS UNIS DE L'AMÉRIQUE DU NORD

PASSPORT.	PASSEPORT.
THE PRESIDENT OF THE INTERNATIONAL SOCIETY OF COLLECTORS INFORMS YOU THAT Mr Thadée A.Bykowski is honorary member and representative delegate of our Society for the Poland.-	LE PRÉSIDENT DE LA SOCIÉTÉ INTERNATIONALE DE COLLECTIONNEURS CERTIFIE QUE M. Thadée A.Bykowski est membre honoraire et delegué representatif de la dite Société en Pologne.-
WE REQUEST ALL THE MILITARY AND CIVIL AUTHORITIES OF FOREIGN POWERS TO AFFORD TO Mr Thadée A. Bykowski ALL POSSIBLE HELP AND PROTECTION.	TOUTES LES AUTORITÉS MILITAIRES ET CIVILES DES ETATS ETRANGERS SONT PRIÉS D' ACCORDER À M. Thadée A. Bykowski AIDE ET SECOURS AU BESOIN.

PHILADELPHIA PA., THE 1th of Marth 192 3.
LE 1. Mars

№ 431/ L/IV.

THE PRESIDENT OF I. S. C.

CHIEF SECRETARY

Figure 1.6. Membership card for the International Society of Collectors in the United States. Labeled a "passport," it had been visaed by foreign officials during a member's travels abroad in 1923 (National Archives, College Park, MD).

the document was issued by the government of the United States, the seal and ornamentation. Such changes were noted by some—and not always for the betterment of the legitimization of the passport's claim to be an official document. "Vox Populi," writing to the *New York Times* in 1874, complained that the recent change in format had produced a passport "issued in unsightly form on a simple half sheet, which is anything but respectable in appearance," with the result that "the sacredness of the instrument is greatly impaired abroad from its miserable appearance."[20] Less than a decade later an article in the same newspaper noted an improvement, although the writer quipped that the U.S. passport had "grown more imposing in the same ration that our influence abroad has waned."[21]

The ornamentation atop a U.S. passport usually took the form of an emblem representing an eagle. This ornamentation seemed to change depending on who engraved the copper plate from which the passports were printed. From 1820 to 1843 the passport actually included the engraver's imprint, but the ornamentation also appeared to provide a space for the personal stamp of the engraver. Ornamentation first appeared on the passport in 1817 in the form of a small representation of the U.S. coat of arms (figure 7.1). In the middle decades of the nineteenth century it had become an eagle with a lyre upon its breast, with 13 stars of varying size forming the constellation Lyra around it. In the 1870s the eagle was removed (perhaps prompting Vox Populi to pick up his pen) before the Bureau of Engraving and Printing prepared its first passport for the U.S. government. The ornamentation on this passport featured a seated female holding a battle ax, an American shield, and an eagle behind the woman (figure 1.7). This changed again a decade later when the woman disappeared, allowing the eagle to once again spread its wings (figure 1.8).

Somewhat surprisingly, the seal used on U.S. passports also changed in appearance, although it was always meant to be the seal of the Department of State—at least according to the text of the passport. An act of Congress established the official seal in 1789 and entrusted its use to the State Department.[22] Early passports had the Department of State seal impressed from the die of 1790, with the legend "Secretary of State's Office" in capital letters on the inside—it measured 1 7/6 inches in diameter. This resembled the design of the Great Seal of the United States, except that the eagle's wingtips pointed downward instead of upward. By 1880 a new die was used that enlarged the seal to 2 5/16 inches. From 1911 the seal used on the passport became a reproduction of the Great Seal, with an encircling legend, "Department of State United States of America." Soon after photographs were added at the end

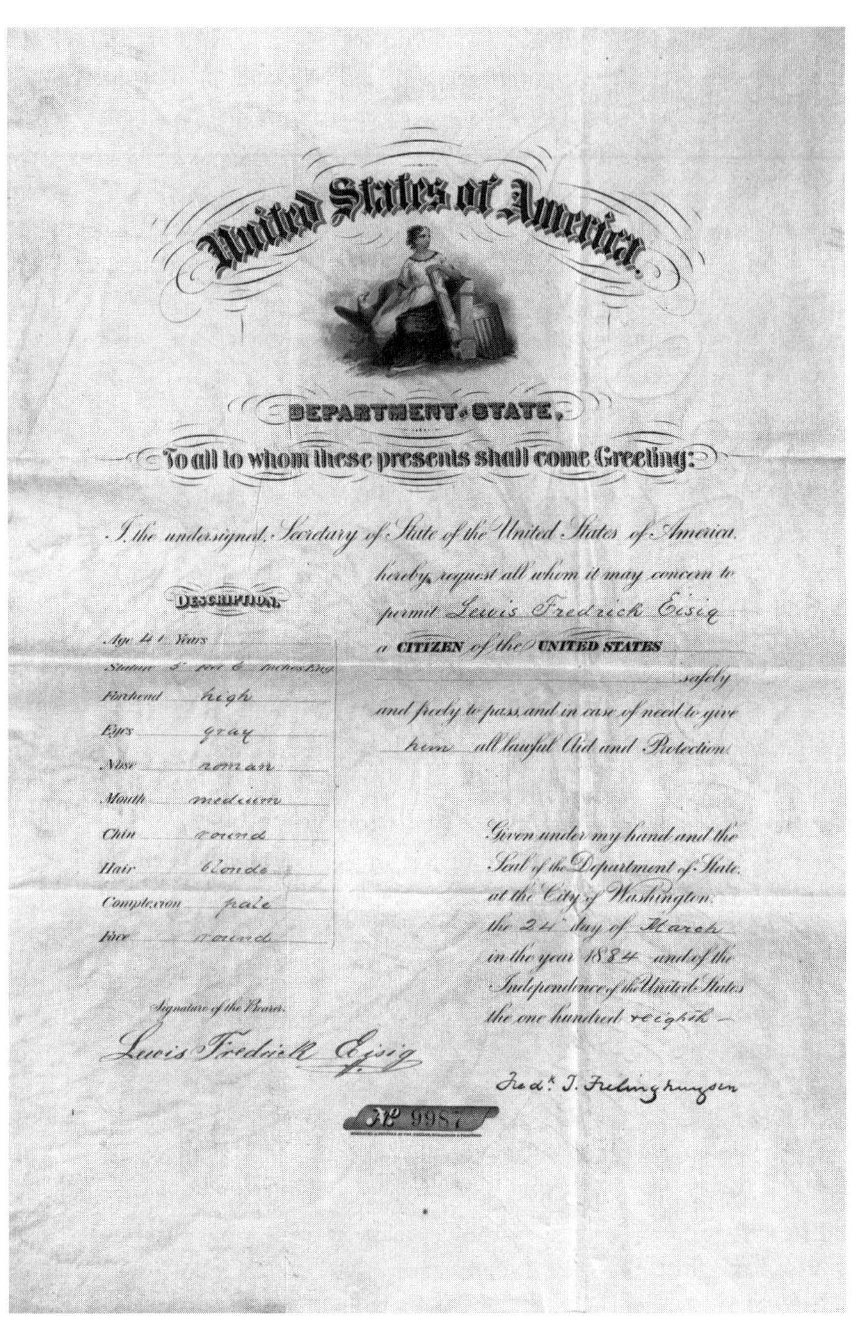

United States of America

DEPARTMENT of STATE,

To all to whom these presents shall come Greeting:

I, the undersigned, Secretary of State of the United States of America, hereby request all whom it may concern to permit Lewis Fredrick Eisig a CITIZEN of the UNITED STATES safely and freely to pass, and in case of need to give him all lawful Aid and Protection.

DESCRIPTION.

Age 41 Years
Stature 5 feet 6 Inches Eng.
Forehead high
Eyes gray
Nose roman
Mouth medium
Chin round
Hair blonde
Complexion pale
Face round

Signature of the Bearer.
Lewis Fredrick Eisig

Given under my hand and the Seal of the Department of State, at the City of Washington, the 24 day of March in the year 1884 and of the Independence of the United States the one hundred eighth.

Fredk. T. Frelinghuysen

No 9987

Figure 1.7. Passport issued in 1884 (National Archives, College Park, MD).

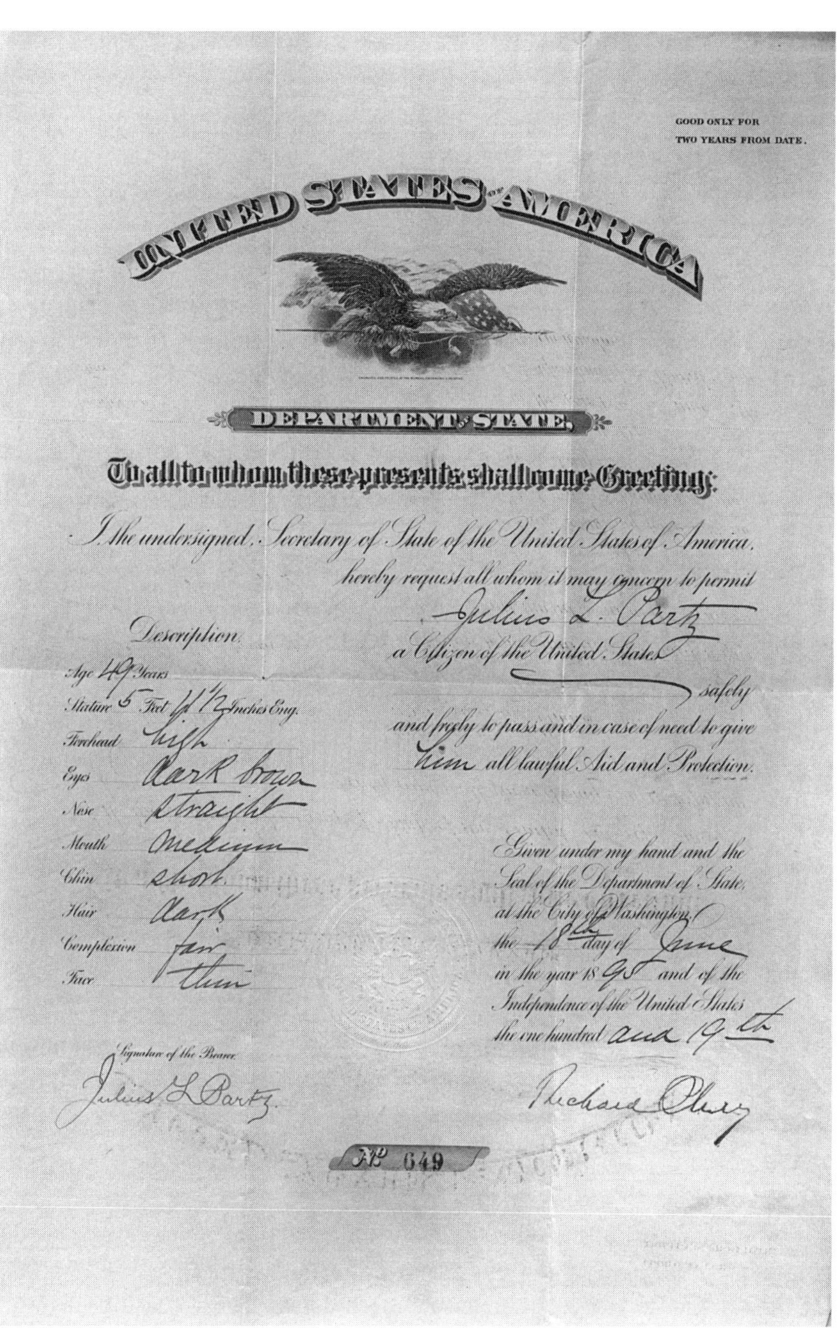

GOOD ONLY FOR
TWO YEARS FROM DATE.

UNITED STATES OF AMERICA

DEPARTMENT OF STATE,

To all to whom these presents shall come, Greeting:

I the undersigned, Secretary of State of the United States of America, hereby request all whom it may concern to permit Julius L. Partz a Citizen of the United States safely and freely to pass and in case of need to give him all lawful Aid and Protection.

Description

Age 49 Years
Stature 5 Feet 4 1/2 Inches Eng.
Forehead high
Eyes dark brown
Nose straight
Mouth medium
Chin short
Hair dark
Complexion fair
Face thin

Given under my hand and the Seal of the Department of State, at the City of Washington, the 18th day of June in the year 1895 and of the Independence of the United States the one hundred and 19th.

Signature of the Bearer.
Julius L Partz

Richard Olney

No 649

Figure 1.8. Passport issued in 1895 (National Archives, College Park, MD).

of 1914 a second seal was attached to the passport to secure the photograph to the document. When the passport design was adapted in 1918 to accommodate photographs more easily, the seal was impressed on a red paper wafer glued to the passport, partly on the photograph and partly on the document.

These changes to the way in which the State Department represented its authority imply an acknowledgement of the importance of such representations to the utility of the passport. However, the link between a document and an external authority such as the federal government was not made in an uncontested fashion, nor was the assumption that a piece of paper could represent an individual's identity and the authority authenticating that identity. The uncertainties and challenges associated with the development of the passport were part of a broader use of printed documents and acceptance of the impersonal nature of their authority in situations where authority traditionally tended to derive exclusively from personal presence or personally established reputation. In nineteenth-century U.S. culture the debate over the authenticity and legitimacy of printed documents and their ability to represent something or someone was more apparent in the development of paper money.

The United States was arguably at the forefront of the widespread adoption of paper money in the Western world, as opposed to the short-term circulation of notes and the "scriptural money" created through bookkeeping that had characterized much of the "money" in Europe prior to this period.[23] This early form of paper money descended from established forms of financial and contractual documentation that included loans, promissory notes, conveyances, and receipts. The successful transformation of these into a document that circulated widely as the representation of value required a negotiation of authority. Paper money had to be accepted as representing something it was not. Coins were understood to be both something of value in and of themselves and a symbol that represented that value. In contrast, paper money was a piece of paper.

In the first half of the nineteenth century currency took the form of banknotes, pieces of paper that represented a certain amount of money in specie. The notes contained the signature of the bank's owner, which indicated that a particular person (the bank owner) possessed the amount of money in specie represented in the note. However, these notes tended to circulate beyond a local context where someone could be expected to personally know, or even know of, the bank owner. Therefore, banknotes produced the still novel situation of documents in everyday interactions being trusted to represent an authority that existed beyond personal knowledge, while employing techniques traditionally associated with personal knowledge and reputation—a personal name and signature. The acceptance of banknotes, their circulation amongst strangers, therefore, demanded the acknowledgment of a new model of communication. Along with other forms of written authority that traveled beyond personal knowledge of the author they constituted a particular form of impersonal communication that required confidence in the medium of printed paper.[24] In a very practical sense, this impersonal mode of interaction necessitated that people learn to work with documents, to understand and accept the authority of a document to represent "reality." For banknotes this involved the acquisition of knowledge to determine if a banknote was authentic—that it was worth what it represented. With over five thousand different state bank notes circulating during the course of the nineteenth century, this was a useful skill to acquire.[25] It was made all the more crucial given the claim by one newspaper that in 1862 counterfeits existed of notes issued by all but 253 of the 1,389 state banks.[26] Aside from what people could find out from the trial and error of personal use, numerous newspaper articles and political tracts were written to help in the quick recognition of telltale signs of a counterfeit note. Specialist publications emerged known as "counterfeit detectors," some with weekly circulations as high as 100,000. That printed publications existed to address suspicion about printed documents underscores the uncertainty and negotiation over the authority of printed words that characterized early life in an increasingly urban and market-driven United States.[27]

The need to establish the authenticity and authority of paper money did not cease when the federal government for the first time began to issue paper money as a way to finance northern mobilization in the Civil War. The federal government, like a bank owner, was in some ways a stranger in the lives of its citizens, even if only to the extent to which hostility to centralized power continued to exist. The government employed a variety of strategies to impose order over the historically chaotic circulation of paper money. It taxed thousands of state-issued paper currencies out of existence and suppressed the private issue of tokens, paper notes, and coins by stores, businesses, churches, and other organizations.[28] Funds were also provided for a secret service to police currency, but with a limited budget and no clear guidelines for how to restrict the activities of counterfeiters it had limited success.[29] However, in 1881 the Chief of the Secret Service did order the destruction of 160 boxes of toy money, and a decade later an agent seized a painting of a U.S. note he found hanging in a saloon.[30]

The novelty of policing the authenticity and authority of documents is also apparent in the frequent changes in the appearance of national currency. The standardization of U.S. currency was a gradual process—only in 1929 did it take on its now familiar size and appearance, sixty-eight years after the federal government began issuing it. These changes had increased the variety of notes in circulation, making it harder to recognize a counterfeit bill. In part this is because the aesthetic features of U.S. currency were more than an anticounterfeiting device. They were intended to convey an arguably more contested form of authority than paper money—that of the political authority of the federal government. On U.S. currency deliberate use was made of aesthetic features such as portraits, allegorical figures, historical scenes, and nationally recognized architecture. In this way national currency allowed the federal government to link its political authority to the more accepted cultural identity of American nationalism.[31]

In the first four decades of use, more than fifteen different historical scenes appeared on currency, along with at least thirty different allegorical figures and over forty individuals. A contributing factor to this was the variety of forms federal currency took, from interest-bearing notes to silver certificates and national bank notes; this further undermined the ease with which currency could be easily recognized as authentically issued by the federal government.[32] These different forms, along with the creation of postal money orders (1864), travelers checks (1891), credit cards (1914), and the first electronic funds transfer (1918), indicate the increased need to trust "abstract" representations of authority and value—the necessity and capacity of money within a rapidly developing national market.

The passport followed a similar gradual path to becoming a standardized document. It appeared in its recognizable contemporary form as a booklet in 1926, three years before U.S. currency took on its now familiar form. The increasingly standardized appearance of the passport, as with currency, had the negative effect of increasing the possibility of fraud. This initially became a subject of concern during World War I but it became more widespread in the 1920s.[33] In this decade, with the introduction of immigration restriction, U.S. citizenship became an increasingly desired identity for immigrants denied entry to the United States through quota restrictions; in the first year of the 1924 quota system a special agent for the Division of Passport Control reported the discovery of fifty cases of passport fraud a month.[34] Newspapers frequently carried stories of the breakup of so-called passport "factories" or "mills," large-scale enterprises that produced fraudulent U.S. passports or visas. The individuals behind these often made use of counterfeit consular stamps and, less frequently, U.S. seals. Another tactic was to alter a legitimate passport either purchased or obtained through theft, and in the case of purported Bolsheviks from passports issued to American citizens sympathetic to the cause.[35]

The State Department sought to counter false passports in two main ways. First, in 1924 it introduced shipside examinations of U.S. passports by its officials at some European ports, though not in France, where the government viewed U.S. officials determining whether an individual could leave its territory as a challenge to French sovereignty.[36] Second, the department tried to make the document more secure. By the 1930s the State Department regularly prepared detailed internal reports on techniques used to illegally produce or alter its passports. Using this knowledge, officials sought to make the passport resistant to tampering by improving binding techniques and the weave of cloth, and introducing a special type of paper on "which the slightest change by any method known to modern science can be readily detected."[37] The most common methods for revealing the majority of fake or altered passports involved exposing unsuccessful attempts to replicate the watermark and inaccurate representations of the seal apparent in the letter size and spacing, and the appearance of the tail feathers (number and width), arrows (shafts, number, shape), and olive branch (number of olives, curve of the stem).[38] However, on occasions the State Department's own officials undercut attempts to secure the passport. The actions of these officials indicate a failure to understand that the authority of the passport depended on the standardized production of the document more than the personal authority of the individual official issuing it. Passports issued abroad were often loosely constructed, thus producing a potentially fragile identification document. In the late 1920s the State Department still had to send reprimands to consuls for issuing passports with unclear seals or for attaching passport photographs with metal clips.[39] The consul in Panama was also asked to stop using a typewriter to fill in passports. Such a request makes clear the ongoing negotiation over standardization in terms of conflicting understandings of trust in its more traditional "personal" and newer "impersonal" form. The department discouraged the use of typewriters as an attempt at standardization, apparently favoring the imprint of the official as form of authenticity; a passport written in long hand was considered harder to alter.[40]

The increased use of identification documents, and the novelty of required passports that came with it, is apparent not only in the concern over ongoing passport fraud but also in the Passport Division's sensitivity to any attempt to replicate the U.S. passport. The official awareness of the importance of the relationship between the image of a document and its authority is highlighted in the attempt of Ruth Shipley, the head of the Passport Division, to prevent the use of passport images in advertising in the late 1920s. Shipley proved to be surprisingly successful in this campaign, considering that no federal law prohibited the reproduction of the passport, in part or whole, for nonfraudulent use.[41] "Offenders" used the image of a passport in print advertisements and window displays. Shipley was particularly concerned when replicas of the passport cover, introduced with the 1926 version, began to appear on the cover of booklets or folders. This commonly occurred as a cover for booklets designed to contain affidavits or other official documents issued by law firms or financial institutions. However, a 1933 *News-Week* advertising campaign based around a replica of the entire passport created more than the usual degree of concern (figure 1.9).[42] Described by a State Department special agent as "the most daring we have yet seen," and rather less dramatically by the assistant secretary of state as "an ingenious bit of advertising,"[43] the mass-mailing campaign used an envelope with the word "Passport" on the outside, and a document resembling a U.S. passport labeled "Passport to the World of News."[44] This "passport" contained a "description of the bearer"—"I am News-Week the most comprehensive, yet lowest prices of all news-magazines"—and subsequent pages headed "Visas" that contained information about the content of the magazine (figure 1.10). In response to letters from Shipley and a visit from a State Department special agent, the publishers removed the word "passport" from the envelope and agreed to change the color of its passport from the red used by the State Department, but they did not stop the campaign.[45] Shipley's comments, endorsed by some letters from confused members of the public, stressed that the word "passport" had only one meaning, and that was the government-issued document.

The use of "passports" in advertising, particularly in an indiscriminate mailing, "cheapened...the high plane to which a passport had been raised."[46] The assistant secretary of state did not agree, suggesting to Shipley "to call attention to the fact that this Department looks with disapproval upon the preparation of booklets simulating an American passport might possibly do more harm than good."[47] The implication that people recognized a clear distinction between the two documents suggests an excessive sensitivity on the part of Shipley in her interpretation of the passport and the sole authority her division possessed to issue them. There is definitely a touch of fastidiousness in the expression of Shipley's concerns; however, the attempt to establish

Figure 1.9. A "passport" used in a 1933 News-Week advertising campaign (National Archives, College Park, MD).

Description of Bearer

NEWS-WEEK

I am NEWS-WEEK, the most complete and yet the lowest-priced of all news-magazines. I was born the 17th of February, 1933, just about a year ago, when, I think you will agree was a poor time to be born, or to be anything — except prepared for the worst.

Yet the best happened! Already more than 65,000 busy, intelligent men and women rely on me each week for an accurate account of world events. Already I have a reputation for sound, impartial interpretation.

I have reached an early maturity because the service I sell is fresh in viewpoint, thorough in fact, brief, bright and strikingly illustrated.

I am an assayer of news. I save you the trouble of reading hundreds of thousands of words every week, yet I let nothing of importance escape you.

I am the first weekly news-magazine to cover the news of the world in *all* its phases: EVENTS — PICTURES — BACKGROUND. Further, I classify news in order of its importance—bringing to your attention first the most noteworthy events.

All things I help you understand.

I am edited by a man with sixteen years' experience judging news values on the New York Times.

I am written by a staff of expert journalists. If you follow me, no frontier of news will be closed to you. There is no news borderline which you cannot cross. You will be more than well informed. You will be *thoroughly* informed.

Figure 1.10. The "description of the bearer" from a "passport" used in a 1933 News-Week advertising campaign (National Archives, College Park, MD).

the legitimacy of the U.S. passport depended on the explicit articulation of its authority and authenticity. The Passport Division's monopoly on the production of passports had only recently been challenged in any significant way through fraud. Therefore, only in the 1920s were attempts first made to secure its authority through a more rigorous standardization in the production of the passport. The articulation of standardization, centralization, authority, and authenticity was not limited to the appearance of the passport. It is also the context for the contested application of identification technologies to the passport, the subject of the remaining chapters in the first part of this book.

2

Name

In 1885 an attorney wrote to the State Department arguing his client should not need to get a new naturalization certificate issued to support his passport application. The department had rejected the application because the name on the naturalization certificate was spelled differently than the name on the application and other accompanying documents. The attorney argued that "there are so many ways of spelling names that this mistake can easily occur, each one thinks his way is the proper one, the Clerk thinks John Schaffer is right I think John Schaffeur [?] is right and still others may have their way of spelling this name and all believe they are right."[1] Irrespective of his motivation, the attorney's argument for discounting the misspelling of his client's name on a naturalization certificate is only plausible in an environment in which a person's written name is not standardized and where an individual is not identified consistently in and through documents. John S__ apparently lived in a world where his documented interactions with a distant centralized authority were so limited that a consistent representation of his name was not seen as a necessary nor even acceptable requirement. In this localized world confusion over identity could presumably be resolved through face-to-face interaction; the recording of legal transactions or events on documents could still potentially be trumped by extratextual knowledge. A person was known and recognized through the dependability of his or her presence and appearance. Consistent with such identification practices, John S__'s attorney tried to use his local knowledge as evidence to support the passport application. He stated that he was present in the courtroom at the time of his client's naturalization. Apparently he believed his presence further verified that the man applying for a passport was the person named in both the naturalization certificate and the application; no doubt as an attorney he believed his professional standing heightened the authority of his individual presence at such an event. While there is no record of a response to this letter, it is doubtful either of these arguments brought the attorney or his client any success.

In the relatively unusual context of interactions with a distant authority such as the federal government, "correct" spelling was fundamental to the bureaucratic standardization that increasingly structured such contact. In official identification this became the belief that to "know" and subsequently "recognize" its citizens the government of the United States needed to fix or stabilize an identity. While a personal name composed of a first or baptismal name and a family name was an established custom in the United States, the bureaucratic demand for consistent spelling to assist in the articulation of identity and information was less accepted. In contrast to the belief that "there are many ways to spell a name" that all have legitimacy, the novel importance of the accurate recording of a personal name for the reliable identification that the passport promised is evident in a revised set of instructions the State Department issued to passport applicants in 1873. These instructions included a new requirement that "the signature to the application and oath of allegiance should conform in orthography to that in the naturalization paper." The ongoing need for such a directive is evident in the above letter, which arrived in the department twelve years after this instruction appeared.[2]

That the State Department had to issue such an instruction in the last quarter of the nineteenth century may seem odd nowadays when the obvious necessity of the personal name for daily social interactions tends to naturalize its function as an identification technology. However, the successful legal stabilization of personal names is a relatively recent process that occurred in parts of Europe contemporaneously with the development of the passport in the United States.[3] The customary stabilization of a personal name as first name and inherited surname is older; while in Western Europe a second name began to be added from about the eleventh century the process by which this developed is difficult to reconstruct. Heritable patronymic surnames were more visible in Europe in the thirteenth and fourteenth centuries, but they were adopted unevenly in reaction to developments in economic and property law, the increased use of documents, and changes in the composition of populations.[4] The earliest official recordings of names in Europe tended to be confessional records kept by individual parishes. By the High Middle Ages the collection of lists of names of delinquents and other criminals had become common, especially in Italian city-states, but neither municipal nor ecclesiastical registers had firmly institutionalized practices—and both subsequently had to deal with the ever-changing ways of spelling late medieval and early modern names.[5] In France the initial attempt at legal and state intervention occurred at the end of the eighteenth century. This was preceded by the emergence of the baptismal register as the normal legal means of recording identity in the mid-seventeenth century and centuries before that by the customary stabilization of the personal name tied in large part to the power of the family. While the stabilization of the name followed different legal paths in Germany than in France, it did so as part of the ongoing development of registration and identity cards. In contrast, in England the personal name was understood to be a matter of common law, not the domain of written law. Therefore, while there were various legal procedures available to people to change their names, they were not necessary to confer a new name—they merely authenticated the change. This English tradition carried over to the United States, where the legal stabilization of the personal name developed not through specific laws but by way of customs and uses, and through the doctrines implicit in court decisions based on them. The small size and scope of the federal government relative to those of European states also produced a context in which the administrative reach of the federal government remained limited regardless of any official desire to more fully know the population. Therefore, in the United States the stabilization of surnames came later than in most European states. According to one expert on naming this only occurred in any substantive way during the second decade of the twentieth century because of income taxes, the draft and ration books during World War I, and in the 1920s and 1930s as car registration, drivers licenses, life insurance, Social Security, and private pension plans increased the number of occasions when names were publicly recorded.[6] Naming, therefore, needs to be understood as a culturally and historically specific practice. This affects the nature of the move from the customary stabilization to the legal immutability of names.

The tension between the official fixing of names and the cultural specificity of naming practices was initially apparent at U.S. borders in the effort to implement the Chinese Exclusion Act after 1882. In an attempt to enforce the complicated identity categories used in the legislation that excluded some but not all Chinese, the Immigration Bureau came to see the need for a comprehensive system to record Chinese names consistently. In one case officials could not issue a certificate to an applicant they considered entitled to the document because they could not locate his original entry file owing to the multiple spellings of the name "Louie Fong." Officials came up with four possible spellings of his name and found four possible matches, but other Chinese immigrants who had claimed the identity "Louie Fong" had already used those files.[7] Situations like this occurred for a number of reasons. With little or no knowledge of Chinese, immigration inspectors could only approximate a spelling in English as they tried to comprehend Chinese tonal nuances. An even greater problem occurred when inspectors sought to write a name in English when the only documents provided used Chinese characters. These language barriers could be further compounded by lack of awareness of Chinese naming practices. The most frequent source of confusion involved the sequence of names. In other cases inspectors did not understand the customs that enabled an individual to claim multiple names, such as a family name and a marriage name. The limited knowledge of Chinese culture was even more apparent when officials understood forms of address or marital status such as "Ah" and "Shee" to be actual personal and family names and identified Chinese on documents and files using these "names."[8]

For all these reasons it was often difficult for officials to link a person to a file, and thus for the state to remember him or her. The initial confusion over naming practices and the spelling of names frequently limited the subsequent retrieval of information. If a person had been recorded under their marriage name or marital status this presented difficulties for a system in which family relationship provided a basis for a claim of exemption to exclusion. While documents were meant to allay some of the official skepticism regarding the trustworthiness of Chinese immigrants, they often furthered it through these problems or even when a name was inconsistently spelled within the same case file.

The enforcement of Chinese Exclusion Acts provides an important insight into the problems associated with documentation that continued to exist when passports extended the world of documents from marginal populations to people not used to having their identity questioned. The difficulties encountered by officials illustrates that anything learned from experience with Chinese immigrants did not spread beyond the specific world of the

Exclusion Acts. As with the Immigration Bureau, the State Department's attitude to an applicant's name makes explicit the growing realization that official documentation required administrative control over both an individual's claim to express his or her own identity, and a local community's claim to verify an individual's identity. However, this awareness encountered a world where not only Chinese names were alien but the rigor required for efficient documentation was equally foreign. In the initial encounters between a local culture of multiple interpretations and the uniformity of an embryonic administrative culture, the discrepancy in spellings of a personal name across documents grew out of a number of circumstances: a clerical error at the time of naturalization, the subsequent formal or informal changing of a name, limited literacy on the part of the applicant, or as noted, sloppiness on the part of the notary or attorney overseeing the application.[9] While the inability to read and write was one cause, all these circumstances stemmed from a limited literacy in documentation. This was accentuated by the fact that officials were initially more concerned with the documentation of "the other"—with the usefulness of documents like the passport in the management of difference. Therefore, most attempts to rigorously verify citizenship occurred with naturalized citizens. The attempts to translate these claims to citizenship into a standardized official identity occurred with individuals whose names also required an act of translation to be recognizable, to become names that could be useful identification tools, not "ill adapted for pronouncing and writing by the majority of Americans," as one Chicago judge commented in 1917.[10]

The importance of names to the relationship between citizenship and control makes clear one function of a personal name—as a symbol of national membership.[11] Assimilation to Anglo-American norms through the formal or informal changing of names was a frequent occurrence in the United States through the middle of the twentieth century. In the mid-1920s an expert on naming estimated that about one-third of Americans with English or Welsh surnames had taken them on after arriving in the United States; in the case of the most popular family name only about half the Smiths in the United States were thought to be of British origin.[12] While the changing of family names could be a choice, on occasion it occurred through the actions of officials either upon an immigrant's arrival or at the time of naturalization. In an unusually explicit example of Anglicizing, the aforementioned Chicago judge refused to naturalize certain applicants unless they took "simpler names than those brought with them from abroad." However, in a society where common law allowed individuals to choose to change their names, this explicit renaming of an individual offended the sensibilities of the editors of the *New York Times*. They argued that the "varying fancies and prejudices of Judges should not be determinative in a matter so purely personal as the family name."[13]

The judge's comments, while lacking in subtlety, illustrated the consequences of the gradual move of the family name into the world of official identification. Although people could change personal names without special legal proceedings, identification understood through bureaucratic procedure privileged an official identity that could only exist in documents; therefore any change ideally had to be explained through documents. This was represented in the logic that emerged through passport-policy decisions that increasingly came to prioritize an identity articulated through a series of appropriately issued and hence apparently "truthful" documents. Thus as the nineteenth century gave way to the twentieth century a set of rules to standardize identity coalesced in the actions of passport clerks. These rules worked to dramatically reduce the number of occasions in which officials issued a passport on an undocumented leap of faith. As a result, the gradual development of documentation led to a situation in which a person's conscious attempt to assimilate to their new nation prevented the state from certifying membership in their new nation-state. Taking on an Anglicized version of their name represented a conscious effort on the part of individuals to adopt a new national culture via its official language, possibly for a combination of patriotic and pragmatic reasons. However, if their U.S. passport application arrived with two different names and no legal document linking the two names the application would more than likely be rejected.[14] This tension between the different membership expectations of the nation and of the state and the role of official identity documents in managing this could still arise even if documents were presented. In one such case, a departmental official informed an applicant with affidavits establishing the relationship between his two names that he did "not feel authorized to omit the name by which you were naturalized." The department issued the passport to "Juda Osiel commonly known as Leon Osiel."[15] The passport, therefore, somewhat oddly (and possibly illegally) functioned as an official record of the name change.

The complicated nature of the tension between the official stabilization of a personal name and cultural practices that encouraged the changing of names is even more visible in a controversy that explicitly linked the family name to the importance of the family within the organizational structure of the nation-state. The controversy was a response to changes in the way married women were identified on a passport. Until World War I State Department practice was to issue a husband and wife a "joint passport" in the full name of the husband only. These passports identified a married woman on her husband's passport through the phrase "accompanied by his wife" or simply "and wife"; neither a wife's name nor her physical description appeared on the passport (figure 4.1). This naming practice reinforced accepted gender roles that clearly located the husband as head of the household and apparently relegated his wife to a public life that ideally required his presence as a preferred chaperone. If a husband and wife decided to travel separately while abroad, only then was it expected that a wife obtain a passport from a U.S. official.

The absence of a name and description specifically identifying a married woman separate from her husband only was an issue in the nineteenth century on the odd occasion a passport was a required document—such as for visitors to Russia, where each adult traveler had to carry a passport. The need for a married woman to be an individual, subject to identification, became an even greater problem when her seeming irrelevance to her own countrymen could in fact lead to the erasure of her original documentary trace, however slight it had been. In the early 1880s when T. B. Aldrich, the editor of the *Atlantic Monthly*, prepared to travel with his wife to Russia, he sent his old passport to the State Department for renewal. Not only did no one alert Aldrich to the fact his wife needed a separate passport, but upon return of his passport he failed to notice that through a bureaucratic error the words "and wife" had been omitted. Through luck the Aldrich's were able to enter Russia on his passport, but that luck ran out when they tried to use the passport to check into their hotel in St. Petersburg. In a subsequent retelling of their ordeal, Aldrich, the angry husband, is said to have exclaimed, "The police at the frontier let us in on one passport and then the St. Petersburg police arrest us because we haven't got two. If we were traveling with a baby I presume they'd want a third: Item: One baby; features undeveloped; stature, knee high to a grasshopper; name not yet decided upon; occupation, tourist chaperoning his parents. But what preposterous nonsense."[16] The reduction of a married woman's identity to that of an appendage to her husband apparent in the joint passport is made even more explicit in Aldrich's ragings. The need for his wife to have a passport becomes equivalent to a baby having a passport—such obvious dependents would certainly not be traveling alone, unchaperoned, especially this far from home. It seems the world of the passport was understood by Aldrich to be a public world where a man's identity and status was all that should be necessary, and definitely the only identity that should be needed if a document was required. In this world gender was a critical component of that status. Because it was issued by the State Department the passport also framed such a gentlemen's club in terms of citizenship. Therefore, the joint passport not only highlighted the gendered nature of identification practices, it also verified the gendered status of the identity it represented. Until 1922 a married woman's U.S. citizenship depended on the citizenship of her husband; that is, a woman with U.S. citizenship would lose that legal identity if she married a noncitizen. And, of course, women who were U.S. citizens had only gained the right to vote in 1920.

Security concerns following the outbreak of World War I lead the State Department to officially stop issuing joint passports. This policy continued following the end of the war, with the additional requirement that a married woman apply for a passport with the family name of her husband. In the context of women gaining the right to vote and agitation over a married woman's citizenship status this new demand saw the launch of a campaign to allow a married woman the option to have her passport issued in her maiden name. The National Woman's Party (NWP) and the Lucy Stone League organized the campaign. In 1921 New York journalist Ruth Hale founded the Lucy Stone League to inform the public that a woman could legally maintain her own name after marriage. Hale did this after her attempt to use her maiden name created problems not only with a passport application, but also in other situations, including voting.[17] Hale named her organization after Lucy Stone, who because of her actions in the second half of the nineteenth century was regarded as the first American woman to publicly assert her right to use her maiden name after marriage. The society was most active in the 1920s when prominent "Lucy Stoners" included Margaret Mead and Amelia Earhart. It also included a number of journalists, which may explain why the group earned newspaper coverage even though it probably only recruited a few hundred women.[18] In the course of its passport campaign the group in the opinion of the assistant secretary of state also gained "considerable senatorial and other political backing."[19] In response State Department officials had to explicitly argue for their right to "fix" the personal name of certain passport applicants in order to enable their full and complete identification.

The debates the campaign generated illustrated both the difficulty in stabilizing personal names in U.S. legal culture and the gendered environment in which it was deemed necessary to verify identity. Both sides of the debate agreed that no court ruling had ever taken away the common-law right of a married woman to retain her maiden name.[20] Therefore, the NWP argued that through its enforcement of the 1920 regulation the State Department had illegally claimed the power to change the name of any married woman who had made the choice to use her maiden name; in the words of the vice president of the NWP, it forced a woman to travel under a "fictitious name."[21] The organization's brief to the secretary of state argued that a "woman's name signifies her identity, her personality, her capacities and her achievements." More specifically, many of the married women who retained their maiden names "are engaged in professions or activities where their names are their trade-marks so to speak." Thus, the rule deprived a woman "of her property without due process."[22] Supporting this point, a newspaper editorial acknowledged that the ruling also seemed to go against developments in "most progressive countries," where a wife was no longer considered her husband's property.[23]

While State Department officials agreed there was no legal requirement for a married woman to take on her husband's family name, in contrast to the NWP's brief, the State Department's solicitor, Richard Flournoy, argued that an acknowledgement of a woman's marriage was necessary to accurately establish and verify her identity.[24] Personal identification was only a successful practice if it followed agreed-upon norms; and within identification practices "the object of a name is to identify an individual." Jurisprudence defined a lawful name as "the designation by which (one) is distinctively known in the community." Therefore, it was not "merely a name which he or she may choose to use at a particular time or upon a particular occasion for a particular purpose."[25] Fundamental to the State Department's argument was the assumption that a married woman was known in the community through her marriage and thus through her husband. Marriage was the source of a woman's public identity, recognized in what Flournoy labeled the "universal custom" of taking a husband's family name. In a letter of support to the secretary of state, Miss Elizabeth Achelis endorsed this argument. She described Lucy Stone League members as women "who have been disappointed and disillusioned in their married life, or are suffering from too great an ego of their own importance, and an equal unwillingness to accept the whole importance of the marriage contract."[26] In contrast, it seems that a husband was at minimum simultaneously always a public figure and a husband, as is implicit in Flournoy's statement that "the argument that a married woman need make no mention of her husband's name, since her husband would not be required to make any mention of his wife's name is specious and unconvincing."[27]

Flournoy and other department officials defended the policy by explicitly defining the passport through its "nature [as] an introduction to the authorities of foreign countries." In this possibly specious argument the passport as a letter requesting the favor of foreign officials needed to acknowledge the legal status of a woman as a wife to comply with conventions of "civilized" nation-states ("including the Far East").[28] Correspondence with twelve diplomatic officials revealed to the State Department that, except in Norway, the failure to identify a married woman through her husband would result in "embarrassment," "confusion," and "misunderstandings" not only for U.S. citizens and foreign officials, but also for U.S. officials abroad who would be "called upon to make explanations."[29] They would be called on to do so because the department believed that "officials of foreign countries will require proof that they are husband and wife."[30] Sites for potential difficulties included not only immigration stations, but also steamship and railway agencies, and perhaps tellingly hotels.[31] A State Department official made it clear that it was this extra work for officials along with their embarrassment that was the point of concern, not the problems it would create for "the individual who thought it worthwhile to insist on her own individuality to the extent of ignoring the question of her marital status."[32] To issue a separate passport to a woman and not acknowledge her legal relationship to the man she traveled with could imply inappropriate behavior and the official sanctioning of such behavior. While Flournoy acknowledged that a passport issued to a woman under her maiden name would not raise such concerns and problems for a married woman traveling alone, the controversy was largely based on the assumption that a respectable married woman would not travel abroad without the protection of both her husband and a passport.[33]

In 1925 the State Department changed its policy to allow a married woman the option of having a passport issued in her maiden name, followed by the phrase, "wife of." This solution emerged largely in the name of expediency—to go further would require a new executive order signed by the president. However, consistent with its position that a name should be able to easily identify an individual, the State Department required married women who wanted a passport issued in this form to provide documentary evidence to support the claim that they still used their maiden name. Nonetheless, according to the NWP magazine, *Equal Rights*, the decision was "hailed with delight by feminists."[34] Thus the new policy apparently averted any potential affront to the family of nations; domestic and diplomatic harmony was maintained.

However, a dozen years later, the Passport Division began with little debate to issue a married woman a passport in her maiden name if she requested it without noting her identity as the "wife of." The suggestion for this change is recorded in a memo from division director, Mrs. Ruth Shipley, who, after acknowledging that passports issued to married men had never stated "husband of," argued that

> because our position would be very difficult to defend under any really definite and logical attack, it seems the part of wisdom to make the change and permit a woman to use on her passport her maiden name if she habitually uses it. There has been much controversy on this point and if you are interested in seeing the Subject File I shall be glad to send it to you.[35]

In response to this new policy the department's ever diligent New York–based passport agent, wanting to be "prepared when the next group of nuns call," enquired if this decision would allow a nun to be identified on her passport simply by her religious name—the established practice was to issue a nun a passport naming her in the letter's example "Bridget McGuiness known as Sister Mary Theresa." In reply Shipley stated she did not see the situations as analogous as she did not consider "that names in religion as a rule sufficiently identify the bearer of passports."[36]

3

Signature

The personal name of the passport bearer appeared on the passport in two places, performing two very different functions. First, the name appeared handwritten within the text that identified the bearer as a citizen and requested safe passage; by the early nineteenth century this was a printed form, though the standardized text was printed to simulate handwritten script. Second, by 1815 the name appeared handwritten below the designation "Signature of the Bearer." The personal name as a signature functioned as a form of identification somewhat distinct from simply being the personal name that verified individual identity across documents. While the handwritten name appears twice, what is of course unique about the signature is that it is assumed to be in the handwriting of the bearer, in contrast to the other occurrence of the handwritten name. A second name, that of the Secretary of State, was also signed onto a passport. This signature guaranteed the authenticity of the document, while also personalizing the authority of the state. The text of the passport, written in the form of a request echoing letters of introduction and protection, carried with it the expectation of the writer's signature. However, the secretary of state's signature, particularly when it was stamped onto the document, suggests the need for a more nuanced understanding of the signature as an identification technology.

The strong belief that a signature can be used to identify a person, like any other identification practice, needs to be seen as a historically specific assumption. To sign a document is to make a mark. However, a signature is not just any mark. It is commonly understood to be a representation of a name, and it is the link between the name and a person that gives the signature value. The importance of the name to the act of signing locates the signature within literate cultures, although in specific circumstances literate cultures tend to accept a signature that does not take the form of a written name. In the case of U.S. passports by the early twentieth century illiterate people were allowed to sign with an "X" as long as they were mentally capable of understanding the significance of an oath and the mark was witnessed by two people who could write; if an illiterate person did not understand the significance of an oath a parent or guardian could sign on his or her behalf.[1] To mark a document with an "X" is a common practice to accommodate illiteracy within a writing-based culture of identification. This is accepted as signing because it is a mark made by a particular individual signifying their understanding and presence. However, because the mark does not make a person's name visible it fails to fulfill the function of identification; the signer remains nameless and thus anonymous. In such situations the person's name is written separately to counter this anonymity. The "X" and the name combined are considered to authenticate the document, to tie the signer to any agreement made in the document; the signature is assumed to do this in one act.[2]

Voicing a long-held belief in the value of a bearer's signature on a passport a U.S. consul wrote the "signature is one of the surest means of identification"[3]—a comment made in 1921 even after the introduction of passport photographs during World War I. The importance of the signature was further recognized when a passport expired or had to be canceled—by the early decades of the twentieth century standard practice called for an official to draw three lines through the signature to indicate the passport was no longer valid. The value of the signature in the verification of identity derived from a specific understanding of the relationship between presence and repeatability. In the second decade of the nineteenth century when State Department regulations started requiring a bearer's signature to be appended to the passport, a space was left for it at the end of a paragraph describing the physical appearance of the bearer. There followed a parenthetical comment: "(whose name is here repeated in his own handwriting, viz)," followed by the bearer's signature.[4] The State Department removed this explanation of the relationship of the signature to the bearer from the passport in the 1820s. However, in the middle of the century officials still considered it necessary to clarify the role of the signature in the process of identification, instructing a passport agent working in New York City during the Civil War, "Care should be taken to ascertain that the persons presenting the same are the 'bona fide' owners and this may be done by comparing the signatures of the persons holding them with the signatures on the documents themselves."[5] In the case of the bearer the signature tied the document to his or her hand making the individual an active participant in the verification of their identity. As an identification technology this signature depended on the possibility of the bearer repeating his or her signature in the presence of any doubtful official and doing so in such a fashion that the official was satisfied the two signatures were identical. This is based on the assumption that people have unique handwriting and that they sign their name consistently.[6] A "proper signature" is generally one that is considered to be distinctive and typical, that is, recognizable and repeatable. The importance this places on developing a unique signature, however, conflicts with the signature as the representation of a name; a signature risks becoming a mark rather than an easily decipherable representation of a name.[7] In the case of passports, with the bearer's name legibly written elsewhere on the document, the repeatability of the signature as a mark seemed to matter more to officials. Although officials received no formal training the assumption was that they would be able to see similarities or differences if a passport bearer was required to repeat his signature in their presence. The belief that most people could accurately compare signatures was challenged by the emergence of "experts" in handwriting analysis. These people argued that the accurate comparison of signatures, and handwriting in general, required training in breaking down writing into its constituent parts. The attempt to advance handwriting analysis as a science brings to the foreground the not always coherent assumptions that allowed the signature to be accepted as an accurate and reliable form of identification.

The development of techniques to verify handwriting offers an important point of entry into the historically specific nature of how handwriting was understood to link a person to a document. In the second half of the nineteenth century the acceptance of evidence from handwriting experts in courtrooms demonstrates important changes in how the relationship between a person and their writing could be proved and hence different conceptions of the relationship between identity and identification. The basis for legal resolution of disputes over the authenticity of written documents changed from personal knowledge of the writer to the belief that accurate identification could be achieved through the articulation of designated "facts" visible to experts who by following a specific set of procedures could analyze handwriting as a series of precisely measured marks. The emergence of handwriting analysis through claims to rationality and objectivity is what turned it into a "modern" form of identification.

The determination of proof in disputes over the authorship of written documents had been an object of legal concern for several hundred years. Until the middle of the nineteenth century U.S. law tended to follow English legal tradition that had established a common-law rule against the "comparison of hands"; courts did not allow multiple examples of writing to test the status of the contested document. Instead, disputes over the genuineness of writing were resolved either by testimony from the writer, a witness who saw the person write the document, or by bringing in an acquaintance of the writer who could testify to the authenticity (or not) of the writing based on knowledge of the person. The circumstances of many cases meant it was an acquaintance of the purported writer who most frequently provided evidence. It was not even necessary for these witnesses to have observed the writing of the specific document under examination—they only needed to have seen the person's writing at some point during their acquaintance.[8] An American edition of an English treatise on evidence made it clear that such a witness was expected to provide "recollection of the general character" of the script, not "the formation of particular letters."[9] This seemed logical for a court in which it was assumed that "one man knows the face of another though he cannot describe the minute particulars, by which he knows it. So it is of hand-writing."[10] Thus, following English practice, some courts were more interested in a witness having a meaningful relationship with the purported writer and therefore only required a general impression of the prevailing character of the writing based on an assumed relationship between a person's character and the uniqueness of their handwriting.[11]

By 1900 the concern over the status of handwriting evidence in disputed document cases had resulted in thirty-seven states permitting comparison of hands to assist in determining the authenticity of handwriting. This was in large part due to a group of self-proclaimed experts who responded to the problems created when changing social structures undermined the social basis that had underwritten the existing method for identifying handwriting. In short, personal knowledge of individuals began to be seen as a problematic basis for evaluating disputes as the small social circles in which documents, especially financial notes, had circulated disappeared by the middle of the century.[12]

Handwriting analysis as a field of expertise also emerged in a period in which it was increasingly accepted that, if properly understood, small variations in appearance and behavior could be seen as meaningful. This belief developed in the last half of the nineteenth century with the emergence of identification techniques such as fingerprinting, anthropometry, and social statistics, along with the popularity of detective novels such as Arthur Conan Doyle's "Sherlock Holmes" series.[13] In line with this, handwriting experts argued the minute particulars of handwriting deemed irrelevant or even irretrievable prior to the first half of the nineteenth century were the only basis for reliable evidence in courts. As legal historian Jennifer Mnookin explains it, an understanding of "not just the shape of the letters, but also the extent of their shading, the existence and nature of various loops, the form of connection between letters, and the presence or absence of retouching" could enable an expert to authenticate handwriting by breaking it down into its component parts; in one instance a signature was broken down into thirty different marks.[14] It was this act of "scientific" reading that courtroom handwriting experts took as the foundation of their work as they sought to identify the writer of a disputed document.

Outside of the courtroom the reading of identity from handwriting more often took the form of graphology. This also sought to attribute the assumed link between personal identity and handwriting to science and thus contributed to moving identification away from the opinion and subjectivity of personal knowledge to the method and objectivity of science. Loosely used, graphology could accredit the so-called handwriting experts who evaluated documents. However, it was more commonly applied to another set of self-anointed experts who sought to reveal a person's true character from their handwriting and to those who sought to do the same using popular manuals.[15] Even if one accepts that handwriting experts sought to identify a more empirically verifiable sense of the individual than the character or personality traits of the graphologist, as practices of identification they shared the claim that a person does not have to know an individual to identify him or her.[16]

Although handwriting identification may seem distant from the passport, its development required the assumption that identity can be verified without personal knowledge and through impersonal means, an assumption that is critical to the belief that identity can be accurately documented. This was particularly the case for a mass-produced document such as the passport, issued by an authority that more than likely did not have personal knowledge of the person identified in the document. The complicated ways in which this changed the relationship between identity and identification is made apparent in both the use and representation of the signature of the secretary of state on the U.S. passport.

Below the text of the passport and immediately preceded by the valediction, which began with the phrase "Given under my hand," was the signature of the secretary of state. The format of the passport as a letter from one official to another no doubt contributed to the perceived need for the secretary to sign the passport, along with an established assumption that an unsigned document implies that no one is prepared to take responsibility for it, thus reducing its value.[17] That the secretary of state's signature was the only signature on early U.S. passports illustrates the late eighteenth century passport was not yet a modern identification document. And the secretary did indeed sign these early passports by hand; the signature remained consistently handwritten until the Civil War. The format of the passport as a letter complete with a signature does give the text an implied autobiographical anchor. However, the signature as a sign of authentication represents the authority of an impersonal entity (the federal government) more than the name of an individual. The bearer's signature was there to connect the person presenting the passport to the document; the secretary's signature, along with the seal, was on the document to stand in for the absent authority that verified the individual identity in the passport.

The importance of the signature as the source of legal authority for the passport was made explicit in 1920 when the confirmation of a new secretary of state went beyond the thirty-day limitation provided for in statutes; this left the United States without a secretary of state. As a result, the State Department considered it necessary to halt the issuance of passports as there was no individual, and thus no signature, "to render a passport effective."[18] While a seal can be understood as an impersonal signature, the secretary's handwritten signature was distinct from the other techniques that represented the state such as the ornamentation that adorned passports. The signed names of secretaries of state personalized what became during the nineteenth century an increasingly large bureaucratic structure. This more personal authority derived from the culturally produced assumption of a link between a person and his or her handwriting and specifically his or her signature. The verification of the state's authority in the form of a handwritten signature resonated with a claim to authority based on an understanding of authenticity, reinforced by the phrase "Given under my hand." The handwritten signature implied the presence of the secretary of state at the creation of the passport and thus its authenticity.

That handwriting could be read to personalize the impersonal authority of official documents granted it the possibility of a very specific role in the development of documentary authority. As part of the contested emergence of print culture, handwritten documents acquired a particular cultural role in contrast to print, which was equated with self-negation.[19] In eighteenth-century Europe print culture gave handwriting a primary role in situations that involved the presentation of the self. Handwriting on calling cards, trade cards, and mercantile letters was deemed more acceptable than the so-called dead letter of print.[20] In the United States in the nineteenth century, the cultural assumptions that considered handwriting personal and unique also played a role in documents issued by institutions in large numbers. As noted, the pre–Civil War banknotes, as documents that circulated beyond the reputation of the banks that issued them, formed part of a new impersonal public discourse that developed separately from personal authority. The authenticity of the banknotes could not be verified through personal interaction and local knowledge, therefore, the authority of these banknotes required confidence in an impersonal medium—the documents through which that claim was expressed. But confidence in the authority of these mass-produced identical documents initially came to depend on the signature of the bank owner that was intended to present the banknotes as a personal agreement. It was anticipated that the signature as a graphic form considered personally distinct would give the notes an aura of uniqueness.[21]

The secretary of state's signature as a sign of uniqueness, something authentic on a passport printed from a standardized template, emphasizes the significance of a personal mark on an impersonal document. In the case of Secretary of State William Seward, whose right hand had been permanently injured, his stenographer believed

> the capitals in his signature were distinguishable, but it was little more than an impatient wave lie, a heavy trailing of the hand, that joined the S and the d. We have wondered whether the foreign officials who scrutinized the travelers' passports could read the signature at the bottom. It reminded one of the shambling gait of Homer's crook-horned oxen.[22]

Of course those hotel clerks, police officers, and border officials to whom the passport was presented more than likely sought to read the signature as an authentication of the document, not to decipher a name; with thirty-two secretaries of state between 1830 and 1900, knowledge of the name of the secretary of state at any given moment would have been quite an achievement on the part of a foreign official looking at a U.S. passport. In this context the pointlessness of a passport having the actual signature of the secretary of state was not lost on some department officials. Seward's stenographer believed "the seal of the Department authenticated by an assistant secretary would be sufficient" for a passport.[23] Without this option, the stenographer believed, the requirement to sign passports turned one of the country's most powerful officials into a "writing machine."[24]

The tension between replication and authenticity that characterized the emergence of mass-produced documents is evident in the concern that the person who signed a passport, who gave the document the semblance of personal authority, was turned into a machine by the excessive need to repeat his signature.[25] A solution adopted by many of the secretaries who succeeded Seward may have allowed them to avoid the mechanical labor of signing passports, but it made this tension even more visible; in the second half of the nineteenth century many secretaries issued passports with their signature stamped on the document.[26] The signature was still preceded by the phrase "Given under my hand," presumably to reassure people that this was the secretary's signature. The introduction of a stamp was probably the result of the dramatic increase in the number of passport issued. From 1801 to 1850 the State Department issued almost 22,000 passports; from 1850 to 1898 it issued a little under 263,000, with another 108,000 being issued between 1898 and 1905.[27] There is no record of why some secretaries reverted to handwritten signatures. However, a turn-of-the-century problem with the stamped signature raises one possibility. In so doing it illustrates the often gradual assumption of documentary claims to authenticity and authority that occurred over the course of the nineteenth century and the early decades of the twentieth century, and it reinforces the importance of standardization to the emerging authority of documents such as the passport.

In 1905, with an increasing number of passports in circulation, the State Department received a series of complaints from U.S. citizens. These expressed the concern that European border guards treated their passports with suspicion because the secretary of state's signature was stamped onto the passport. Secretary of State Elihu Root seemed to agree with the logic implicit in these complaints, acknowledging in a memo, "Passports are more valuable if signed by the pen than if signed by the stamp."[28] The use of a stamped signature likely challenged the authority of a document in two ways. The suspicious foreign officials possibly sought authority in the personal imprint of the issuer, an expectation encouraged by the representation of the passport as a letter. That is, the officials more than likely read into a handwritten signature a personalized token of authenticity. In appearance a handwritten signature had potentially greater value as a sign of individual identity than a stamped signature; the strokes of the pen linked the secretary personally to the document, he had to be present at its creation, and therefore performing the function of personal knowledge traditionally associated with identification. On a more practical level, also possibly in line with Root's comments, foreign suspicion of the U.S. passport could have been a direct result of concerns about authenticity in the more narrow terms of fraud—a stamp could be stolen or easily copied.

These concerns foreground the changing notions of the relationship between replication and authenticity in mass-produced documents. The signature was intended to verify the authenticity of the passport through the uniqueness of the script and the consistent replication of that script. Following this logic, a stamp, or some other way of reproducing a standardized signature, would be more desirable than a handwritten signature as it is virtually impossible to consistently repeat exactly the same signature. However, the cultural assumptions behind the signature as a graphic symbol of authenticity and legitimacy made clear Root's belief that a document is "more valuable if signed by the pen than if signed by the stamp."[29] A handwritten signature gave the passport authenticity through an assumed relationship between body, pen, and paper. A stamped signature gave the passport authenticity through a logic of standardization.

Despite Root's acknowledgment of the significance of a handwritten signature, the State Department's response to these complaints about the lack of a personal touch in its passport moved the passport further in the direction of a standardized document and thus towards its emergence as a modern identification document. Department officials stopped stamping signatures onto the passport, instead, a facsimile of the secretary's signature was engraved on the plate used to print the passport. While this continued to ensure that people did not have to sign fifteen-thousand passports by hand annually, it further clarified that a passport derived its authenticity from its standardization. This change is part of the gradual move away from a culture of identification in which authority derived from the implication or assumption of knowledge of one person by another person.

At the beginning of the twentieth century the passport preserved the form of a letter, complete with salutation and signature. However, the official authority of the passport did not come from an attempt to represent a personal relationship or even to imply that each document was produced with the personal knowledge of the secretary of state, but increasingly from uniform appearance (although the passport still identified the bearer through a name, physical description, and signature, all applied to the passport by hand). In an era of mechanical reproduction authenticity continued to be thought of in terms of a singular, unique object. This was still based in the idea of an original. But because this singular object was the engraved plate from which passports were printed it articulated a new understanding of "original," albeit one that was still unique to a particular place.[30] The possibility for authenticity to be understood in terms of repeatability was thus achieved through its articulation to a technologically derived understanding of standardization.[31] Trust in the reliability of identification became trust in the impersonal standardized form of a document, rather than in the personal knowledge of a reputable person. The impersonal authority was represented in the very nature of the standardized document. A facsimile of the secretary's signature being added to the engraved plate indicates the authority of the passport would not come from the signature of an individual authenticating and authorizing the document to which it was appended but from people recognizing the entire document as a passport issued by "the state." This increasing reliance on uniformity and standardization as the measure of authenticity and reliability also affected how a document such as the passport came to verify the physical appearance of the bearer, much to the concern of those citizens who considered their behavior, background, and appearance to be more than socially acceptable.

4

Physical Description

The perceived absurdity that people of an "acceptable" class, behavior, and background would have to carry an identification document is nicely captured in a piece from *Punch* (a useful reminder of the international nature of the anxiety over passports), reprinted in several U.S. magazines. Published soon after the outbreak of World War I made the passport a required document for most international travel, it recounted the attempts of an English gentleman to fill out the physical description on his passport application. He asks his wife for help on the grounds that he rarely sees himself. When she asks who needs to know what he looks like, her husband replies with the personal name of the foreign secretary, not the British Foreign Office. The personalization of the request locates, intentionally or otherwise, an understanding of "society" in which knowledge of personal identity does not involve interaction with institutions. The novelty, or indeed inappropriateness, of institutional intrusion sets the scene for what follows. His wife describes his nose as fine and substantial. He replies that he will only agree if fine means delicate and substantial means handsome, offering instead "Roman." When she disagrees, he fills in the appropriate blank with "non-Roman." The color of his eyes is described as green-grey (a compromise), to which he adds "gentle." However, much to the relief of his wife, he mistakenly enters this information as the description for his hair—she had never known how to describe his hair. Thus for "eyes" he writes, "see hair." His wife rejects "fair" as a description of his complexion, so he describes it as "normal," having observed that "most people who fill up blank spaces always use the word "normal" at least once." Now waiting for his passport to be sent to him, he concludes by taking "this opportunity to warn the French authorities that within a few days a gentleman with a non-Roman nose, grey-green and gentle hair, see-hair eyes and a normal complexion may be seeking admission to their country."[1]

Trivializing the need for certain people to have a passport in this manner also celebrates the absurdity associated with the inherently subjective nature of attempts to describe the body, itself an example of the difficulty of translating the visual into words. When describing someone, what physical features does one focus on? How does one describe someone's face or nose? And can everyone be expected to describe (i.e. see) the same nose as common, the same eyes as green? The emergence of a standardized physical description was an initial attempt to increase accuracy by limiting this discretion. The development and use of a physical description on the passport, therefore, provides further insights into both the contested transition of documentation from marginal groups to the population as a whole, and the importance (and novelty) of standardization in documentation.

As with the use of the bearer's signature, a physical description had been included on some U.S. passports issued abroad in the late eighteenth century, but not on passports issued in the United States.[2] This was the result of the actions of U.S. government representatives who issued passports that adhered to the format of the states in which they were appointed. The extant examples of U.S. passports issued abroad are from Europe when, in the last decade of the eighteenth century and first decade of the nineteenth, numerous states at certain times required passports of aliens and residents.[3] The introduction of physical descriptors on passports transformed the passport into a document that sought to establish the "unambiguous identity" of the bearer; that is, it pushed the passport in the direction of a modern identification document.[4] These passports were an administrative response to the increased rights associated with citizenship in an era in which individuals had begun to move around states and territories more frequently. Increased mobility is a common explanation for the emergence of state-issued identity documents; simply put, movement beyond one's community introduces the need for the proof of identity. It is important to note that the novelty of mobility meant no great distance had to be traveled for documentation to be required; in 1809 the Kingdom of Westphalia required that anyone who was more than eight miles from his or her home had to have what was labeled a passport.[5]

By the second decade of the nineteenth century, passports from the State Department did contain a space for the physical description of the bearer (figure 7.1). This followed the greeting from the secretary of state, and preceded his request for free and safe passage. Written in the form of a paragraph, blank spaces were preceded by descriptors: name, age, height (in feet and inches), complexion, hair, eyes, and a space of approximately two lines which was used to describe any distinguishing physical marks or features (such as scars and tattoos). In the 1820s, as the format of the passport changed once more, a more comprehensive physical description was added: age (years), stature (feet, "inches Eng."), forehead, eyes, nose, mouth, chin, hair, complexion, and face. Officials also relocated the description; it now appeared as a vertical list of categories down the left side of the document; the State Department kept this format until the first booklet passport was issued in 1926 (see figure 4.1).[6]

Although the State Department added a physical description of the bearer to the passport relatively early, the development of the U.S. passport as a source of "unambiguous identity" was not consistently recognized as a goal by all officials or members of the public. The addition of a physical description, along with the signature of the bearer, formalized the move away from a passport's original role as a diplomatic communication. However, in a society with no tradition of registering citizens, it was not guaranteed that a passport would be thought of primarily as a document to prove identity; in fact, the demand to prove identity through a passport could still be greeted with shock. We have already encountered one such example—the *Atlantic Monthly* editor, T. B. Aldrich's adventures with "his wife" and the Russian bureaucracy of the early 1880s, recounted thirty years later in the *New York Times* in the midst of the dispute over the Russian refusal to accept U.S. passports from Jews. In Russia the required passport was most definitely intended to clearly and specifically identify an individual within a larger system of registration and identification. In this context a passport was understood to be an identification document that verified facts about both personal identity and legal identity. A physical description of the bearer played a vital role in ensuring the system of identification documents could be counted on to keep the government accurately informed about the movement of people within its territory. A traveler to Russia required "an identification paper setting forth name, nationality, age, height, color of eyes and hair, shape of nose and chin and other such personal peculiarities as would definitely connect the document with the bearer and thus prevent illegal substitution

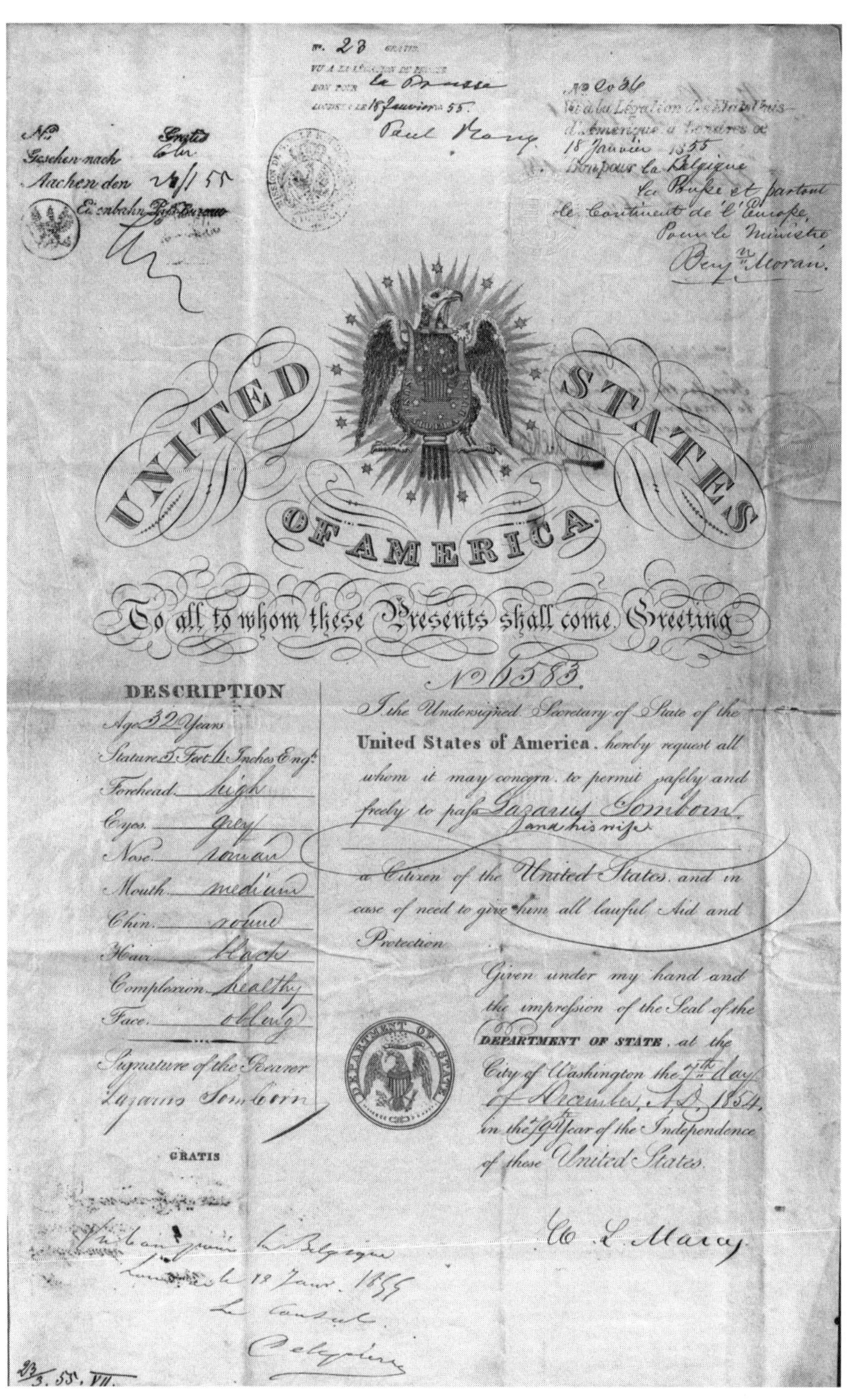

UNITED STATES OF AMERICA

To all to whom these Presents shall come, Greeting

№ 6583

DESCRIPTION

Age 32 Years
Stature 5 Feet 4 Inches Eng.
Forehead high
Eyes grey
Nose roman
Mouth medium
Chin round
Hair black
Complexion healthy
Face oblong

Signature of the Bearer
Lazarus Somborn

GRATIS

I the Undersigned Secretary of State of the **United States of America**, hereby request all whom it may concern, to permit safely and freely to pass Lazarus Somborn and his wife a Citizen of the United States, and in case of need to give him all lawful Aid and Protection.

Given under my hand and the impression of the Seal of the DEPARTMENT OF STATE, at the City of Washington the 7th day of December A.D. 1854, in the 79th Year of the Independence of these United States.

W. L. Marcy

Figure 4.1. Passport issued in 1854 following the format introduced in the 1820s. It is issued to the named bearer "and his wife" (National Archives, College Park, MD).

and transfer."[7] Here the physical description has a specific purpose, one that locates the passport as an identification document in an environment where it is acknowledged that its legal necessity produces the possibility it could be fraudulently used. In contrast the U.S. passport was generally issued on the assumption that it was an optional document, and it was trusted that it would be used as intended, that is, "legally" in the most general sense.[8] This is not to say that people did not attempt to illegally acquire U.S. passports in the nineteenth century, but that no rigorous system was set up to prevent it—this did not occur until the outbreak of World War I turned the passport into an important tool for ensuring national security.

In a country that did not demand passports at its borders and did not require its residents (citizen or otherwise) to register with government officials, the passport frequently appeared as a certificate of citizenship in official correspondence of the U.S. government. This moved it well beyond a letter of introduction in the eyes of most officials, but within a context in which identification documents were not required, the passport still had an ambiguous relationship to a modern identification document. The State Department required documentary evidence of citizenship by midcentury; in the last quarter of the century officials even began to rigorously enforce the demand for supporting documents. But, significantly, State Department officials stopped short of adapting the physical description to more "modern" forms of personal identification technologies: anthropometry, fingerprinting, and photography.

The limited interest in the passport as an identification document can be attributed to what is a recurring argument throughout this history: popular thinking considered only marginal populations—especially criminals—to be the appropriate targets of official identification practices. Identification practices should target "them"—those without power—not "us"—those with power. It is in this sense that the passport is an example of a contested move from the excessive documentation of "the other" to the inclusion of an entire population in a regime of documentation. Through the first decades of the twentieth century (and arguably beyond), fingerprinting and photography were identification practices that were associated with criminals, not the segment of the population who could afford the luxury of international travel. This indeed is the theme of the *New York Times*'s lengthy recounting of Aldrich's 1880s Russian adventures, in which the failure to have a passport is presented through what is seemingly intended to be read as an incongruous invocation of criminality; the retelling of Aldrich's journey ends with the image of designated cells for the "passportless" in "gloomy" prisons. The article makes explicit that this could have been the temporary home for this esteemed American gentleman and his wife; as we know from the previous chapter, the absence of her passport had made them probable objects of a "suspect file." Such a scenario was only averted because the U.S. consul in St. Petersburg personally vouched for their identity. The tale thus provides an example of the personal world of reputation and status within which the passport partially and awkwardly took on the role of an identification document; hence the "incongruity" that structures the *Times* article. In the face of the happy ending, the absurdity of pursuing this demand for documents beyond a polite request provides a somewhat humorous recounting of Aldrich's travels. In "knowing" criminals the official need for an external source of identity was apparently obvious. In contrast, an honest and trustworthy person, it seems, did not need an identification document. Such documents were considered to be necessary only for suspect populations, at least by those people who felt that their own appearance clearly verified they were honest and trustworthy.

In this context even the requirement of a physical description was seen as a somewhat delicate request, if not an affront to the sensibilities of a passport applicant—for this reason British passports in the mid-nineteenth century did not have a physical description.[9] In 1882 a notary public described how he assisted people in filling out a U.S. passport "blank," or application.

> We generally mention the chief peculiarity of each feature mentioned in the blank. I remember one passport in which the nose was described as 'common.' Most persons would object to such a description. Single ladies who apply for passports sometimes blush or even show signs of anger when I ask them their age or perhaps the length of their feet but I show them the law on the subject and they are generally satisfied.[10]

The request for age in this explicitly gendered example is seen as an intrusion, an invasion of privacy even for a document intended to facilitate public movement. It should be noted that the State Department did not require the recording of the length of a person's feet. If anything, this type of intrusion was precisely what officials seemed to avoid either on the grounds of sensitivity, or, more pragmatically, because such detailed descriptions (or degrees of accuracy) were not considered necessary for the nineteenth-century passport to do its job. A possible source of the mistake could have been how the application form requested height ("Stature:___ feet, ___ inches, Eng") which, if it indeed led the notary to believe that he was required to provide a measurement of the applicant's feet in inches, provides another example of the argument that filling in forms required a distinct literacy. However, while that specific example is inaccurate, the general tone of the notary's explanation accurately captures the discomfort caused as the passport became a document that required a version of identity that many applicants considered to be an inaccurate representation of their sense of who they were. The notary's concern over the "common nose" further indicates how the requirement of a physical description revealed that the documentation of individual identity was changing the relationship between identity and identification. The stark, simple adjectives used to describe a person's body turned the complexity of a "romantic" perception of the personal uniqueness of appearance and character into a standardized and thus simplified list of physical traits.

The use of a discrete list of features and descriptors was an early way in which the passport entered the world of standardization, a world that characterized modern identification practices in terms of precision and economy. These practices were driven by an ad hoc flight from subjectivity to objectivity—in this specific example, a boilerplate text that sought to avoid any unique flourishes in attempts to clearly describe individuals so they could be more easily recognized. The introduction of an application form in the 1830s that included the list of features on the passport encouraged applicants to describe themselves according to the criteria the State Department had chosen; likewise, the early-nineteenth-century listing of physical categories on the passport itself served a pedagogical function for clerks writing up passports.[11] The *Punch* parody acknowledged that this was the official strategy by illustrating the applicant's "subversive" description of his eyes as gentle. In another example an English author was said to describe himself as "of melancholic appearance."[12] Thus, the ascription of character traits to these physical features, while perhaps also ridiculing people for reading too much into such features, also stressed that the application and the passport turned personal identity into something very generic and impersonal. This was not an understanding of identity drawn from the palate of the "romantics"; it was most definitely not the identification of people through their character and social status. In practice a small number of physical descriptors came to dominate. Eyes and hair were described by color, a face was generally either round or elongated, a nose was common, large, or small. But even with a limited set of options, space still existed for different interpretations. As the article from *Punch* illustrated, people could disagree, and "common" could be all too common if the alternative was a "large" nose. Or, as a nineteenth century commentator noted, an applicant would more than likely "contest the terms applied to their nasal organ in a passport, insisting upon a kindly adjective to designate the shape thereof, although it may cast a doubt of identity."[13]

Problems raised by the possibility of different descriptions of physical appearance are problems of mediation. Standardization was an attempt to prevent descriptions from being too subjective, but as a form of mediation it introduced other problems. While the increasing belief in the need to standardize the collection and presentation of information made some sense as an attempt to stabilize an official identity or a legal identity such as citizenship, it could be more problematic when personal identity was abstracted into a physical description. Applicants recognized an aspect of this when, in renewing passports, they alerted officials that features of their appearance had changed. When people applied for a new passport they sometimes mentioned the graying of hair, or that a previously "round" face had become "elongated"—perhaps indicating a loss of weight.[14] In producing a stable identity to facilitate identification, the passport had artificially fixed physical appearance in the midst of the natural aging process. Another problem of mediation came from the mechanism used to record physical appearance on a passport; the physical description was not only translated through the subjective assessment of one person, but also remained susceptible to transcription errors in the writing up of a passport—the physical description was filled in by the hand of a passport clerk using details handwritten onto the application form. On occasions a clerk would incorrectly transfer information from the application to the document. Such errors resulted in applicants "officially" aging ten years or more overnight, having their hair color changed, or their wife omitted. These were generally noted by the bearer and returned for correction, but, as recounted earlier, this was not always the case.

The problems associated with mediation were potentially troubling because they affected the consistency with which a document could reliably represent an identity. A documented identity was deemed useful when it could be counted on to accurately link the bearer to the document. Although application forms and identification documents allowed state officials to dictate the parameters of a physical description, the translation of a person's physical appearance into words still relied on the specific perception of individuals. Even with the policing mechanisms of a form and a clerk reviewing the form, the brief, standardized formality of the description could not be guaranteed to abstract an individual's physical appearance into a document so it could always be seen as an accurate resemblance by all those who looked at the document and the bearer. Possibly motivated by this concern, a high school teacher applying for a passport in 1896 submitted a "picture" with his application. From the accompanying letter it appeared that he believed the picture (probably a photograph) provided an accurate representation of his face; noting his age, height, and the color of his eyes, he added "the rest can be seen from the picture."[15] Simply put, the physical description favored the potentially particular observations of an individual. By the second half of the nineteenth century, in some parts of the state apparatus the translation of observations into verbal descriptors was considered neither sufficiently accurate nor useful as an identification technology. Beyond the documentation of individual identity in a passport, identification practices in the world of policing became structured by attempts to limit discretion in the name of objectivity—both scientific objectivity and bureaucratic objectivity.

While the increased disposition in favor of objectivity was more pronounced in the nineteenth century development of criminal identification practices, the purported objectivity and, therefore, assumed accuracy of modern identification technologies were important to the articulation of the passport's usefulness during (and after) World War I. Thus, although the passport was not at the forefront of the new identification technologies developed in the nineteenth century to police suspect populations, these developments are critical to understanding the move toward documenting everyone, and therefore to comprehending how the passport became an acceptable answer to the question "Who are you?"

New policing techniques and technologies initially emerged on the European continent and reached broader public consciousness when Alphonse Bertillon, a French police clerk, applied anthropometry (the scientific measurement of the human body) to criminal identification. With a father who was a pioneer of nineteenth century social sciences, Bertillon had grown up in a household filled with anthropometric tools and a belief in Adolphe Quetelet's groundbreaking "social physics." After his father, in an attempt to settle his wayward son, found him a job in the central Paris police station, Bertillon quickly became appalled at the chaotic identification and record-keeping practices he encountered. To solve the problem he invented a system that became known as "Bertillonage," or sometimes erroneously as anthropometry. It differed from the preexisting practice of anthropometry in two important ways: it was directed toward the identification of individuals, not types; and it used techniques other than measurement. This technology of identifying individuals through the precise measurement of the body and the statistically based storage of files experienced both a rapid growth and decline in the last decades of the nineteenth century—the former through an understanding of identity that linked it to phrenology and physiognomy, and the later largely as a consequence of fingerprinting.[16]

Bertillon's intervention occurred in a century in which European police officials became increasingly anxious about procedure, specifically that inadequate physical descriptions jeopardized the attempt to thwart criminals.[17] While the development of a standardized form was an initial step toward solving this, anthropometry offered a potentially more significant move, as it replaced personal memory with a set of techniques to establish identity through the collection of measurements. Bertillon required eleven different anthropometric measurements: height, head length, head breadth, arm span, sitting height, left middle finger length, left little finger length, left foot length, left forearm length, right ear length, and cheek width. These were believed to be the proportions least likely to be affected by weight change or aging. Each measurement was recorded with specially designed calipers, gauges, and rulers. To ensure the required accuracy and the ability of different measurers to achieve the same result, Bertillon outlined precise instructions that delineated the position of the body of not only the prisoner but also the officer who measured the prisoner's body. For example Bertillon prescribed twenty distinct movements just to measure the left foot. Bertillonage did not finish with these anthropometric measurements. The prisoner's physical appearance was also recorded in a detailed and standardized fashion using a system of precise terminology Bertillon developed that included more than fifty types of eye color. The prisoner was also photographed twice: a frontal image and a profile shot. A clerk then recorded all this information onto a card. Bertillon also introduced a system of standardized abbreviations for clerks to use.[18]

The cards at the center of Bertillonage did not record the biography of an individual; rather, their contents prioritized the body, which was assumed to be harder to alter than the details and evidence of an individual's social identity. The formalized physical description combined anthropometrical measures and a standardized description of physiognomic and bodily details. In contrast to the identity forms that had become more common in this period, there was no information about birthplace, place of residence, religion, or other biographical details.

In this manner Bertillon organized the recording of identity so it provided only those aspects of an identity that would be useful in identifying a recidivist who had been subjected to Bertillonage. His goal was to create a system that produced the very identity it needed to be a successful identification technique. Bertillon did not make use of an existing (social) identity; he used Bertillonage to produce a new identity. He did this by delimiting the nature of the identity he recorded to privilege anatomical and physiological categories. And, of equal significance, this system recorded the identity it produced in such a way that it could easily be retrieved; thus Bertillon created an identity that adhered to the conditions of bureaucratic objectivity. The description on the card derived its logic from what Bertillon saw as the needs of identification—information arranged systematically and according to relevance. It was common for a description of the face to begin with hair and end with the beard to recreate how they appeared in "natural" facial order to facilitate easier identification. However, Bertillon recorded hair and beard next to each other, following the logic that they belonged to the same group of physical characteristics. He also ordered the information on the card so that it began with the features he considered most relevant to identification (forehead, nose, and ear).[19] In this manner Bertillon hoped to produce an identity that could more easily be retrieved from the large volume of records modern states had begun to compile.

The purported accuracy of Bertillonage came from not only the information that was prioritized—anatomically "factual" evidence—and how it was recorded, but also most importantly how the resulting cards were filed. This system could only be used to identify someone successfully if the card could subsequently be found; the lack of a successful system of classification had limited the usefulness of photography as an identification technology. Bertillon created a complex system of filing that began by separating the identification cards by sex. The cards were then arranged into successive subdivisions, each divided into below-average, average, and above-average figures; these categories were defined through statistical studies of prisoners in Paris. The first subdivision was head length. This was then subdivided into head breadth, followed by middle finger length and so on as the classification system made use of measurements recorded on the cards. The resulting groups were filed into drawers ultimately being arranged by ear length. If done correctly this system could break a collection of over 100,000 cards into groups of no more than a dozen.[20]

In contrast to Bertillonage (but more faithful to anthropometry), physical appearance read off the surface of the body could also be used in attempting to identify the behavioral and character traits of a particular social group. This specific understanding of the exterior of the body developed outside of administrative police work. Criminology and broader medico-legal approaches interpreted the surface of the body in the name of "science"—the former originating in anxieties over the physical and mental degeneration of the European race, the latter in concerns over urban disorder and population growth. In both cases the goal was to isolate a typical set of characteristics. Criminology focused on identities like "the criminal" or "the prostitute" that overwhelmed the individual identity Bertillon sought.[21] While this is also in contrast to the individual identity that was the goal of the passport, it does point us in the direction of an identity that could be read off the body. This was an identity that many individuals and officials believed made a document such as the passport redundant.

The faith in the reading of the body was not limited to experts. Outside the police station and the university, a preexisting, everyday amateur reading of appearance provided what many considered a satisfactory way to identify people. By the turn of the twentieth century people in the United States increasingly saw bodies as the surface reflections of interior characteristics.[22] The development of this belief can be traced to the popularization of physiognomy and phrenology.[23] Physiognomy sought to establish a person's character through external appearance, particularly the face and profile. More popular in the United States was phrenology, which argued that the personality traits of a person could be derived from the shape of their skull.[24] Modernity (in the form of the bustling, overcrowded metropolis of the second half of the nineteenth century) did present a challenge to the belief that people could read identity off bodies, while simultaneously granting new legitimacy to these pseudo sciences. In response to the increased mobility in the nineteenth century "crimes of mobility" emerged based largely on the deceptiveness of appearance, particularly swindles and the work of "confidence men."[25] Cultural historian John Kasson reads such crimes as suggesting to the public "that character was not permanent but malleable, that identity was not coherent but fragmented, and that social appearances were not dependable but subject to the most cynical manipulation."[26] However, while in this context the value of such signs as evidence of identity may have been questioned, neither they, nor the identity they verified, lost their authority in identification. An explanation for this is offered in the emergence of etiquette and manners books (as well as detective novels). In response to the possibility of deception such books popularized a concern with the need to accurately read appearance from signs by developing specific modes of looking. Their authors sought to simultaneously give readers various techniques of inspection to ascertain the appearance of others and to advise them on how to become anonymous and to disappear safely into the crowd.[27] Despite the mutability of the body that such techniques demanded (and that various forms of "passing" also illustrated), faith continued to exist in the subjective observation of the visual as critical evidence for determining identity. The emergence of the rogues' gallery in the second half of the nineteenth century provided another forum in which people were encouraged to think of looking at the body as an important form of detection. These galleries were rooms, usually in police stations, that displayed wall-mounted photographs of criminals to enable crime victims to identify suspects or police to compare the faces of people in custody to see if they had previously offended (possibly under different names). However, they quickly became viewed as a form of popular entertainment, so popular that the New York City Police Department closed its gallery; New Yorkers could continue to visit a rogues' gallery at P.T. Barnum's museum. While the photographs were originally intended to assist in the identification of specific individuals it is fair to suggest that in the context of physiognomy and phrenology the photographs encouraged visitors to view the images as evidence of the existence of a "criminal" type.[28]

In the absence of voter registration and official documents, the mid-century identification of voters at polling booths drew from this belief in the ability to use social and physical markers to identify other people. In this case individuals did not read the body to determine character or individual identity but to verify race and ethnicity. When race in particular was in dispute, prior to the Fifteenth Amendment guaranteeing African Americans the right to vote, concerned parties sought evidence from the body of the voter. This generally occurred when a voter had what were seen as ambiguous features. At this time voter eligibility was established by a process involving community members assigned by parties to challenge people as they voted, with a final decision made by an "election judge," often under the influence of the assembled community. Race was usually determined by employing a checklist of four features through which the community believed the "presence of black blood and its proportion" could be detected, particularly in a person unknown to them: hair, nose, lips and complexion. Telltale signs of African American identity could be seen in "kinky" hair, "flat" noses, "protruding" lips and a "dark" complexion. A list such as this was developed to try to bring rational order to the potential problem of verifying racial identity. This form of voter identification was used more frequently in urban areas where the size of the precincts produced an anonymity that prevented the assembled public from appealing to communal knowledge to establish an individual's genealogy. In cities, in the absence of documents, ethnicity was somewhat similarly verified. However, bodily accoutrements such as speech, behavior, and most importantly attire were read as evidence of ethnic identity.[29]

In a similar manner officials at the U.S. border believed they could read the individual bodies and appearances of new arrivals and identify individuals as members of suspect populations (such as prostitutes or excluded Chinese laborers). An individual's physical appearance along with his or her general deportment (including clothing) was viewed as providing sufficient evidence of identity to enable that individual to be, if not specifically known, at least trusted (Aldrich) or not (Chinese laborers). In this context the surface of the body was "read" through increasingly complex understandings of race (and class) that drew categories of "inferior" and "superior" from Darwinism, eugenics and physical anthropology.[30] Ultimately, this identification of some*body*, not some*one*, produced a useful identity by attaching individuals to a group of behavioral expectations based on their adherence to certain physical types.

The assumed correspondence between physical appearance and an individual's essential identity, particularly the ways class, gender, and race were articulated to embody privilege or not, offers a parallel history to that of the passport—or more accurately, a framework for understanding why documents were not considered necessary. From this perspective we can return to the "absurdity" of T. H. Aldrich's passport woes in Russia. Aldrich's presence, the racialized, classed, and gendered body he presented, was thought by some to make explicit that he was a person who could be trusted, a person whose word (made manifest in his body) should be sufficient to establish identity; he only had to be looked at. In the case of "Americans" like Aldrich, the encoding of class and whiteness as status and privilege was so naturalized as to be practically invisible. Their identity allowed them to do what they wanted and to go where they wanted; it was something that did not need to be commented on. Within the world of the Aldriches a demand for the verification of identity beyond the "obvious" constituted an affront. In one sense it took away from individuals the control of their identity. The indignation, the occasional awkwardness of anything that associated the passport with "requirements" (in either description or use), challenged the sense of self and rights; it denied the understanding of self-control that most passport bearers used to distinguish "us" from "them."

To clarify; what someone like Aldrich offered to be "read" was less the body itself and more a body's social accoutrements. While, in the words of the *Punch* parody, the "normal complexion" of whiteness was important, beyond race the reading of people's appearance also privileged their social distinction through the way the body was clothed, the way it moved, and the voice that came out of the body. Further within the complex articulation of public and private that constituted decency and deportment, for those with privilege the body itself was off limits, in contrast to "the others" whose bodies revealed their lack of privilege. Thus neither the precise measurements of anthropometry nor its successor, fingerprinting, were considered acceptable ways to establish the identity of "us" as opposed to "them"; nor, it seems, were "abnormal" physical features (such as tattoos and scars) that on other bodies could be used to "verify" identity.[31] In the case of the U.S. passport, this appeared to be a very conscious choice, albeit for reasons that are unclear. The paragraph allotted to the physical description on early passports included two lines to describe any distinguishing physical marks or features.[32] In the reformatting of the passport at the beginning of the 1820s, the State Department increased the number of physical features listed, but did not provide any space for distinguishing physical marks or features. There is no record of the rationale for this decision. The use of the body over facial features was perhaps seen as inappropriate—scars and tattoos not on the face would more than likely be hidden under clothing.

The removal of references to bodily "deformities" may have had less to do with people and more to do with the hesitant entrance of the U.S. passport into the world of efficient, standardized, and objective identification documents. It could be that officials presumed that distinctive markings such as tattoos and scars appeared so infrequently on the body of "Americans" that it was unnecessary to allocate space on every passport for the occasional noticeably blemished body. Thus the lack of space to describe physical markings could perhaps be more fully located in the belief that efficiency and standardization were necessary for more useful and reliable identification. In contrast to the presentation of the physical description in paragraph form, the move to vertically listing specific features implied a conscious effort to produce a document that would be more effectively and efficiently filled in and read. Two blank lines also provided empty space that could be filled at the discretion of the official or the bearer. Such discretion ran counter to the ideal of objectivity to which modern identification was increasingly being held. Objectivity in the form of standardization was in large part used to control the creation of identity by limiting the opportunity for an official's discretion to influence the creation of a document.

However, the complexity of the emergence of the passport as a modern identification technology is evident in the return of a designated space for distinguishing marks in the twentieth century. The twentieth-century passport developed as a document required in the name of national security. Unlike its nineteenth-century relative, the priority of this passport at the border was the identification of suspect individuals such as Bolsheviks and aliens who sought to avoid immigration laws. Although after 1914 U.S. passports contained a photograph of the bearer the retooled physical description remained on the passport to help a suspicious official establish that a photograph had not been altered or substituted; the U.S. government no longer thought of its passports as a courtesy document for travelers. Therefore, any concessions to privilege disappeared as all parts of the body became appropriate objects for the gaze of officials. In fact, all aspects of a person's identity came to be viewed as potentially valuable to what was now viewed as a useful and necessary act of identification. In deference to the international standardization of the passport, U.S. officials added "occupation" as a category in the description of the bearer.[33]

5

Photograph

On 21 December 1914, Secretary of State William Jennings Bryan issued an order requiring two unmounted photographs no larger than three inches by three inches to be submitted with passport applications—one attached to the application, the second to be put on the passport.[1] Citizens who had been issued passports without photographs were required to have a photograph added. Photographs were introduced to make the passport a more accurate identification document in a time of war.[2] The use of the passport in the name of national security also brought with it an increased concern to make the document more secure. Less than a month after adding photographs to passports, the State Department acknowledged the need to more effectively ensure that the correct photograph was connected to the correct document. When applications were submitted to local courthouses, clerks were now requested to affix photographs to the application with a seal to avoid subsequent substitution of the photograph prior to the issuance of a passport.[3] In Washington and at embassies around the world, officials stamped the seal of their office over the top left corner of the photograph when they attached it to the passport instead of the initial practice of simply pasting it to the document. A rubber stamp was also introduced to apply a legend across the photograph. In addition to being an attempt to secure the passport, the legend made explicit the purpose of the photograph and the authority that legitimized the identification process. The legend stated: "This is to certify that the photograph attached hereto is a likeness of the person to whom this passport is issued. In witness whereof the seal of the Department of State is impressed upon the photograph." In 1928, as part of continuing attempts to make the passport a more secure document, the State Department began to use a machine that perforated a legend across the lower part of the photograph after it was attached to a passport. This made it more difficult for someone to cleanly remove the photograph, and it was assumed to be more difficult to replicate than the rubber stamp.[4]

All of this effort was necessary because officials considered the photograph to be an authoritative likeness of a person—hence their concern that a substituted photograph would allow someone to easily claim the citizenship and identity the state had intended for someone else. The concern with fraud led officials to employ the relatively less "accurate" identification technologies of the signature and the physical description to further ensure the photograph on the passport was indeed that of the person the State Department had issued the passport to. Officials reduced the categories in the physical description to height, hair, and eyes, but as noted retained the recently added category for "distinguishing marks." From 1924 applicants had to sign the back of the passport photograph. According to a State Department publication, this signature "provided a written record to identify the rightful bearer in the passport, reduced the possibility of fraud, and insured that the proper photograph was attached to the application and the passport."[5]

During the 1920s the State Department also clarified its policy to ensure that all passports carried a photograph of the bearer. In 1921 the secretary of state ruled that applicants had to provide a photograph regardless of religious beliefs; this was in response to an applicant intending to travel abroad as a missionary who had quoted Exodus 20:4 against the making of graven images to support his belief that he should not have to provide a photograph.[6] At the end of the decade the State Department issued a requirement that all infants had to have a photograph on a passport.[7] The department also sought to stop its officials, both at home and abroad, from accepting photographs that did not satisfy the increasingly specific requirements: thin paper, light background, and dimensions between 2.5 inches by 2.5 inches and 3 inches by 3 inches.[8]

The passport photograph, if it adhered to this particular form, was considered to produce a "truthful" image that could be used to reliably link a person to a passport and thus accurately establish an individual's identity. The promise to deliver accurate identification was based in a faith in the mechanical reproduction of the camera over the lingering subjectivity of the written physical description. It is therefore important to establish how the photograph came to be considered an objective, trustworthy technology that satisfied the new modern criteria for reliability in official identification. It is equally important to recognize that this visual authority was contested, both implicitly and explicitly. The "truth" that state officials granted the passport photograph in documenting a person's face and thus their identity coexisted with a public perception of what a newspaper called the "distortion of passport photography."[9] This "distortion" was the product of the clashing of two particular traditions of photographing people: the portrait and the "scientific" image (generally used in criminal identification photographs). Most passport applicants associated representational truth with the specific articulation of realism in photographic portraits. This association gave rise to complaints that a standardized passport photograph was unflattering, and in fact did not look like the bearer. From the inception of passport photographs, people experienced "a pang of horrid surprise, almost disbelief, upon first looking at the photograph which [was] to identify them in a foreign country;"[10] at least according to a *New York Times* editorial from 1930 (which will be discussed in detail below.)

In the nineteenth century photography developed rapidly from the unique image of the daguerreotype in the 1840s to the arrival of the first Kodak handheld cameras in the 1880s. While this involved numerous technical advances, including a move from wet plates to dry plates and the introduction of flexible film and faster lenses, throughout this period most people encountered photography in one form—portraits. In the United States portraits were produced in the form of the phenomenally successful daguerreotype and the subsequently popular carte de visite. The former produced a unique picture directly onto a polished silver-coated plate; made as a positive image without a negative, it was extremely fragile and therefore was kept in a protective case like a piece of jewelry. The latter was a photographic visiting card 2½ by 4 inches that arrived once paper prints could be produced from glass negatives. Early histories of photography cited these particular forms as evidence that photographs democratized portraiture; images of individuals were made available to members of the lower classes who had not been able to have painted portraits. The simple facts of the arrival of the daguerreotype can be read to support this claim. In the 1840s it became the most successful commercial concern in the United States, with people spending $8–12 million a year on daguerreotypes; by the mid-1850s, with the fad subsiding a little, an estimated three million daguerreotypes were still produced, selling at two for twenty-five cents (making them more expensive that the new paper prints that had recently emerged).[11] More recent histories of photography have argued that although such numbers indicate that the ability to access a portrait had permeated the population, this supposed democratization of representation arrived as a commodity to secure developing class relations and in the form of a portrait style that, it is argued, transmitted bourgeois values.[12] While this argument developed in debates about the extent to which a recognition of resistance and multiple uses can challenge the power of the state and the market, it is the claim to "likeness" in the development of the photographic portrait style that is of primary importance to the history of photography as an identification technology.

A discussion in the early issues of the New York Camera Club magazine about the relationship between art and photography highlights an important distinction in early photographic portrait practices—namely, between "photographic likeness" and "photographic portrait." This debate from the late 1890s drew on popular physiognomic understandings of the relationship between the surface of the body and interior identity or true character.[13] The "likeness" was an image almost entirely associated with physical attributes that apparently enabled only a perfunctory identification. In contrast, it was argued that a more accurate representation could be elicited if photographers followed the conventions of portraiture. This accuracy lay in the successful capturing of "the imprint of the subject's personality."[14] True "resemblance" was thus not due to any specific insights on the part of the camera, nor was it to be found on the surface of the body. Rather, it was due to the discursive construction of the body as a portrait, which the camera could then merely represent. Cultural historian Alan Trachtenberg has argued that the portrait as a camera image was made to "resemble a resemblance, to give an effect of likeness" achieved "only under controls (focus, framing, lighting) derived from a formula of likeness" taken from an adjacent formal system of representation in portraiture.[15] Posture and expression were critical to the construction of this "likeness"; it has been argued that this arrangement of head and hands needs to be understood through the typologies of physiognomy.[16] In the United States the earliest and most infamous example of the articulation of the physiognomic appeal of photography to class and national identity was Matthew Brady's portraits of "illustrious Americans." These were images of people in three-quarter profile looking away from the viewer.

Brady exhibited his daguerreotypes of famous Americans in New York in the 1850s and 1860s before selecting twelve portraits for a print edition called *The Gallery of Illustrious Americans*.[17]

As the nineteenth century progressed another style of gallery became equally famous—the rogues' gallery that made photographs of criminals available to the public with great success as a form of entertainment. By the 1880s these images were circulated more widely, such as in *Professional Criminals of America*, a book written by the chief detective of the New York City police.[18] In comparison with Brady's *Gallery* the distinction between "portrait" and "likeness" in the rogues' gallery becomes a stark division between the artistic and technical. This new "juridical photographic realism" drew from the imperatives of medical and anatomical illustration rather than the traditions of portraiture.[19] These photographs, stripped of the accoutrements of the portrait in the name of a "scientific" rigor, produced the image of the head-on stare, which was in direct contrast to the cultivated asymmetries of a portrait pose.[20] As photography was more fully recruited into the policing of criminals, it is possible to make a further distinction between the "technical" and the "scientific." While each approach turned on the relationship between individual and group/species, they sought to reveal a different aspect. The technical was the particular image of the mug shot, used to identify a specific individual. But photography was also employed to define the generalized look of the criminal. As criminology emerged to produce a typology of criminals, photographs were used to define the generalized appearance of these types. This occurred most prominently in the work of Francis Galton, a cousin of Charles Darwin. In the 1870s, before he moved on to develop eugenics, Galton used photographs of individuals to produce composite images of criminal types.[21] Although different in intention, the scientific and the technical collectively created a culture of photographic documentation, which art historian John Tagg describes as one of "precision, measurement, calculation and proof, separating out its objects of knowledge, shunning emotional appeal and dramatization, and hanging its status on technical rules and protocols whose institutionalization had to be negotiated."[22]

The acceptance of photographic authority also occurred gradually in other areas. In the world of science the photograph emerged to challenge the scientific drawing. While the quality of early photographic images was often less visually accurate than that of scientific drawing, photographs were seen as being more reliable, as their automated image was understood to eliminate any chance of suspect human mediation. The faith in this new "mechanical objectivity" put a new preference for automation over precision at the forefront of the creation of the scientific image. This definition of reliability, grounded in moral terms as the exclusion of the scientist's will, produced the early trust in the photographic image over and above individual actions.[23]

In U.S. courtrooms the claim that photographs provided accurate evidence was not as readily accepted. At the beginning of the twentieth century, photographs had become a routine evidentiary tool in the courtroom, but this only occurred through a complicated and not entirely consistent process.[24] The legal debate over the authority of photography illustrated the two paradigmatic understandings of photography: as objective machine-made truth ("a mirror with memory,"[25] as Oliver Wendell Holmes famously put it) and as artifice (the product of human agency and skill). While supporters believed in the accuracy of a photographic image, the photograph came to be accepted as legal evidence on the grounds that it only "might" be a true depiction.

Prior to the middle of the nineteenth century, words constituted most of the evidence in a courtroom. By the 1870s, although photographs were frequently used to prove identity in criminal cases, they remained such a novelty in the courtroom that lawyers often contested the authority of photographs. The photograph officially entered the courtroom, along with maps and diagrams, as an example of "illustrative evidence." A photograph was thus understood to be open to dispute. As illustrative evidence it was not independent evidence, and therefore a witness had to authenticate the image and confirm it was an accurate representation before it could be used. That is, judgment as to the truth of visual representation was identical to the assessment of the veracity of any witness. However, the power of the photographic image was such that, when used in courtrooms, photographs became more than mere illustrations. They trumped other visual tools as the idea of a photograph as an unmediated image of reality permeated the courtroom; if not official evidence, photographs were at least an increasingly compelling, independently persuasive form of proof. Therefore, through contested claims to truth, photographs entered the courtroom as a legal fiction—"a formal rule that coexisted with a reality that contradicted it."[26]

The competing understandings of photographs as unmediated depictions or constructed artifacts meant the "reliability" of photography did not arrive uncontested. While a common result saw photographs viewed as dependable and objective, this outcome was the product of debate and negotiation that both purposely and inadvertently exposed the precise terms under which photography could be seen to accurately represent the world. In the development of identification documentation in the United States, the enforcement of the Chinese Exclusion Acts provides an early example of how this negotiation over the authority of the photographic image often originated in an initial blind faith in photographs to document the "truth." The addition of photographs to the identification documents used to verify Chinese who were exempt from the act was the first example of government-issued photographic identification in the United States.[27] Photographs were added to prevent potential Chinese immigrants from selling, exchanging, or creating fraudulent documents. They were initially considered to provide an accurate representation as they came from the camera, not from Chinese, who were not trusted to truthfully represent themselves through documents. However, most Chinese who sought entry to the United States exercised some control over their photographic representation. In this way they maintained a more active involvement in their representation than officials intended. For at least the first fifteen years in which photographs were required, Chinese regularly submitted their own photographs with few official guidelines—and it was not until 1926 that regulations specified a uniform photographic size or pose, at which point they codified what had become standard practice.[28] The limited requirements were that a photograph should not be retouched or mounted, and it had to accurately represent the face—"1½ inches from base of the hair to the base of the chin."[29] As a result, the submitted photographs ranged from elaborate studio portraits to simple headshots. Subjects stood, sat, faced the camera, or looked to the side. While most wore Chinese clothes, some men presented themselves with the markers of Western masculine respectability: suits, ties, and even facial hair. Others adopted a very traditional Chinese cultural appearance. The majority of these images were rectangular vertical portraits, but some had trimmed corners and others were in the shape of arches or ovals.[30]

The initial lack of official interest in standardizing images stemmed from a simple understanding of the photographic process that led to a belief that because of the mechanical creation of the image there was no suspect mediation in the use of the camera. However, by the end of the nineteenth century most immigration officials had grown more cautious about photography, owing to the recognition that the conditions in which a photograph was taken could affect the veracity of the image. What skepticism there was about photography was linked to the object of the image. A belief that Chinese were untrustworthy was translated to mistrust of the photographs (and documents) they presented.[31] One response to this was to photograph Chinese immigrants as they arrived in San Francisco. In these outdoor shots the person's face was frequently in shadow and less clear than in the photographs immigrants brought with them. However, these were considered more reliable, as the production of the image had been taken out of Chinese hands.

Two decades after Congress required photographs on Chinese identification documents, the State Department introduced a similar requirement for passports. In the 1920s, with the country no longer in a wartime state of emergency, citizens began to speak out against required passports. The passport photograph became a focal point for these middle-class and upper-class concerns about demands to prove personal identity through official documents and official photographs. The stark frontal image of the passport photograph revealed the unease that many travelers felt towards a required passport. For these travelers this style of photograph indicated the proper target of identification documents should be populations considered suspect and marginal by those who traveled for leisure. A magazine writer stated with apparent certainty, "No one has ever been known to admit that his passport picture looks like himself and usually it presents him as a candidate for the Rogues' Gallery or the psychopathic ward."[32] The belief that passport photographs are unflattering is clearly not a recent development. A late-1920s anecdote captures this, describing "the sage reply sent by the editor of a woman's page to a love-sick damsel who asked if she might know if her sweetheart were really true to her. The answer was: 'Send him your passport picture, and if he withstands that shock, you can depend upon it he loves you.'"[33]

Such sentiments constituted the perception of the "distortion of passport photography" that occupied a *New York Times* editorial in 1930. The editorial was a commentary on an article in the *New York Evening Post* that compared the professional portraits of celebrities with their passport photographs. The *Post* had published the passport photographs of five well-known Americans alongside their professional photographs. The *Times*, in commenting on the exercise, saw in the professional photographs "subjects [who] appear beautiful, amiable, pretty, jolly or generally attractive." In contrast, "in the line-up of passport evidence they beggar description. A criminal or imbecile cast of countenance is marked in most of them. If the lovely Ethel Barrymore can look 'like that' to the eye of any camera, ordinary mortals have no kick coming."[34]

It was not the "eye" of any camera that made Ethel Barrymore look like a criminal, an imbecile, or, for that matter, beautiful, but rather differing conventions of visual representation. The "distortion" occurred when a claim to the "mechanical objectivity" of the camera in producing a scientific image encountered the tradition of photography as portraiture. As discussed, the former gave the photograph an important function as an objective, empirical form of visual verification, but the object of the passport photograph—a person—produced expectations of the latter style of representation. The perception of passport photographs as depictions of the criminal or the insane was the result of the association of an untouched image of a person's face staring straight at the camera in front of a light background with images of members of suspect populations. In contrast, the coding of the professional photographs as beautiful drew from the tradition of portrait photography specifically its language of poses and the skill or manipulation of the photographer. The less direct pose of the photographic portrait had become an inscription of class and a manifestation of social identity. This is made clear in dancer Isadora Duncan's 1916 passport, which has a photograph portrait of her sitting on a sofa, illustrating that social status could grant an exemption to requirements then that it apparently could not in the following decade.[35] The frontal image of the passport photograph therefore captured the discomfort that many travelers felt toward the increasingly pervasive demands associated with the official documentation of individual identity.

The passport photograph was prepared with the intention of highlighting an individual's unique facial features as part of an attempt by the state to know its population on an individual basis. The image of a face looking directly at the camera, with no headdress, in front of a light background followed the logic of standardization that underwrote the emergence of modern identification documents. Alphonse Bertillon made one of the first attempts to standardize identification photographs. He stipulated the exact distance of the subject from the camera and created a special chair on which the subjects sat to control their physical position and posture. He also specified the type of lens and introduced the combination of direct frontal and profile angles that have come to characterize mug shots.[36] Through practices of standardization, identity was "simplified" to facilitate state officials recognizing and remembering individuals.

Standardized passport photographs emerged in a somewhat ad hoc manner. The style and size of the photographs applicants submitted provided a recurring problem for officials throughout the 1920s and into the 1930s. The State Department often responded to problematic photographs simply by accepting them, though in 1924 the State Department clarified for its officials that photographs that failed to adhere to the accepted size and paper type would no longer be accepted.[37] While this was enforced with increasing rigor in the issuance of passports in the United States, some degree of flexibility remained for consuls who issued passports abroad, at the margins of the U.S. government. Senior officials in Washington simultaneously expressed concern about passports issued abroad and regularly tolerated deviations from the specifications for photographs. In the 1930s the State Department still occasionally issued passports to a family in the primary name of the husband and father as head of the household. In situations where a consul issued such a passport abroad, a group photograph was preferred over individual photographs; until 1930 infants did not need to be photographed.[38] These group photographs tended to approximate portraits; they were still taken by a professional photographer in a studio. In one instance, even the requirement of a studio photograph was waived when the demands of U.S. administration reached beyond the realm of commercial photography. The consul in Curaçao (in what was then called the Netherlands West Indies, now the Netherlands Antilles) was allowed to accept family snapshots after it was explained that a visit to a professional photographer would entail considerable expense because the applicant would have to take several days off work to travel with his young child.[39] Back in the United States frequent complaints about the cost of passport photographs did not result in the acceptance of snapshots, but neither did they fall on deaf ears. Most photographers advertised a standard rate of seventy-five cents for the three photographs required, but many, after taking a photograph added an additional charge of $3 or $4 for immediate delivery. In the busiest passport agency in the country in New York, following complaints about cost in the early 1930s, the staff only allowed one photographer to advertise in the agency.[40]

Official attempts to standardize photographs constituted an effort to ensure that the image on the passport fulfilled the promise of accuracy through which officials understood the utility of photography. While this was done primarily through codifying the precise pose and format of the image, it was also done via other regulations that continued to frustrate some applicants—even more than the cost. This frustration came as people encountered requirements that overrode an expected trust in their character. By the early 1930s State Department practice resulted in the demand that no passport photograph should be more than two years old—any older and it was believed the image could not be guaranteed to offer a sufficiently accurate likeness.[41] This demand for new photographs was considered an affront. In requiring recent photographs the state's claim to know someone became read as a claim to know what they looked like over and above their own perception.[42]

The comments of a consul assigned to inspect U.S. passports abroad offer another example of the official struggle to determine if a person looked like a passport photograph; in this case the problem different visual practices created at the moment of official recognition. In contrast to what a person may have worn for a passport photograph, he complained, "When the passport is presented to the inspecting officer the holder of it is always dressed for travel with complete headgear and with wraps. It is therefore often impossible for the inspecting officer to determine at a glance whether the person who presented the passport and the person who sat for the photograph are one and the same."[43] In the technical specifications of the passport photograph, state officials sought to emphasize the "natural" features of a person's face to highlight uniquenesses and differences. But amid the cultural accoutrements of travel, that individuality was harder to discern. The visual effects of travel fashion, closer to the visual coding of leisure in the conventions of portraiture, affected the utility of the passport photograph to provide an effective comparison at this early moment in its "modern" history. In this particular example the official effort to stabilize identity according to specific requirements, to freeze it in time, failed because the inspection process went by too quickly.

Thus, while a photograph was thought to provide a more objective representation than a written description, the "accuracy" of the photograph had to be read against an individual's changing appearance. The purported strength of photographic representation was that it produced a stable and fixed object that provided an accurate point of comparison for state officials. This belief in a stable identity provides the fiction at the heart of the modern identification project—the broader version of the "legal fiction" that introduced the photograph into the courtroom. This formal identity (which coexisted with a reality that contradicted it) would be increasingly naturalized as the twentieth century progressed. However, in examples such as the "distortion of passport photography," this identity was viewed as anything but natural. Similarly, the consul's complaint about dress shows that the authority attributed to identification photography depended in part on a need to learn to recognize the precise likeness captured in a photograph. As Trachtenberg argues, a "portrait is a picture 'of' someone, the 'of-ness' consisting of a likeness, a correspondence of features between what the image conveys and what the living figure looks like."[44] The ability to see a correspondence between a person and the features highlighted in the photograph was just that, a skill that had to be acquired.

Another way to understand the standardization of the passport photograph is therefore as the production of a useful and easily seen "of-ness." The regulation of the passport photograph is an attempt to improve the accuracy of the "likeness" in a photograph. Initial difficulties in using the photograph to verify the identity of the person who presented the passport and complaints from people that their passport photograph did not resemble them make explicit that the identity in the passport was an official standardization or bureaucratic expression of personal identity; it was an identity distinct from a person's understanding of his or her personal identity. A photograph shorn of accoutrements represented the "simplification" at the core of modern identification: the official representation of only that part of a person's identity relevant to the particular governing practice.[45] The "modern" practices the identification photograph made visible facilitated the production and verification of an identity that the state could use to both verify and remember individuals. The difference between this identity and a more romantic sense of individualism and self-knowledge is offered in a Passport Division anecdote recounted in a newspaper profile of the office. As part of her passport application, an Illinois woman sent two photographs as required along with her passport application to Washington, D.C. But these were purportedly different photographs: "along with the 1928 model she sent one with leg-o-mutton sleeves."[46] The applicant seemingly sought to give historical depth to her claims to identity; she had always been the person she claimed to be. However, her attempt to establish her identity temporally was in contrast to the new intentions of identification. While she sought to connect the present to the past, modern identification practices were organized to link the present to the future. The standardization of the passport photograph across multiple copies was demanded in anticipation of the need for future verification through comparison with the photograph on the passport—to put a face on the information contained in the file according to the anticipatory archival logic of identification practices. As the following chapter makes clear, the claims to objectivity that determined the visual representation of identity in the passport photograph can be also seen to constitute the verification of citizenship through documents as an administrative fact useful to the changing governing practices of the long nineteenth century.

6

Application

Until the 1840s most passport applications arrived in the State Department in the form of a personal letter addressed to the secretary of state (figure 6.1). The letter usually included some description of physical appearance, occasionally a declaration of citizenship, and more frequently a brief outline of the writer's travel plans. While applications were returned because of insufficient evidence of citizenship, passports were also issued to people not entitled to them.[1] The returned applications were usually from naturalized citizens, as is apparent from the printing of an application form for naturalized citizens, which took the form of an affidavit from a notary, though it seems to have been rarely used after it was introduced in 1830.[2] In the mid-1840s the State Department issued formal guidelines for applicants, including a description of the documents that now had to be submitted to prove personal identity and citizenship. However, it seems that only in the last decades of the nineteenth century did officials start to consistently enforce these requirements; in 1896 the State Department changed the name of its guidelines for applicants from "General Instructions in Regard to Passports" to "Rules Governing Applications for Passports," indicating this new attitude to the passport application (figure 6.2).

With the ad hoc enforcement of application requirements, it is perhaps not surprising that at the end of the century an applicant could express "considerable annoyance and exasperation" when officials deemed his word insufficient evidence of citizenship.[3] In 1897 this particular applicant, Donald McKenzie, applied for a passport on behalf of his elderly mother. Although not born in the

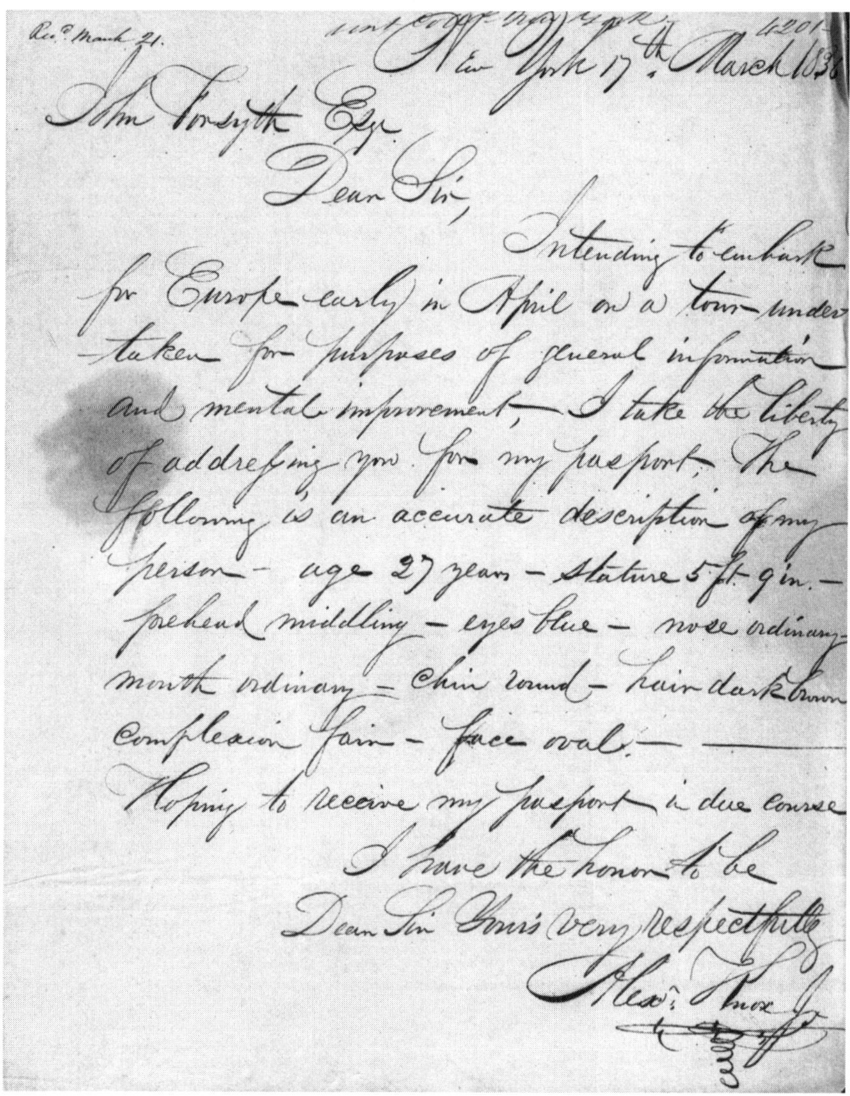

Rec.d March 21.

New York 17th March 1836

John Forsyth Esqr.

Dear Sir,

Intending to embark for Europe early in April on a tour undertaken for purposes of general information and mental improvement, I take the liberty of addressing you for my passport. The following is an accurate description of my person - age 27 years - Stature 5 ft. 9 in. - forehead middling - eyes blue - nose ordinary - mouth ordinary - Chin round - hair dark brown Complexion fair - face oval. —

Hoping to receive my passport in due course

I have the honor to be

Dear Sir Yours very respectfully

Alex.r Knox Jr.

Figure 6.1. Application for a passport, 1836 (National Archives, College Park, MD).

United States, she claimed citizenship through the naturalization of her father while she was a minor and her later marriage to a naturalized citizen.[4] Both men had died by the time of her passport application and neither of their naturalization certificates could be found; a courthouse fire was assumed to have destroyed one record, and the other could not be found nor the location of

GENERAL INSTRUCTIONS IN REGARD TO PASSPORTS.

Department of State, U. S. A.,

Washington, April 15, 1885.

Citizens of the United States, visiting foreign countries, are liable to serious inconvenience if unprovided with authentic proof of their national character. The best safeguard is a passport from this Department, certifying the bearer to be a citizen of the United States. Passports are issued only to citizens of the United States, upon application supported by proof of citizenship.

Citizenship is acquired by nativity, by naturalization, and by annexation of territory. An alien woman, who marries a citizen of the United States, thereby becomes a citizen. Minor children, resident in the United States, become citizens by the naturalization of their father.

When the applicant is a native citizen of the United States he must transmit his own affidavit of this fact, stating his age and place of birth, with the affidavit of one other citizen of the United States to whom he is personally known, stating that the declaration made by the applicant is true. These affidavits must be attested by a Notary Public, under his signature and seal of office. When there is no Notary in the place, the affidavits may be made before a Justice of the Peace or other officer authorized to administer oaths; but if he has no seal, his official act must be authenticated by certificate of a court of record.

A person born abroad, who claims that his father was a native citizen of the United States, must state in his affidavit that his father was born in the United States, has resided therein, and was a citizen of the same at the time of the applicant's birth. This affidavit must be supported by that of one other citizen acquainted with the facts.

If the applicant be a naturalized citizen, his certificate of naturalization must be transmitted for inspection, (it will be returned with the passport,) and he must state in his affidavit that he is the identical person described in the certificate presented.

Passports cannot be issued to aliens who have only declared their intention to become citizens.

Military service does not of itself confer citizenship. A person of alien birth, who has been honorably discharged from military service in the United States, but who has not been naturalized, should not transmit his discharge paper in application for a passport, but should apply to the proper court for admission to citizenship, and transmit a certified copy of the record of such admission.

In issuing passports to naturalized citizens, the Department will be guided by naturalization certificate; and the signature to the application and oath of allegiance should conform in orthography to the applicant's name as written in the naturalization paper.

The wife or widow of a naturalized citizen must transmit the naturalization certificate of the husband, stating in her affidavit that she is the wife or widow of the person described therein.

The children of a naturalized citizen, claiming citizenship through the father, must transmit the certificate of naturalization of the father, stating in their affidavits that they are children of the person described therein, and were minors at the time of such naturalization.

The oath of allegiance to the United States will be required in all cases.

The application should be accompanied by a description of the person, stating the following particulars, viz:
Age: years. Stature: feet, inches, (English measure.) Forehead: .
Eyes: . Nose: . Mouth: . Chin: . Hair: .
Complexion: . Face: .

If the applicant is to be accompanied by his wife, minor children, or servants, it will be sufficient to state the names and ages of such persons and their relationship to the applicant, when a single passport for the whole will suffice. For any other person in the party, a separate passport will be required. A woman's passport may include her minor children and servants.

By act of Congress approved June 20, 1874, a fee of five dollars is required to be collected for every citizen's passport. That amount should accompany each application. Postal money orders and bank checks should be payable to the Disbursing Clerk of the Department of State. Checks to be available for the full amount must be drawn on banks at principal business centers. Individual checks must be certified by the banks upon which they are drawn.

* A passport is good for two years from its date and no longer. A new one may be obtained by stating the date and number of the old one, paying the fee of five dollars, and furnishing satisfactory evidence that the applicant is at the time within the United States. The oath of allegiance must also be transmitted when the former passport was issued prior to 1861.

Citizens of the United States desiring to obtain passports while in a foreign country must apply to the chief diplomatic representative of the United States in that country, or, in the absence of a diplomatic representative, then to the Consul General, if there be one, or, in the absence of both the officers last named, to a Consul.

Passports cannot be lawfully issued by State authorities, or by Judicial or Municipal functionaries of the United States. (Revised Statutes, section 4075.)

To persons wishing to obtain passports for themselves, blank forms of application will be furnished by this Department on request, stating whether the applicant be a native or a naturalized citizen. Forms are not furnished, except as samples, to those who make a business of procuring passports.

Communications should be addressed to the Department of State, indorsed "Passport Division," and each communication should give the Post Office address of the person to whom the answer is to be directed.

Professional titles will not be inserted in passports.

* Mr. Whilden's application for a new passport requires a fee of five dollars,
Jan. 28, 1886. N. Benedict
Passport Clerk

Figure 6.2. General Instruction in Regard to Passports, 1885 (National Archives, College Park, MD).

the naturalization remembered. In lieu of these documents McKenzie offered the statement that her "two living children are both native born and voters and that fact together with mother's 47 years of continued residence, should give her citizenship even disregarding 'naturalization papers.'" But in the absence of verification through the proper documents, McKenzie's *statements* were simply that; they were not the "*facts*" the clerk wanted and that McKenzie assumed them to be. The demand for impersonal documentary evidence over personal vouching defied McKenzie's sense of logic; "The absurdity of your asking for naturalization papers which were taken out probably 45 years ago (in the case of her father) and a quarter of a century ago (or more) in the case of her husband, is too evident to be gainsaid."[5]

The frustration passport applicants like Donald McKenzie felt in response to demands for documents originated in a failure to comprehend that increasingly in official interactions, proof of identity no longer depended on the authenticity of personal claims; identification was not contingent on an individual's personal reputation or character, or simply his word. In contrast to these expectations, official identity was in the process of becoming a bureaucratic expression, an identity distinct from other ways in which individuals represented themselves publicly. As the number of interactions between individuals and the federal government increased, officials began to rely exclusively on the information contained in documents; they wanted facts that could be understood from afar, without need of any local knowledge as they sought to establish the passport's credentials as a certificate of citizenship. This required the *intentional* collection of specific documentary evidence within the purview of the state. But the attempt to standardize official identification in this manner developed in an ad hoc manner as the problems associated with the name, physical description, and photograph illustrate. The State Department's inconsistent but increasingly rigorous adherence to documentary evidence of citizenship contributed greatly to both the aggravation applicants felt when they could not comply and also to their confusion about why state officials could not trust their word as to who they were. The localism that had dominated governing practices in the United States throughout much of the nineteenth century undoubtedly accentuated the perception of this new mode of identification as a relatively impersonal form of governing; somewhat surprisingly the earlier introduction of a fee for passports had apparently not signaled to applicants this more impersonal relationship between state and citizen. In 1862 a passport fee of $3 was introduced, which was subsequently increased to $5 before being reduced to $1 in 1888; from 1871 to 1874 there was no passport fee.[6] Officials viewed the fee as an important source of revenue, especially as the number of passport applications dramatically increased in the second half of the century, as did the number of clerks required to issue them. Although many applicants considered a passport to be something like a letter of introduction or protection, the fee appears not to have been viewed as an affront, barely even registering as an annoyance.[7]

The initial attempt to verify citizenship claims through specific documents authorized by designated officials occurred in the second half of the nineteenth century, when most individuals still considered personal statements and relationships the primary ways to confirm individual identity.[8] Voting, another forum in which citizenship had to be verified, underscores the limited importance of record keeping and identification documents to interactions between individuals and government. The community surveillance organized on election day occurred in the absence of voter registration and with the assumption that voters could not prove their right to vote with documents.[9] While the verification of race and ethnicity were important to voter eligibility, concerns also existed over the age, residence, and mental competence of potential voters. At the polling booth the party appointed challengers and the "election judge" used three main sources of evidence to resolve these concerns: physical appearance, the collective memory of the community, and the word of the would-be voter. Community practices and norms determined the viability of any evidence, with the result that the decisions made at the polls often had a limited foundation in formal electoral law. Age was frequently decided through collective memory, sometimes by connecting a birth to an extraordinary event, or whether it was known the voter was able to grow a beard. Where a man's washing was done was commonly considered sufficient evidence of residence and his right to cast his vote in the precinct.[10] In urban areas voting often could not depend on such communal knowledge, but with few if any documents available, the body and personal appearance also played an important role particularly when race and ethnicity became contentious issues at polls. Voter registration laws first appeared in urban centers to counter concerns about residence. However, these laws offered only limited assistance in the verification of voters. Before the regular adoption of typewriters, the lists were handwritten and could not necessarily be read with accuracy. Many voters were unable to spell their names, with the result that election judges and clerks attempted to make phonetic matches. This task was made all the more difficult as early lists were not alphabetized. Voter registration also did not immediately solve the problem of verifying residence, as most cities lacked systematic criteria to identify individual houses.[11]

The attempt to standardize the application process through preprinted forms, official documentary evidence, and designated officials encountered the practices and etiquette of this relatively undocumented world. Even when documents were used in local interactions, there was still the assumption that they could be supported by (or even trumped by) local extratextual evidence, as in the attempt of John S__'s attorney to connect his passport application and naturalization certificate through personal knowledge despite a difference in the spelling of his name. The use of documents was intended to marginalize the predominately face-to-face interaction and the (seemingly) unmediated culture in which they occurred. The dramatic increase in geographical size and population of the United States also challenged the on-going viability of localized forms of verification. In both instances, this lead to more geographical mobility that challenged the social relations that had underwritten identification practices in local communities. This points to the often-recited argument that the documentation of individual identity originated to provide proof of identity in the absence of a communal group as part of the displacement of the modern world. Cultural historian Matt Matsuda describes this as the belief that centrally-issued identification documents developed to replace "the assurance and authority of the 'small circle' of familiars who could attest to the good name of an individual... [with] the distant authority of an 'official' document, the assurance of an encompassing administration distilled down into a card."[12] However, in the United States until well into the twentieth century, the assurance of the state could not be *purely* recorded. The small size of the federal government relative to the geographic size of the United States meant the federal government was limited in its administrative reach and frequently struggled to function successfully without relying on local practices and what was perceived as their potential for bias.[13]

In 1845 Secretary of State James Buchanan issued the first departmental circular regarding the passport application process, but only in a subsequent circular in 1846 did the department describe the specific documentary evidence required before a passport could be issued.[14] In the absence of critical twentieth-century seed documents such as the birth certificate and driver's license, the circular introduced a combination of documents and designated local officials and individuals to provide the basis for claims to citizenship and personal identity. All applicants had to provide an affidavit witnessed by a notary public and signed by another citizen to verify their personal identity and claim to citizenship. To facilitate this, by the 1860s the application form was printed as an affidavit. The top half of the form contained text that stated the applicant was a citizen, and the applicant inserted his name, place of birth, and the country or countries he intended to visit in the appropriate blanks. Below this was a space for the applicant to sign, and then underneath that a space for a notary public to record the date of the application and affix his signature and seal. The lower half of the form was a statement in which a witness declared his personal knowledge of the applicant and the truth of the applicant's statement. There was a space underneath for the witness's signature and for the notary public to sign and date this declaration. At the bottom of the form was a space to fill in the physical description of the applicant.[15] Notaries public frequently had their own version of the application form printed (figure 6.3). Naturalized citizens also had to send in their naturalization certificate. From 1861 applicants were required to submit additional proof of citizenship in the form of an oath of allegiance—the start of the Civil War motivated the demand for verification of more than the mere fact of citizenship (figure 6.4).[16] In contrast to the affidavits and certificates used to establish citizenship, the department considered an oath to offer evidence that a citizen retained ongoing loyalty to the nation-state. While oaths are a relict of medieval statecraft, in the modern state they tend to appear in response to general climates of fear and particular crises such as war and rebellion.[17] In the United States the need for a citizen to affirm supreme loyalty to the nation and the federal government was significant in establishing the nation-state as a tangible site for loyalty and identity over local ties and affiliations.[18]

The oath of allegiance, along with other documents demanded as evidence of citizenship, existed not only within the project of reifying the nation, but also as part of an attempt to establish a centralized administrative state through standardized practices that eliminated local modes of information collection. The attempt to assert control over the production of knowledge was hindered by the ad hoc use of bureaucratic procedures in the second half of the nineteenth century. This derived from the less than rigorous application of procedures and the limited range of the federal government's administrative structure. In the case of the passport this was further accentuated by the lack of federal interest in the document, particularly outside of the diplomatic and consular service. The acceptance, albeit inconsistently, of

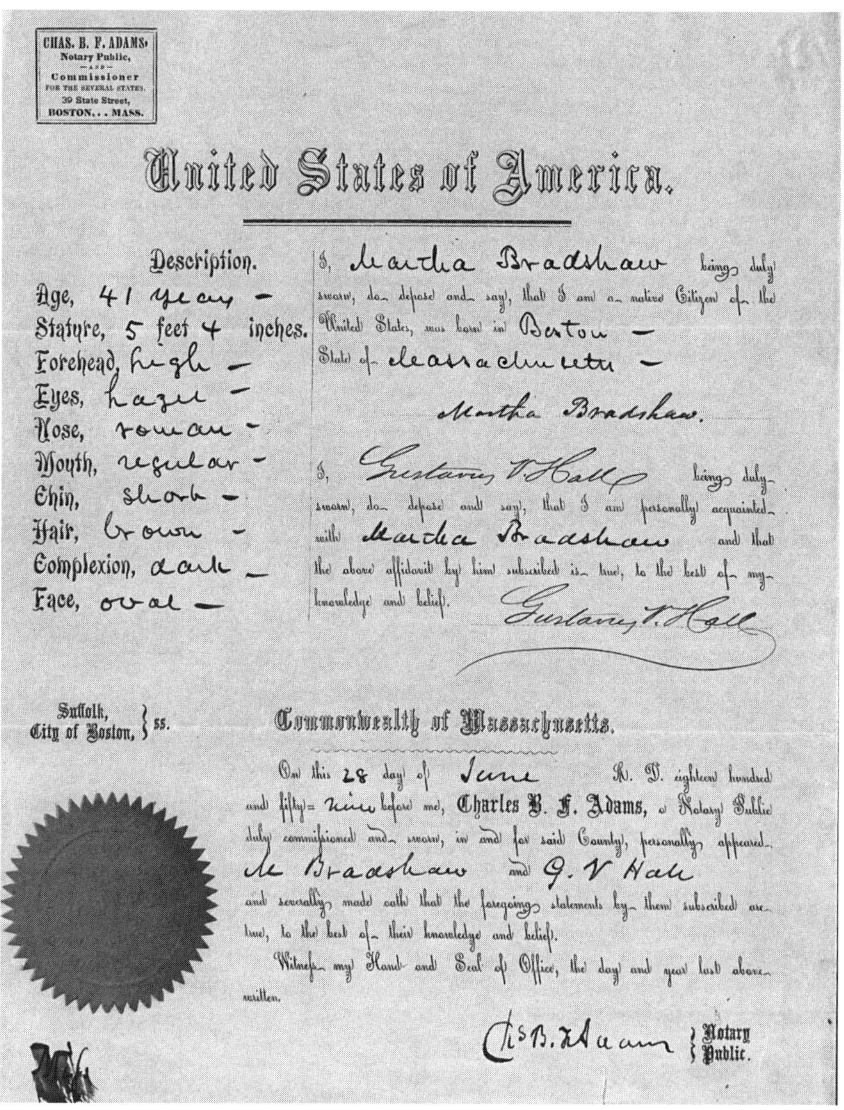
CHAS. B. F. ADAMS,
Notary Public,
—AND—
Commissioner
FOR THE SEVERAL STATES,
39 State Street,
BOSTON, . . MASS.

United States of America.

Description.
Age, 41 years —
Stature, 5 feet 4 inches.
Forehead, high —
Eyes, hazel —
Nose, roman —
Mouth, regular —
Chin, short —
Hair, brown —
Complexion, dark —
Face, oval —

I, Martha Bradshaw being duly sworn, do depose and say, that I am a native Citizen of the United States, was born in Boston — State of Massachusetts —

Martha Bradshaw.

I, Gustavus V. Hall being duly sworn, do depose and say, that I am personally acquainted with Martha Bradshaw and that the above affidavit by him subscribed is true, to the best of my knowledge and belief.

Gustavus V. Hall

Suffolk,
City of Boston, } ss.

Commonwealth of Massachusetts.

On this 28 day of June A. D. eighteen hundred and fifty-nine before me, Charles B. F. Adams, a Notary Public duly commissioned and sworn, in and for said County, personally appeared M Bradshaw and G. V Hall and severally made oath that the foregoing statements by them subscribed are true, to the best of their knowledge and belief.

Witness my Hand and Seal of Office, the day and year last above written.

Chs B. F. Adams } Notary Public.

Figure 6.3. Passport application form printed by a notary public, 1859 (National Archives, College Park, MD).

alternative oaths until the end of the nineteenth century was but one example of the way in which secretaries of state and department officials undercut attempts to create a uniform passport application process.[19]

A more significant consequence of the partial reach of the state in the passport application was the need to the use affidavits witnessed by notaries

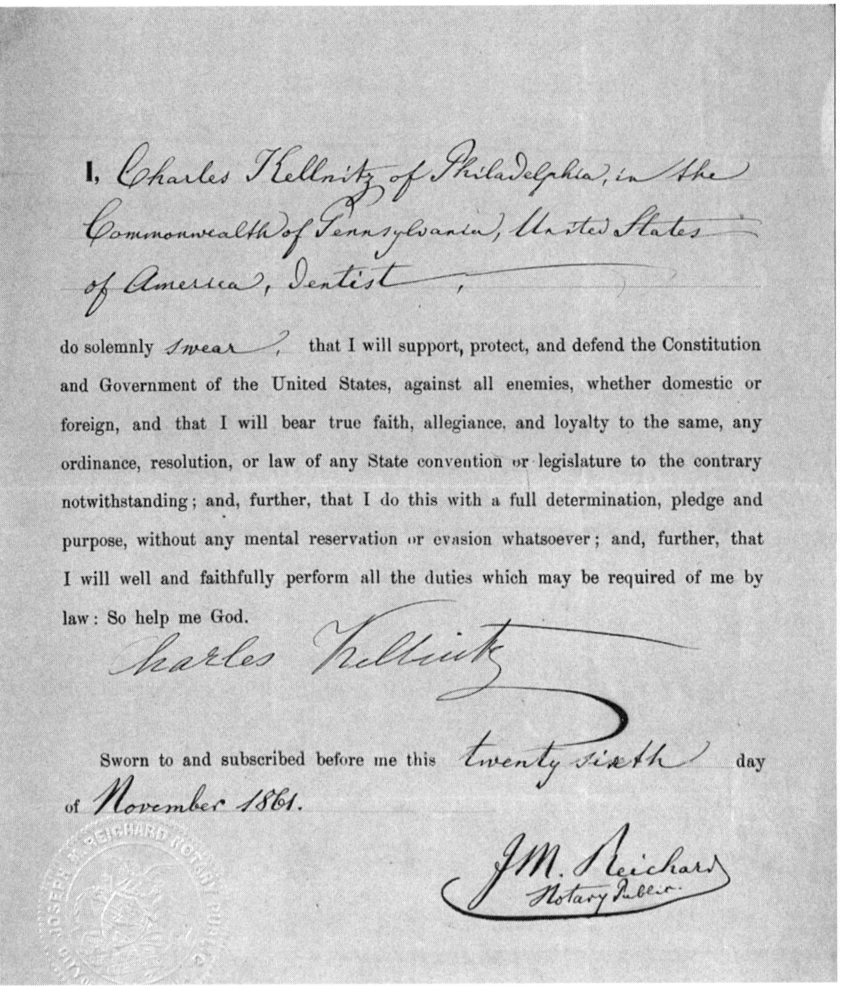
I, Charles Kellnitz of Philadelphia, in the Commonwealth of Pennsylvania, United States of America, Dentist,

do solemnly swear, that I will support, protect, and defend the Constitution and Government of the United States, against all enemies, whether domestic or foreign, and that I will bear true faith, allegiance, and loyalty to the same, any ordinance, resolution, or law of any State convention or legislature to the contrary notwithstanding; and, further, that I do this with a full determination, pledge and purpose, without any mental reservation or evasion whatsoever; and, further, that I will well and faithfully perform all the duties which may be required of me by law: So help me God.

Charles Kellnitz

Sworn to and subscribed before me this twenty sixth day of November 1861.

J.M. Reichard
Notary Public

Figure 6.4. Oath of Allegiance from passport applicant, 1861 (National Archives, College Park, MD).

public. With insufficient direct knowledge of specific local interactions, the federal government had to rely on preexisting structures such as notaries public to verify evidence of identity. Though usually a stranger to both the applicant and the State Department, these people were "known" to department officials through the recognition of the official position of the "notary public." As both an official stranger and official witness, the notary public recorded the applicant's statements about personal identity and citizenship on behalf of the federal government in the absence of locally deployed federal officials. Affidavits sworn in front of notaries were an attempt to establish an acceptable degree of reliability in personal identification that adhered to the new standards of bureaucratic objectivity, not trust in self-verification of identity. However, in the absence of birth certificates, the fact of citizenship still originated in someone's personal claims, not in official record-keeping practices; most states did not pass laws requiring the registration of births until the first decades of the twentieth century. Further, the precise nature and authority that made a notary's official witnessing useful to the federal government often appeared to be unclear to both applicants and notaries. Applications arrived in the department without the signature or seal of the notary and with the applicant's place of birth omitted. Aside from sloppiness, these incomplete applications also point to a failure to fully grasp that in the developing articulation of reliability through documents, the successful translation of a personal statement into a legal and administrative fact required that a document contain evidence of the presence and authority of the appropriate official. To simply record an oral statement on a piece of paper did not turn the statement into what was coming to be seen as an official and usable fact. An affidavit could only give legal authority to a claim to citizenship and identity if it recorded the notary's presence at the swearing of the statement, which was understood to authenticate the document and therefore the statements that appeared on it. It was not to be assumed through implicit association, but rather verified through a seal, signature, and date that located the source of authority in the actions of a designated official. The number of applications received without verification of the notary public's authority was one reason the department printed forms to be returned with incomplete applications. These forms were in regular use by the 1880s and represent the move toward a more consistent enforcement of application requirements and, therefore, a more assertive attempt to claim control of the issuance of the passport. Beyond an attempt to further standardize the application process, their use indicates that the department received incomplete applications in sufficient numbers to warrant the printing of specific forms—illiteracy in documentation was not unique to notaries public.

The notary public's role as an "official stranger" in the application process ended with the outbreak of World War I.[20] From the end of 1914 passport applications had to be executed in front of a court official before being sent to the department. Another measure that brought the application process more securely into the legal and administrative realm of the state was the postwar decision to open passport agencies in port cities. The State Department employees who staffed these agencies took passport applications and, if necessary, issued emergency passports.[21] In the 1920s the department continued to actively police the individuals involved in the application and issuance of a passport. Instructions were issued to officials about evaluating the "witness" used in passport applications. Although notaries public were no longer involved, the process still required an individual who could verify the personal identity of the applicant and, therefore, that the applicant was indeed the person the supporting documents had established as a citizen. The witness was required to appear in person at the time of application rather than signing the form prior to the applicant going to the agency or courthouse. This "inconvenience" became a frequent source of complaints.[22] State Department circulars described an appropriate witness as a "respectable citizen," but this category was not defined, leaving individual officials to police it at their discretion. These respectable citizens not only had to establish their own credentials; they also had to convince officials that they knew the applicant. Enforcement of the latter was given regulatory teeth in the late 1920s, when the Passport Division declared a "professional witness" unacceptable. This regulation was intended to exclude people with a financial interest in the issuance of passports, usually either steamship company employees or lawyers.[23] Similar regulations were enacted in regards to people eligible to witness an oath of allegiance. These witness requirements were relaxed in the case of passports issued abroad. On occasion, if conditions prevented an applicant from traveling to the nearest consulate, departmental regulations allowed an oath of allegiance to be sworn in front of a foreign official authorized to administer oaths. However, another U.S. citizen had to be present at this act so that the U.S. state witnessed the application in surrogate form.[24] Another instruction from the State Department added that if the witness to a passport application was not personally known to the consul, "he" was still allowed to witness an affidavit if "his personal appearance, as well as that of the applicant, indicate[d] American nationality."[25] In the early 1920s the equation of citizenship with a particular definition of whiteness (and its association with respectability) meant that in certain circumstances personal appearance was still accepted as evidence of U.S. citizenship in lieu of paper documents; this form of verification had been useful to enforcing immigration restrictions from the 1880s.

Witnesses, in the form of notaries public and citizens, had been used to verify the personal identity of all applicants but only the citizenship of those who claimed birth in the United States. The "birth" of naturalized citizens was documented in the form of a naturalization certificate. Therefore, as the initial application requirements made clear, the claim to citizenship of a naturalized citizen called for this document instead of the affidavit demanded of people claiming citizenship through birth in the United States. In the 1880s the different evidence and statements required of naturalized and native citizens resulted in the State Department issuing three different sets of instructions and application forms for native citizens, naturalized citizens, and for people claiming citizenship through the naturalization of a husband or parent (figure 6.5).[26] The necessity that naturalized citizens submit a naturalization certificate was frequently seen as a hardship—aside from Donald McKenzie's incredulity, we have also seen frustration resulting from the requirement that the name on the certificate and application be the same. For other applicants this requirement was also discriminatory, in contrast to what they perceived as the more easily satisfied demand for an affidavit from applicants claiming birth in the United States. The State Department rejected this assertion, and with it the implicit privileging of a particular understanding of whiteness and citizenship. In 1888 Secretary of State Thomas Baynard wrote, "The rule of proof applied to each class of citizens is the same." He clarified that this was the "legal rule," that "in all cases the proof to be submitted of the existence of a fact must be the best proof of which the case is in its nature susceptible."[27] For naturalized citizens the best proof was the legal record of their naturalization. In the developing practice of official documentation, the naturalization certificate also represented the ideal evidence of citizenship. As a record of the bureaucratic "birth" of the citizen, a naturalization certificate is produced by designated officials within the apparatus of the state. The "birth" could not take place outside of the state and its official record. It required the actions of officials who were located more comfortably within the state than the notary public, who, while an official, was not fully accountable to the state. The judge presiding over a person's naturalization possessed a clearly defined authority derived from his position within the state, an authority that provided the sole way in which an alien could become a citizen. A judge did not merely witness an event, but the event could not happen without him. Therefore, this "birth" was documented in court records and through a certified copy issued under the seal of the court. This pointed toward an ideal scenario in which a passport would be created exclusively from documents that were rationally and objectively produced within the administrative control of the state. In such a documentary regime

[Edition of 1889.] [FORM FOR NATIVE CITIZEN.]

No................. Issued...............................

UNITED STATES OF AMERICA.

State of Kentucky } ss:
County of Hardin }

I, C. R. Shacklette, a Native and Loyal Citizen of the United States, hereby apply to the Department of State, at Washington, for a passport for myself, accompanied by No one as follows: ...., born at ...., on the ....day of ...., 18....., and ....

I solemnly swear that I was born at Meade County, in the State of Kentucky, on or about the 6th day of March, 1867; that my father is a native citizen of the United States; that I am domiciled in the United States, my permanent residence being at Elizabethtown, in the State of Kentucky, where I follow the occupation of Dentist; that I am about to go abroad temporarily; and that I intend to return to the United States within two years, with the purpose of residing and performing the duties of citizenship therein.

OATH OF ALLEGIANCE.

Further, I do solemnly swear that I will support and defend the Constitution of the United States against all enemies, foreign and domestic; that I will bear true faith and allegiance to the same; and that I take this obligation freely, without any mental reservation or purpose of evasion: So help me God.

Sworn to before me this 16th day of May, 1892. C. R. Shacklette

[signature]
Notary Public.

DESCRIPTION OF APPLICANT.

Age: 25 years.	Mouth: Medium Size
Stature 5 feet, 6½ inches, Eng.	Chin: Square
Forehead: Medium	Hair: Light
Eyes: Blue	Complexion: Fair
Nose: Medium	Face: Full & Round

IDENTIFICATION.

........................, 18.....

I hereby certify that I know the above-named........................ personally, and know him to be a native-born citizen of the United States, and that the facts stated in his affidavit are true to the best of my knowledge and belief.

A. B. Montgomery M.C. 4th Ky Dist.

[Address of witness.] ....

Applicant desires passport sent to following address:

To his home Elizabethtown Kentucky

C. R. Shacklette
Elizabethtown
Kentucky

Figure 6.5. Application form for Native Citizen, 1892 (National Archives, College Park, MD).

of verification, documents would beget documents to successfully articulate an official identity in a well-documented life.

The lack of a system of birth registration was far from this ideal, especially once government officials began to take the passport more seriously in the early decades of the twentieth century. There had been a history of calls for universal birth registration, but although a 1903 congressional joint resolution had endorsed the American Public Health Association's suggested standard certificates for births and deaths and its proposal for enforcement, Congress gave it no financial support.[28] Although some cities and states (notably Pennsylvania) enforced birth registration laws, the United States in the early decades of the twentieth century remained in a "barbarous state of existence without complete vital records," according to a 1916 report from a former chief statistician for the Census Bureau.[29] The federal government slowly oversaw the achievement of national birth registration, with Texas being the last state to implement and enforce registration of births in 1933.[30] Despite the limited history of birth registration, the State Department made birth certificates a requirement in 1921 for applicants born in the United States, following the initial introduction of the demand during World War I. While it signaled another attempt to bring the issuance of a passport closer in line with the practices of modern identification practices, the demand for a birth certificate was only a gesture towards this. As late as 1942 the Census Bureau estimated 40% of the population (54 million people) did not have birth certificates.[31] Further research clarified that in 1948 the claim to universal birth registration represented the registration of 95% of the population, up from 90.7% in 1935. The complicated social context in which any identification practice occurs is evident in statistics that estimated that while 97.1% of the births of white babies were registered, this dropped to 85.9% for non-white babies. A higher percentage of births outside of hospitals and rural residence for non-whites were offered as possible explanations for this difference.[32] In the realistic expectation of the absence of birth certificates, the State Department required affidavits from people who they thought must have witnessed the birth (mother, doctor, or midwife) or a document issued close to birth (such as a baptismal certificate). If the approved witnesses had either died or could not be located and no document had been issued contemporaneously to the birth, and the applicant had satisfied an official that he or she had made a genuine attempt to locate this evidence, the department resorted to the previously accepted evidence of a sworn statement of a "respectable" person who knew the applicant to be a citizen—this statement was also required if the applicant presented a baptismal certificate, as it was a document issued outside of the authority of the state.

The demand for a birth certificate and the ranking of the alternative evidence of citizenship indicated the importance of proximity for the reliable documentation of an event as an accepted fact. Ideally, an event would be documented close to its occurrence. A less ideal alternative was proximity to the applicant in the form of a personal relationship. Therefore, while officials were instructed to accept a sworn affidavit by someone not present at the birth as a last resort, they were told to reject "birth certificates" that local health departments issued retrospectively to adult citizens; in response to the demand for documentary evidence of birth, state and local health departments and hospitals had begun to issue these certificates to people who claimed birth in their state. State Department officials decided to reject this document because it was not issued contemporaneous to the birth—it did not adhere to a definition of reliability based on proximity. The authority of these birth certificates tended to derive principally from the word of an individual or, less frequently, a document such as a baptismal certificate, and even less often, a hospital record that the State Department considered unreliable. In the former two cases the passport application already required a statement from the applicant and, if necessary, a baptismal certificate, thus making a document produced from them redundant. In the case of the latter, the perhaps questionable belief of department officials that record-keeping practices were unreliable was supported by occasional examples of the dubious manner in which some retroactive birth certificates were issued. An investigation of certificates issued by the New York State Department of Health revealed an institutional failure to grasp the precise nature of documentary authority. In 1924 passport officials discovered that standard office practice had different health department officials signing the certificates in the name of the designated official, thus limiting the usefulness of the signature as a sign of authority and authenticity. The certificates under review also all had the same date from 1912 because staff had been unable to change the date on the stamp for a dozen years.[33]

While the demand for a particular type of birth certificate can be located in an increased belief in the reliability of documents produced within systematic and rational bureaucratic procedures, such a belief existed alongside other criteria of reliability that could trump adherence to process and documentary authority. In 1926 the State Department decided not to accept any passport applications without birth certificates from the territory of Hawaii even if they included one of the affidavits allowed in lieu of a birth certificate, described to applicants in a footnote to published regulations. The new policy was explained to the secretary of the interior in the following way:

> In this connection it may be added that while the footnote above quoted is contained in forms of applications prepared by this Department, these forms were prepared primarily for use in the continental United States after an examination of the conditions existing in this country with reference to the difficulty sometimes encountered in obtaining evidence of birth by applicants for passports claiming to have been born herein.[34]

An internal State Department memo was more explicit as to why continental conditions could not be assumed to apply in Hawaii:

> The substitute evidence which we will take in the cases of persons born in this country of white fathers and mothers is appropriate when the circumstances warrant our taking such action, for we may do so with reasonable safety; but when it comes to extending the same practice to members of the Japanese race, with their well-known racial tendency to equivocate and their racial similarity of physical appearance, we cannot do so without danger of being imposed upon, both in the matter of the identity of the applicant and in the matter of his alleged birth on the soil of the United States.[35]

The explanation for the decision fits into the dominant understanding of citizenship and race in the United States. The specific concern over Asians drove the restrictions on Japanese immigration introduced in the early twentieth century and the passage of the first Chinese Exclusion Act two decades earlier. The deployment of documentation within a racialized conception of citizenship is a useful reminder that while the documentation of individual identity is articulated through claims to objectivity (against the subjective bias of "local" practices), it is always enacted within a distinct social context with very specific cultural understandings of identity.

By the 1920s the privileging of documents issued by designated officials securely located in the state apparatus was still an emerging ideal. This piecemeal and contested process can be traced back to the mid-nineteenth century. Its gradual development was a product of a lack of trust in some citizens (naturalized, and non-"white") but not all (native born) citizens, and the inconsistent documentation of important facts such as birth in the United States. The development of application procedures was an attempt by the state to control an individual's claim to be a citizen. This involved not only the authority to issue documents, but also establishing who had the authority to verify identification in the absence of documents. The developing faith in documentation could still be trumped by undocumented leaps of faith. In the same correspondence from 1888 when Secretary of State Baynard stated the necessity for a naturalization certificate, he allowed a passport to be issued to a naturalized citizen in the absence of any supporting documents on the grounds that "the personal knowledge of a minister of the United States necessarily obviates the necessity of more formal proof."[36] The fact that the U.S. representative in Paris knew the applicant rendered not only a naturalization certificate unnecessary but also the alternative evidence of an affidavit allowed in exceptional circumstances.[37] The possibility for a personal relationship between a citizen and the state harkens back to the identification practice that the increased scale of social interactions had made unreliable. Therefore, at the periphery of the state, where the state (such as it was) interacted regularly with a small number of citizens, the possibility for reliable official identification without documents could exist. However, the issuance of a passport in the absence of supporting documents was the privilege of the state. Donald McKenzie's frustration with his mother's passport application arose from his belief in the reliability of a relationship of identity and identification based on a trust in self-identification, reputation, and local knowledge. In this situation the State Department did not share this belief. McKenzie's mother was not "known" to the state either through the documents it produced or the personal knowledge of one of its trusted senior officials.

A 1906 law digest included Baynard's decision to issue a passport on the word of the U.S. minister, implying it was still an extent precedent; it was not in an abridged section on evidence of citizenship in the subsequent digest, published in 1942.[38] After World War I the emerging rationale was that the state could only accurately "know" people through documents. If no documents existed to verify birth prior to a passport application, the application process had to create them; the verification of identity required a more visible documentary trace than what had been acceptable in the nineteenth century. However, the absence of prioritized documents could not be resolved by the mere translation of individual statements onto paper. The conditions in which documents were created had became critical to their reliability, especially who produced them.

7

Bureaucracy

Who actually read passport applications in the State Department? Which officials were responsible for issuing passports? Over the course of the nineteenth century the answer to these questions changed, as State Department staff increased in size and adopted administrative practices that can be recognized as bureaucratic. These changes were typical for government departments in this period. However, their consequences for the passport were significant. The standardization of the personal name, signature, physical description, photograph, application, and appearance of the passport can all be viewed as a consequence of the broader development of bureaucracy. The changing designations of the clerks and officials responsible for the passport further illustrate how a developing bureaucracy was utilized in an attempt to improve the processing of the document.[1] Before 1806, it appears that the chief clerk issued passports. In 1818 an executive order was issued that specifically stated the duties and salaries of a number of clerks. The production of all credentials and certificates, including the few hundred passports issued annually now became the responsibility of a junior clerk. Bureaus and divisions were established in 1833 in response to an increase in the number of clerks in the State Department to a dozen. In this structure, the Translating and Miscellaneous Bureau initially issued passports, before the Home Bureau took responsibility for what in the 1830s was an annual average of close to a thousand passports. By the 1840s seven clerks worked in the Home Bureau, with three clerks allocated to a collection of tasks that included responsibility for passports; in 1857 there were twenty-eight officials and clerks in the department, including the secretary of state. As a result of a major overhaul, a Passport Bureau was created in 1870, only to be eliminated three years later as a result of budget cuts; in 1873 the passport clerks were transferred to the Bureau of Archives and Indexes. Over the next two decades the number of clerks in the State Department continued to increase. In 1889 there were forty-eight clerks (including eleven women) in a staff of eighty-one; less than a decade later clerks comprised sixty-six of the eighty-six State Department employees. The same bureau continued to issue passports until 1898, when the passport clerks were moved to the Bureau of Accounts when it became responsible for collecting passport fees. In 1902, with the State Department receiving over ten thousand applications annually the issuance of passports became the responsibility of a separate bureau with multiple staff members. In the following decades this bureau had various names, reflecting the changing status and role of the passport, which subsequent chapters will address—the Passport Bureau (1902–7), Bureau of Citizenship (1907–17), Division of Passport Control (1917–25), and Passport Division (1926–52).

The changes in the administration of passports seemingly occurred in response to the volume not only of passport applications but of the work of the State Department in general; in 1909 the department employed 135 clerks.[2] These administrative developments manifest not only a belief in bureaucracy but also an increasing faith in rationalization. While bureaucracy increases control by improving the capability to process information, rationalization increases control through decreasing the amount of information to be processed.[3] The dependence on standardized documents, along with the policing of the personal name, signature, physical description, and photograph, are all ways in which the passport was altered to produce a more rational identity. In this manner the reliability of identification that came to depend on a belief in the objectivity and neutrality of bureaucratic procedures over the subjectivity and discretion of individual action was directed not only at applicants but also officials. Bureaucratic rationality was the logic that, consciously or not, drove the transformation of the passport into a modern identification document. The reliability that came to be associated with the documentation of identity derived from the increasingly pervasive belief that bureaucratic objectivity produced useful knowledge on a scale large enough for effective government in a nineteenth-century nation-state.[4] More than as a context for understanding the development of the modern documentation of identity, bureaucracy needs to be understood as being as important to the passport as the signature or the photograph. Bureaucracy in this argument is not a neutral mechanism for representing identity; it is an active process that affects the form and nature of the identity verified by the passport. This new form of identity made it possible for people to think that it could in fact be documented accurately. While attempts were made to standardize identification techniques to assist in the verification of identity, bureaucratic rationality was equally important in the rethinking of identity as the collection of information, if not more so. Standardized application forms and supporting documents turned it into a problem centered on the collection, classification, and circulation of information—the archival problematization of identity that remains critical to the documentation of everyday life into the twenty-first century. Therefore, a fuller appreciation of the novelty of the assumption that identity could be documented requires locating the passport within the equally novel and contested introduction and implementation of bureaucracy in the second half of the nineteenth century.

Bureaucracies of some sort had existed in a variety of forms in the West from at least Roman times, but they lacked the distinct structures and specialization of tasks that came to characterize the modern form of bureaucracy that emerged to organize and administer commerce and government in the era of industrialization.[5] The reorganization of the State Department into bureaus in the 1830s is an example of how a more modern bureaucratic practice began to appear in the federal government. The move in little over a decade from a junior clerk with multiple responsibilities to different bureaus signaled an attempt to create a more clearly defined administrative structure to process information. Previously, the creation of documents was arranged around the act of writing, but with the introduction of bureaus the content of documents became the formal organizing principle that determined which clerk prepared a document.[6] This was a response to the increasing size of government and with it the number of documents produced. However, while the federal government increased in size in the early decades of the nineteenth century in 1831 only 665 civilians ran all three branches of government in the nation's capital. The dramatic increase in size occurred throughout the rest of the century. By the 1880s there were approximately thirteen thousand civilian employees, and twice that number a decade later, although a majority of those worked outside of the capital in the postal service.[7] By this point the growth of government offices had prompted experimentation with more bureaucratic methods of administration and evaluation. The cabinet-level agencies, previously divided into bureaus, were subdivided into divisions devoted solely to functional duties. The technical, legal, and administrative duties once performed by clerks were often transferred to bureau "chiefs" or "assistant secretaries."[8] Within this structure were a large number of clerks, members of the new middle class who were brought in to handle the increasing amount of paper the burgeoning bureaucracy produced.[9] Despite these changes in organization and structure, according to U.S. historian Cindy Sondik Aron, for much of the nineteenth century, government offices continued to operate "in ways that were more reminiscent of small, informal, and even family-run businesses." This was arguably the result of the shared class background of supervisors and clerks, and the patronage system that provided the majority of the workers.[10] The reform of civil service through the introduction of a merit system in the 1880s was intended to make the labor of governing more efficient. However, a few years after the passage of this reform, work within departments and bureaus remained sufficiently fluid that the majority of those in charge could not tell a select committee exactly what duties each worker performed.[11]

The State Department fits into this hesitant adoption of bureaucratic methods and new office technologies that were intended to facilitate an efficient, modern office environment. Through the nineteenth century and into the twentieth century, the department frequently relied on the memory of two long-serving officials, William Hunter and Alvey Adee. Their overlapping careers spanned ninety-five years, beginning with Hunter's appointment as a clerk in 1829 and ending with Adee's death in 1924 at the age of eighty-two. Hunter became second assistant secretary of state in 1853, a position formerly known as chief clerk that had been changed with the creation of the position of assistant secretary of state. He remained the department's number three until his death in 1886, having worked for fifty-seven years under twenty-one secretaries of state. Adee, appointed to a temporary position in the State Department in 1877, succeeded Hunter and remained in that position until his death. Throughout their careers Adee and Hunter's encyclopedic knowledge was regularly noted.[12] In the 1870s Hunter's immediate superior described him as the "personification of the department's work... its memory, its guiding hand."[13] In one instance Hunter alerted the secretary of state that a treaty the Dutch government had recently made a claim under had in fact been abrogated; in this instance it took considerable time to confirm his suspicion, as Hunter's initial memory of the date proved inaccurate.[14] Although, Hunter's memory, the State Department's primary (re)collection of knowledge, was not always accurate through his almost six decades of service, it was critical in an office that until the 1870s lacked a bureau in charge of archives and collected its papers in chronological volumes, each with its own index. Adee took on a similarly crucial role, described in 1915 by a colleague as the "anchor of the State Department."[15] His importance to the daily functioning of the department was recognized in the establishment of an Office of Coordination and Review in the State Department soon after his death. Although, as the personification of the department's memory, Adee challenged the impersonality of the newer forms of bureaucratic administration one of his final wishes acknowledged the erasure of subjectivity critical to bureaucratic objectivity—he ordered all his personal papers burned at his death.[16]

Particular individuals who possessed a broad knowledge of all that mattered in a government department, men who could claim impartiality and authority through personal reputation, became less critical to government as the prioritization of specialization and efficiency increased.[17] Thus, somewhat appropriately, Gaillard Hunt, who did much in his bureaucratic career to secure the history of the federal government in documentary form, began work in the State Department in 1887, a year after the death of Hunter. A decade later Hunt, then a passport clerk, completed the 233-page book *The American Passport: Its History and a Digest of Laws, Rulings and Regulations Governing its Issuance by the Department of State*. This book, including a detailed table of contents and an index, centralized the previously dispersed correspondence and memoranda on passport policy; it is primarily a collection of excerpts from the State Department's external and internal correspondence, to which Hunt provided limited commentary.[18] Outside of this book the documents existed within the general State Department filing system based on bound volumes of correspondence created to store information, not to facilitate retrieval. While the digest as a collection of quotes had long been a model for codes of law, it is significant that the application of this format to U.S. passport policy occurred in a period in which the federal government was increasingly adopting bureaucratic practices in its day-to-day administration. Beyond its legal origins, the compilation of *The American Passport* signaled an attempt to produce knowledge that was logical, rational, retrievable, and ultimately "reasonable." The verification of precedent through retrieval no longer required personal knowledge of when and who wrote a letter or memo in order for it to be found in bound volumes. It simply required the clerk or official to read the book's index. The book pared down the vast amount of passport correspondence to those extracts that critically Hunt and the current department believed mattered.[19]

However, such innovations were only one aspect of the gradual emergence of bureaucratic practice. The year Hunt's book was published, John Hay was appointed secretary of state. He arrived at a State Department described as an "antiquated, feeble organization, enslaved by precedents and routine inherited from another country, remote from public gaze and indifferent to it. The typewriter was viewed as a necessary evil and the telephone an instrument of last resort."[20] Despite Hay's overseeing such initiatives as the Passport Bureau, comments from his successor illustrate that introducing bureaucratic practices was no easy task. In 1905 Secretary of State Elihu Root described himself as "a man trying to conduct the business of a large metropolitan law-firm in the office of a village squire."[21] A request for correspondence on any specific topic provided one source for his frustration. Because of the department's record-keeping practices, any such demand usually led to the delivery of several large volumes, if indeed the requested documents could be located. Incoming and outgoing correspondence was stored in chronologically ordered bound volumes. Until 1870 records were indexed in the front of each volume. After 1870 the department made use of folio index books.[22] While these changes lessened the reliance on personal memory, the records themselves were still stored in multiple places. Reportedly annoyed at being brought several bound volumes after he requested a handful of documents, Root insisted a more efficient system of storage and retrieval be adopted.[23] In 1909 the department began to use a numerical subject filing system with the files stored in folders in filing cabinets; this was further refined by the introduction of a more comprehensive decimal filing system in 1917.[24]

Innovations such as the filing cabinet and compilations like *The American Passport* provided a basis for a more impersonal and mobile memory that could be consulted in the absence of any specific individual; it facilitated the production of what Matt Matsuda labels the "memory of the state."[25] These developments illustrate the "modern" recognition of the need for a systematic approach to information rather than the mere awareness of the

UNITED STATES.
vouched by Clem. C. Biddle

***To all to whom these Presents shall come,* GREETING:**

THE bearer hereof, Alexander Benson — — — — *aged* twenty three — *years, or thereabout, of the height of* five — *feet,* seven *inches,* dark — *complexion,* dark brown — *hair,* and blue — *eyes,*

(whose name is here repeated in his own hand writing, viz.)

a citizen of the United States of America, having occasion to pass into foreign countries about his lawful affairs, these are to pray all whom it may concern, to permit the said Alexander Benson

(he demeaning himself well and peaceably) to pass wheresoever his lawful pursuits may call him, freely and without let or molestation, in going, staying, or returning; and to give to him all friendly aid and protection, as these United States would do in like cases.

In Faith Whereof, *I have caused the Seal of the Department of State, for the said United States, to be hereunto affixed. Done at the City of Washington, this* fifteenth — *day of* April — *in the year of our Lord,* 1818 *and of the Independence of these States the forty-second.*

SECRETARY OF STATE.

[GRATIS.]

Figure 7.1. Copies of early passports were stored in a press book. This example from an 1818 volume shows that the file copy was used to note who had vouched for applicant (National Archives, College Park, MD).

need for information.[26] Akin to the move to use impersonal modes to verify identity, the demand for these techniques occurred in response to an increase in scale, specifically the volume of documents an office such as the State Department now produced. Information was organized so the state could have a memory over and above that of the individuals who worked in it. In most early nineteenth century large scale offices the memory of long-term workers (like Hunter and Adee in the State Department) had been required to locate relevant material on a topic because outgoing and incoming correspondence had been stored in two separate places. Incoming correspondence was usually stored in bound volumes and/or boxes, and copies of outgoing correspondence were created in tissue press books; in the first decades of the nineteenth century the State Department issued passports out of a press book (figure 7.1).[27] In each case documents were not indexed by subject but by author or destination, if at all. Initial attempts to store documents by subject in a centralized location through flat filing (pigeonholes and letter boxes) had limited success. In contrast the introduction of vertical filing solved these problems so successfully that it won a gold medal at the 1893 Chicago World's Fair; it ensured that after enabling officials to communicate, correspondence could become part of the state's memory.[28] Rather than being a consequence of origin and chronology, storage could now be determined in anticipation of future use; carbon paper and typewriters assisted this development. With storage made more systematic the filing cabinet, combined with an appropriate indexing system, effectively increased the amount of readily available information on a particular subject by gathering all files on a topic in a location where, importantly, new files could be added easily. In making information available that had previously been hard to locate, the filing cabinet functioned to produce new knowledge.

The development of complex systems of filing played an important role in the first attempt to use documents to verify identity at the U.S. border as a result of the Chinese Exclusion Acts.[29] From the beginning of the twentieth century, extensive cross-referenced files centralized in Washington, D.C., were constructed as part of an attempt to improve channels of communication between the Bureau of Immigration and its agents at ports of entry; this attempt was also extended to State Department officials in China who issued documents to Chinese verifying their claim to be exempt from the act. The systematic ordering of files was necessary because of the ongoing attempt to limit discretion and ensure predictability through an increasing reliance on procedures and documents. The turn to documents was a response to initial problems with the general enforcement of the act in the 1880s and 1890s and to specific instances of corruption.

The standardization of procedures, the documentation of decisions, and the centralization of records were more successful within the Bureau of Immigration in the United States than with the Asian-based diplomatic and consular service of the State Department. By the second decade of the twentieth century, with the prioritizing of structure and predictability, officials and clerks at the newly opened Angel Island immigration station near San Francisco were regularly rotated between cases in a further effort to limit personal attachment and emphasize the impartiality of the rules and procedures of the inspection system. In China the State Department had the most success in standardizing the methods of investigation that its representatives used to make Chinese people correspond to bureaucratically defined categories of exemption such as "merchant" or "student." In this case the increasing use of documents was intended to remove both Chinese and officials from their local environment and relocate them into a centralized bureaucratic network. Except for the category of familial exemption, the social relations and interactions that usually defined an applicant's identity were no longer relevant to the identity categories associated with Chinese exclusion. The act provided the identity that an official had to verify and the State Department generated a set of procedures to ensure this was done effectively and with a claim to objectivity; with this system of enforcement a migrant could only be a "merchant" if that identity could be verified through the appropriate standardized forms and cross-referenced files. In this scenario local Chinese were considered "interested parties," in contrast to the purportedly bureaucratically neutral U.S. government officials whose attempts to enforce the act did not apparently come with any "interest."

The attempt to create a bureaucratic system of predictability to manage Chinese immigration was frequently viewed as a clash of cultures between a modern, rational United States and an uncivilized, illogical China.[30] However, in the United States the hesitant development of the passport as a standardized identification document also led to a cultural clash when this rationalized administration encountered localized practices of trust and identification. In this manner the Chinese Exclusion Acts illustrates the formation of a documentary regime of verification, but the pervasive appearance of such a regime in U.S. society cannot be explained without acknowledging the contested extension of documentation practices to the wider population. The passport as one of the first wider encounters with documentation is a critical example of how people initially responded to official identification. While the novelty of bureaucracy was challenged or only gradually accepted in the offices of business and government, such practices were more frequently perceived as foreign when they were applied to the identification of certain individuals; the objectivity critical to bureaucracy challenged the subjective claims long considered inherent to any authentic claim to identity, even the popular understanding of the legal category of citizenship. When a more rigorous documentation of identity was applied to marginal populations such as criminals and Chinese, it tended to make sense to the population at large, but it made much less sense to the larger population when they themselves became subjected to bureaucratic identification practices and found their word increasingly discounted. As previous chapters have noted, this marginalization of people's opinion and socially produced reputation created for some a sense that the identity being asked for in the application and presentation of a passport did not necessarily belong to them. In issuing a passport in this manner, the State Department seemed interested in a distinct, if not altogether new, identity separate from people's cultural and social understanding of who they were.

The awareness that the documentation of identity did not necessarily verify a preexisting identity is an example of how documents generated in a bureaucracy help make the world they inhabit.[31] A passport was not a neutral representation of identity, despite its emergence within claims to neutrality articulated in the logic of bureaucratic objectivity; to standardize and centralize identification is to exclude. As noted a document such as the passport reduced or "simplified" identity to merely that which could facilitate the official recognition of the inhabitants of a territory by creating an official identity that enabled a person to exist within a bureaucracy.[32] Identity had to be broken down into recordable evidence in the form of specific facts. Critically, each fact had to be intentionally processed so it could be placed in an organized and meaningful relationship with other facts to constitute an individual's identity.[33] The passport then had to be produced in such a way that it accurately and reliably represented this identity to people outside of the bureaucracy that created it. The previous chapters have taken specific identification technologies to trace how a correspondence was created between them and a person, or at least how they came to be accepted as offering the possibility of facilitating the accurate identification of a person by linking that person to a document. The ad hoc development of these newer, more objective claims to identity, and the tension between them and the subjective claim to identity creates the contested emergence of the passport as an identification technology.

The attempts to control the production and representation of identity beginning in the mid-nineteenth century through bureaucratically issued documents were intended to reduce personal discretion and leaps of faith in official identification. These attempts would eventually coalesce into a widely accepted documentary regime of verification. This occurred as officials came to depend more and more on specifically issued documents in the belief that they returned an acceptable degree of certainty to the official identification of individuals. However, in the attempt to realize these aspirations, the passport in the United States emerged as an accommodation to a variety of disputes over its authority and function. While the stabilization of identity was articulated through bureaucratic claims to objectivity, its manifestation in the passport was subject to numerous logical and local contingencies. Therefore, while the preceding chapters have offered a sketch of how it became possible and practical to assume that identities could be documented, the following chapters seek to understand the establishment of that authority specifically in the passport. The emergence of the passport as a document used by officials and the public makes explicit that who could document official identity, or the social or institutional purposes for which it was documented—indeed the very nature of citizenship or nationality as a documented identity—were all subject to historical contingencies. In a time of racial instability the targeting of naturalized citizens (as an indication, possibly unconscious, of the privileging of a native-born, Anglo-Saxon whiteness) is an important reminder of how documents can be used to "fix" identity and thus "objectively" resolve culturally specific problems of identification. The contested and negotiated emergence of the passport as documentary proof of identity in such situations provides the passport with the history the remainder of this book outlines. Episodes from the passport's role in debates about citizenship and the control of immigration and travel provide important insights into the difficulties associated with the expansion of the documentation of identity from the margins to the center of society. While many of the issues raised in these disputes and deliberation were not immediately resolved, they contribute to our understanding of the piecemeal development of modern identification documents. These episodes illustrate how this key category of contemporary public and private life emerged, and how over several generations officials and public alike negotiated the new forms and types of knowledge that it depended on and generated.

To understand how the U.S. passport as a piece of paper became a reliable identification document demands breaking it down into its various components. However, an equally important perspective on the identity supposedly fixed in the document can be found by locating the passport in its use in historically specific administrative and political contexts. The passport did not simply arrive as an identification document, ready to enforce border security and manage international mobility at the moment when politicians and officials decided such a document was necessary. Rather, it emerged with its contemporary authority and function through confusion and contestation that challenged its status and that of the institutions that sought to deploy it, as well as the identity categories the passport purported to merely verify.

Part Two: Using the Passport

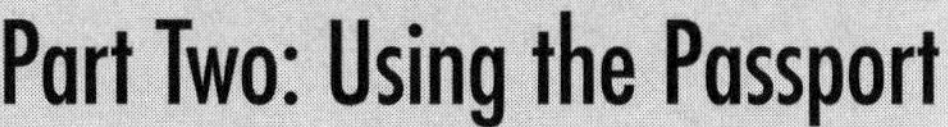

8

Dubious Citizens

Although the Continental Congress authorized the issuance of a U.S. passport in 1782, it was another fifty years before any branch of the government gave serious consideration to the precise nature and authority of the passport and its relationship to citizenship. In 1835 the Supreme Court offered its first comments on the legal status of the U.S. passport. As part of an appeal, the court had to determine whether a passport was legal and competent evidence of citizenship—in this case a passport John Quincy Adams had issued as secretary of state in 1824. The Court ruled that a passport did not provide sufficient legal proof of citizenship.

In writing the Supreme Court decision, Justice Thompson outlined two functions for a passport. He argued that within international law a passport, through its usage to facilitate the freedom of travel, had come to be accepted as evidence of the fact of citizenship. However, while custom had made it evidence of citizenship, in origin a passport was a "political document." By this Thompson meant that the purpose of the passport was not to provide legal proof of citizenship; rather, it was a document "which from its nature and object is addressed to foreign powers, purporting only to be a request that the bearer of it may pass safely and freely." As a "political document," the majority of the justices believed, it could not function as a legal document in a U.S. courtroom. Outside of the world of diplomacy, when presented in a courtroom, a passport became merely an "ex parte certificate" that did not offer any evidence of citizenship. In the eyes of the Court, as a letter from the secretary of state, a passport had no legal standing. To determine citizenship a court would require the evidence that had been presented in the passport application—assuming that some evidence had indeed been presented, and that it was evidence "of a character admissible in a court of justice." The Court, however, was skeptical as to whether evidence was ever actually demanded in a passport application. Thompson outlined how the justices understood the issuance of passports in the United States.

> There is no law of the United States in any manner regulating the issuing of passports, or directing upon what evidence it may be done, or declaring their legal effect. It is understood as a matter of practice, that some evidence, of citizenship is required by the Secretary of State before issuing a passport. This, however, is entirely discretionary with him. No inquiry is instituted by him to ascertain the fact of citizenship, or any proceedings had, that will in any manner bear the character of a judicial inquiry.

Therefore, the Court believed, a passport offered no legal proof of citizenship. From a legal perspective, a passport was merely the opinion of the secretary of state, who, as a member of the executive, had no judicial authority to rule on citizenship.[1]

This Supreme Court opinion provides a useful starting point for examining an important transition in the emergence of the United States passport as an identification document—the development of the passport from a "letter" to a "certificate of citizenship." The Court's ruling would be invoked by other courts and government documents for more than a century, but it had little impact on the use of the passport. Outside the courtroom, it became a document that was considered evidence of citizenship. However, the Court's decision to use the form of the letter to define its purpose, over and above any other use, does offer an important insight into the nature of the use and authority of the passport, as it indicated that the passport functioned within a system of diplomatic accommodation. For officials, applicants, and bearers, the passport—particularly in the first half of the nineteenth century—was in practice a document more akin to a letter of introduction or letter of protection than an identification document. It satisfied occasional regional demands that a document be presented to local officials when a visitor stayed in the area, or it offered the possibility of entry into certain social circles abroad. In this tradition of documentation, the authority of the writer and the character of the bearer were critical. A letter of introduction was not thought of as a document offering absolute proof of identity; rather, it was a letter that referenced a person (and therefore only identified them) through their name. It did not claim a legal status for the bearer, nor did it have to include a physical description, signature, or any other technique intended to link the bearer unambiguously to the document; it was not a document intended to prove identity. The association of the passport with this tradition of documentation limited attempts to constitute the passport as a document that could be consistently trusted to verify an individual's identity. We have encountered numerous attempts to make the document a more reliable and accurate presentation of individual identity, but, as the Supreme Court's decision accurately stated, in terms of passport applications, no laws existed to establish evidence, nor were there any departmental rules guiding issuance—the latter did not appear until 1845, a decade after the decision.

In his early twentieth-century law digest, John Bassett Moore described the system for issuing passports during the first half of the nineteenth century as "exceedingly loose."[2] In this period State Department officials issued passports to noncitizens; on occasions this was done deliberately, as the passport was considered a letter of protection or introduction not a document that had anything to do with citizenship. Passports also ended up in the hands of noncitizens out of confusion over who exactly could be a U.S. citizen. This confusion created "dubious citizens." With citizenship a disputed and contested category, the passport lacked the stable identity critical for its development as an accurate identification document. How could a passport be considered a reliable certificate of citizenship if citizenship itself was not clearly defined? To answer that question, this chapter focuses on nineteenth century citizenship debates as they affected the development of the passport as an identification document—that is, when, as a result of social and legal debates about citizenship, it became difficult to document identity and, therefore, to position the passport as a reliable document to verify citizenship. In the first half of the nineteenth century, immigrants who had declared their intention to be citizens and free African Americans who applied for passports, provide important examples of two kinds of noncitizens who challenged the definition of citizenship. The attempts by free African Americans to obtain passports in the mid-nineteenth century link the problem of documentation both to challenges to the racial constitution of U.S. citizenship and to tensions between individual states and the federal government. The endeavor to make the passport a reliable certificate of citizenship also encountered problems when naturalized citizens returned to their countries of origin and sought to renew passports repeatedly throughout what increasingly seemed to be a permanent residence abroad. Such long-term absences from the United States called into question the loyalty that officials considered reciprocal to the promise of protection made by the passport. Beyond the unclear legal boundaries of categories of citizenship, the novelty of the practice of documentation also created another type of dubious citizen. While these people were apparently legitimate citizens in the eyes of the law, their citizenship became doubtful when they presented what they thought was a passport to U.S. officials abroad. Instead they were presenting a document issued without the authority of the State Department by a more proximate and local official such as a state governor, a mayor, or a notary. It was becoming apparent the stabilization of identity through documentation depended on a knowledge of the protocols and formalities associated with identification, particularly how identification practices trumped the authority of certain officials to issue documents.

Although the U.S. constitution did not define American citizenship, it did give Congress the authority to define naturalization. Congress did this in 1790, a few months after the ratification of the constitution, when it limited naturalization to free white persons who had lived in the United States for two years; in 1795 it increased the required period of residence to five years.[3] In 1802 the residence requirement was reduced back to two years. Eligible aliens who intended to become U.S. citizens could declare their intention to do so before a court official and receive a certificate recording this fact. The uncertain nature of the relationship between these "declarants" and their future nation-state complicated the somewhat ad hoc passport policy that secretaries of state created in the 1820s and 1830s. In a period when fewer than five hundred passports were issued annually, conflicting decisions were often made in the name of the same secretary of state. In 1826 Secretary of State Henry Clay issued a document that entitled a declarant to "all lawful aid and protection...in the case of need." A year later he stated that only on naturalization did someone acquire the full and same rights as a native-born citizen.[4] Perhaps this apparent inconsistency can be explained by the actions of Clay's predecessor, John Quincy Adams, who issued a passport to a declarant, but not as an "actual citizen."[5] By the 1840s, when annual passport issuance was at more than a thousand, Secretary of State James Buchanan clarified that a declarant should not be given a passport. A year after issuing the first instructions regarding passport applications, he informed an applicant, "The passport certifies that the bearer *is* a citizen.... His intention to become so may be ever so manifest, and his right to become so at any moment he please may be ever so clear and unquestionable; still, this does not make him one; on the contrary, it renders it certain that he is not one."[6] However, other contexts blurred this distinction for immigrants. By the middle of the nineteenth century, in an attempt to attract new residents, some states and territories allowed declarants to vote in local elections. At the same time the U.S. Senate debated the merits of declarant-alien suffrage.[7]

Despite this articulation of the passport as a certificate of citizenship, no law prevented U.S. passports from being issued to aliens. When passports were deliberately issued to noncitizens, its function as a letter of protection seemed to trump any burgeoning authority it had to certify citizenship. In most instances, such passports were issued abroad, often with the words "citizen of the United States" crossed out. In the early 1850s, a U.S. official outlined the general chaos around the status of U.S. passports in Turkey owing to the issuance of passports to noncitizens. There were three groups of noncitizens affiliated with the failed Hungarian revolution against the Austrian Habsburgs who were in Turkey with U.S. passports. One was a group that had emigrated to the U.S. but returned with "passports" from U.S. legations, consulates, or other authorities identifying them as "American affiliated citizens." A second group had received passports from the Constantinople legation "not noticing their nationality at all, but merely describing them as persons 'emigrating to America.'" A third and much larger group, numbering in the hundreds, had arrived in Turkey with passports from the consulate in Rome that described them as U.S. citizens. Many of these passports had been purportedly sold or exchanged. In an attempt to halt occurrences such as this, a State Department dispatch threatened diplomatic and consular officials with deprivation of office for issuing such documents to aliens.[8] Nevertheless, a year later a new secretary of state issued a personal instruction that permitted aliens to be issued passports under special circumstances; it is unclear whether such a passport would have specifically identified a bearer as a noncitizen.[9]

In the midst of this inconsistent policy, it seems fewer declarants were being issued passports; at least that is one possible reason for the increase in the use of declarant certificates abroad, often called "first papers." In an 1852 letter to the minister in London over the increasing use of these certificates in lieu of a passport, Edward Everett, at the end of his four-month tenure as secretary of state, argued that in most dealings with foreign officials a passport and a declaration of intention would serve the same purpose. He considered that declarants, as bearers of first papers, "had disabled themselves from procuring passports from their own governments," and therefore that "they seem to have some claim to all aid...we can with propriety give them."[10] Everett did not specify exactly what that was. Other diplomatic correspondence from this period indicates the nature of this assistance while attempting to establish the difference between first papers and a passport. Officials and agents of the U.S. government could endorse a declarant's certificate as genuine,[11] and, if the bearer required protection, offer their "friendly offices," but they could not "interfere officially."[12] In practice, this distinction between "friendly offices" and official interference only further contributed to the blurred boundaries of the passport and the declarant's certificate. In these two roles, both documents offered a form of assurance—they allowed someone to be known (as a friend) among strangers.

The passport and declaration of intent reveal the somewhat incoherent nature of official documentation in the mid-nineteenth century. The declaration of intent was a small certificate recording an event, not a document that contained any attempts to identify the declarant beyond a name and signature. In contrast, the passport was a document that officials wanted to be accepted as a certificate, but it was presented in the form of a letter, albeit one with features that were intended to ensure it could be accurately linked to the correct bearer. The addition of a physical description and signature was meant to contribute to the separation of the passport from letters of introduction and court-issued documents such as the declaration of intent. By claiming a practical equivalence between the declaration and the passport, Everett indicated the limited need for, and utility of, the passport as an identification document. A court-issued declaration of intent and a traditional letter of introduction or protection referred to an individual's identity, but not with the purpose of proving it. If the passport was understood as belonging to this category of document, the attempt to prove identity became a minor function of the passport. This did in fact seem to be the case with most midcentury passports. The most significant role of the passport abroad (one that it shared with the declaration of intent) was apparently to document a personal name, and to endorse the bearer's character or reputation through a relationship to a known body (the U.S. government), not to articulate citizenship (as an official identity) to an individual. Further, in most instances when citizens abroad needed their citizenship recognized, it was to obtain travel advice from a U.S. government official.[13] Therefore, regardless of attempts to present the passport as a certificate of citizenship, it continued despite changes in its appearance to bear a strong resemblance to letters of introduction or protection.

Challenges to citizenship law from individuals and, directly and indirectly, from states further complicated the boundaries of the official identity that federal officials sought to stabilize and verify with a passport. In the decades preceding the Civil War, free African Americans attempted to exploit the tension between federal and state citizenship and occasional inconsistencies in State Department policy to obtain U.S. passports to support their citizenship claims. They took the State Department's assertion that a passport was a certificate of citizenship at face value. This linked the passport to the murky antebellum right of states to declare individuals citizens of the United States.[14] These passport applications were partly intended to contrast the ease with which free African Americans could get forms of citizenship from some states with the lack of recognition from the federal government.[15] The strategic nature of these applications is even more apparent given that only in 1856 did Congress give the State Department sole authority to issue passports. Prior to this legislation, governors, mayors, and notaries public could legally issue passports. Within these contested practices of documentation, the State Department in fact did issue free African Americans a document that identified them as citizens, albeit not a passport. Black sailors received a seaman's protection certificate that stated the bearer was a "Citizen of the United States of America." Introduced at the end of the eighteenth century, these documents were regularly used until 1940. It is estimated that many thousands of them were issued to free black sailors from 1796 to 1868. As a runaway slave, Frederick Douglass escaped disguised as a sailor and carried a borrowed seaman's protection certificate to "prove" that he was a freed slave.[16]

In 1847 in a letter to an applicant Secretary of State James Buchanan wrote department policy was to issue "free negroes" a special certificate, not a regular passport.[17] This did little to discourage free African Americans from applying. Harry Hambleton, "a respectable colored man from Pennsylvania,"[18] unsuccessfully applied for a passport in 1849. However, his case was successfully used by abolitionists to highlight the contradictions between states and the federal government over African-American citizenship. Once the letter of refusal from John Clayton (Buchanan's successor) was made public, sympathetic newspapers criticized the decision. The *New York Evening Post* labeled Hambleton a citizen of the United States; another newspaper supported this, citing the certificate of nativity the state of Pennsylvania had issued him on the grounds of his birth in the United States.[19] Supporting his right to a passport, the abolitionist *National Era* castigated the State Department's policy as "purely arbitrary, without warrant from the Constitution, and in conflict with the sovereignty of every State which chooses to recognize colored persons as citizens."[20] In another article the newspaper argued that without a passport Hambleton would be identified as an "outlaw," as most foreign officials would not accept the undocumented claims of a "colored person" to be a citizen.[21] Clayton further angered abolitionists in the one instance in which he held that an African American was entitled to the protection of U.S. and foreign officials while abroad—a "person of color...in the service of diplomatic agents" could be offered the protection the U.S. government requested for its citizens in a passport. To Clayton's opponents, this statement reinforced the belief that "wherever the colored man goes he must carry with him the badge of slavery to receive the protection of the Americans."[22] In attacking both Clayton's rejection of passports for free African Americans and his outline of an exception, the escaped slave and abolitionist William Wells Brown argued, "None but an American slaveholder could have discovered that a man born in a country was not a citizen of it."[23] In a letter generated by Hambleton's application, Clayton was explicitly asked if he was a slave owner. The secretary retorted that he was not "though I do not perceive of what importance it can be to know."[24] By this point Clayton's original letter to Hambleton had become the center of a controversy for President Zachery Taylor who had recently been elected representing the anti-slavery Whig party.[25]

In the course of the controversy it became known that in the 1830s the State Department had issued passports to two free African Americans that identified them as U.S. citizens. In one case, Reverend Peter Williams in 1836, Clayton brought forward the former department clerk who issued the passport to state that this was a bureaucratic error as the application did not identify Williams as a "person of color"; Williams was the first African American Episcopal priest.[26] Bureaucratic error could not explain the second case. In 1834 Robert Purvis, a "wealthy free man of color" from Philadelphia, received a passport but only after applying a second time after he had initially received the alternative certificate Buchanan described. When reapplying Purvis got a reputable and politically connected white Philadelphian to write a letter arguing for his right to receive a passport. The letter writer contended the refusal contradicted State Department policy of issuing passports to black sailors before invoking Purvis's wealth and light complexion. In claiming the issuance of this passport did not constitute a precedent Clayton explained that the then secretary of state understood Purvis to be "a gentleman, a man of property, of scarcely perceptible African descent." He therefore stated Purvis had been issued a passport, "but not as a colored man."[27] Clayton's articulation of this decision shows not only the racial underpinnings of U.S. citizenship law, but also the ongoing importance of the body as evidence of identity in excess of any claim made in a document and, with it, the seeming redundancy of the "complexion" category in the passport's physical description. While abolitionists had argued that without a passport Hambleton would be identified as an "outlaw," their interest in the symbolic potential of a passport perhaps overemphasized not only its necessity abroad but also its practical usefulness. The "badge" a "colored man" carried in his "complexion" could potentially undercut any authority a passport could have to verify a claim to citizenship, his body identified him as democracy's "Other."

With citizenship an increasingly contested category the official belief that that passports should only be issued to citizens became more prevalent by the mid-nineteenth century; this despite the fact that while the text of the passport identified the bearer as a citizen no law stated that passports could only be issued to citizens. Clayton's successor, Secretary of State Daniel Webster made this clear when he wrote that African American men could not be issued passports because as "colored men" they were not citizens. Buchanan and Clayton had justified their refusals on the grounds of the color of the applicant but not explicitly linked that to legal understandings of citizenship.[28] The issuance of a special document that promised protection to free African Americans (however inconsistently enforced) indicated a further attempt to make the passport a certificate of citizenship first and a travel document second. However, despite these attempts the public perception of the passport as primarily a travel document that offered protection and character endorsement continued to exist, at least among white men who were deemed eligible for it. In 1846 the State Department received a passport request on behalf of a family who were not even going abroad but were planning to travel from Massachusetts to Oregon. On the possibility that they were traveling by sea not land the State Department issued a passport.[29] The ease with which a passport was issued when it would likely not be needed was in sharp contrast to the issuance of documents to free African Americans. In addition the request for an internal travel document stood out against the expectation and occasional demand that free African Americans carry documents when they traveled within the United States.[30]

The purported basis in citizenship of the request for protection (and the implicitly acknowledged promise of protection by the United States) was complicated by the issuance to free African Americans of a document with the same request found on a passport. The existence of the two documents made clear that in the eyes of the State Department (on most occasions) African Americans were not citizens, while acknowledging some relationship between them and the federal government. In contrast, declarants were denied such a document. This possible inconsistency spoke to the complicated and often contradictory understandings of citizenship within different presidential administrations, and the racial underpinnings of those interpretations. The question of whether any protection would ever be offered to free African Americans abroad who carried letters of protection was further muddied when in one particularly complicated case a declarant traveling abroad without a State Department issued document received protection from the U.S. government in a relatively spectacular manner.

A diplomatic controversy over the rights of a former Hungarian revolutionary to the protection of the United States offers a different articulation of race, citizenship, and documentation. After the unsuccessful 1848–49 revolution against the Austrian Habsburgs, Martin Koszta had fled to Turkey before eventually arriving in the United States in 1851 (though, significantly, he was not issued a U.S. passport for the final leg of the journey as some of his compatriots were). The events of the revolution had captured the imagination of the U.S. public; it was perceived as one of the last opportunities for an American-style republic to develop in Europe. The most notable leader to end up in the United States, albeit on short fundraising trip, was Lajos Kossuth, who arrived in December 1851. He called on a receptive public to support the Hungarian cause; his speeches drew large audiences and were printed in full in newspapers and Americans were fascinated with the "Hungarian Washington." By the time of his departure in July 1852, Kossuth's popularity had begun to wane, partly because he refused to become involved in U.S. politics, particularly to support abolition.[31]

Around the same time Martin Koszta also left the United States on a journey to Europe, possibly at the request of his employer, three months after declaring his intention to become a U.S. citizen. The following year while Koszta was in Smyrna(now Izmir, Turkey), Austrian representatives seized him from a coffee shop and held him on a navy vessel. When he had fled Austria following the revolution, Turkey had refused to extradite Koszta to Austria, but released him on the understanding he would not return to Turkey. Following his arrest Koszta claimed the protection of the United States. However, before the local U.S. consul in Smyrna and officials in Constantinople could verify the documents Koszta carried to support his request for protection, the captain of a U.S. naval sloop in port in Smyrna rescued him; as a result of this action the captain was awarded a medal from Congress. Several months later, when news of the events reached the United States, newspapers gave the subsequent diplomatic controversy between Austria and the United States detailed coverage, reprinting full transcripts of the lengthy diplomatic dispatches on their front pages. The disagreement centered both on the right of the U.S. government to "rescue" an individual on foreign soil, and given the complex legal nature of Koszta's relationship to the United States, whether he had any right to receive U.S. protection.

The Koszta controversy derived from the murky relationships among citizenship, protection, and documentation. The vagaries of U.S. citizenship law and the uncertainty associated with the modern practice of documenting identity meant that four different documents issued by four different authorities were offered to support Koszta's claim to the protection of the United States: a declaration of intention to become a U.S. citizen issued by a New York court, a Turkish *tezkereh* issued by the U.S. legation in Constantinople, a copy of Koszta's declaration made by a U.S. diplomatic official, and a certificate of "affiliated citizenship" issued to Koszta by a New York notary. As none of the officials involved questioned Koszta's personal identity, the verification of a legal identity, and the reciprocal acceptance of official identification between states, became the issue in this controversy. Collectively, these documents also help clarify the authority and status of a document Koszta did not offer to support his claims—a U.S. passport—the one document that explicitly linked citizenship to a right to protection while abroad. However, he apparently did not need it to receive the protection of the U.S. government.

Koszta had with him the document certifying his declaration of intent to become a U.S. citizen at a New York court. Newspapers gave particular attention to his status as someone who had declared an intention to become a U.S. citizen. This liminal status was almost universally understood in the United States to entitle the bearer to the benefits of U.S. citizenship, as the frequent use of a declarant's certificate abroad indicates. In addition Koszta's actions against the Habsburgs seemed to rekindle memories of the revolutionary origin of the United States and made him the embodiment of the revolutionary man.Therefore, it is fair to believe that the historical context in which the Austrian empire sought to claim someone who was viewed as "American" in spirit, if not in fact, trumped any public uncertainty about his status and right to protection.

While the declaration of intention was popularly understood as an oath of allegiance, it was not the primary evidence the State Department offered to support Koszta's claim to protection and to justify the actions of U.S. government representatives. A lengthy letter to the Austrian chargé d'affaires in Washington, D.C., signed by the recently appointed Secretary of State William Marcy but written by long-time clerk William Hunter, defended the United States' action on the grounds that Koszta's "kidnapping" by Austrian representatives occurred in a neutral country that did not claim his allegiance.[32] In such cases, Marcy argued, international law "looks only to the national character in determining what country has the right to protect."[33] In this defense of U.S. actions, while Koszta was not legally a citizen his domicile and declaration of intention meant he nonetheless had under international law gained a "national character" as American. This contestable claim had little legal standing outside of the complicated specifics of Koszta's case but given the coverage of the case it not surprisingly resulted in the State Department receiving numerous requests for protection from declarants throughout the rest of the nineteenth century.[34] The letter also clarified that U.S. actions were further justified by the document Turkish law required Koszta to carry.

A contributing factor to the uniqueness of Koszta's case was his possession of a "tezkereh." Variously translated as "passport," "guaranty certificate," "traveling permit," or "nationality credential," it existed to fulfill the requirement that all foreigners "whose religion and social manners do not assimilate with the religion and manners" of Turkey had to have the protection of a state which shared their religion. In practice, this meant that Christian visitors had to be under the protection of a Christian state that had official representatives near the courts of the sultan. This made Turkey one of the few nineteenth-century states that consistently required foreigners to carry documentation within its borders. However, unlike with the passport, it was on the basis of their religious beliefs that foreigners gained the required document to facilitate safe travel. Turkish authorities had no interest in whether the individual had any preexisting relationship with a specific state—shared religious history was the only factor that mattered. Although it challenged claims to the primacy of nationality as an identity to facilitate international travel, the *tezkereh* was ultimately issued in a manner associated with "national character," which reinforced the authority of states. It was issued by a state (not a church), and from the perspective of the head of the U.S. legation in Constantinople, the Turkish demand meant that "some nationality is necessary to every foreigner."[35] He explained to Secretary Marcy that when a representative

> consents to receive [a foreigner]...they are treated in all respects as the subjects of the protecting power. This is every day's practice; and for a long period there has not been a Legation at Constantinople or a Frank Consulate in Turkey which has not had foreign non-naturalized Franks under its full protection and jurisdiction. In some cases the protégés have been counted by hundreds and even thousands.[36]

Koszta's possession of a *tezkereh* sponsored by the U.S. consulate in Constantinople became the rationale by which U.S. action was most easily explained. While the appeal to international law still raised doubts about the meaning of "domicile," the possession of a *tezkereh* located the rationale for action in the specifics (and ultimate peculiarity) of Turkish law. And it illustrated the authority a document could exhibit if it was issued under clearly marked lines of authority to verify a specific identity.

The U.S. legation in Constantinople produced another document that played a part in the diplomatic controversy—a copy of Koszta's declaration of intent. However, in contrast to the *tezkereh*, it further fueled Austrian claims to the illegality of U.S. actions. The concerns over the authenticity and accuracy of this documentation of his declaration originated in the actions of an official who seemingly struggled to grasp the developing relationship between identity, identification, and documentary authority. Shortly after Koszta's "rescue" by the U.S. navy, Austrian officials contacted the U.S. legation in Constantinople to demand evidence of his claim to U.S. citizenship. John Brown, a career official who was acting chargé d'affaires of the legation during the Koszta controversy, explained his response in a subsequent dispatch to Marcy. "I, at that period, did not possess a copy of Koszta's declaration of allegiance; but having its date, I filled up one with it and sent it to the Internonce."[37] It was the nature of Brown's attempt to document Koszta's declaration that angered Austrian officials. In a letter of complaint, Johann Georg von Hülsemann, the Austrian chargé d'affaires at Washington, D.C, questioned how this document could prove anything:

> It is difficult to conceive how the representative of the United States [in Smyrna] could have sought to found proof of the pretended naturalization of Koszta upon a document destitute of all authentic character, seeing that the form of legalization which is affixed to it, and which alone could have invested it with that character, leaves in blank both the name of the tribunal before which the declaration of Koszta must have been made, and the name of the Clerk, who is supposed to be the depository of the original document, and that, moreover, this pretended legalization has neither signature nor official seal attached to it.[38]

While this is possibly a strategic misreading of the document on the part of von Hülsemann (as may be his understanding of it as conferring naturalization), it does highlight that the practices of documentation were still in formation. Brown was no diplomatic novice—he had held various positions at the legation since 1835—and his reputation as a fine translator of Turkish literary classics into English suggests he was perhaps more intelligent than many administrative assistants.[39] However, while he had acquired a noteworthy reputation in the classical literary world, Brown apparently struggled to be literate in the changing world of modern documentation. His action in producing a copy of Koszta's declaration was likely the result of the infrequency of situations in which documented identity mattered, or perhaps simply the novelty of documentary authority in a world of diplomatic accommodation and trust. Whatever the causes of Brown's actions, Austrian officials were able to take advantage of the contested formation of a new documentary regime and his apparent lack of understanding about how authenticity and authority were increasingly being translated onto official documents. The documentation of individual identity depended on the successful translation of an individual's subjective statement into a legal and administrative fact through a document that contained evidence of the presence and the authority of the appropriate official. The certificate of declaration was a document generated by the judiciary, not the executive, branch of the government to which Brown belonged as an employee of the State Department. In the developing documentary regime of verification, an agent of the executive branch was denied the authority to record a declaration of intent. A diplomatic official was now ideally meant to do no more than verify the document's authenticity. Individuals' specialized positions within an established hierarchy underwrote their authority; an official's authority was circumscribed by his or her duties, and not a consequence of his or her reputation or personal character. Brown's actions indicated he was unaware of (or rejected) how this "logic of location" produced a particular kind of authority. He seemingly believed that his reputation as a government official would carry sufficient authority to produce a "truthful" documentary record, to translate the fact of Koszta's declaration into a document. But Brown could only offer the date of Koszta's declaration on the document, not the evidence that gave it the legal significance that a documentary regime demanded—the name of the courthouse and the signature of an official with a title that indicated his authority to witness and record the declaration, which could trace the origins of the document to the time and place when the event occurred.

Koszta carried a fourth document to verify the legality of his relationship to the United States. Upon his request, a New York City notary public, Joseph Nones, had issued Koszta a document certifying his declaration of intent.[40] Although it was issued outside of any federal or diplomatic channels, Brown was suitably impressed with this document and the category of "affiliated citizenship" it bestowed on the bearer.[41] Beyond Brown's comments, this document received little attention. This is surprising because in large part the controversy turned on the exclusive right of the U.S. government and its representatives to determine U.S. citizenship. While this rhetoric was directed against the claims of the Austrian Empire, the notarial certificate that Koszta carried with him is evidence of an internal challenge to the federal government's exclusive claim to document its citizens. The State Department did contact Nones, but not until the following year, in response to a complaint from the U.S. minister in London about Nones's so-called "passports."[42] Nones responded that, as a notary public, he believed he was entitled to issue certificates "proving existing facts—to be noticed abroad." He argued further that he issued this particular certificate because of the inadequate documentation produced by the courts. Nones contended his "Notarial Certificates of Affiliation and Identification" countered the possibility of fraud created by the "loose and imperfect" certificate of declaration issued by the courts. He believed his documents reduced the possibility of fraud as they "exemplify facts by a careful description of the bearer's person, signature &c." Nones also claimed he clearly outlined the purpose and function of his certificates to applicants, "impress[ing] upon persons the fact that no 'passports' are issued in America, but 'Certificates of Citizenship' by the State Department, and Certificates as foresaid, by me as a notary—and similar ones by the Mayor of our city and by other Mayors and State Officers which abroad are called 'passports.'" He enclosed a copy of one of his certificates, duly stamped and signed by foreign officials, to illustrate that they fulfilled their intended function of entitling "the possessor to respect in his position."[43]

In reply, Secretary of State Marcy again requested that Nones stop issuing such certificates, especially to noncitizens. At this point these certificates were not illegal, so Marcy could merely request. However, he also challenged the distinction between a passport and a certificate of citizenship:

> You have erred in stating to persons as you say you have done that no passports are issued in America, but only certificates of citizenship by the State Department. Although the passport of this department is substantially only a certificate of citizenship, still it is a passport and believed to be almost identical in form with that issued by other governments. The head of the Department is the only officer in the United States who can be recognized by the authorities of foreign governments.[44]

A passport structured as a letter from one government authority to another required the mutual recognition of specific government officers, and in the United States, in the absence of other documentation, the passport happened to also serve as the only evidence of citizenship issued by the government. Therefore, although Nones's "passport" incorrectly stated that a declarant had declared allegiance, it was his request to foreign officials that "all whom it may concern" permit the bearer "safely and freely to pass" that made the document a passport; in this case a greater threat to the authority of the State Department than claims to citizenship. However, these documents were perfectly legal and would be for another three years, at which time Congress established that the State Department was the only authority entitled to issue passports; even after this Nones maintained his right to issue such documents.[45]

The initial congressional intervention in the issuance of passports was a response to the Koszta controversy.[46] On August 18, 1856, as part of an act that reorganized the diplomatic and consular services, Congress declared that passports could only be issued to citizens. It also gave the secretary of state the sole authority to issue passports and made it illegal for any other authority to issue a passport or a document in the nature of a passport. The act stated the secretary of state "may grant and issue passports."[47] Although passports could now be issued only to citizens and exclusively by the secretary of state on a discretionary basis ("may issue") they were still understood as prima facie evidence of citizenship. As outlined in subsequent diplomatic correspondence the State Department remained adamant that "determination of the fact of citizenship is not an executive function. What is reserved to the executive is the use of its proper discretion as to the protection of a person abroad when the facts prima facie establish his citizenship by origin or naturalization, and the issuance of a passport is part of the exercise of that discretion."[48] Therefore, the refusal to issue a passport or to recognize a document issued outside of the State Department as a passport did not annul an individual's citizenship. However, the discretion read into the department's legislative mandate to issue passports became crucial to the development of the passport as a certificate of a very particular form of citizenship centered on a specific understanding of loyalty. The discretion granted to the secretary of state initially carried over to what constituted a passport application—the act did not specify the exact nature of the application process, but instead clarified that the president would proscribe the necessary rules. Until 1896 this was interpreted to mean that the State Department could simply issue instructions; that year a reinterpretation of the act meant subsequent passport application rules and amendments had to come as executive orders from the president.

With a passport law on the books the U.S. government was able to make use of passports in a time of crisis, as European governments had periodically done since the beginning of the nineteenth century. However in practice this turned the U.S. passport into something closer to a travel permit. During the Civil War Secretary of State William Seward issued more stringent passport regulations than any the U.S. government would attempt to enforce until World War I. From August 1861 until June 1865, the arrival and departure of persons at U.S. seaports were subject to a series of regulations and the State Department issued circulars that specified passport requirements along the Canadian border.[49] The federal government sought to use passports to manage the movement of military-aged males who might be leaving the country to avoid military service or arriving to fight for the South. With the exception of immigrants, everyone entering the United States had to have a passport, and nonimmigrant aliens had to have their passport visaed (signed) by a U.S. minister or consul. Everyone leaving the country had to have a passport, and those with non-U.S. passports had to have their passports visaed by the secretary of state. Within U.S. borders people could not pass the lines of the Union army without a passport. In all situations Seward requested the assistance of civil, military, naval, and municipal officials in the attempt to enforce demands for a passport. The additional requirement that passport applicants had to swear an oath of allegiance was a further manifestation of the articulation of loyalty and citizenship at the core of Seward's Civil War passport policy. However, these passport requirements, issued under the authority of the 1856 act, were also accompanied by a suspension of part of that act to allow the granting of U.S. passports to nonnaturalized foreign-born residents or declarants. With this suspension, the State Department could issue passports to noncitizens who were eligible for military service but were leaving the country, having paid a bond. However, the issuance of passports to noncitizens meant that subsequent secretaries of state rejected so-called "Civil War passports" as evidence of citizenship, arguing that they were issued only as permits to leave the country.[50]

While the 1856 act enabled the federal government to use temporary passport requirements with some apparent success, the passport continued to be somewhat of a novelty for officials and travelers. The use of the U.S. passport frequently resulted in disputes centered on three key aspects of the 1856 act: the issuance of passports only to citizens, the sole authority of the secretary of state to issue passports, and the discretion read into that authority. In contrast to the passport's wartime use at the border, the challenges and disagreements centered on the presentation or issuance of U.S. passports abroad. Many of these disputes originated in the uncertainties of U.S. citizenship law. The unsettled nature of the law made the problem of verifying citizenship in a document even more problematic especially as both government officials and applicants often sought to turn the vagaries of citizenship to their advantage by exploiting whatever authority a passport might have as evidence of citizenship.

In the decade between the 1856 act and the Fourteenth Amendment, the ability to document citizenship in a period of racial contestation continued to provide a challenge to the attempts to establish the passport as a certificate of citizenship. This called into question not only the effort to form an exclusive relationship between the passport, citizenship, and protection, but also the notion that a passport was primarily a certificate of citizenship.

In 1859 Sarah Remond, a thirty-three-year-old "freed person of color," arrived in London with a U.S. passport.[51] In the two years she spent in London, Remond delivered more than forty-five antislavery lectures as she studied for a degree at Bedford College for Ladies. Neither of these activities attracted the attention of major U.S. newspapers. What did get their attention was the refusal of a State Department official in London to verify her U.S. passport for a trip to France (this act of verification was referred to as a visa, and in practice could be done by any foreign official; in this case it did not have to be either a U.S. official or a French official). The *New York Times* approvingly reprinted Remond's indignant letter to the official who had refused to recognize her passport and, therefore, her claim to be a citizen; the letter had already been published in English newspapers generating much criticism of the United States. The article commented: "On the face of the passport there could be no question as to the right of Miss Remond to demand a visa from the American representative. But the Secretary at the Legation seems to have been instructed to take his cue from the face of the bearer rather than from that of the document."[52] The *Times* was to some extent correct. While the State Department "expected that a person...will not omit to mention in the application that he or she is a person of color," officials were aware that this trust could be abused.[53] Correspondence prior to the passage of the 1856 act, suggests that "persons of color" presented passports frequently enough for rejection to have become, if not policy, at least an acceptable response.[54] If a "person of color" presented a passport, department officials remained confident that, as with Remond, "such a passport would not be countersigned by the Ministers of the United States abroad [and therefore] it would be of little or no use to the bearer."[55] The latter was not necessarily the case if the bearer intended to use passport to make a point in debates over African American citizenship.

The State Department had received a passport application on Remond's behalf from a notary public in her hometown of Salem, Massachusetts (figure 8.1). Rather than use a preprinted application form, the notary applied for the passport with a one-page handwritten affidavit that he, Remond, and a witness signed. While the application did not mention Remond's race she argued in her letter of protest to the London legation that the notary "saw my *color* which is very *apparent*."[56] In the affidavit the notary had described her hair, complexion, and face as dark; in contrast, the official in London described her as "dark mulatto with wooly hair and negro features."[57] The affidavit subtly addressed Remond's citizenship status. The notary, in his cover letter and at the beginning of the affidavit, carefully stated that he knew her to be a citizen of Salem; the affidavit recorded that Remond "made oath that she is a native citizen of the United States." In accordance with passport regulations, the affidavit also included a statement from a citizen who knew Remond. In contrast to Remond, the notary identified that person, Samuel Andrews, with the phrase, "known to me as a native citizen of the United States." For his part, Andrews stated he was well acquainted with Remond but limited his statement about her citizenship to the comment that he "verily believed that she was born in Salem."[58]

The passport issued as a result of this application identified Remond as a citizen when she legally could not be one. In a world of few documents and limited administrative reach, the State Department still had to trust the honesty of local officials and applicants. Although her application thus constituted an abuse of this trust, somewhat ironically the *Times* used Remond's experiences to make a case for the passport as something like a letter of introduction that would vouch for an individual's character. The editorial acknowledged that Remond was not actually a citizen and therefore moved the issue away from an explicit statement about race and U.S. citizenship to a critique of the post-1856 passport. The *Times* defined the passport as "simply a declaration on the part of the authorities of the country to which the holder belongs that his name is Brown or Smith, and that he is not a fugitive from justice." Described as such, the passport should only be a document to introduce to officials abroad those individuals who sought their assistance. The editorial writer further proclaimed with confidence that "no European government cares a straw whether they are [citizens] or not." Therefore, "this solemn refusal on the part of a great nation to grant a valid document

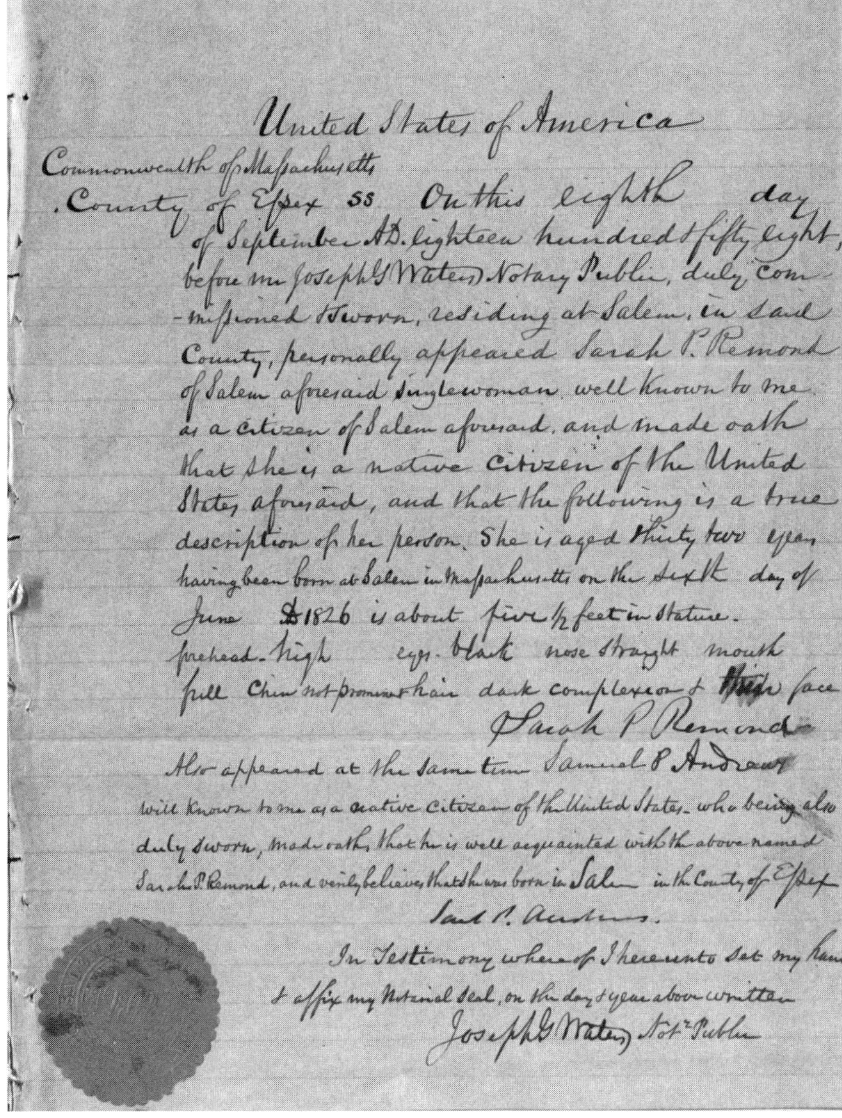
United States of America
Commonwealth of Massachusetts
County of Essex ss On this eighth day
of September A.D. eighteen hundred & fifty eight,
before me Joseph G. Waters Notary Public, duly com-
-missioned & sworn, residing at Salem, in said
County, personally appeared Sarah P. Remond
of Salem aforesaid singlewoman, well known to me
as a citizen of Salem aforesaid, and made oath
that she is a native citizen of the United
States aforesaid, and that the following is a true
description of her person. She is aged thirty two years
having been born at Salem in Massachusetts on the sixth day of
June AD 1826 is about five ½ feet in stature.
forehead - high eyes - black nose straight mouth
full Chin not prominent hair dark complexion & [illegible] face
Sarah P Remond
Also appeared at the same time Samuel P Andrews
well known to me as a native citizen of the United States - who being also
duly sworn, made oath, that he is well acquainted with the above named
Sarah P Remond, and verily believes that she was born in Salem in the County of Essex
Saml P. Andrews.
In Testimony whereof I hereunto set my hand
& affix my Notarial Seal, on the day & year above written
Joseph G Waters Not. Public

Figure 8.1. Affidavit in support of Sarah Remond's passport application, 1858 (National Archives).

of this kind to an unprotected colored female on her travels is something not only unjust but very ridiculous."[59]

The special certificate the State Department issued "free persons of color" seems to be the type of document suggested in these comments (figure 8.2). However, while the *Times* (perhaps strategically) viewed the passport

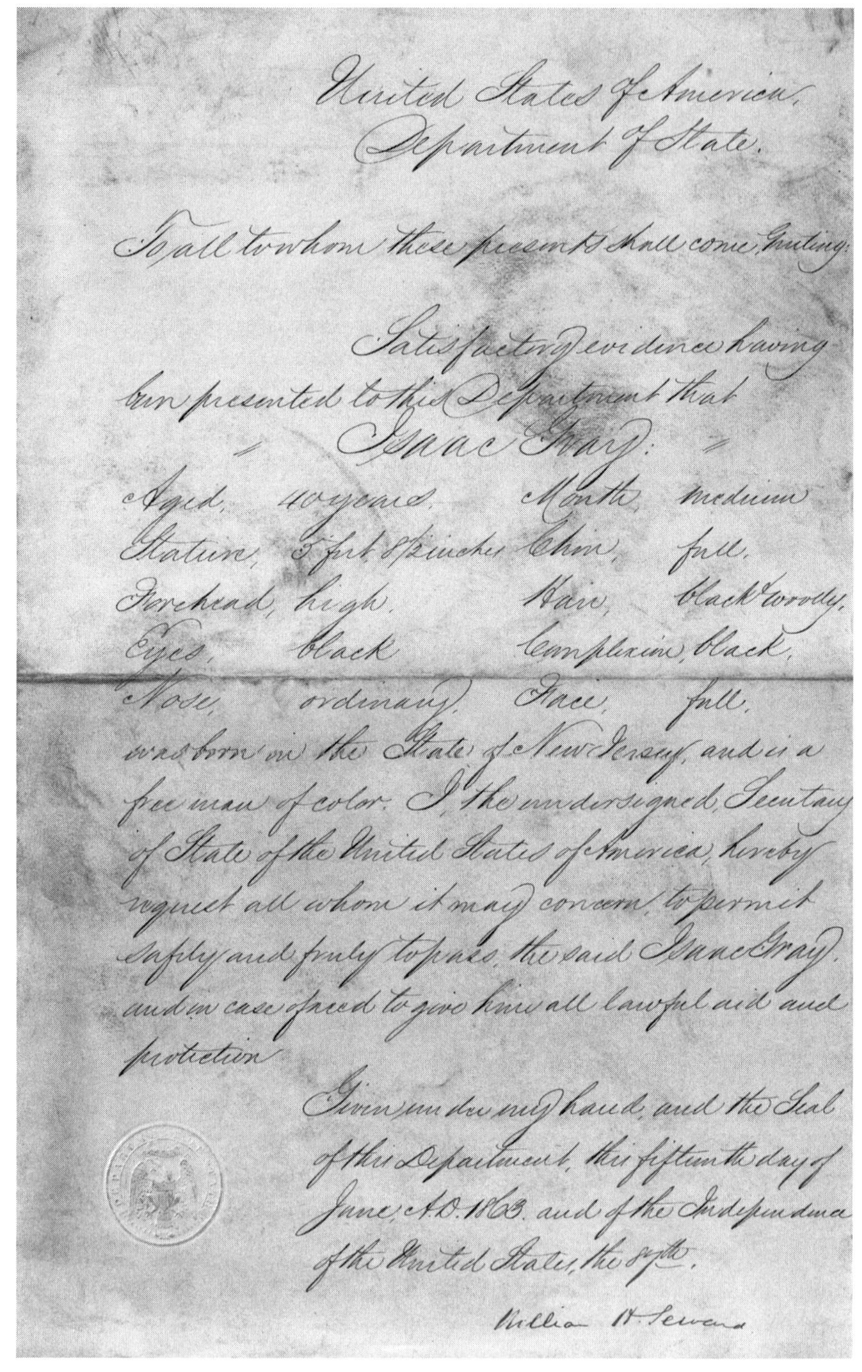

United States of America,
Department of State.

To all to whom these presents shall come, Greeting:

Satisfactory evidence having been presented to this Department that

Isaac Gray:

Aged,	40 years,	Mouth,	medium
Stature,	5 feet 8½ inches,	Chin,	full,
Forehead,	high.	Hair,	black & woolly,
Eyes,	black	Complexion,	black,
Nose,	ordinary,	Face,	full.

was born in the State of New Jersey, and is a free man of color. I, the undersigned, Secretary of State of the United States of America, hereby request all whom it may concern, to permit safely and freely to pass, the said Isaac Gray, and in case of need to give him all lawful aid and protection.

Given under my hand, and the Seal of this Department, this fifteenth day of June, A.D. 1863, and of the Independence of the United States, the 87th.

William H. Seward

Figure 8.2. "Certificate" issued to a freed man of color, 1863 (National Archives).

as simply a letter of introduction and protection the State Department was becoming adamant that its passport was primarily a certificate of citizenship; a claim that could now be supported by the 1856 act. A few months after the 1856 act (and a few months before Taney's *Dred Scott* opinion denied citizenship to "colored persons"), a group of eleven black minstrel performers were refused passports in Washington on the grounds that they were not citizens of the United States, despite their birth on U.S. soil and their being "highly respectable, and worth considerable property."[60] The assistant secretary of state explained the denial on the grounds that the constitution prevented the applicants from being regarded as citizens; therefore he argued when beyond the jurisdiction of the United States they could not claim the full rights of citizenship a passport represented. As had been practice prior to the 1856 act he offered to issue what he labeled a "certificate" that would state the bearers were born in the United States and "that the Government thereof would regard it as its duty to protect them if wronged by a foreign government, while within its jurisdiction for a legal and proper purpose."[61] The claim to birth while not grounds for "full" citizenship did apparently entitle individuals to protection regardless of their skin color.

Half a dozen years later, Attorney General Edward Bates endorsed the type of document offered to the minstrels, but like the *Times* identified it as a passport. He "confidently believe[d] that there is not a government in Europe which, in view of our laws of citizenship, would question the validity of a passport which declares upon its face that the bearer is a free natural-born inhabitant of the United States"; Bates used this claim within a larger argument that a "free man of color," if born in the United States, was a citizen of the United States.[62] He deliberately referred to it as a "passport" because he believed that, in substance and fact, it was. Bates supported this belief with the argument that the 1856 act did not prescribe any form for a passport, and as these documents were letters from the secretary of state to foreign officials, requesting safe passage, they fit the definition of passport. Therefore, contrary to the intentions of the 1856 act, but in the context of disputes over African American citizenship, the *Times* and Bates both downplayed the importance of the verification of citizenship as the primary function of a passport. Instead they viewed it as a document that established a relationship between the bearer and a recognized authority, and on this ground offered individuals protection abroad and made them known to whomever they might encounter on a journey.

In the same opinion Bates contended U.S. citizenship lacked a clear legal definition. He argued he could find "no such definition, no authoritative establishment of the meaning of the phrase [citizen of the United States], neither by a course of judicial decisions in our courts nor by the continued and consentaneous action of the different branches of our political government."[63] The most recent attempt to offer clarity to citizenship law had been Chief Justice Taney's landmark Dred Scott vs. Sandford ruling in 1857.[64] Taney argued that African Americans were not citizens. His ruling was largely based on the argument that they could not be citizens because they were not treated as citizens; the State Department's refusal to issue passports to free African Americans provided part of Taney's evidence for this argument. Perhaps encouraged by Taney's ruling Secretary of State Lewis Cass declared the passport had always been a certificate of citizenship and therefore "never since the foundation of government [has it] been granted to persons of color."[65] In 1866, Congress passed the Fourteenth Amendment, which defined national citizenship to include "all persons born or naturalized in the United States" and prohibited states from violating the privileges of citizenship without due process of law. In practice, this resulted in the contested citizenship of black men both at a legal level (frequently in terms of disputes between states and the federal government) and in nonlegal situations.[66] But in terms of the U.S. passport, the clarification of the citizenship status of African Americans seemed to reduce, if not completely eliminate, the privileging of the face of the bearer over the face of the document; an African American could now legally be a U.S. citizen. The contested category of African American citizenship had affected initial State Department attempts to consistently establish the passport as a document that could only be issued to citizens. For at least two decades prior to 1856 the State Department had sought to make that its policy without any legal backing. But with on-going disputes over who could be a citizen, the department continued to respond to those debates with changes in issuance policy. Two years before the passage of the Fourteenth Amendment granted African Americans citizenship the State Department passport clerk informed an attorney in a letter published in anti-slavery newspapers that in terms of passports "there is no distinction made in regard to color." Although the passport was purportedly a certificate of citizenship it could at this moment seemingly be granted to people whose citizenship status at best was dubious.[67]

Outside of citizenship law, the attempt to enforce the documentation of citizenship according to the 1856 Act created another category of dubious citizens.

The act described the secretary of state, and diplomatic and consular officials specified by him, as the only people who could issue passports. Prior to 1856 a number of state governors and mayors, along with notary publics like Nones, had issued passports. Despite this, in 1857, in response to Taney's Dred Scott ruling the Massachusetts senate passed an act that allowed the commonwealth to issue passports "to any citizen whatever his color may be."[68] In contrast to this deliberate action the officials who issued passports outside the authority of the secretary of state appeared to do so out of ignorance of the law or confusion over what constituted a passport. In most cases a mayor or governor expressed surprise or regret when they received a letter from the State Department pointing out the legal implication of a rhetorical flourish or an elaborately designed document.[69] These passports tended to be deemed illegal owing to a combination of their appearance and the request for safe passage they contained. In many cases, local officials perceived a passport as a formal letter of introduction, and even if they modeled the documents they issued on the national passport, they did not consider any type of passport dependent on specific evidence of citizenship, nor did the people who carried these documents on their travels.

In 1889 John Jagger, a resident of Minnesota, walked into the U.S. legation in Vienna with a document that he believed provided "all the evidence necessary to establish his right to consideration as an American citizen"; instead, it made that claim, if not questionable, at least unverifiable. In this case, the diplomatic agent who declined to endorse a document issued by the governor of Minnesota admitted that, while it did not purport to be a passport, the document did "appear susceptible [under the 1856 act] to criticism as an instrument in the nature of a passport." When he informed Jagger that he did not have a passport, and, therefore, the consulate could not endorse his document, the Minnesotan seemed "surprised to hear this and remarked that he had intended to get a passport at Washington but that his friends in St. Paul told him the Governor of Minnesota would give him a paper which would answer the same purpose and he had therefore applied and got this document."[70] In response to a letter from the State Department, the governor of Minnesota wrote that he never intended his letter to be a passport and in the future would make it clear to people requesting such a letter that it was simply a "certificate of good citizenship," and that if they wanted a passport, they needed to apply to Washington.[71] Because many people understood a passport in this manner, such an explanation would probably confuse them or fail to convince them they did not already possess a passport, as was apparently the case with Jagger. His confusion over the document he carried was seemingly grounded in the belief that a passport served as a letter of introduction and, possibly, a letter of protection, but not a certificate of citizenship. Such a "passport" introduced and endorsed an individual—it did not provide proof of a legal identity; it allowed bearers to be known by name and reputation while they traveled abroad and carried with it the request for safe passage. In the words of the document Jagger carried, he was a "worthy and respected citizen," which is in keeping with the governor's description of the letter as a "certificate of good citizenship." It more than likely made sense that such a "passport" would be issued locally, where a greater possibility existed that reputational knowledge could provide whatever form of evidence would be required.[72] Citizens like Jagger had yet to learn the institutional purpose of a U.S. passport as a certificate of citizenship and, therefore, to recognize who had the authority to issue a passport that verified the legal category of U.S. citizenship.

In the second half of the nineteenth century, citizenship as an important identity for most travelers remained somewhat of a novelty, which could also only perpetuate an understanding like Jagger's of the passport and its relationship to identity. Passport regulations were "visibly relaxed" throughout Europe from the mid-1850s.[73] Demands for passports at borders practically disappeared, leaving the passport system to function (if at all) as a registration system. Under this arrangement a traveler could, on occasion, expect a request to register with local officials upon arrival in a town; registration systems often relied on the incorporation of tavern keepers into the state apparatus through the threat of fines.[74] The potential for inconvenience in this unpredictable system meant that by the 1870s, while guidebooks primarily listed passports as useful at post offices and banks, or to obtain entrance to museums, they urged travelers to carry them, because a passport could still be demanded at any time.[75] What remained of the passport system functioned as it had in early nineteenth-century Europe—in an arbitrary manner heavily informed by social bias. The majority of U.S. citizens who increasingly traveled abroad as tourists thus did not need the passport they carried unless they were going to Russia or Turkey. They found them useful, however, for geting the attention of U.S. officials abroad. This was rarely for "protection," but for assistance in the form of travel advice from officials, or to gain an invitation to 'society.'[76] In this context the passports epistolary form could only foster a perception that the passport was a document akin to a letter of introduction.

Throughout the second half of the nineteenth century the State Department's difficulties in positioning the passport as a certificate of citizenship came to center on an intensification of the demand for evidence of loyalty to the United States. The lack of a legal definition of what constituted loyalty and therefore an indication of what was required to prove loyalty created problems for officials who attempted to document citizenship in a consistent and standardized manner. In this void the State Department utilized the secretary of state's right to exercise discretion in issuing passports, following its interpretation of the 1856 Act.

At the end of the century, long term State Department employee Alvey Adee summed up how the discretionary policy of passport issuance had evolved: "Discretion has been generally confined to requiring full establishment of the citizenship of the applicants, and of the conservation, in good faith, of the character of citizenship, to the end that the statute may be obeyed and that passports may issue to none but citizens."[77] The citizenship verified in a passport was therefore not determined solely through claims to birth in the United States or naturalization but also through the behavior of citizens when abroad. Officials primarily defined this "full" citizenship through loyalty in relationship to the passport as document that promised official assistance and, if necessary, protection while the bearer traveled abroad ("his right to protection as a citizen abroad will depend on his purpose to fulfill the obligations of good citizenship, whereof allegiance is the highest").[78] For State Department officials, the right to protection existed within a liberal conception of citizenship as a reciprocal and active relationship between citizen and state; "if the applicant has no intention of performing the duties of an American citizen he has no just claim for a certificate of such citizenship."[79]

In the context of this policy loyalty was more easily defined for citizens who applied in the United States. The State Department took their U.S. residence as evidence of loyalty, which continued to be verified through an oath of allegiance. However, this criterion produced a particularly vexing problem when "citizens" applied to renew a passport while abroad. The exercise of discretion in passport renewals for U.S. citizens living abroad long term, particularly naturalized citizens residing in their country of birth, produced another type of dubious citizen. The origin of the word "dubious," the Latin *dubius*, meaning moving alternately in two opposite directions, from the word *duo*, conveys the doubtful loyalty that department officials perceived in these "citizens." The State Department came to understand long-term residence abroad as potential evidence of reduced allegiance, and therefore a questionable entitlement to the protection offered by the passport. These "dubious citizens" only became visible when they sought to renew their U.S. passport while abroad.[80] Thus, in large part passport policy developed through diplomatic and consular correspondence, particularly in response to actual and potential consequences of claims to protection that U.S. officials received from citizens living abroad, not from the short-term travelers for whom the passport was thought to exist.

The State Department's association of protection with loyalty caused passport policy to become intertwined with broader attempts to define expatriation in a world of increased mobility. Government and legal officials read the 1868 Naturalization Act as granting citizens the right to expatriation through the "abandonment of perpetual allegiance" even if this right was not intentionally exercised through long-term residence abroad.[81] However, the act did not outline how citizens could expatriate themselves, voluntarily or otherwise.[82] In 1873, in a long letter, Secretary of State Hamilton Fish informed President Ulysses Grant this gap in the law produced "much doubt and correspondence" for the State Department and its diplomatic and consular officials, especially in response to the "constant occurrence" of naturalized citizens who had permanently returned to their former homeland.[83] That many of the applications to renew expired U.S. passports only originated as part of an attempt by the applicant (and his sons) to avoid the military service his former homeland required of its citizens only encouraged such misgivings.

In attempting to determine loyalty in applications from long-term foreign residents, officials decided that expatriation did not require an explicit renunciation of citizenship; citizens could expatriate themselves through the "silent withdrawal" of long-term residence outside of the United States.[84] This raised the question of when absence from the U.S. became long-term and therefore turned into an exercise of the right to expatriation. The State Department determined that it was after two years; hence in 1873 it extended the validity of a passport to two years. This time frame was based on naturalization treaties the U.S. had signed with individual countries. However, Fish argued in his letter to Grant that in the absence of a specific law, this did not "relieve the decision in each case of much embarrassment and of much doubt"; it would be another thirty years before Congress passed a law defining expatriation.[85]

The absence of any law outlining the criteria for expatriation hindered the already hesitant attempts to document citizenship as an administrative fact within clearly defined bureaucratic practices of objectivity and standardization.

The documentation of identity relied on a stable and fixed identity, or, to be more precise, it produced a stable and fixed identity, to allow for verification. The frustration within the State Department stemmed from the concern that, without standardized criteria for determining citizenship, the passport could not gain authority as a reliable certificate of citizenship. Lacking this, the issuance of passports came to depend on the particularities of specific case, which meant in those cases it relied on more "localized" forms of identification in contrast to the ongoing attempts within the United States to centralize its issuance. In the absence of standardized criteria, the department came to believe that each application had to be considered on its own merits, hence the potential for "much embarrassment" and "much doubt." With loyalty and expatriation positioned as critical to a citizenship defined beyond the fact of birth or naturalization, the issuance abroad of a passport as a certificate of citizenship pushed passport policy into the realm of subjective judgment.

Determining each case on its own merits meant that the evaluation of citizenship beyond the "fact" of either birth or naturalization became the responsibility of U.S. officials abroad. The manner in which consular and diplomatic officials were appointed did not guarantee confidence in their judgment—in fact such officials frequently inspired as little confidence as notaries did in domestic passport issuance. According to one senior department official, there were two classes of inefficiency within the diplomatic and consular service: the first was a lack of natural qualifications and experience, and inadequate professional education; the second was apathy and indifference.[86] Consular and diplomatic officials were not appointed on the basis of a merit system.[87] For all intents and purposes, they were appointed on the basis of proximity—in the case of consuls, proximity to a specific geographic location, and for diplomats, proximity to political influence and wealth. Most consuls were "commission merchants" who were appointed by the government to assist in the expansion of U.S. trade. Few consulates were established on the initiative of the federal government. Instead, when a merchant arrived at a port to discover a lack of U.S. representation, he lobbied for an appointment in the name of U.S. trade, frequently also in an attempt to increase the local prestige of his own name. While consuls did not always have the responsibility to issue passports they did have to assess whether a passport holder was entitled to aid and protection and the exact nature of that aid and protection. Diplomats were appointed on the basis of political connections. Wealth was a prerequisite for these ministers and consul-generals. The U.S. government tended not to own any residences abroad; therefore, in the first few weeks of their appointment, ministers (from 1893 the United States appointed ambassadors) and consul-generals looked for whatever accommodation they could afford. As a consequence of this system of appointment, people with no training and limited knowledge frequently made judgments on the status of citizenship applications. This arguably became less likely after the introduction of merit systems for the diplomatic and consular services early in the twentieth century, though these reforms were more immediately successful in the consular service.[88] A lack of any books that outlined citizenship law, especially as it related to the issuance of passports in consulates or embassies, compounded this ignorance; hence the importance of Hunt's 1898 digest of passport policy.[89] This was further exacerbated by a reluctance on the part of some secretaries of state to issue circulars, owing to fear of having to deal with the correspondence such documents generated from consuls and diplomats "eager" to understand the applicability of the new rules to their purportedly unique situation.[90]

In reviewing an application to renew a passport, ministers and consul-generals had to establish that the applicant manifested a clear intention to return to the United States, where subsequent residence would provide evidence of loyalty. This demonstration gradually took the form of applicants swearing in front of a diplomatic official that they would return to the United States within two years—that is, before their new passport expired. While one official abroad argued that this was something that "might be said to come under the class of obligations denounced by the law for uncertainty,"[91] officials in Washington disagreed, at least in the realm of diplomatic correspondence. The department assured another diplomat that it "trust[ed] to the oaths of the applicants and his witnesses, as in reality it is obliged to do, unless extraneous circumstances suggest the statement to be false."[92] Diplomatic officials were further instructed to renew passports only when an applicant presented "competent evidence" that they possessed the "state of mind" to return; that is, when "the honesty and good faith of this intention shall satisfactorily appear."[93] The necessary "state of mind" could be considered absent by "the patent circumstances of…continued domicile abroad."[94] Beyond this, the State Department did not demand definitive evidence of the actual desire to return in the form of a ticket or fixed date of travel. Instead, its officials abroad were instructed to assess "the manifestation of a fixed intention to return within some reasonable time."[95] The downplaying of an actual date stemmed from the primacy given to the specifics of any case: "It is obvious that no inflexible rule fixing a permissible period for residence abroad can properly be laid down, since the intent to return may actually exist in one case for many years after leaving the United States, and in another case may be nonexistent as soon as a person leaves our shores."[96] In the case of an elderly man of poor health who had not lived in the United States for forty years, a secretary of state advised that the specific facts in this case "might properly operate to produce a lenient construction of the requirement of definite intention to return to the United States. However, being on the spot you are the best judge of whether as a fact, Mr. Bernheim has forfeited a right to the protection of the U.S., and should consequently be definitely refused a passport."[97] Face-to-face assessment remained an important, if not the primary, mode to assess the ongoing possession of full and substantial citizenship. But with the regular change of secretaries of state, no consistent policy developed. While some secretaries of state sanctioned a liberal construction of passport regulations to privilege the word and judgments of the State Department's overseas officials, others still emphasized that these officials should not treat the declaration of intention to return as "an empty phrase."[98]

However, in practice, subsequent secretaries of state used Fish's 1873 letter to President Grant to generate a set of "general principles" to compensate for the lack of "fixed rules."[99] Specifically referring back to the letter, late nineteenth-century diplomatic correspondence isolated three situations in which citizens living abroad were considered exempt from expatriation regardless of the length of their absence from the United States—ones involving health, religion, and commercial activity. The citizens in these circumstances were determined to be loyal because, through their actions abroad, they were considered to be contributing to the development of U.S. society in either the short or long term. In this manner, the State Department utilized its right to refuse passports in order to police what it defined as practices of good (and bad) citizenship. A small exempt category was constituted by people who needed a long-term stay abroad to recover from illness; the assumption existed that, once recovered, they would return home to become productive citizens.[100] A second, slightly larger category, was that of missionaries. Passports were granted to missionaries living abroad long-term for two reasons; first, that they were pursuing "their religious calling" by attempting to convert the "uncivilized" world to Christianity, and second, because missionaries living indefinitely in a "semi-barbarous country" had to remain U.S. citizens "since obviously they [could] not become subjects of the native Government without grave peril to their safety."[101]

The largest group of people the State Department excluded from expatriation were citizens living abroad long-term who could claim an ongoing economic relationship to the United States. These economically determined good citizens tended to be businessmen living abroad—those who worked for an "American business house," not for a "local calling."[102] From the 1860s, when William Seward became secretary of state, the State Department maintained sympathy for business abroad. Seward and others perceived the establishment of U.S. businesses abroad as an informal form of economic penetration into an international market in which the forces of industrialization had reorganized the frontiers of labor migration and export distribution.[103] The resulting conception of the world had at its core an economic vision that determined the actions of State Department officials abroad. Therefore, the work of these citizens was considered to "be essential to the maintenance of some of our great industries." Such citizens were to be treated as "if they were on a mere transient visit of inquiry," no matter how long they remained abroad.[104] This was in contrast to a person whose claim to citizenship was considered dubious because in the words of a secretary of state his "moveable wealth is purposely placed where it may never contribute to the national necessities, and his income is expended for the benefit of a foreign government and his accumulations go to swell its taxable wealth."[105]

Outside of expatriation, the State Department also deployed its policy of discretionary issuance both to promote good behavior and to discourage behavior that could be considered inappropriate. The latter situations involved "dubious citizens" who in some way had deviated from the acceptable Anglo-Saxon, protestant foundations of responsible republican citizenship. The idealized citizen remained a white property-owning male, the head of a productive household. Throughout the nineteenth century, passport policy encouraged this ideal through the issuance of one passport per family or household that traveled abroad. A man's wife and his minor children were included on his passport "inasmuch as they necessarily and legally share the status of the husband and father."[106] While women could obtain a passport ("the sex of the [applicant] is immaterial"[107]), as noted earlier, most wives traveled without any documents, instead being identified on their husband's passport by the phrase "and accompanied by his wife." Officials often appealed to efficiency and the savings of multiple passport fees to actively encourage a family to travel together.[108] However, wives and adult children could carry their own passports, though "reasonable cause" had to be shown before they would be issued, such as "the intended residence of one of a family in a foreign land."[109] The family traveling abroad often did so as a household, taking servants with them, who, prior to 1856, were also noted on passports. However, following the 1856 act, these servants could only be added to a passport if they could prove they were U.S. citizens.[110] A more explicit attempt to police a particular vision of the family is evident in the decision not to grant U.S. passports to Mormons, a decision that is the subject of a brief but tantalizing correspondence from 1886. Thomas Bayard, the secretary of state at the time, clarified that "inasmuch as polygamy is a statutory crime, proselytism with intent that emigrants should live here, in open violation of our laws, would seem to be sufficient warrant for refusing a passport." He, therefore, instructed officials not to issue passports to "emissaries of the polygamous Mormon sect who were seeking to make proselytes" in Europe.[111]

However, officials did not want the passport to be perceived as explicitly enforcing particular moral codes. Alvey Adee, after the discussion of discretionary passport policy quoted earlier, explicitly clarified that although Congress had granted the secretary of state discretion, the department had no jurisdiction to make "conduct or deportment" a basis for refusing passports. Adee made these comments in an instruction to officials in China in 1899; moral character had become a point of interest for officials after federal immigration laws listed morality as a factor in determining the admissibility of immigrants to the United States. Adee informed the minister in Beijing he had to accept passport applications from two known prostitutes if the applications were "made out properly." But in his instruction Adee did not condemn the subsequent decision by the consul not to forward the two women's passport applications to be issued at the Beijing legation, because the applicants apparently wanted "travel certificates" required for Russian territory.[112] In this manner, it seems, department officials could broaden the statutory jurisdiction over passport issuance by utilizing a bureaucratic and administrative structure created to "objectively" assess passport applications to in fact subjectively judge and police the behavior of citizens abroad. This was recognized as such by a subsequent assistant secretary of state, who in 1907 commented that "the conduct and character of an American citizen may under certain circumstances influence the department as regards the discretionary act of granting a passport." Though he too later clarified, "A passport is not to be refused to an American citizen, even if his character is doubtful, unless there is reason to believe that he will put the passport to improper or unlawful use."[113] The improper use in this example was blackmail and a perceived general disposition to disrupt U.S. relations with foreign states; in an opinion from 1901, the attorney general offered the example of anarchists applying for passports as a circumstance "which would make it most inexpedient for the public interests of this country to grant a passport to a citizen of the United States."[114] However, secretaries of state did not generally offer the breaking of laws in other countries as the sole grounds for refusing a passport, particularly as passports were intended to offer protection and aid when foreign officials detained a citizen in such circumstances.[115] Nonetheless, on "rare" occasions it was acknowledged that the department had denied passports to citizens who violated U.S. laws while abroad.[116]

From the middle of the nineteenth century in the diplomatic and consular correspondence of the State Department, the passport appears as a certificate of citizenship and one which had value as a document that the executive could use to police the loyalty of its citizens by refusing to issue it to "dubious citizens." However, outside of this context a passport was still not always recognized and used as a legally authoritative document. At the turn of the century, the U.S. ambassador in Paris informed the State Department that the passport primarily served the function of a personal identification document. According to him, French officials

> do not attach to the possession of this document the importance that we do. For a French police officer it means nothing at all. In Paris it is usually asked for at the Police Headquarters for registration; at the post offices for obtaining registered letters and it is sometimes convenient for securing admission to monuments and various other places; but a certificate of identity, such as we issue to students and scholars who desire to study in the public libraries and galleries, would do just as well.[117]

This attitude was endorsed the same year in a French legal text that described passports as "a 'curiosité' of the science of jurisprudence, a subject for a doctoral dissertation, but not one of wider significance."[118]

The comments from the U.S. ambassador to France came in response to a survey initiated by a commission established to report on citizenship, expatriation, and protection abroad; the report of this commission was intended to help the drafting of what would become the 1907 "Act in Reference to the Expatriation of Citizens and their Protection Abroad."[119] The authors of the commission report (three men affiliated with the State Department including Galliard Hunt) recommended that Congress use the general principles the State Department had utilized to determine expatriation since 1873.

Following this recommendation, the 1907 act finally defined the actions that led to a presumption of expatriation and to the overcoming of expatriation albeit three decades after Secretary of State Fish's request. The commission report also argued the passport should be "returned to its original purpose to provide free and safe passage through foreign territory on a temporary sojourn abroad."[120] Acting on this recommendation a system of registration for citizens living abroad was introduced to avoid such citizens using the passport as a document to certify citizenship. The department "invited" U.S. citizens living abroad to register with diplomatic or consular officials, whereupon they would be given a certificate of registration. This certificate, issued on the same rules of evidence the department had used for the passport, would then serve as evidence of their citizenship. Although such certification remained optional, diplomatic and consular officials were instructed to read a refusal of the "invitation" to register as a presumption of expatriation. The introduction of this alternative certificate of citizenship as an attempt to make the passport a temporary travel document did result in the certificate of registration being used illegally as a travel document, as a second-tier passport.[121] Despite such attempts, the passport remained the most prominent certificate of citizenship issued by the U.S. government in the eyes of many officials and members of the public. However, at the beginning of the twentieth century, citizenship was no longer a critical source of problems for the development of the passport as an identification document. The passport continued to be important in debates about citizenship, but, unlike in the second half of the nineteenth century, these debates did not create problems for the documentary verification of identity. While there were debates in the early twentieth century over the citizenship of women and residents of "insular possessions" such as Puerto Rico, these did not significantly affect the development of the practices necessary for the passport to be accepted as a reliable identification document.

9

Suspicious People and Untrustworthy Documents

Although in the latter half of the nineteenth century, the State Department sought to establish the U.S. passport abroad as a certificate of citizenship, passports had no official use along the borders of the United States in this period. Regulations at these borders included some restrictions on the entrance of goods, but allowed freedom of movement for most individuals; until the 1870s individual states were responsible for regulating the arrival and departure of people along the national border.[1] After the federal government took control of U.S. borders, customs officials (and later immigration officials) did not perceive the passport as a useful border document, or, in fact, as a border document at all. For these officials, the U.S. passport, even as a certificate of citizenship, retained its primary purpose as a travel document. The passport was a document of courtesy to enable citizens to elicit assistance from officials within the borders of the countries visited in their travels.

When entry was policed at the border, it tended to be through the reading of bodies and personal appearances, not the reading of documents. The body was held to provide something close to absolute evidence of an individual's true identity. The essentializing properties associated with appearance (and clothing) solved the problem of identification at U.S. borders by allowing officials to identify a person as a member of an excluded group. After the Supreme Court ruled in 1875 that individual states did not have the authority to regulate immigration, Congress began to restrict the entry of certain groups. In 1882 Congress passed legislation excluding Chinese laborers. That same year it also passed an immigration act that excluded the entry of "idiots," "lunatics," convicts, and people unable to look after themselves who were likely to become "public charges"; the 1891 Immigration Act added polygamists, persons convicted of crimes of "moral turpitude" (prostitutes), and those suffering from loathsome or contagious diseases to the list of those excluded.[2] In the absence of a regular need to identify and know a particular individual, the body could provide the general evidence needed to secure the border; without any required documents officials did not use knowledge of immigrants' past behavior to assess entry nor did they use documents to collect information to increase knowledge to assist in governing the population and society.

The assumption that the body provided easily accessible evidence of identity was popularly accepted, with occasional corroboration from scientific and medical expertise. The authority of science was useful when it supported the belief that citizenship as a racial identity could be confirmed by not much more than a fleeting look.[3] However, in the early decades of the twentieth century, when leading anthropologists began to label Syrians and Asian Indians as "Caucasian," the legal evidence for whiteness as a criteria for naturalization was explicitly articulated through what a Supreme Court ruling labeled "common knowledge." The Court made this comment in a 1923 decision that, legal and political historian Mae Ngai argues, seemingly ended a struggle "to reconcile race as a popular concept, as scientific classification, and as judicial and congressional precedent."[4] Rejecting the scientific manipulation of "Caucasian," the Court stated,

> It may be true that the blond Scandinavian and the brown Hindu have a common ancestor in the dim reaches of antiquity, but the average man knows perfectly well that there are unmistakable and profound differences between them to-day.... We venture to think that the average well-informed white American would learn with some degree of astonishment that the race to which he belongs is made up of such heterogeneous elements.[5]

The dismissal of origin, of the not–immediately visible "dim reaches of antiquity," underscored that racial identity was something that could only be accurately verified by presence in the present. Recognizing racial identity by looking at the person in question championed the authority of the average man over that of science.

At the border the average men who read not only racial identity but also morality and criminality were initially officials from the customs service, who maintained a significant degree of local autonomy. After 1891 they came from the Bureau of Immigration, which the federal government created to implement its authority to police the U.S. border. Initially located within the Treasury Department, and subsequently in the Department of Commerce and Labor, the Bureau argued that effective exclusionary work needed a broad policy that allowed for problems (anticipated or not) to be dealt with quickly and efficiently. Efficiency thus required the uncontested authority of officials on the spot.[6] By the turn of the twentieth century, in the name of efficiency, men of science joined these average men. Unlike anthropologists who provided "evidence" that Asian Indians were Caucasian and therefore eligible to become citizens, doctors from the Public Health Service (PHS) provided expertise that supported the administration of immigration according to the categories constructed by immigration law. They were employed to read the body not for a racial identity but for signs of disease; in practice these were not necessarily distinct, as health authorities tended to work with the belief that disease was both foreign and nonwhite.[7] The percentage of immigrants denied entry for health reasons increased from 2% of those denied entry in 1898 to over 50% by 1913—but throughout this period the overall rate of exclusion hovered around 1% of all immigrants.[8] Although doctors brought expert eyes to the body to enforce the exclusion of those with loathsome or contagious diseases, disease had become a useful way to police the "public charge" category of exclusion; people could be excluded if it was believed their health would prevent them from working, thus making their support the responsibility of the state. In reading the body at immigration stations, inspectors and doctors frequently came to privilege what medical historian Amy Fairchild labels "industrial citizenship" in determining admission. In their inspections PHS doctors were in effect asking "Are you capable of working?" rather than "Do you have a contagious disease representing a threat to the health of the nation?"[9]

Illness and physical deformity fit into the dominant enforcement practices used at the border, as they were considered to be visibly obvious.[10] A commissioner general of immigration declared in 1902, while "vice may come in the cabin or the steerage, in rags or fine raiment, and escape detection, . . . diseases . . . proclaim their presence and are their own detectors."[11] However, inclusion of the eye disease trachoma as one of only two "contagious diseases" leading to deportation required a different form of visual verification. It was a disease whose diagnosis needed an examination of the eyelid by experts; this was not a "truth" that clearly proclaimed itself upon a cursory glance. The identification of trachoma employed a scientific method in which a doctor's expertise was used to define health and disease, not simply to cure what others could see. It also fit into the expectation of which national bodies were most likely to bring disease to the United States, and more generally, those bodies that were thought to pose a threat to the nation. In a 1912 article from *Popular Science*, an Ellis Island doctor made clear that that trachoma was mostly found in "Russians, Austrians and Italians, although it is of common occurrence in Oriental and Mediterranean countries. It causes a large percentage of the blindness in Syria and Egypt."[12] These groups were important constituents of the undesirable "new immigrants" who came to be policed by the immigration quotas introduced in the 1920s, quotas that represented a complex and contradictory redefinition of whiteness different from that used in debates about naturalization.[13]

Identification documents had no significant role in the assessment of people under immigration law. However, it is precisely this absence that makes a more detailed analysis of turn-of-the-century immigration enforcement critical to understanding the emergence of the documentation of individual identity. In a space where documents have come to play a critical role, their nonappearance provides examples of the identity and identification practices that made a document such as the passport unnecessary in this period. Outside of immigration law, though, documents did have a role in the enforcement of Chinese-exclusion laws. However, these documents were used in an environment in which they both challenged and were challenged by the assumption that the body and appearance provided a useful way to verify not only racial identities, but categories exempt from exclusion such as "merchant." The restriction of Chinese laborers came to rely on a reading of both the body and documents creating what Chinese immigration historian Estelle Lau describes as a complicated relationship of "hyper-bureaucratization and hyper-discretion."[14] Although in the attempts to control Chinese immigration from the turn of the century, documents started to have increasing authority, their use beyond this marginal and targeted population was not considered necessary, nor, it seems, did techniques of documentation and bureaucratic skills move easily from this domain to other areas of the federal government.

From 1892, when the federal government opened Ellis Island, officials worked to establish an inspection process to more effectively distribute and organize the immigrants who were arriving in steadily increasing numbers. The authority of these officials had been established three years earlier, when a Supreme Court decision positioned the exclusion of aliens as a sovereign right, rather a right derived from the control of foreign commerce.[15] This decision, endorsed through subsequent court rulings and federal regulations, was read to effectively deny aliens any claim to due process and therefore to locate absolute sovereign power in border officials. Identification documents did not have any utility or authority within this conceptualization of border control. Not only did they verify an individual identity that was deemed unnecessary, their issuance outside of the Bureau of Immigration was seen as a challenge to the sovereign authority recently granted to federal officials to determine entry at U.S. borders. Of equal importance was the fact that those officials had little faith that documents in any form could identify a person more accurately than the body an immigrant presented to them. Official discretion was recognized as expertise because of the dual sources of the authority granted to presence—this authority derived from the legal understanding of immigration law and from the popular belief in the body and personal appearance as reliable evidence of identity and character. Thus, with tautological certainty, an official's discretion could be justified through the privileging of an identity that could only be verified through an official who was present at a port of entry.

A brief walk through the inspection procedures at Ellis Island provides important context for why passports were not considered necessary when border security was defined through a racialized understanding of what made the nation productive and healthy, and when, as in the case of United States, the primary "border" was a seaport. The individual identity utilized at Ellis Island, befitting the nature of immigration, was a transitory one, with only hesitant attempts made to record that identity for future reference by government officials. When immigrants needed to be identified individually, it was to ensure their movement through the main hall, and this identification was achieved through something akin to a premodern logic of badge and uniform.

The successful movement of more than five thousand people a day through Ellis Island in the peak years of immigration at the turn of the twentieth century depended on an efficient choreography of bodies that utilized the structure of ships and buildings to facilitate inspection. This was in part due to the limited federal money budgeted for enforcing immigration law; the greater resources allocated to collecting customs duties was read as a constant reminder of border priorities by at least one commissioner in charge of immigration at Ellis Island.[16] Personal appearance was integral to the implementation of an efficient system where race and class provided useful shorthand for establishing identity according to the categories created in the law. The examination process for steamship passengers began by initially sifting them through a specific understanding of class and identity. There were two stages to the process: an inspection on the ship for first class and cabin passengers and an inspection at Ellis Island for steerage passengers. Because immigration laws did not apply to citizens, this inspection was limited to "aliens" with the assumption that a citizen would be easily recognizable as such. The inspection of first-class and cabin passengers occurred as a ship made its way from quarantine to the port of New York, when the boarding divisions of the medical inspection and immigration services performed their duties.[17] Immigration officials utilized the tripartite division of the steamship into first class, cabin, and steerage to determine differing degrees of inspection. The structured mobility of ocean travel was viewed through the articulation of class and race that underwrote immigration restriction. First-class passengers were rarely inspected, and second-class cabin passengers received "cursory examination,"[18] apparently distinct from the expert glance steerage passengers received during their onshore inspection at Ellis Island. Officials assumed that most immigrants traveled in the cramped quarters of steerage, therefore, those who did not were not thought likely to be subject to exclusion. The inability of immigrants to afford a more expensive ticket marked them as poor and thus, in the eyes of immigration officials, more susceptible to disease and the lack of morals which made their right to live and work in the United States questionable. Potential immigrants became increasingly aware of this, and often tried to find additional money for a nonsteerage ticket to reduce the possibility of exclusion.[19] However, whether out of necessity or genuine belief, officials continued to treat the ability to afford a cabin ticket (first or second class) as evidence of the cultural suitability necessary for admission. A ticket above steerage was read to exhibit wealth (that is, a productive capacity) and a belief in the importance of hygiene (self regulation).

Until 1912 the official confidence in the ship's sorting mechanism was such that claims to admission through citizenship from cabin dwellers were rarely challenged. But on the occasions they were, the documents offered by "passengers who appear to be aliens" were of little value. Documents would be easily trumped if the inspector's "cursory and hasty examination" offered evidence to suspect either the "bona fides of the passenger or the genuineness of the paper."[20] An Immigration Service commissioner clarified the nature of the appearance that aroused suspicion, writing that "experience shows that those from southern, south-eastern and eastern Europe are more likely to be ineligible than those from northern Europe";[21] this despite the fact that prior to 1921 immigrants from these areas were not restricted because of race or ethnicity.

At the beginning of the twentieth century those who successfully passed this on-board inspection were issued with a card to present when they disembarked that verified their right to enter the United States. When the ship arrived all immigrants from steerage and any non-citizens in second class who had failed the on-board medical inspection were transported to Ellis Island on barges. The first barge from each ship also carried what was deemed relevant documentation: the steerage manifests, the landing tags of any citizens in steerage, and a list from the steamship company of passengers rejected at embarkation.[22]

Once at Ellis Island immigrants entered the main building in two lines, at which point the four PHS doctors on duty at the line performed the medical examination.[23] The point at which an immigrant turned right soon after entering the building determined the placement of the doctors. The immigrant's entry into the building under the eyes of these officials became, in the words of one doctor, a "system, silent, watchful, swift, efficient."[24] The complete medical examination usually took no more than forty seconds, with some claiming no more than six seconds.[25] As one writer noted, "The examination can be superficial at best; but the eye has been trained and discoveries are made here, which seem rather remarkable."[26] In 1912 a PHS doctor explained to readers of *Popular Science Monthly* how these discoveries occurred:

> At this turn stands a medical officer. He sees each person directly from the front as he approaches, and his glance travels rapidly from feet to head. In this rapid glance he notes the gait, attitude, presence of flat feet, lameness, stiffness

> at ankle, knee, or hip, malformations of the body, observes the neck for goitre, muscular development, scars, enlarged glands, texture of skin, and finally as the immigrant comes up face to face, the examiner notes abnormalities of the features, eruptions, scars, paralysis, expression, etc. As the immigrant turns, in following the line, the examiner has a side view, noting the ears, scalp, side of neck, examining the hands for deformity or paralysis, and if anything about the individual seems suspicious, he is asked several questions. It is surprising how often a mental aberration will show itself in the reaction of the person to an unexpected question.... At the end of each line stands a second medical officer who does nothing but inspect eyes.[27]

It should be noted that a year after the publication of this article, its author, Dr. Alfred C. Reed, resigned in frustration at the inefficiency of the medical examination at Ellis Island, complaining, "the staff is too small and the administrative policy is passive, rather than aggressive, reactionary rather than progressive."[28]

A little under one-fifth of immigrants failed the medical examination. If they did fail, an official marked their clothing with a chalk symbol "indicating the nature of the suspicious circumstance": for example, a "C" signified an ocular condition, and an "S" signified senility.[29] They were then removed for further examination. If the subsequent examination confirmed the initial diagnosis, the immigrant was issued a medical certificate signed by at least two doctors and rejoined the line, where the certificate would become evidence for the final decision, which an immigration inspector would make.

After the medical inspection, the line of immigrants entered the main hall. This could hold approximately two thousand immigrants, most of who would make a two-hour journey through the hall before they were finally examined by an immigration inspector.[30] The movement of immigrants through the hall was initially managed by "groupers" who were employed to ensure that immigrants ended up in the correct line. The manifest compiled by steamship officials determined the right line; it listed passengers' names along with information requested by the Immigration Bureau. Immigrants had cards attached to their clothing with the number and line of the manifest that recorded their information. A series of numbered aisles corresponding to manifest numbers divided the hall. The grouper thus attempted to ensure immigrants were lined up in the aisle appropriate to their ship by looking at the number on the cards attached to their body. At the end of each line, an inspector sat behind a desk to ask questions based upon the "facts" recorded on the manifest and any other additional documents. On a busy day, this inspection normally lasted no more than two minutes; each inspector had to examine four hundred to five hundred immigrants a day. In 1909 inspectors were required to ask thirty-eight questions during the inspection and note any new information or discrepancies briefly on the manifest; they were then expected to enter the changes in longhand at the end of the day.[31] Along with the immigrants' answers, inspectors were also instructed to evaluate their "appearance and general demeanor."[32] Although officials made use of an identity derived from a belief that "race" could be read off a body, this understanding of race combined elements of language, culture, and physical appearance. In this conception of race, the essentializing function given to clothing could turn immigrants' clothes into evidence of race and nationality. While this particular representational function of immigrants' clothing was made visible in newspaper and magazine articles where immigrant clothing was usually described as "national costume," it also allowed officials to determine how detailed their inspection needed to be.[33] If the cross-examination failed to verify the immigrant as a viable and productive future citizen, the inspector marked the individual's coat or shirt lapel with chalk and sent him or her to wait for a hearing in front of a review board; different colored markings indicated the reason for the initial exclusion. While about 20% of potential immigrants failed this initial examination, as noted earlier, only 1% of potential immigrants were eventually excluded.

In an inspection that privileged the body and physical appearance over documents, the most important document was the manifest. It gave an individual an identity that enabled immigration officials to inspect him or her. First, and perhaps primarily, the manifest was intended to organize an individual's passage through the main hall in the hope of "obliviating dire confusion," in the words of the official in charge of Ellis Island.[34] It was also intended to make the immigrant appear before an inspector in another sense—it attached the body of an immigrant to information deemed necessary to assess an alien's suitability to work and live in the United States. In a review of the manifest's implementation as part of the 1893 act, the immigration commissioner contended the detailed manifest ensured that the inspection of immigrants would no longer be "mere census taking," making it "possible to identify each and every one of them."[35] It did this by substantially augmenting the basic information (name, country of citizenship, last residence, and destination) steamship companies had had to provide to officials since 1819.

To be more than "mere census taking," the manifest had to comply with the requirements of immigration officials. The manifest was a large sheet of paper, ruled with horizontal lines and vertical columns. There were thirty lines intended to record thirty names, with twenty-nine numbered vertical columns for steamship officials to record the information immigration officials required to ascertain admission. However, in the decade after its introduction, the manifest had apparently become little more than census taking. In 1902, William Williams, a young Wall Street lawyer with some experience in government legal services, was appointed commissioner of immigration at Ellis Island by President Theodore Roosevelt to clean up the running of Ellis Island following a number of scandals. The rigorous collection of information on manifests became one part of his crusade. Soon after his appointment Williams began to impose fines on steamship companies for "instances of very bad manifestation"[36]—occasionally, the only information on a manifest was an immigrant's name.[37] Not only were many categories not filled out (a common omission was the address of the relative with whom the immigrant would initially stay), but, to Williams's mind, several categories seemed to have been filled out in advance with standard answers (for example, health was uniformly described as "good").[38] With limited success he offered steamship companies a variety of methods to collect the necessary information from passengers during the voyage: "Inquiry, direct or indirect, by hearsay, by observation, or by any other method that may seem to you appropriate." However, Williams was careful to remind company officials that their staff should not rely on direct questioning to obtain the necessary information, because "if an alien is suffering from a dangerous contagious disease, or if he is a noted criminal, he will generally avoid admitting that such is the case."[39] Many steamship companies had also taken to listing more than thirty names on each sheet; there could be anywhere from twenty to fifty additional names crammed onto the document. This practice developed in response to the requirement that a ship's officer had to swear to the completeness of a manifest's list of passengers before the U.S. consul at the ship's port of departure. Because a steamship company had to pay a notary a fee for each sheet of the manifest, the fewer sheets, the lower the cost.[40]

The need for a complete manifest also came from Williams' belief in its importance as a record of arrival. He appeared to be keenly aware that "imperfect manifestation" affected how immigrants would subsequently appear in the memory of the state. In an attempt to follow the law as he understood it, Williams ensured that after the immigration inspection but before being filed, manifests were corrected in long hand, though he was angry that his "expert" inspectors had to spend as many as six hours doing this, after they had each inspected four to five hundred immigrants.[41] As it was a document that could be referred to in the future, Williams worked to ensure both that it would survive until needed, and that any required information could be easily retrieved. This translated into an attempt to standardize the appearance of the manifest and to introduce a better indexing system. Early on, he requested that steamship companies prepare manifests on "good quality paper," since they would "become permanent Government records."[42] That request appears to have been ignored as Williams eventually took control of printing and distributing manifests to the various steamship lines to ensure uniformity of appearance and to facilitate their eventual binding. At this time he introduced different-colored manifests for aliens reflecting their location on the ship: first class on light pink paper, second cabin on light yellow, and steerage on white.[43]

In his first months on the job, Williams also sought to ensure that the federal government would be able to use manifests to remember immigrants after they had left Ellis Island and entered U.S. society. To that end he introduced an alphabetical card index organized by name according to nationality—when in doubt as to which name was an immigrant's surname, clerks were instructed to index the immigrant under both names. As he explained it in a report, each card contained a "reference to the sheet of the manifest on which the name appears, so that data not transferred to the card can be readily obtained from the original source."[44] Within a year this indexing required the "constant work" of seven clerks.[45] It is unclear how successful these clerks were in maintaining this as a useful and retrievable collection, especially when immigrants subsequently needed to verify when they arrived, usually for the purpose of naturalization. Thanking Williams for providing such information, a letter writer acknowledged the "unfailing devotion to an ideal and stick-to-it-iveness of purpose that characterized your search and discovery."[46]

Despite these hesitant efforts to establish a system of documentation to record the arrival of immigrants, their inspection primarily relied on an official reading of their appearance and bodies. Identification at Ellis Island was organized around the body as it was presented. Officials visually surveyed immigrants to see if they matched their understanding of a noncitizen and then of a member of undesirable social groups. The writing of marks on, and the attachment of cards to, clothing emphasized that the individual identity produced in the immigration inspection process was both site-specific and temporary. This system apparently solved the problem of identification as immigration officials understood it. These measures were sufficient to adequately enforce immigration policy along borders that were not set up for the rigorous enforcement of laws, as the nearly 99% admission rate indicates; the complaints about resources from officials at both seaports and land borders imply that this low exclusion rate was not the product of an efficient inspection system. However, the use of the manifest with a card index points towards the archival logic that would soon come to ports of entry when the federal government needed to be able to know, recognize, and remember individuals. But prior to World War I, immigration officials primarily understood the problem posed by immigration regulations to be the identification of some*body*, not some*one*—the articulation of an individual to a racial group or set of behavioral traits via their body or personal appearance. That the privileging of appearance over documents was a result of lack of a perceived need for documents is evident in the contemporaneous existence of a system of documents to police movement across U.S. borders introduced, not under immigration law but through the Chinese Exclusion Acts. However, in practice, the frequently limited authority officials granted to those documents, in contrast to the information they saw in Chinese bodies, further fleshes out why a document such as the passport had no significant role at the U.S. border prior to World War I.

In 1882 Congress passed the first Chinese Exclusion Act. This was a response to the complex economic, racial, and cultural context in which opinion had turned against Chinese during the preceding three decades, when nearly 300,000 Chinese immigrants had entered the United States. Throughout the 1870s, national party and labor politics fueled the perception of the economic threat of Chinese labor and, along with racial and cultural arguments about the impossibility of Chinese assimilation, created a situation in which the federal government instituted its first significant action to police a part of the U.S. border.[47] While labeled an "exclusion act," this legislation in fact only restricted Chinese immigration. The target of the 1882 Act was new laborers. It limited Chinese migration to the United States to merchants and their families, college students, and travelers, and allowed laborers resident in the United States to remain; Chinese women could only enter if married to a man in the exempt categories. The difference between the exclusion of all Chinese people and the restriction of most provided the space for the federal government's first comprehensive attempt to regulate entry to the country. In contrast to other immigrants, whom officials excluded by looking for physically marked individuals within a largely admitted group, the management of Chinese exclusion involved identifying admissible individuals within a largely excluded group. To enforce the 1882 act and its subsequent revisions and renewals, the federal government introduced what an early historian of Chinese immigration regulation labeled, "an elaborate system of registration, certification and identification"[48]—a system that continued to develop until the legislation was overturned in 1943 and initially replaced with an annual quota of 103 Chinese immigrants. However, recent scholarship has shown that this system of documents, while elaborate in design, was far from successful as a mechanism through which to verify the identity of applicants, particularly before the early years of the twentieth century. For although the introduction of identification documents acknowledged the difficulties associated with verifying the identity categories of the act through the appearance and bodies of Chinese, the documents created the additional need to record information accurately and to link the document to the correct person.

The initial act, along with subsequent renewals through 1892, created a series of documents to ensure that Chinese immigration was restricted according to the law: return certificates, "Section Six" certificates, and registration certificates.[49] Return certificates were issued to already resident Chinese laborers who temporarily left the country, though San Francisco customs officials issued them to merchants as well. The Chinese government issued Section-Six certificates to exempt individuals; after 1884 they had to be visaed by a U.S. consul. Registration certificates were introduced in 1892 for all Chinese laborers legally living in the United States. The arbitrary nature of a system based on documents was made evident by an 1888 act that invalidated return certificates; it is estimated the act stranded at least twenty thousand laborers abroad, as U.S. officials now claimed these were merely certificates of identity, not a guarantee the bearer could enter the United States.[50] As an identification document, these certificates exposed the difficulties in unambiguously identifying an individual to ensure that a document remained in the hands of the person to whom it had been issued. Despite the legislation requiring that the certificate include "all facts necessary for identification of each such Chinese," these facts frequently proved insufficient for accurately connecting a person to the document, and at some ports, notably Portland, Oregon, a limited administrative infrastructure meant the certificates were not even issued—a fact that, once known, led many Chinese who entered the United States without documents to claim they had departed from Portland. The assumed physical similarity of Chinese also negated the usefulness of identification documents in the eyes of officials. The very similarities that allowed an inspector to identify an individual as a "Chinaman" became the characteristics that prevented the reliable identification of that "Chinaman" as a distinct individual through a document. Chinese were seen to be similar "in color of skin, eyes, hair and style of their features," as a collector of customs wrote in 1885.[51] Therefore, the physical description on certificates was organized around "significant marks or peculiarities."[52] An example of the pattern of physical description that resulted is evident from a return certificate for a store porter in the mid-1880s: "Small brown spot left corner left eye. Small pock pit right corner right eye. Small pit near each corner mouth. Pit near right side nose."[53] While this could only but "confirm" the uncivilized status of Chinese that justified exclusion, it did little to assist in the enforcement of that exclusion. Inspectors became increasingly frustrated with the one short line provided for writing a description and the lack of guidelines for what constituted a significant mark or peculiarity.[54] Although there were attempts to introduce the more "scientific" methods of fingerprinting and Bertillonage on later certificates, these did not last; the latter was dropped as part of a series of deals to end the Chinese boycott of American goods in 1905.[55] While the addition of photographs was a potentially more reliable representation of appearance, it did not change the fact that many officials claimed Chinese looked similar in appearance.

As well as trying to link individuals to documents, officials had to connect potential Chinese immigrants to the identity categories outlined in the acts. In assessing whether an arrival was a merchant or a member of one of the other exempt categories, officials rarely privileged the Section-Six certificate issued in China verifying the bearer as exempt. While various acts sought to define "merchant" more clearly, at border stations officials read the body for signs of a life of manual labor. The majority of the denials of admission to Chinese with Section-Six certificates were largely based on a reading of class derived from "personal appearance," a criterion upheld on appeal.[56] The confidence of a judicial declaration in 1882, that "it would not be easy for a Chinese laborer or coolie...to simulate the dress, manners and general appearance and bearing of the merchant, student, teacher or traveler," continued to influence the evaluations of officials in the early years of the twentieth century.[57] The bodies of people who claimed to be Chinese merchants were read for evidence of labor: calluses, sunburned legs or arms, the size and shape of fingers, were all interpreted as proof that the applicant was in fact a laborer. In their decisions inspectors sometimes also argued more generally that an individual did not look like a merchant: "He makes statements to the effect that he is a man of wealth and standing in his own country, yet comes in the garb and manner of the poorest laborer....He is undoubtedly a fraud"; or, more simply: "[He has] a non-mercantile personal appearance."[58] Clothing, appearance and manner, and even handwriting, were thus assumed to be reliable ways to connect someone to one of the categories in the act. Any occasional inconsistency was of limited concern in a system of enforcement that gave discretion to the officials who were face to face with potential immigrants. However, in the initial years of enforcement, unsuccessful Chinese arrivals enjoyed almost overwhelming success in having courts overturn officials' decisions, in part because the burden of proof shifted to the government. The range of nondocumentary evidence the courts accepted also challenged the authority of documents, with one judge arguing that nonproduction of a document was not conclusive evidence of the fact of exclusion.[59]

Although the body was considered more reliable than a document, Chinese arrivals could manipulate the bodily evidence deemed "essential" to determining their right to enter the United States. While documents could be passed from hand to hand, the identity read from a body could also be passed from body to body. Race reduced to skin color allowed Chinese laborers to "pass" successfully into the United States, especially outside of San Francisco. In the 1910s and 1920s, government officials uncovered an apparently common strategy of "painting the Chinese black," either to disguise them as part of steamship crews docking in New Orleans, or to "disguise the Chinamen as negroes after they had arrived in Mobile, Alabama."[60] In 1907 an immigrant inspector reported on Chinese who had used fake Mexican citizenship certificates to enter the United States. He expressed surprise that it was "exceedingly difficult to distinguish these Chinamen from Mexicans."[61] Other Chinese laborers, after being schooled in Mexico on appropriate language and manners, entered successfully under the false status of either U.S. citizens or merchants.[62] The ability to manipulate the signs of race and class used to identify a "Chinaman" indicate that while a faith in visual symbols and markers remained possibly the most effective form of verification, it could not guarantee successful identification, or even consistent identification.[63] However, immigration officials considered it less fallible than documents. That is, they trusted the authority of their own perceptions over the authority of unknown officials represented in a document, especially a documented presented by a person who belonged to a racial group they did not trust.

However at the turn of the century, some officials had become frustrated with the system used to enforce the Chinese Exclusion Act. For many senior officials the problem lay with the acts, which had created laws "as fragmentary, inefficient, and unreasonable as might be possible to suppose."[64] While the discretion of officials continued to be important for restricting Chinese immigration, from the early years of the century an increasing faith in recordkeeping practices (if not in documents carried by Chinese) developed. From this period on the actions of officials (in the United States and as previously noted in China) became more closely restricted by a system of standardized forms and cross-referenced files. In the United States the implementation of more coherent rules associated with Chinese exclusion, including recordkeeping practices, began to increase in rigor after its administration was moved to the Bureau of Immigration, initially under the Treasury Department in 1903 and then the Department of Labor and Commerce in 1905. Beyond assessing the information in any particular case, immigration officials worked to standardize and routinize the collection, classification, and storage of information.[65] Prior to this a file on a Chinese arrival was usually less than five pages and offered little if any attempt to reconcile evidence. Inspectors did not use a standardized set of questions; therefore comparison between "interviews" or files was of little use. The early fragmented nature of the administration of exclusion had left many blanks in the memory of the state, as different ports followed different procedures and each used a unique filing system. The 1906 San Francisco earthquake destroyed City Hall and, with it, the birth certificates of many Chinese—an event that allowed Chinese to claim exemption through a birth certificate purportedly lost in the destruction of City Hall.

With limited faith in the reliability of documents already issued, Chinese immigrants were interviewed several times. The search for discrepancies through a comparison of answers from these interviews became critical to the assessment of any claims the prospective immigrants made. The assumptions behind the harsh questioning were twofold. Officers had genuine difficulty verifying information Chinese offered, and they generally believed most Chinese were attempting to enter illegally. Unlike the use of manifests in the two-minute cross-examination at Ellis Island, the appeal to consistency to verify truth led to the creation of a complex bureaucratic structure. Intensive examinations became particularly critical for evaluating claims of paternity to expose "paper families." These "families" were produced when, after returning to China, a man exempt from exclusion through U.S. citizenship would sell his status as a "father" to other men, who could then enter the United States as the child of a U.S. citizen. (It is estimated that in 1950 nearly 25% of Chinese immigrants in the U.S. had illegally entered as paper children.) Official questioning focused increasingly on the "son's" life in China in an attempt to discover inconsistencies with subsequent interviews with, or the files of, other "family" members. By the end of the 1920s, standardized forms, along with an improved indexing system, meant that inspectors were able to efficiently cross-check a "son's" answers with those provided in any previous interview with other purported family members, even if those interviews had taken place several years earlier and at another immigration office. The Chinese immigration archive was such that in a typical case twelve other files would be pulled for comparison, each containing a single-spaced typed manuscript around thirty pages long, and a multipage explanation of the decision, all prepared in anticipation of subsequent retrieval.[66]

However, even within an administrative system that relied on documents to verify truth through consistency, officials made extensive use of other techniques to establish the veracity of claims; especially as officials correctly believed that many Chinese arrived in the United States having received considerable coaching on the relationships in their "paper family." Thus age, often a key fact in establishing paternity claims, was verified by considering facial and/or body hair, teeth, and genitalia. Expertise was sought in the form of opinions from doctors and the occasional use of X-rays to analyze bones. In less scientific ways, an inspector's visual assessment of physical appearance also continued to be important in these examinations: the analysis of demeanor and appearance to determine if an immigrant was lying, and the attempt to establish family resemblance through comparison with any relatives, either present or represented in photographs in the retrieved files.[67] While there is not a clear consensus among historians as to the balance between discretion and bureaucratic control, inspector discretion in the form of reading bodies and personal appearance continued to play some kind of role in the processing of Chinese immigrants.[68] This was in response to the very system of documentation introduced to limit discretion, a product of both the lack of faith in documents issued outside of the administrative reach of the United States and because of the manipulation of documents by Chinese.

Given the underlying distrust in the usefulness of documents to identify individuals, it is perhaps fittingly ironic that the first use of passports to limit immigration to the United States occurred in a context that defined itself, at least rhetorically, through trust. From 1906 to 1908 the United States and Japanese governments exchanged a series of diplomatic notes that came to be known as the "Gentlemen's Agreement"—an accord in which the Japanese agreed not to issue passports to laborers, in an attempt to prevent them entering the United States. The restriction on passports to the U.S. mainland had been part of a more informal agreement made in 1900, but in this second version the Japanese government promised to enforce it rigorously. The U.S. government facilitated that enforcement through an executive order that prevented noncitizens (Japanese) using neighboring countries or insular possessions (Hawaii) to enter the U.S. mainland.[69] The passport restricted immigration within its recognized legal boundaries; that is, as a letter between two states. State Department officials could trust the passport within a mode of diplomatic accommodation. Adopting this agreement between "gentlemen" in place of an exclusion act originated in part in President Roosevelt's recognition of a public demand to limit Japanese immigration and his belief that the Japanese were racially different, but not racially inferior—the Japanese victory over the Russian navy in 1905 appears to have been an important factor in this judgement.[70] However, the immigration officials who had to enforce the new diplomatic arrangement saw a Japanese passport as no more trustworthy than any document issued under the Chinese Exclusion Act.

The problem with identification documents for U.S. immigration officials once again stemmed from their lack of trust in the authorities who issued passports under the Gentlemen's Agreement. While this mistrust was undoubtedly racial, these documents could not even be issued under the veneer of official bureaucratic objectivity that was beginning to be applied to Chinese exclusion documents at this time. As with most states at the turn of the century, the Japanese government lacked a sufficient offshore bureaucracy to adequately police exemptions to the agreement, primarily Japanese laborers who were U.S. residents along with their family members.[71] In the absence of its own representatives, the Japanese government utilized local Japanese associations to determine the socioeconomic status of Japanese in the U.S., to record marriages and births, and, crucially, to ascertain if a man had the right to bring his wife to the United States. The associations introduced an arbitrary figure of $800 in savings as necessary financial support for a wife—the annual income of a railroad worker, a common Japanese occupation, was $677. To fulfill this requirement, assets were pooled into "show money" with the result that, the same $800 could provide travel documents for a number of female relatives.[72] Skepticism about the origin of these documents translated into distrust when they were presented to U.S. border officials.

The doubt U.S. border officials felt toward identification documents also included the U.S. passport. A passport was challenged on the grounds of its uncertain legal authority at the U.S. border and the lack of belief that it could accurately identify an individual. This was the source of a dispute between the State Department, which issued passports, and the Department of Commerce and Labor, which had the responsibility of enforcing immigration regulations. The attempts of some Chinese to enter the country as U.S. citizens initiated the first significant debate between the two departments about the U.S. passport. A second case centered on the need for naturalized citizens to identify themselves after the Immigration Bureau introduced a requirement that steamship companies provide a manifest of citizens as well as aliens.

Although Chinese could not be naturalized, the Supreme Court clarified the status of Chinese born in the United States when it recognized Chinese birthright citizenship in 1898.[73] Soon after the decision, the State Department began to forward all Chinese applications for passports to the immigration officials in the Treasury Department, in recognition of an assumed expertise in dealing with Chinese. When the newly formed Department of Commerce and Labor took control of Chinese exclusion, it discontinued this practice on the grounds that its Immigration Bureau budget did not contain an appropriation for it, and more significantly, on the belief that immigration officials could legally determine citizenship only in regards to reentry, not evaluate the initial fact of citizenship.[74] However, in an effort to maintain authority at the border, immigration officials required that passports issued to Chinese carry a disclaimer that they did not guarantee entry to the United States. This ended two years later when, in 1905, recently appointed Secretary of State Elihu Root had this "unseemly" notation removed. Root refused to accept that passports issued under his authorization should be "discredited by the officers of another Executive department."[75]

In response, Victor Metcalf, the secretary of commerce and labor, justified the continued nonacceptance of U.S. passports on the grounds that the document merely offered prima facie evidence of citizenship, and had no legal authority at the U.S. border. He contended that the only legal outline of a U.S. passport's function, the 1835 Supreme Court case, not only declared it prima facie evidence of citizenship, but also indicated that a passport granted a status to a traveler *abroad* as an act of courtesy. Metcalf used this case to argue that passports were accepted out of convention, not law, and, further, that no legislation indicated that the U.S. passport had any role at *home*, along the U.S. border.[76] In the case of Chinese arrivals, Bureau of Immigration officials specifically doubted the authenticity of U.S. passports, reiterating the belief that Chinese possessed an inherent disposition to dishonest behavior. Therefore, along with the removal of the notation, immigration officials explained their refusal to accept passports as proof of citizenship from Chinese on the grounds that they "contain no certain means of identification and are easily transferred from hand to hand."[77] Consequently, Chinese who claimed exemption through U.S. citizenship had to show signs of "Americanness" that were obvious to immigration officials: the ability to speak English, the extent to which they behaved and dressed "like Americans," and their knowledge of U.S. history.[78]

Despite the State Department's identification of the passport as a certificate of citizenship, the passport's uncertain legal status continued to provide grounds for U.S. officials to ignore it. A second example of this occurred at Ellis Island when, in his ongoing campaign to tighten up inspection, William Williams required steamship companies to manifest citizens; steamship officials were instructed to list individuals as citizens only if they had no doubt about their citizenship. The decision to introduce additional manifests for citizens was an attempt to ensure that the underresourced Bureau of Immigration maximized all possible funding sources; in this case, the head tax from aliens, with the logic being that the need to prove citizenship would result in the identification of more aliens. Williams outlined to steamship officials and immigration inspectors ways they could eradicate any doubt about citizenship through a combination of visual and oral evidence and, if necessary, documents. The division between native-born and naturalized citizens determined the weight given to the possible forms of evidence an individual could offer to prove their citizenship. Significantly (but not surprisingly), in neither case did Williams consider a U.S. passport primary evidence of a claim to citizenship. Immigration officials on the east coast followed their colleagues on the west coast and considered passports apparently little more than travel documents.

Williams assumed that the status of native-born citizens could be easily and effectively verified through appearance. Because they would "obviously" look like citizens, he merely requested that native-born citizens "state with accuracy their place of birth" as evidence of citizenship beyond their appearance. On the rare occasion when this visual and oral evidence failed to convince inspectors, they (or, later, a review board) were encouraged to seek evidence from documents and the corroboration of waiting relatives. In this scenario the passport did appear as one such document, but on equal footing with documents such as birth certificates and baptismal certificates that were intended to record an event, not document an identity.[79]

The concern about the enforcement of citizen manifests centered on naturalized citizens. In contrast to citizens born in the United States, officials assumed that many if not all naturalized citizens would not look or sound "American," hence the demand for documents as primary proof of citizenship. Within the increasingly problematic association of citizenship and whiteness, the beginnings of a practical need for documents appeared, and with it a disposition to look more favorably on documentary proof of identity. However, because officials wanted verification of citizenship as a legal category, the passport was not given a primary role. Immigration officials requested naturalization certificates, as they were the official legal documentation of naturalization, although they were not issued with a physical description or photograph to link the certificate to a specific person. In contrast, while the passport contained numerous aids to connect it to a particular person, it remained only prima facie evidence of citizenship, which immigration officials continued to believe the State Department issued on the basis of "superficial investigation."[80]

The limited utility of U.S. passports at the border highlights that a documentary regime of verification, such as it existed in the first decade of the twentieth century, did so in a very particular context, limited to specific documents. At this time identification documents existed within practices of verification determined by logical and historical contingencies in which the general authority of documents to determine identity was not trusted.

This distrust occurred both as a product of the dispute over which executive departments could control entry at the U.S. border, and because of the status of passports as "documents." Two practices that the State and Labor Departments introduced in this period hint at an environment in which identification documents could be made a trustworthy and useful tool for securing the border.

After the 1905 dispute with the Department of Labor and Commerce over U.S. passports, the State Department attempted to counter the assumed dishonesty of Chinese, and thus to increase the authority of its passports when presented by Chinese. When Chinese applied for passports, they were required to send the name of their return port and two photographs with their applications. However, if they were issued a passport, neither photograph would be attached to it. One photograph was included in the application file held by the State Department, and the second photograph was sent to immigration officials at the port of reentry. As a result, the State Department argued, "the means of identification would be in the hands of the officer at the return port."[81] In this manner the two departments added an element of trust to the practice of documentation, but one that did not dispel the disbelief that a document alone could identify an individual. The authority of the second photograph to verify identity came from its separation from the document; the photograph was not in the "quick hands" of the bearer. Locating a photograph in the files of executive departments to be retrieved by the steady hand of an official guaranteed that it could be reliably used to link the document to the bearer; such reliability was not considered possible if the photograph was attached to the passport, where it could easily be substituted. The separation of photograph and document helped establish a relationship between the bearer and the passport without enhancing the status of the passport as a document that verified either an individual's personal or official identity. The Bureau of Immigration continued to report that their own investigations had revealed that in "several cases" since 1905, Chinese bearers of U.S. passports were not actual citizens, confirming its belief that passports were issued on negligible evidence of citizenship.[82] In contrast, the bureau had sufficient trust in documents it issued, in 1908 reintroducng a return certificate, complete with a photograph, albeit as an optional document.[83]

The placing of photographs on file and the thorough investigation of applicants indicated conditions through which identification documents could be trusted in practice to assist in securing the border—trust in the authorities who issued them, and a faith in bureaucratic procedure to ensure the verification of identity. In the absence of these conditions, identification documents were seen to be evidence only of opinions not objective facts. In this instance, to create reliable "facts," the production of the documents had to be located in bureau offices where supporting documents were filed. Documents in the hands of the immigrant could not secure identity as authoritatively as those in a filing cabinet.

However, the practical application of documentary authority through the objectivity of archival memory was not pervasive; many departments and officials still thought it unnecessary, if not impractical. In contrast to the systems being developed to administer Chinese exclusion, the bureaucratic infrastructure at Ellis Island and other ports of entry remained in a very embryonic state. This prevented much of the potential for information collected within the inspection process from becoming an effective part of the memory of the state. The practices of collection, classification, and circulation critical to the construction of an effective state memory of identifications was of low priority in administering a border with few resources. Only in a hesitant and lazy way did the inspection of general immigrants seek to capture and fix immigrants in a mass of documents. Immigrant identity remained transitory; the limited documentation accumulated at Ellis Island during an immigrant's arrival was intended to assess an individual's suitability for entry to the country, not to follow them into the United States as the basis of their identity as aliens, declarants, or naturalized citizens. Although manifests were kept, they were rarely consulted when aliens who sought naturalization required certification of their arrival date; instead, documents were issued on the word of the immigrant.

The gradual recognition that identification practices associated with immigrants could provide information for later use only occurred in the more traditional context of identifying criminals—in this case, plans to more accurately identify those who might attempt to return to the United States following deportation. However, these plans would have affected all immigrants. In the decade before World War I, immigration officials at Ellis Island investigated the possibility of photographing or fingerprinting arriving immigrants so their identities could be sent to police officials for verification.[84] These records would be consulted away from the border, and therefore could only alert authorities to the presence of alien criminals in the country; they could not prevent their admission. In contrast, retired rear admiral Casper F. Goodrich (who helped establish the Naval War College and the U.S. Naval

Institute) advocated branding the shoulder or tattooing the inside upper arm of convicted alien criminals with the letter U (for Undesirable). He argued that this identification practice, "hallowed by the gentle ranchman's practice on his beloved calves and ponies," provided a more efficient way to ensure that, once convicted and deported, an alien would be easily identified and excluded by immigration inspectors at the border.[85] Goodrich appears to have been a lone voice. However, his critique of documentation was answered a year after he announced his proposal; in 1913 162 aliens were excluded after a comparison between names on manifests and a confidential list of inadmissible aliens.[86] However, the extreme suggestion of branding is a reminder that documentary identification was still not positioned as an effective mode of state control. The body "documented" identity such that information was always co-present with the appearance of a person. A branded alien was easily visible to the state at a specific moment of direct control. The emergence of a large-scale state archive of identity could only offer a more indirect form of state control through which an individual was made permanently visible to the government through presence in a file. This external identity needed a complex documentary regime of verification to have any claim to reliably articulate a person to the archive. If such a system functioned, the state could always locate knowledge of the individual, if not always physically locate the individual. The sudden need to have information about individuals following the outbreak of World War I redefined border security away from an exclusive focus on the admittance of productive workers toward the collection of information on individuals. In this new environment, identification documents could offer a practicable solution to the problem of border security.

10

Reading Bodies, Reading Documents, and "Passport Control"

In October 1915 the *New York Sun* ran a short article about William K. Vanderbilt, at the time considered the head of the Vanderbilt family. The article did not mention anything about his business dealings; rather, it reported on his application for a passport at a federal courthouse under the headline "W. K. Vanderbilt Tries to Identify Himself." The article both expressed curiosity at the novelty of a passport application and also educated the public on what to expect. Readers were informed that

> "Mr. Vanderbilt after telling of his intention to go abroad had to describe the color of his hair and the shape of his nose, chin and forehead. Then Mr. Vanderbilt had to stand in front of... [the] desk and swear that while on his travels he would defend the Constitution of the U.S. whenever the occasion arose. He also had to furnish a photograph which was pasted on the application for the passport and stamped with the Federal seal in accordance with the Department's plan for preventing aliens from getting passports fraudulently. Mr. Vanderbilt's application... will be sent to Washington and examined carefully by an employee of the State Department."[1]

The main point of the story seemed to be that, with the war in Europe a little over one year old, new passport rules were apparently not being waived even for someone like Vanderbilt; by the end of World War I, Woodrow Wilson needed a passport to travel to Versailles—the *Sun* made this front page news, with the claim he was the first president to be issued a passport.[2] The limited role of the passport at U.S. borders had changed. Now articulated to national security, the passport had an important role at the border, both in the minds of government officials and also in the popular imagination. The *New York Sun*'s attention to the passport was typical of newspapers and magazines, which regularly ran articles on the passport during the war. These ranged from brief State Department announcements of new requirements to lengthy feature articles, usually on either the history of the passport or the attempts of German agents to use U.S. passports. As the chief of the Bureau of Citizenship noted in a memo written at the end of 1914, "Passports were not taken very seriously, but now they have assumed an importance which they never had before."[3]

This new importance took the form of wartime "passport control." It manifested itself in two ways: an attempt to have all people who entered and left the United States present a passport, and, as the Vanderbilt article indicates, the introduction and enforcement of new application requirements. Through "passport control" the document became associated with a new regime of international travel and bureaucracy in which the passport was recognized more as a border document and less as the travel letter of the nineteenth century. Significantly, the passport's new role as a modern identification document did not disappear after the war. However, in the absence of suspected German agents, but with the purported presence of thousands of "aliens" trying to enter the United States illegally, new, more direct forms of border control soon joined the passport. The development of a border patrol after the war captured the public imagination as the symbol of a new approach to border security and of the new focus on the land border, not seaports. But, that being said, the passport continued to have a far more significant role at the border than at any time prior to 1914. The claimed success of the documentary surveillance of borders during the war gave identification documents legitimacy in the postwar administration of immigration. The passport grew in importance as the acquisition of knowledge about individuals became fundamental to an official understanding of national security and border control. The state had to know and remember everyone who crossed its borders. Documents did not replace the body as an important source of information; however, a document like the passport was read to provide information that could not easily be seen on a body, but which was now considered necessary to the enforcement of border security. After 1921, annual quotas limited immigration based on nationality. Therefore, the state had to identify an individual's nationality and know that he or she had been counted and accepted within their nation's annual quota. The identity of "immigrant" (and "alien") became the product of administrative facts, not simply the outcome of an official's glance. While the nationality quotas enforced a specific racial hierarchy, in practical terms the articulation of race through nationality privileged an identity that needed to be verified through documents.[4]

Initial attempts at passport control came in the form of State Department proclamations and executive orders per the act of 1856. In November 1914 the State Department released an announcement stating that all citizens going abroad "should" carry passports. A year later President Wilson issued an executive order to the same effect, stating that the regulations of European countries made passports a necessity, though the order did not require aliens or citizens to have passports to enter and leave the United States.[5] The lack of a requirement for citizens to carry passports continued to be a concern for State Department officials, especially those responsible for passports in the Bureau of Citizenship.[6] However, although no law existed requiring U.S. citizens to have a passport to leave the country, federal officials pressured steamship companies to refuse to carry passengers without passports on the grounds that European nations required them.[7] Newspapers also fostered the belief that a passport was needed, as they continued to publish ambiguous statements that implied it was required to leave the country.[8] Despite regular announcements to this effect, in the middle of 1915 citizens were still "shocked to learn" of these "requirements."[9] In June 1917, two months after the United States entered World War I, the secretary of commerce sent a letter to all steamship lines to "formally request" that they not accept passengers without passports examined and approved by customs officials.[10] Therefore, as the chief of the Bureau of Citizenship commented, "in a very informal and haphazard way," the executive required passports of all people leaving the United States during the war; or, in the words of one approving congressman, the federal government effectively required passports by "stretching the law and stretching its own regulations to meet the situation."[11]

The first attempt to legally control the entry of aliens to the United States came in a joint order of July 26, 1917, issued by the State and Labor Departments. This required that all aliens who intended to enter U.S. territory have a visa issued by a U.S. consul. At the end of 1917, despite the precedent of passport requirements during the Civil War, the attorney general ruled that the executive did not have authority to control the departure of aliens, nor the departure and entry of U.S. citizens.[12] While the attorney general offered the possibility of issuing certificates to U.S. citizens, the State Department wanted the U.S. passport to remain the only certificate of citizenship issued by the executive. Secretary of State Robert Lansing argued, "I can not with propriety or out of regard to the proper conduct of international relations sanction any plan which would tend to minimize the importance and significance and value of the American passport. On the contrary I believe that every effort should be made to enhance its dignity and integrity amongst nations."[13] As a result Congress passed the Passport Control Act of May 22, 1918, which delegated to the president the power in wartime to control the travel of citizens and others to and from the United States, and the authority to give executive departments the power to enforce it. In congressional hearings for this bill, executive officials argued that, while steamship companies had cooperated in controlling arrivals and departures at ports, the government needed more authority to enforce passport requirements on the land borders, particularly with Mexico, "where most of our trouble has come."[14] With the war in Europe in its last days, President Wilson proclaimed rules and regulations in an executive order on August 8, 1918, governing departure and entry into the United States. This gave legal backing to the visa system, passport requirements, and the restriction on the issuance of passports unless in proven cases of need; it also made legal the use of departure permits for aliens.

The prime object of passport and visa requirements was to "control the transmission of information in and out of the country."[15] This was how State Department officials explained the rationale behind the need for passports to the House Committee on Foreign Affairs during hearings for the Passport Control bill. One official stated that since the beginning of the war

> one of the very perplexing questions has been how best to control travel into and outside of the United States for the purpose of preventing persons who are spies or enemy agents from coming into the United States and doing damage, and also persons from going out, and carrying with

> them, perhaps, data or information or in some other way seeking to injure the United States.[16]

Officials believed this question could best be answered through a system of required documents anchored by the passport. The requirement for noncitizens to have a departure permit, introduced shortly after the United States declared war in 1917, had been suggested as a way to even more successfully control the flow of information. It not only promised to provide the U.S. government with information on departing aliens, but also, if not to prevent, at least to delay the departure of possibly valuable information from the United States.[17] Similarly rigorous enforcement of more comprehensive passport applications allowed officials to know the travel plans and purposes of its citizens, and to track their movement through requiring them to renew passports more frequently. Outside of the country it was suggested that officials could use the requirement for a visa to bar the entry of a German even if there was incomplete proof that "he is dangerous as a means of communication from Germany."[18]

Passports and visas not only controlled the flow of information by stopping the movement of "knowledgeable" bodies, they also facilitated governing over distance by making knowledge mobile; the passport contained information for officials to read. Once acquired, this knowledge could be assembled in the war effort, to be made available to government representatives, whether they were at the nation's capital, its borders, or its diplomatic and consular outposts. However, security could only be guaranteed over distance if knowledge acquired throughout the governing apparatus could be successfully coordinated and transmitted. In contrast to prewar levels of bureaucracy, wartime administrations attempted to develop elaborate schemes for the classification and coordination of information that illustrated the possibilities documentary surveillance offered for governing over distance. Newspaper reports on the apprehension of suspects and the confiscation of passports abroad supported the idea that the improved circulation of information in the form of documents was making the United States safer.[19] If this occurred, it was because during the war, the information diplomats, consuls, and military officers gained from interviewing visa applicants abroad became suspect lists that could be distributed throughout the government, in contrast to the prewar period when, in the words of one official, "there was no suspect list...other than in the brain of the minister himself."[20]

However, while the usefulness of identification documents became apparent, suspect lists had to be compiled, information had to be collated, evidence requirements had to be enforced, and, critically, government departments and agencies had to cooperate. The new conception of a passport within a broader documentary regime of verification still had to be accommodated to ongoing problems of authority and coordination and contradictory policies in governing practices both within and outside the United States. The extent to which initiatives around passport control were actually put into practice is unclear. Although passport control was premised on a faith in documentary surveillance, only in March 1918 did government officials float a proposal that customs officers who examined and stamped the passports of aliens and citizens as they left the United States should use this requirement to compile a record of people leaving the country. On the suggestion of the chief of military intelligence, Secretary of State Lansing requested that this record of names, passport numbers, nationalities, and destinations could then be forwarded to representatives of military and naval intelligence.[21]

Any attempts to institute the intensive surveillance of the arrival and departure of citizens and aliens depended on the cooperation of various federal departments. Policing the arrival and departure of aliens involved the following departments: the Department of Labor, which administered the laws governing the immigration of aliens; the Treasury Department, which supervised customs officials who examined the passports of people who left the United States; the Department of Commerce, which controlled the clearance of ships carrying passengers from ports; the Department of State, charged with the conduct of foreign affairs, which received daily information from its agents abroad about the activities of hostile aliens who should not be allowed into the country; the Department of Justice, which prosecuted aliens who violated U.S. laws, and which through its Bureau of Investigation gathered information on enemy agents in the United States; and the Departments of War and Navy, which were directly charged with conduct of war, and hence the safeguarding of ships and troops against the machinations of enemy agents. Therefore, despite public statements celebrating the success of passport control, it is fair to say that a tradition of independence amongst these departments undercut its effectiveness. For example, the inspection of documents at U.S. ports continued to be a problem. After a visit to New York, Richard Flournoy, who as chief of the Bureau of Citizenship was in charge of issuing passports, noted that the requirement that customs officials check the passports of U.S. citizens against duplicate applications as they boarded ships was not being followed—no one had established a system to get copies of the applications to the office of the customs collector. Flournoy wrote to his superior, the secretary of state, complaining, "Under the present system, or lack of system, each office in any way interested in this work seems to expect the responsibility to be carried somewhere else."[22] Although he believed that officers at the ports looked to the State Department for direction, the constantly forthcoming guidance from the department was often unwelcome, and frequently ill-informed. A State Department request that customs officers closely scrutinize any passports issued out of Germany revealed the legal problems involved in the enforcement of passport control. Interdepartmental turf wars prevented the "stretching" of the law utilized in other situations with nongovernment agencies such as steamship companies. The secretary of the treasury informed the secretary of state that customs officials could only detain people for customs violations, and similarly, that his officials had no authority to turn anyone over to immigration officials. He did suggest that, on the approval of the secretary of labor, he would instruct customs officials to immediately report any suspicions to immigration authorities.[23] Customs officials did begin to control foreign travel under the 1917 Espionage Act, and soon assembled a staff of five hundred to handle the work. However, after the Passport Control Act gave legal authority to wartime border control practices, the State Department issued a supplemental order that divided control of foreign travel between immigration and customs officials—but without consulting customs officials.

The need for cooperation also existed outside of the United States. The 1917 joint order required all aliens to have a visa issued by a U.S. diplomatic or consular official; this was intended to procure information to protect the United States. The visa application, which included basic identification details along with the intention of the visit and destination and contacts in the United States, had to be signed in triplicate at least two weeks prior to departure. The consul was expected to attach a copy to the alien's passport, send another ahead to immigration and customs officials at the port of entry, and retain the third for the consulate's records. However, distance and a lack of coordination often resulted in travelers considered suspicious arriving in the United States before consular concerns could be transmitted via the State Department to the appropriate immigration officials.[24] Military and naval attachés were to assist consuls in ascertaining the intention and necessity of an alien's planned visit to the United States. The State Department granted wide discretion to consuls. It only limited their authority through the suggestion that laborers, students, and businessmen with adequate evidence be granted visas. If a consul refused a visa, he was meant to contact consular officers in all countries through which the unsuccessful applicant could subsequently travel and reapply. This system appeared to function with some success, though on occasion naval attachés believed that, as passport control was a war measure, they should have the final decision on the issuance of a visa, not a consul.[25]

The reality that a passport was now required for international travel was initially discovered by those U.S. citizens already abroad. The initial weeks of the war witnessed chaos at U.S. consulates in Europe, as U.S. citizens fleeing the continent sought a passport or some other official document to satisfy the demand of steamship companies that all passengers have an officially issued identification document—a process that, according to one newspaper, revealed "a contingent [of U.S. citizens] whose numbers had never been suspected until the flight from war disclosed them."[26] Officials tended to issue passports and certificates on their discretion, not according to the State Department's rules for determining citizenship; often times the words "American citizen" were crossed out and "American resident" written on the passport.[27] These "passports" and so-called consular certificates later caused problems when individuals presented them as proof of citizenship to other consuls, or when foreign officials accepted them as passports certifying citizenship.[28] The limited apparatus in place for efficient administrative control also meant the time lag involved in the centralized collection of applications made it difficult to prevent any intentional misuse. The legation in Berlin reported that between late October and late November 1914 one individual had obtained three passports from three different consulates in Germany.[29] When the State Department sought to counter such lax practices with more rigorous enforcement of issuance procedures, officials at home and abroad encountered a problem that had already come up in the decades before the war—many "citizens" did not have a document that recorded their birth or naturalization. In the context of a limited documentary culture, the immediate wartime requirement that officials only issue passports on "unquestionable evidence" became (at least at the London embassy), in the absence of birth certificates but the presence of complaints from citizens, "identification by reputable persons," with the documentary evidence of letters and traveler's checks being of secondary value.[30] However, officials were instructed to apply "special strictness" to passport and emergency passport applications from persons born in the United States of foreign-born parents. A State Department dispatch asked the U.S. ambassador in Paris to require these people to produce affidavits and evidence that established the cause of their foreign residence, that provided evidence of continuing ties to the United States, and that proved they had indeed chosen to become U.S. citizens.[31]

Passport applicants encountered these attempts to enforce more rigorous requirements in a Europe in which a passport was required at most borders within the first nine months of the war. Navigating these novel requirements was made all the more difficult by the fact that a uniform passport system did not emerge.[32] Travel in France proved particularly bewildering, as officials demanded other documents in addition to a visaed passport. According to newspaper accounts, these difficulties were enhanced by French officials who rigorously sought to compare the facts of the documents to the person who presented them, especially physical descriptions and photographs.[33] In Britain the need to carry a passport for travel within parts of that country confounded many of the estimated eleven thousand U.S. citizens who lived there. Many of these were long-term British residents who struggled to comprehend that they could not provide satisfactory evidence of their U.S. citizenship, thus according to one reporter "adding corrugations to the heavily-lined brows of secretaries and clerks" at the embassy in London.[34] While some citizens were able to get a passport on appeal, there were many who became known as "twilight-zone Americans"; unable to prove their citizenship (after living abroad for up to thirty years in some cases), they were thus prevented from moving in "restricted areas."[35]

In another attempt to more effectively control the issuance of passports outside the United States and, therefore, to manage the movement of its citizens abroad, the State Department issued passports that were valid for only six months, with two renewals allowed. Prior to the war a combination of protocol and practice had historically made the passport valid for one journey or two years. Any citizen already abroad who held a valid passport now had to report to a consul to swear an oath of allegiance and get his (and only occasionally her) passport verified. Verification took the form of the consul writing "Good" on the passport and signing and stamping it. For those citizens who lived too far from a consulate, an oath could be taken before any local official authorized to administer oaths, "provided the signature of the person applying for amendment of his passport is witnessed by at least one other American citizen."[36] On instructions from the State Department, U.S.

customs officials asked returning citizens to surrender any unexpired passports. The Bureau of Citizenship (renamed the Division of Passport Control in 1917) would hold these passports, and citizens who wished to travel while they were still valid would have to "apply" to the State Department for them before their next departure. The State Department had no right to ask citizens to surrender their passports; therefore, those who exercised their right to keep their passport had their names recorded and sent to the State Department instead of their passports.[37]

The centralization and rationalization of passport applications occurred in the United States with rigor similar to efforts abroad. In the early years of the war, numerous requirements were introduced in an attempt to locate the application process more securely within the state apparatus. The removal of notary publics from the application process was greeted with much delight by the official in charge of passports.[38] As the Vanderbilt article illustrated applications now had to be taken at a federal courthouse or a state courthouse authorized to naturalize citizens, before being sent to the State Department in Washington, D.C.[39] In 1917 applications had to be received in Washington at least a week before the applicant departed, rather than the five days previously mandated.[40] The State Department took even more direct control of applications when it opened an agency in New York City devoted exclusively to passports.[41] At either a courthouse or the passport agency, sworn passport applications had to be made before a designated clerk in the presence of a witness; the latter being a U.S. citizen "known" to both the applicant and the clerk. In 1917 the State Department required a person making an application outside of their place of residence to give contact information for a "reputable professional or business man having his office or place of business in the place where the applicant resides."[42] The department also instituted what they labeled an "intensive examination" of each applicant. This "intensity" referred to the requirement that all applicants provide documentary support of most of the claims made on their application. This included not only their identity as U.S. citizens, but also the purpose and necessity of their journey. The list of countries to be visited and a brief statement of the journey's purpose was written on the passport, and, from late 1914, a photograph was attached. An applicant also still had to provide a physical description and swear an oath of allegiance, the latter "while the penetrating eye of the clerk is holding him."[43] According to one reporter, "This part of the procedure is the most impressive, and the most cynical of applicants is charged with a spark of patriotism as he solemnly answers: 'I do.' " The new "seriousness" with which the passport was taken meant that "the road toward getting the precious bit of paper is a hard one and must be proved a straight one."[44]

In the first year of the war in Europe, fifty thousand citizens successfully walked the hard and straight road to get a passport, but not all applicants completed the journey.[45] As the war progressed, the State Department adopted procedures that restricted the issuance of passports to various occupational and social groups; no passports were to be issued to missionaries, to students for studying abroad, or to journalists who did not work for accredited news organizations.[46] Naturalized citizens were "discouraged" from traveling to their country of origin, particularly if that country was at war and did not have an expatriation treaty with the United States. The concern was that, with U.S. citizenship not being recognized, a male could be drafted into the army of his country of birth. In the eyes of the department, "very few satisfactory explanations" were offered; thus most applications from naturalized citizens in this situation were rejected.[47] More generally, the State Department tried to prevent citizens from traveling in the war zone—apparently, the traditionally popular destination of France was for some U.S. citizens even more alluring with a war going on. In a statement from the secretary of state explaining the policy, it was noted, "The department believes that the presence of American tourists in and about places where military operations are being carried on is most undesirable, and can give such persons no assurance that they will be immune from arrest and difficulties if they persist in attempting to visit such places."[48] The need to provide proof of the necessity of a journey was subsequently extended to travels in neutral neighboring countries. After the United States entered the war in 1917, "proof of necessity" was required in all passport applications, though this was more strictly enforced for travel to Europe. The State Department's attempt to exert more direct control over the passport, and therefore indirect control over the movement of its citizens, was not limited to the issuance of a passport. A passport could only be used to enter the specific countries officials wrote on it, and only for the purposes that were listed on it; in this sense it functioned somewhat like visas do now. If citizens changed their itinerary, they had to apply to a consul for an emergency passport for their new destinations.

The intensification of passport requirements in the United States and abroad was partly a response to the early wartime reputation of the U.S. passport as the "forger's friend."[49] The threat of German spies carrying a U.S. passport loomed large in the initial years of the war, owing to several German spies being caught in possession of stolen U.S. passports, and also because of two cases that captivated U.S. newspapers, in which Germans were charged and sentenced in the United States for conspiring to obtain passports for German reservists residing in the country.[50] The second of these cases revealed the difficulties involved in policing passport applications when it was discovered that the conspirators had overcome the obstacle of the required photograph that the State Department had trumpeted as a way to prevent fraud. As the *New York Sun* explained the Germans had bypassed this through the "simple expedient of having the reservist apply for the passport in person, using the name of an accommodating American citizen, but submitting his own photograph."[51]

U.S. officials became even more concerned when, in the middle of 1915, it became apparent that the German government was producing its own fake U.S. passports, no longer merely seeking to acquire legally issued passports. The first and most celebrated case involved George Breeckow, who used a fake U.S. passport to enter England, copied from a legitimate passport issued to Reginald Rowland, who had had his passport temporarily taken for inspection by German officials when he had checked into a Berlin hotel several months earlier (figure 10.1). Despite carrying a copy of this passport and arriving as Reginald Rowland, Breeckow was arrested on suspicion of espionage soon after his arrival in England. The discovery of his fake passport received substantial newspaper coverage in the United States because, in the words of one newspaper, it provided the first evidence of "the abuse by one nation of another nation's sacred seal and of the deliberate forgery by agents of one nation of the signature of the Secretary of State of another and friendly power. Officials here are amazed that it has been possible to procure such definite proof."[52] According to the report on Breeckow's passport forwarded to the State Department by the U.S. Ambassador in London, although the passport was a good enough copy to "deceive a casual observer," a "chemical analysis and comparison" revealed "unequivocally" that the passport was a fraud.[53] Thus the war saw the passport enter the world of modernization and rationalization, both in its production and, gradually, in the determination of its authenticity—the passport could be as much the object of an "objective" gaze as the person who carried it. The report on Breeckow's passport included the results of tests on fiber, dyestuff, and "the Biuret test" on paper type; close examination of the eagle at the top of the passport also revealed discrepancies in the wings, tail feathers, and the background of the thirteen stars.[54] Final confirmation that the passport was a fake came when State Department agents located Reginald Rowland, who had "preserved his passport in a beautiful way." As was common among travelers of the period, he had framed it as a souvenir of his European vacation.[55] Breeckow was executed by firing squad in England on October 26, 1915. Prior to his execution, he told a U.S. consul "he had no

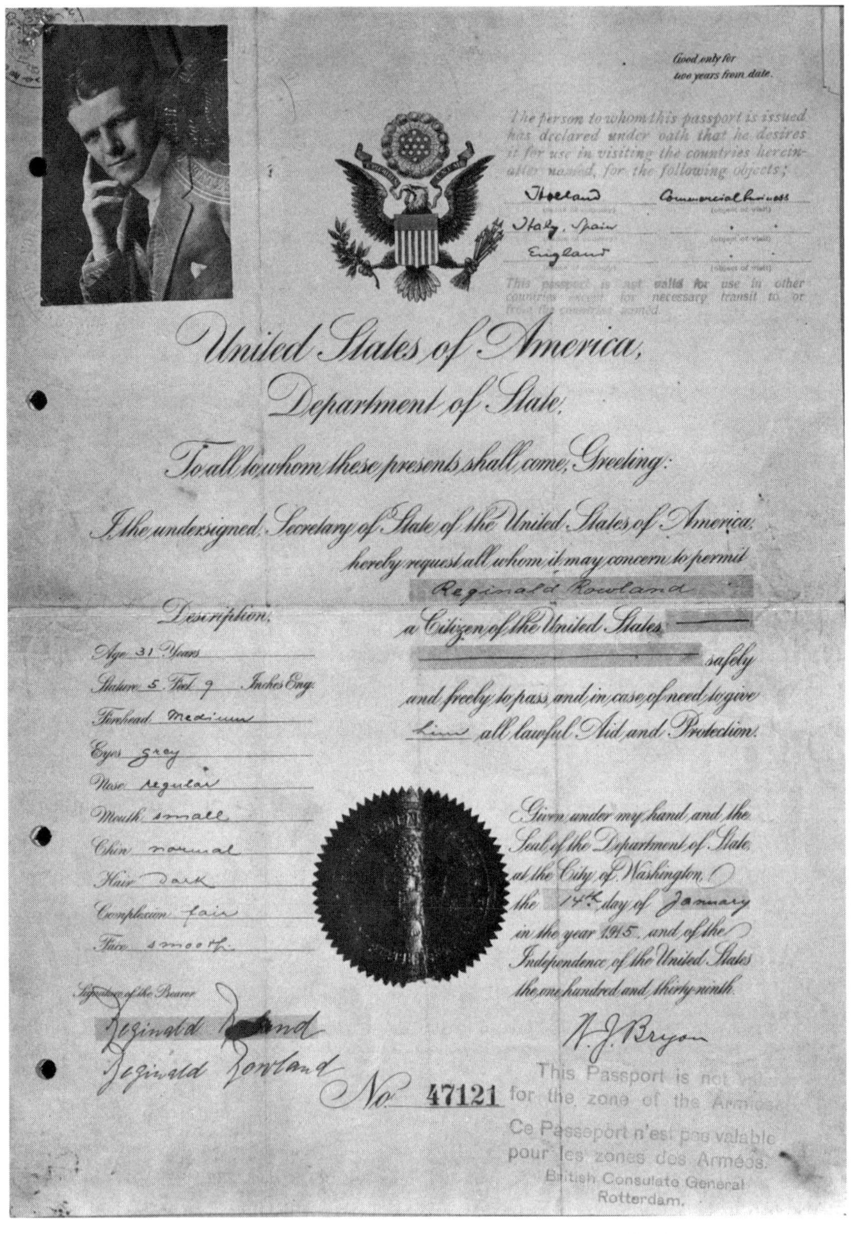

Good only for two years from date.

The person to whom this passport is issued has declared under oath that he desires it for use in visiting the countries hereinafter named, for the following objects;

Holland — Commercial business

Italy, Spain

England

This passport is not valid for use in other countries except for necessary transit to or from the countries named.

United States of America,

Department of State,

To all to whom these presents shall come, Greeting:

I the undersigned Secretary of State of the United States of America, hereby request all whom it may concern to permit Reginald Rowland a Citizen of the United States safely and freely to pass, and in case of need to give him all lawful Aid and Protection.

Description.

Age 31 Years

Stature 5 Feet 9 Inches Eng.

Forehead Medium

Eyes gray

Nose regular

Mouth small

Chin normal

Hair dark

Complexion fair

Face smooth

Signature of the Bearer

Reginald Rowland

Reginald Rowland

Given under my hand and the Seal of the Department of State, at the City of Washington, the 14th day of January in the year 1915, and of the Independence of the United States the one hundred and thirty-ninth.

W. J. Bryan

No. 47121

This Passport is not valid for the zone of the Armies.

Ce Passeport n'est pas valable pour les zones des Armées.

British Consulate General Rotterdam.

Figure 10.1. George Breeckow's fake U.S. passport, 1915 (National Archives).

complaint to make except that he felt that as he had not succeeded in transmitting any information to Germany, the punishment was rather severe."[56]

While fraud and forgery showed potential faults in the documents and procedures used to implement passport control, officials along the Mexican border viewed the entire system of passport control as flawed and illogical. Although verifying citizenship at the Mexican border was invoked as a reason for the 1918 Passport Control Act, officials on the ground saw little value in the passport owing to the large number of daily border crossers and the vast stretch of land under official watch. Their experiences made clear that the top priority for passport control and wartime border security was seaports (particularly New York, the sole port for wartime Atlantic crossings after 1916), where, to state the obvious, people arrived and left the country in ships, "closed containers" that people could not easily leave or enter until arrival at a specific location.[57] In contrast, along land borders people could simply enter the United States over the open stretches of land between the major cities. An initial attempt to prevent this came in the form of a small group of inspectors hired to patrol the border, intended to make inspection more mobile. Known as "passport employees," these were mounted inspectors who policed the land border toward the end of World War I. According to one former inspector, these "fairly rough characters," hired from "local ranchers and cowhands," rode in groups of three or four. They "proved themselves of considerable value particularly deterring cattle and horse thieves from running livestock across the border into Mexico."[58]

Passport control was further hampered by the limited number of officials assigned to designated entry points. It was estimated that if the document requirements were to be rigorously enforced in any useful way, an additional sixteen inspectors and two stenographers would be required to keep record of the approximately four thousand Mexicans who crossed the border daily through the towns of Nogales, Naco, and Douglas; this estimate did not include the work of inspecting the documents of other foreigners.[59] As a result, inspectors often felt that personal knowledge should trump the time-consuming effort of verifying identity through documents; most of the Mexicans who crossed the border did so on a daily basis as part of their "commute" to work. While one report noted "there is very little of the looseness of personal recognition"[60] at El Paso, pressure there and from local chambers of commerce not to impede the flow of laborers created a less-than-rigorous documentary regime along the Mexican border. Officials in Washington, D.C., continued to be frustrated even in situations in which documents replaced personal recognition. U.S. and Mexican border officials regularly accepted documents other than the passport, including passport applications and certificates issued by local authorities.[61]

Therefore, while the commissioner general of immigration praised the effectiveness of passport control at New York in the 1918 Immigration Bureau annual report, in that same report Frank Berkshire, who had been in charge of immigration inspectors along much of the Mexican border since 1907, complained that enemy agents simply avoided official ports of entry along the land border; "Therefore, the passport regulations as now enforced discommode thousands of loyal, or in any event, not unfriendly persons whose legitimate business or innocent pleasures naturally take them through the regular channels, while the frontier elsewhere is inadequately guarded. This is wholly wrong, illogical, wasteful and dangerous."[62] His frustration grew when he saw a role for the passport in targeting the actions of disloyal citizens who sought to cross the border for what he considered was not innocent pleasure. After the introduction of Prohibition, Berkshire sought permission to deny passports and other necessary documents to citizens who wanted to travel to Tijuana to drink. Despite endorsements of this initiative from local civic officials and religious groups, the State Department continually refused to allow Berkshire to act as a "censor of morals," and instructed that passports and border permits be issued to the so-called "thirsty tourists" who crossed into Mexico to drink alcohol.[63]

Berkshire's argument, that the focus of passport control on "loyal" and "not unfriendly persons" created a border system which was "illogical, wasteful and dangerous," inadvertently pointed to a strength of documentary-based systems of border management. In this sense, the passport was not simply a technology of exclusion; it introduced citizens to a developing documentary regime of verification. The passport and visa applications and their potential use as records of the movement of citizens and aliens are examples of a "modern" form of government based on more complete knowledge of the population and society. This could be used not only in the logic of wartime surveillance, but also as the basis of statistics that could inform practices of governing. The war created a need for information, and not necessarily for any known purpose; rather, it gave rise to the belief that the government simply had to know and be able to remember all possible knowledge about its population and society. Prior to the war the limited collection and analysis of information meant that the government did not know with any accuracy facts that became critical to mobilization such as the country's net financial reserves, total industrial production, and the potential combined transportation capability.[64] In reaction to the outbreak of war in Europe, mobilization saw the importation of the management logic that had developed in major industries into parts of the federal government.[65] After President Wilson sanctioned the Civilian Advisory Commission for the collection of information, centralized agencies concerned with specific economic sectors were created, such as for food and fuel, that prioritized systematic gathering of data and centralized administration.[66] While it is not clear if any government official explicitly articulated the passport to this project, the war showed how identification documents could manage difference, not simply through the documentation of identification categories, but more astutely through the knowledge of the individuals who comprised these categories, and the production of more precise identification categories, a role that immigration and passport policies in the 1920s would increasingly make apparent.

Beyond attempts to document the identity of aliens and citizens entering and leaving the country, the federal government instituted surveillance practices to monitor what it considered suspect populations within the country in the context of this increasingly pervasive project to collect information. These early attempts to gather knowledge on specific individuals within the United States illustrated the potential of a systematic administrative structure for the acquisition of information about people rather than more benign objects such as the growth of corn or the production of automobiles. Beginning with German spies and sympathizers, the initial attempts at domestic surveillance moved to labor and left-wing political organizations.[67] The initial targeting of Germans took the form of informal surveillance within unofficial attempts to limit German presence in the United States. Preexisting Progressive Era concerns about immigration evolved into efforts to target German music and books, and more specific instances of a loosely conceived sense of German cultural identity: the hamburger became the liberty sandwich, sauerkraut was renamed liberty cabbage, and, somewhat more illogically, German measles became liberty measles.[68] However, following the entry of the United States into the war, a series of laws formalized such prejudice through the legal surveillance of citizens of German descent: the Espionage Act of June 15, 1917; Trading with the Enemy Act of October 6, 1917; and the Sedition Act of May 16, 1918. Presidential proclamations were also issued that labeled all German males aged fourteen and over "enemy aliens" (April 6, 1917) and required the registration of all German males (November 16, 1917) and then German females (April 19, 1918). Non-German U.S. citizens were not exempt from state-sponsored attempts at surveillance. Although not necessarily thought of as such the Selective Service Act functioned to register, and thus collect information about, citizens eligible for military service. By the end of the war, it resulted in more than 24 million male citizens aged eighteen to forty-five being registered for the draft through the establishment of local draft boards; about 12% of them would eventually serve.[69]

How effective was the employment of the powers of surveillance in these acts and regulations? The responsibility initially fell on a woefully understaffed federal police structure centered on the Department of Justice's Bureau of Investigation. Created in 1908, it had gained a semblance of responsibility following the passage of the Mann Act in 1910, in which Congress utilized the federal government's right to control interstate commerce to make it a federal offense to transport a woman across interstate lines for immoral purposes. But in 1914 the Bureau of Investigation still only had one hundred agents; by the end of the war it had four hundred agents operating among a population of 100 million. Under the leadership of Bruce Bielaski (whose sister Ruth Shipley would later run the Passport Division for almost three decades, from the late 1920s to the early 1950s), the bureau attempted to both consolidate and centralize information on suspicious individuals. It also employed agents, largely recruited from the Pinkerton National Detective Agency, to investigate both suspected German spies and radical agitators. It was further assisted by the American Patriotic League (APL), which at the end of the war counted 250,000 members. In his 1918 report the attorney general called the APL "invaluable to the government as an auxiliary force"; in his history of the United States and World War I David Kennedy labels them "a rambunctious, unruly *posse comitatus* on an unprecedented national scale."[70] The main target of APL chapters became citizens who did not register with local draft boards; large-scale raids tended to discover small numbers of "slackers," identified by their failure to produce an identification card that showed they had registered for the draft. The Selective Service Act was in fact implemented through volunteer groups, befitting the purportedly voluntary nature of the draft, but more practically, an acknowledgment that the federal government was not the massive bureaucracy such an act required. Volunteers staffed draft boards in smaller towns, with President Wilson appointing prominent local citizens to boards in larger cities.[71] In contrast, the registration of Germans made use of existing state apparatus. Germans had to report to a local police station or post office to fill out detailed forms, supply several photographs, and give fingerprints. They were then issued an identification card with their name, address, photograph, and thumbprint, which they were required to carry at all times. Through the information collected in the registration process, officials believed they could identify possibly hostile aliens and, if not deport or incarcerate them, at least keep them away from vital resources.[72] By the end of the war, surveillance practices had become part of the twentieth-century U.S. state in the form of the Bureau of Investigation and the enforcement of these acts and regulations, along with their accompanying procedures such as internment, denaturalization, and deportation. This new form of state and its relationship to citizens and aliens also included immigration offices and passport agencies.[73]

Wartime practices of administrative surveillance produced an understanding of identity as a problem of information, particularly its collection and circulation. After the war the individuals that officials sought to expose through information changed from German spies to political agitators, specifically Bolsheviks and anarchists, but the public pronouncements of the success of documentary surveillance remained the same. A belief in the rigorous collection of information at the point of application continued to generate the confidence that passport control could capture individual identity and thus keep the United States safe. President Wilson urged the peacetime continuation of the visa system for aliens, arguing that it worked to "exclude practically all persons whose admission to the United States would be dangerous or contrary to the public interest."[74] In 1919 a correspondent for the *New York Times* celebrated the difficulties individuals encountered with U.S. passport and visa requirements (note that "passport" continued to be the catch-all label for state-issued travel documents): "Only a man who has struggled to get a passport on his way back to the United States can sense to the full the trouble which the present wartime regulations make. It is easier for the camel to get through the needle's eye than it is for the Red to escape the vigilance of our Consuls abroad at the present time."[75] However, in 1920 the chair of the House Committee on Foreign Affairs told a hearing that it was well known that the visa investigation and interview was "extremely imperfect." For him this was specifically due to the limits of a U.S. official's local knowledge when "strangers" arrived in a town and applied for a visa; a more lax peacetime attitude to the compilation of suspect lists also contributed to this situation.[76]

The continuing use of passports and visas at the U.S. border after the end of the war occurred in a period of transition in both official and public understanding of the consequences and implications of official attempts to document identity. While the need for these documents at the border seemed to be recognized, questions about the system remained: Who exactly should be required to carry these documents? Who should issue them? How should they be issued? One important debate centered on whether passport requirements should continue for both citizens and aliens. At a 1919 House Committee on Foreign Affairs hearing, senior State Department official Wilbur Carr made explicit what he considered the impracticalities of partial documentary requirements at the border:

> If Americans are not going to have some sort of document to enable them to get onto a steamer, it does not seem clear to me how it is going to be possible to distinguish between the two, because there are many aliens and many Americans who can not be distinguished by any other means, except some kind of proof which they can carry with them.

A member of the committee endorsed this concern with the following question, which highlighted the perceived redundancy of prewar border identification methods: "How do you distinguish whether the man is an American citizen or not, if all he has to do is say 'I am an American citizen,' and not produce a passport?" This question remained unanswered, aside from a somewhat ambiguous comment from the committee chair that "of course in all laws of that kind that is merely a matter of proof."[77]

Outside of the need for information, officials who wanted to maintain passports understood the border as a place where trust or leaps of faith should not be used as part of identification practices. People could no longer be relied upon to verify the identity that officials needed to establish; that role belonged to documents. In contrast, for those who sought to abolish passports, some individuals could still apparently be trusted, and, similarly, an element of faith remained in the utility of personal appearance in the verification of identity. To eliminate passports only for U.S. citizens indicated a belief that the body could provide the necessary proof of citizenship; that someone akin to the Supreme Court's "average man" could tell a "true" white man from a nonwhite man and, by implication, a U.S. citizen from an alien. But Carr's comments, referring as they did to naturalized citizens, emphasized that the conflation of whiteness/

nationality and nonwhiteness/foreignness that grounded this form of verification was being increasingly eroded. Although this presented a problem to which universal identification documents at the border appeared to offer a solution, in 1921, two years after this hearing, Congress dropped the requirement that citizens have passports to leave or enter the United States. Concerns over the extent to which peacetime passport requirements would limit the assumed right of citizens to travel abroad (a problem Carr had acknowledged in his testimony in 1919) and the burgeoning Red Scare provided sufficient rationales to get rid of a universal requirement for passports at the U.S. border but retain it for aliens; in 1920 the requirement for aliens to have a departure permit was also removed.[78] The Passport Control Act was revoked as part of a joint congressional resolution that repealed all wartime measures. Although Congress had appropriated money for the continuation of the consular viasing of passports, it was initially thought that without the Passport Control Act there was no longer any authority for the consular visa system. However, the attorney general "clarified" that a provision in the diplomatic and consular appropriation act provided the legal underpinning for the United States to demand visas from aliens.[79]

The belief that documents could keep specific individuals out of the United States still did not translate into the recognition that to achieve this, official identification on a large-scale had to occur within a system of clearly demarcated administrative authority. This was evident in the system in which visas were issued abroad by representatives of the State Department under criteria distinct from those used by representatives of the Labor Department to assess the right of entry at the U.S. border. The frustrated chief of the Visa Division (created in the State Department in 1919) informed a shocked congressional hearing in early 1921 that although a consul could attempt to exercise discretion and not issue a visa to a leper (excluded under immigration law), if the consul was not emphatic enough, and the leper insisted, the consul would have to grant a visa.[80] Or, as the State Department put it to a confused letter writer, a U.S. official abroad could only be of "assistance to an applicant in determining his admissibility" under immigration law.[81] State Department officials were clear that the visa system existed for the sole purpose of "shutting out anarchists and Bolsheviks."[82] To assess and possibly refuse an alien under the immigration act would "trespass upon the prerogatives of the Department of Labor."[83] However, an informal system was introduced that sanctioned a small degree of intrusion. Consuls occasionally alerted immigration inspectors to possible grounds for exclusion through a set of symbols written on a visa that represented categories of exclusion.[84] In a similar act of cooperation, immigration inspectors were told that if an individual was admissible under immigration law but arrived without a visa, he or she could not be admitted without State Department approval.[85]

This problem became even more acute following the introduction of immigration restriction based on nationality in 1921.[86] Temporary annual quotas were set at a maximum of 3% of a total nationality present in the United States according to the 1910 census.[87] However, the 1921 Immigration Act did not provide for the issuance of a document to verify admission. This became a significant administrative problem because the act departed from the formal guiding principle of individual selection to restrict immigration on a group basis.[88] Although immigration had arguably been *enforced* prior to the war through the articulation of individuals to group identities, it had been legally *defined* in terms of assessing individuals based on their ability to be productive citizens. After 1921, while the preexisting criteria relating to disease and morality remained, an individual's right to entry was initially assessed based on their nationality, bounded by the specific number of nationals allowed under the annual quota; a criterion the informal system of symbols could not assist in ascertaining.

Therefore, the federal government attempted once again to have steamship companies compensate for the limitations of U.S. administration and bureaucracy abroad. Steamship officials continued to "inspect" alien ticket buyers to avoid fines for bringing ineligible immigrants to the United States, and most steamship companies required non-U.S. citizens to have visas. However, the two shipping conferences that ran the trans-Atlantic route did not have a system to administer ticket sales on the basis of nationality, especially when aliens crossing U.S. land borders also contributed to monthly quota numbers.[89] Therefore, no centralized bureaucracy existed, officially or unofficially, to coordinate ticket sales with the numbers of immigrants allowed to enter the United States under nationality quotas in any given month—a maximum of 20% of a nation's annual quota. As a result, quotas were regularly filled soon after the beginning of the month. The commissioner at Ellis Island claimed that it was not unusual for inspectors to admit five thousand immigrants in one day, and consequently fill the monthly quota for eight nations before the month was seventy-two hours old.[90] The most powerful symbol of this mismanagement of the border occurred when steamships failed in their "midnight races" to be the first to arrive on the first day of each month. On August 31, 1923, four steamships slightly miscalculated their arrival at New

York, or what a newspaper called the "imaginary line between Fort Wadsworth and Fort Hamilton"; port officials recorded their arrivals at 11:54 P.M., 11:55 P.M., 11:57 P.M., and fifteen seconds before midnight.[91] As the ships had failed to arrive on September 1, the immigrants on board were counted against the already-filled August quota. While the Labor Department fined the ships' owners $200 for each over-quota immigrant on board, the Secretary of Labor ultimately used his discretion to admit those passengers subject to the quota on humanitarian grounds.[92] This discretionary treatment was not always applied in less spectacular cases. In 1923–24 aliens who arrived after quotas had been filled comprised 40% of excluded immigrants at Ellis Island, albeit part of the mere 3.3% of alien arrivals who were rejected at the border.[93]

The writers of the 1924 Immigration Act sought to utilize a more efficient documentary system to rigorously administer the border.[94] Section 2(f) of the act gave consuls authority to inspect individuals as potential immigrants. The act required immigrants to have an "immigration visa" issued by consuls prior to their departure to the United States; nonimmigrant aliens had to have their passports visaed per the existing law. The administration of quotas was centralized in each quota country through the principle consular officer, who generally established waiting lists; the reduction of monthly quota maximums to 10% of the annual total further assisted in making the system more efficient.[95] Therefore, an official could refuse a visa on the grounds that either the monthly or annual quota had been filled. A successful immigrant visa application form became the visa when an official signed it, stamped it, and attached it to a passport. Immigration inspectors at Ellis Island quickly came to accept this visa as proof of a thorough inspection.[96] By the 1930s less than 5% of immigrants who arrived at the port of New York were sent to Ellis Island for inspection. This amounted to a daily average of only three hundred immigrants. These individuals were most frequently sent for further inspection because they were considered potential "public charges," or because their sponsoring relatives were not at the port; it was less common that their papers were out of order. Ultimately, an annual average of 0.2% of immigrants with visas were refused entry. In the first four years of enforcement, this equaled 2,783 rejected immigrants out of a four-year total of 1,182, 213 arrivals.[97] The medical inspection of immigrants by PHS doctors at foreign ports further enhanced the perceived reliability of overseas inspection.[98] However, PHS doctors could only report on the health of immigrants, the authority to reject a visa remained exclusively the State Department official's.

With the introduction of immigration quotas, U.S. citizenship had become an increasingly valuable identity, and therefore the passport became a sought-after document for gaining admission to the United States. While this resulted in the establishment of large-scale enterprises that produced fraudulent U.S. passports or visas (so-called passport "factories" or "mills"), through the 1920s noncitizens outside of the United States regularly attempted to obtain authentic U.S. passports by using fraudulent supporting documents. Multiple types of fake documents were produced to prove citizenship, such as birth certificates, baptismal certificates, marriage certificates, and naturalization certificates.[99] Utilizing another strategy, noncitizens acquired authentic versions of these documents and then used fake local documents to falsely link the real citizenship documents to the applicant. In some cases the person originally issued the document had died; in one case a number of original documents were stolen from a local municipal archive.[100] The emergence of fake documents exposed the ease with which a document produced an identity as opposed to merely verifying a preexisting identity. Therefore, while the State Department sought to make its passport a more reliable and secure document, the existence of a culture of suspicion directed at noncitizens meant that when they issued a passport abroad, circumstances pushed officials to rely more on the evidence produced by their observation of individuals and less on locally produced supporting documents. Regardless of the documents offered, officials abroad were encouraged to rigorously question suspicious-looking applicants, particularly first time passport applicants with limited or little English.[101] Following the purported success of a system of questioning such applicants in Warsaw, the State Department encouraged using another version of the intensive examinations of applicants and identifying witnesses.[102] The State Department also used the authority and value of an official's face-to-face evaluation to argue against the establishment of review boards in the United States to evaluate appeals, particularly for those applicants rejected abroad after President Herbert Hoover instructed the department to more rigorously enforce the broadly defined "public charge" exclusion clause to limit the arrival of new workers in the early 1930s.[103]

While the move to verify immigrants and documents abroad did lessen the number of inspections at Ellis Island, it did little to alter the problems associated with using documents to police the land border, where officials not only had to identify people, but they also needed to stake a claim for the actual existence of a border. The articulation of face-to-face observation with locally generated knowledge played out in the enforcement, as opposed to the issuance, of documents, thus producing a different set of tensions for officials, citizens, and potential immigrants. These tensions manifested themselves in the handling of a distinct group that was not encountered at seaports or consulates and embassies: commuters. Unlike with seaports, which existed as a space of transit, people lived along the land borders and regularly crossed them on their way to work. The requirement to identify the people who crossed the border via nationality affected the movement of workers. In these situations, the enforcement of nationality quotas required documents to make practical and visible the identities demarcated in immigration laws. In 1927 a controversy developed on the Canadian border in response to a strategy employed by some unsuccessful European immigrants. These individuals, who had been unable to move to the United States because of nationality quotas, located themselves in Canada close to the U.S. border, where they obtained commuter permits to work in the United States. To curb this practice, all workers who crossed over daily from Canada were defined as immigrants. As a consequence, native-born Canadians were required to get visas, and foreign-born Canadian citizens were to be counted against the quotas of their country of birth. The Department of Labor, and eventually the Supreme Court, refuted various arguments offered in support of the Canadian commuters, including the argument that the act of immigration had to involve a change in domicile.[104]

The conflict between commuters and attempts to exert sovereignty at the border was more visible on the Mexican border, where it arose for different reasons and was solved in very different ways. Mexicans had historically been racialized as inferior. In 1917 a typhus panic, combined with the Progressive-inspired public bath movement, led to a system in El Paso and other major border towns in which medical inspectors examined and bathed Mexicans who crossed the border. Regular border crossers were issued a bath certificate that verified that the bearer had been "deloused, bathed, vaccinated," and all their clothing and baggage had been disinfected at least once a week. Embracing this, groups of "habitual bathers" emerged. They were not converts to "modern" standards of hygiene, but individuals dirtying their hands through a little deception. These "bathers" subjected themselves to multiple daily disinfections to obtain certificates, which they then sold to the "unwashed."[105] The bathing requirement was a manifestation of an ongoing colonial mentality that saw labor needs along the border with Mexico differently from that with Canada. Following the 1924 Immigration Act, the local movement of Mexican labor was viewed through a new cultural and racial lens. Within the act's increasingly complex understanding of race and nationality, Mexicans were classified as white, but their whiteness was of a very particular form. Mexican immigration was not restricted by an annual quota, but visibly different from white European immigrants, Mexicans who commuted to work in the United States, or crossed the border as "temporary visitors" became the target of immigration inspection. This created the image of the Mexican as *the* illegal immigrant on the southern border.[106] Although in this context Mexicans were identified as members of a racial group they could also be identified as specific individuals through local knowledge and the familiarity of personal recognition. In a 1932 report on the Mexican border, some officers were still criticized for not rigorously checking the authenticity of documents; the face of the bearer regularly continued to trump the document.[107]

Reading personal appearance was in fact required to correctly identify one eligible group—citizens who entered the United States at entry ports along both the northern and southern borders. Although U.S. citizens were not required to carry passports, most citizens who returned on ships from Europe carried passports to fulfill the laws of other nations. This was not the case along the land borders, so in 1929, in an attempt to avoid confusion, individuals were required to offer proof of U.S. citizenship upon request on return from Canada. While it was reported that this was "rigidly enforced at all customs houses,"[108] it appeared to be a much more fluid system than that imposed on noncitizens. This did not prevent it from frustrating many U.S. citizens—especially those citizens taking up the increasingly popular pastime of day excursions in cars. Although passports were the preferred document, birth certificates, naturalization papers, and documents issued by the Board of Education to verify voting rights were also listed as acceptable. Drivers' licenses were not accepted; as officials repeatedly stressed, noncitizens could get a driver's license. However, officials were apparently confident noncitizens could not be members of clubs or fraternal societies—membership cards for such groups were reportedly often accepted. The rationale for accepting such documents was made clear by the assistant secretary of labor, who told a newspaper reporter that along the Canadian border "the inspectors, well trained in their work, have ways of sizing up an applicant for admission even when the applicant does not possess what would be regarded as evidence in court."[109] The breadth of this sizing up was explained in a Senate hearing two years later; a Labor Department official argued his staff was adept at recognizing citizens without passports because "an American's manner of speech, his appearance and bearing betoken the American citizen."[110]

Land borders were not exclusively a place of transit, a fact that made the novelty of attempts at rigorous border enforcement visible in numerous ways. The security concerns of the northern border, articulated through a distinct understanding of whiteness, made issues with identifying the actual border more visible and the racial underpinnings of national security less visible than in debates over the Mexican border. The existence of houses built across the international boundary line—so-called line houses—clearly attested to the historical lack of interest in locating and enforcing that line as an international border. In actualizing the metaphor of the land border as the United States' "back door," line houses demonstrated the difficulty of enforcing a border in a space where people lived. A 1928 *Saturday Evening Post* article informed readers that in houses that straddled Rock Island (now Stanstead), Quebec, and Derby Line, Vermont, "families cook their food in Canadian kitchens and eat it in American dining rooms."[111] To counter the domestication of the national border by these houses, a row of brass tacks would be nailed to the building's exterior so authorities of both countries could see "where the line entered the house and where it passed through the rear."[112] The power to officially inspect these houses depended upon which country the building's front door opened onto.

In the 1920s stories about line houses became a useful way for newspapers and magazines to show the change in the official attitude of the United States to its international boundaries and with it the peacetime requirement for documents. Boundaries were now officially thought of as borders, understood as places to secure the nation against perceived threats. The trumping of a house's back door by the United States' "back door" produced what immigration officials labeled "line bound" individuals. One such individual, Arthur Plante, was a Canadian citizen who was considered a U.S. resident by virtue of the fact that the front door of his line house opened into the United States; the boundary line apparently ran *exactly* along the rear of his house. In the late 1920s Plante traveled into Canada, but without getting the documents he now required to return. As a result, U.S. officials denied him entry when he attempted to return home through the nearest official port of entry. Thus, according to the Associated Press, Plante had spent the four years since that ill-fated trip to Canada, still in Canada. That is, he lived in his woodshed, which was located in Canada. While the woodshed abutted his house, he could not legally enter the backdoor of his American home.[113] As recounted in the AP article, Plante's life in his woodshed represented an ideal for border enforcement in which all parts of the border could apparently be seen by an immigration official. How else to explain Plante's situation, except through the presence of a permanent official stationed at his property? Another possible explanation provides a second ideal scenario—life in a woodshed without a guard but with respect for the border turns Plante into a poster child for the respect for the border (albeit with equal institutional encouragement). This and other news stories are difficult to make sense of in hindsight. Nonetheless, they are useful to an analysis of early attempts to identify the border through officials and documents. They speak to the cultural confusion and shock over the policing of a national border between Canada and the United States. In the 1920s the boundary line began to matter in ways it had not previously. The attempt to consistently police this "new" border made the line something that people needed to see—not only immigrants, but also those locals who lived close to it, or even on it. The border had to be introduced and understood as a line that could not be crossed without the permission of the federal government. Therefore, these articles collectively performed a pedagogical role in making clear that the "back door" needed to be thought of as a space of exclusion; the boundary line had in fact become a border, not a mere line marked on the land.[114]

Another symbol of the new border but one that emphasized the limited role of documents was the establishment of a border patrol. Although prior to the 1920s a small force had patrolled the border their job had been merely to compel people crossing the border to go to ports of entry. However, in the 1920s advocates called for a patrol that could apprehend people seeking to illegally cross the border to avoid quota restrictions. In arguing for such a patrol, an immigration official informed a Congressional hearing that "a port of entry is the last place in the world that an alien seeking to come in . . . would approach;" instead,

> they cross the borders in wide gaps of unguarded stretches . . . [and] unless these stretches are patrolled by a force of sufficient strength, efficiency and authority to at least make attempts to cross the border dangerous and to hold illegal entry down to small proportions, our whole system

> fails, and we might just as well abandon our ports of entry and give up the expensive stations maintained thereat.[115]

Congress granted funding for a border patrol in 1924. The number of subsequent newspaper and magazine articles on the topic suggests that in the popular imagination this replaced passport control as the symbol of border security. However, in practice initial congressional efforts to establish a border patrol amounted to little more than a symbolic acknowledgment of the desire to rigorously enforce immigration restrictions along the land border. Contrary to positive reports in newspapers and magazines, it was introduced with the same administrative and legal shortcomings that had characterized other initiatives to manage the border and immigration. Specifically, the new border patrol of immigration inspectors was located squarely within a battle with customs officials over inspection authority, and was thus a dispute between the Departments of Labor and Treasury; an attempt in the early 1930s to create a unified border patrol failed. The federal government's priorities in this turf war were made explicit in 1924 when the Department of Labor received an appropriation of $1 million to create the border patrol; the same year $12 million was appropriated by the Treasury Department for enforcement of Prohibition. In the initial years, the exact role of the inspectors assigned to the border patrol was subject to both formal and informal negotiations with the Treasury Department's customs officials. In 1925 border patrol inspectors were given the power to arrest aliens and search vehicles, but by the end of the 1920s, they had gained and lost the right to apprehend aliens who were smuggling alcohol, but retained the right to examine aliens and search houses. This apparently did not stop them regularly questioning and arresting aliens for a variety of smuggling offenses, beyond the illegal "importation" of individuals. By 1930 the border patrol consisted of 847 officers. Therefore, less than one thousand men were responsible for turning the long spaces between ports of entry into a governable border along both the northern and southern boundaries.[116]

For the officials who policed it, a land border required a different mode of surveillance than that prioritized at seaports and abroad. It was believed the direct surveillance of the border patrol could prevent illegal immigration more effectively than the indirect administrative surveillance of the documentary regime used at seaports. In this environment, the increasingly complex understandings of whiteness, nationality, and the border still provided a role for personal appearance as a useful and efficient way to verify individual identity and keep the nation secure.

By the end of the 1920s, identification documents, specifically the passport and visa, had developed a particular and at times important role at the U.S. border. This role was frequently tied to the record-keeping practices of immigration restrictions, as well as the precise identities outlined in the quota acts. While a system of identification based on documents could not solve all problems at the border, officials continued to see documents and record keeping as a way to facilitate greater official awareness of individuals, particularly in the more manageable border environment of seaports. An example of this was the establishment of a requirement that aliens be issued certificates of arrival and reentry permits. The ultimately successful introduction of these documents was predicated on an official belief that archived records generated a more accurate memory than that of individuals. It was through such a belief that practices of individual identification gained an authority they had lacked prior to the war. The 1907 Immigration Act had required the issuance of certificates of arrival, but it is unclear how long, if at all, this practice lasted. In the absence of these documents, and given the limited enforcement of any immigration laws regarding record keeping, officials had issued certificates of arrival for naturalization proceedings on the basis of "nunc pro tunc" (now for then); officials rarely consulted the ship's manifest to confirm the date of arrival, assuming the individual had accurately remembered the name of the ship and the date of arrival. After 1927 the arrival of an immigrant was recorded through the filing of the papers required to enter the country, verified by issuing each immigrant a certificate of arrival. These certificates were subsequently used to obtain reentry permits and eventually to prove an immigrant had satisfied the residency requirement for naturalization. In this manner a documentary regime of verification emerged for aliens in which documents verified documents, and the authority of the state remained to some extent continuous; it did not need to rely on the individual opinions or memories of its subjects.

However, for such a system to work, documents had to be retrieved; the state had to be able to "remember." The novelty of a documentary regime, of the need to remember through the consultation of documents, increased the awareness of the importance of the physical act of filing. In 1924 the

State Department warned consuls against using excessive ribbon on visas. This followed a complaint from the secretary of labor that "it has been found, in filing these visas that the excessive quantity of ribbon attached, and the manner of applying it to the visas, unnecessarily consumes a large amount of the file space and the tangling of the ribbon makes exceedingly difficult the access to these visas in the file."[117] Half a decade later, these initial concerns about the material construction of a retrievable memory for the state became a constant concern regarding the inability of overworked clerks to complete and file documents. By the 1930s staff at Ellis Island annually issued fifty thousand reentry permits and twenty thousand monthly verifications of arrivals.[118] There were long delays in getting reentry permits, accentuated if an alien chose not to get a reentry permit prior to departure. The *New York Times* cited a 105-day delay as an extreme example of the problems created by a lack of staff to enforce the use of records to prove arrival for nonnaturalized long-term residents.[119] Ten short-term staff assigned to Ellis Island in 1929 took a year to clear the backlog in the card index of immigrant arrivals, only for the Ellis Island office to then be given the additional responsibility of maintaining an index of visitor arrivals and departures, which often involved searching through manifests from other ports. This new index quickly fell five months behind. The Ellis Island commissioner, in requesting that three of the ten temporary clerks become permanent, promised that with "prompt and effective action it should never be more than 60 days in arrears."[120]

While this system indicated the possibilities (as well as practical limitations) offered by documents for collecting information about people, the need for official documentation of identity was still treated with skepticism by some sections of U.S. society. An attempt to introduce a system to register aliens failed; this campaign generated much more publicity than the actual introduction of the system to record the entry and departure of these same individuals. The attempt to establish registration and documentation into the everyday lives of people brought with it accusations of a "Soviet model of espionage" and the oppressive and intrusive relationship between state and citizen this was understood to represent. Opponents viewed alien registration as a form of government surveillance that was in opposition to the spirit of the constitution and a purported American tradition to treat citizens and aliens alike; partially driven by the association of identification practices with criminals or the insane.[121] Advocates, notably Secretary of Labor James Davis, tried to position registration and documentation as the efforts of a benevolent government to look out for its population. Davis often referred to it as an enrolment plan to assist aliens in accessing citizenship education programs, equivalent to the requirement that citizens register to vote. He less frequently admitted that registration would facilitate the arrest of aliens who had entered the United States illegally.[122] Promoting the former, an editorial in the *Saturday Evening Post* argued in favor of alien registration and the identification cards that would enable it, contending that

> It would exhibit for him what he is and it would entitle him to all the consideration which is owing to duly admitted foreigners who are peaceable, law abiding and industrious. The more positive the means of identification employed, the more serviceable they would be to the alien if he were unjustly accused in a court of law. The fuller the record, the more the accused would enjoy the benefits of an honorably earned good repute. Only the lawless and the criminal would have anything to fear from the working out of such a system.[123]

Opponents also believed that documents and their bureaucratic support system marked individuals with identities that would affect how they negotiated their daily life, but they considered that this would be an identity that invited the state into the private lives of its individuals, something that law-abiding people had done nothing to deserve. While the United States did not implement national registration for aliens, the application for a required passport, like the various documents required of aliens, was perceived by some citizens as part of the extension of state-sponsored information gathering into the private lives of citizens, which problematized the relationship between the state and individuals.

"The Passport Nuisance"

In the aftermath of World War I, U.S. officials were not alone in seeing the value of requiring aliens to have passports and visas in peacetime; foreign governments made the same demand of U.S. citizens. Therefore, when the number of U.S. citizens traveling abroad dramatically increased in the 1920s, so did the number of citizens who came across the demand to identify themselves through documents. The initial responses to this situation made clear that using identification documents was a novelty for the majority of the population. The reactions also indicate that this was typically not an enjoyable first encounter. Having completed a journey through Europe in 1919, one traveler considered the passport a "souvenir of the persisting doubt, the official suspicion of your character."[1] An article in the *Washington Post* declared, "It is difficult for any one who has not actually gone through it to realize the feelings of personal humiliation which the process implies. In many instances passport officials went apparently on the theory that every applicant was to be considered a spy until he had proved the contrary."[2] The causes of frustration with the process of obtaining a passport included the demand to apply in person along with a witness, the need to submit a photograph, and the requirement for documentary proof of citizenship—an application process that was less acceptable outside of a wartime state of emergency. The humiliation stemmed from the request for these documents over and above an individual's word. Travelers took this rejection of their word (and appearance) as a sign that officials considered them dishonest and untrustworthy—a response grounded in the association of identification documents with suspect individuals such as criminals. The annoyance with the system intensified when it became clear that the required passport was not going to disappear like other emergency wartime measures. This increased when a combination of an increase in population and a decrease in the price of transatlantic steamship tickets exposed more people to passport demands. The Passport Division authorized the issuance of 1.6 million passports in the 1920s (compared to 200,000 in the decade prior to World War I, when passports were optional).[3] Newspapers and magazines labeled the negative response to postwar passport requirements the "passport question," or more frequently the "passport nuisance"; the additional cost of travel as a result of increased passport and visa fees was another source of this frustration.

The passport nuisance implicitly referred to the perception that an element of mistrust had entered the relationship between the federal government and its citizens, as well as more visibly structuring U.S. citizens' interactions with foreign governments. The relationship with the federal government had been a somewhat limited one as it was.[4] Most applicants had only had infrequent interactions with their government; it was only in the 1920s that income taxes become a centerpiece of the federal tax system. The historically limited interactions between citizens and state officials had produced a perception that only people whose (mis)behavior drew the attention of the state deserved official intervention, particularly in the form of the collection of personal information; travel was not considered a form of behavior that warranted official attention. For the "us" who simply wanted to travel, the "them" of criminals, the insane, the poor, and (less consistently) immigrants represented populations whose behavior and appearance indicated insufficient self-control to warrant trust and, therefore, the need for the state to keep track of them through the production of files and identification documents.

The move away from the sometimes excessive documentation of "the other" to an attempt to document all citizens did not, of course, originate with the passport, nor was it limited to the passport. However, the passport became an important site for the negotiation over the documentation of individual identity and the general paperization of everyday life—the pervasive demand for documentary verification that many people increasingly encountered in various aspects of their lives. From the perspective of the federal government, passports seemed to fit into the wartime emergence of the "will to know," to document "facts" in order to produce information about the population it governed. This was also articulated to the domination of bureaucratic methods in the federal government. The State Department wanted all claims to citizenship to be verified by specially designated officials according to specific documents; to widen the use of official documents was to narrow the opportunities for individuals to invoke a "local" or personal practice of identification. To some applicants, it seemed officials ignored the respectability that most assumed they naturally exhibited, and which therefore should have automatically verified the truth of their statements. A *New York Times* letter writer, unclear who the State Department now considered respectable, asked with minimal humor and evident frustration, "Who ever heard of an irresponsible philatelist or a frivolous certified public accountant?"[5] The State Department was attempting to replace respectability with the standardization of documentary practices. Through these practices, officials sought to make the population visible, to simplify people and objects so facts could be collected and governing could become more efficient. The fees associated with the passport system also angered applicants. This increase in the cost of travel was identified as both inefficient and in opposition to the government's perceived function to encourage U.S. businesses. It was also considered an affront to the reciprocal bonds of loyalty and protection at the heart of the relationship between state and citizen that the passport was understood to represent.

In this manner the passport changed from something like a letter of introduction and protection into an identification document in a very public way. The benevolent state offering protection in the form of a letter addressed to foreign officials became a nation-state practicing surveillance to gain knowledge about its citizens. The official processes of acquiring facts made it clear to many applicants that they had lost control of one aspect of the public representation of their identity; that identification practices produce a new identity is evident in the awareness that the "formalities" associated with a passport application turned citizens into objects of inquiry.

The passport nuisance developed in the early 1920s, as European countries struggled to rebuild a tourist infrastructure in a world with a changed understanding of national security. After the end of World War I, U.S. citizens did not vacation in Europe in significant numbers until 1922. A shortage of ships and coal had limited the number of available passages in the first two years of peace, and major tourist destinations such as England, France, and Italy did not allow tourists until the summer of 1921. In the years of limited tourism, newspapers and magazines published numerous articles on the problems tourists would encounter when they returned to the new Europe.

One journalist described central Europe in 1921 as "a mapless, bewildering and intensely annoying world in which to travel. Roughly re-made by the Treaty of Versailles, it has not yet become used to itself and its new boundaries and multitudinous regulation."[6] Lingering wartime control of international travel through passport and visa regulations was invoked to explain a continent where "every frontier that one used to slip over without knowing...now bristles with high military formalities. Everywhere in your path are sheds and offices crammed with bureaucrats who scribble on your passport for a consideration."[7] Magazine and newspaper readers were treated to detailed descriptions of the many hours needed to obtain the numerous documents required just to travel between two countries. In 1919 Gilbert Fuller, the president of the American Association of Tourist and Travel Agents, recounted how, for his journey from London to Paris, he had to get visas from the U.S. consul, the English police, the French consul, the French military control, the inspector on the boat crossing the Channel, and the police in Paris.[8] Two years later a journalist reported he had had to add six pages to his passport to accommodate the 131 rubber stamps he had accumulated in his travels through postwar Europe—the visa had become formalized as a rubber stamp in an attempt to reduce the time involved in inspection.[9] A 1922 *New York Times* article informed potential travelers that "the passport system gives employment to an army of officials who have become adepts in the art of using rubber stamps on documents with one hand and collecting fees with the other."[10] The simultaneous significance of the redrawing of European boundaries and the annoyances it produced for tourists was humorously expressed in the suggestion of one reporter that "we shall undoubtedly read in years to come learned dissertations on Europe in the Reign of the Rubber Stamp."[11]

By the middle of the 1920s, the awkwardness of the lingering wartime reign of the rubber stamp had become the peacetime efficiency of "the passport regime"; the label the League of Nations gave its attempts to intervene in travel documentation. The League's Organization for Communication and Transit held two passport conferences (in 1920 and 1926).[12] Both conferences began with the stated intention of abolishing what was considered to be an expensive and restrictive wartime passport system. However, in spite of this aim, these conferences ended up cementing the wartime system. The conferences created the standardized object that is now recognized as a passport, and, with the assistance of non-League members such as the United States, sketched the conditions that established the passport as the "conventional inter-state permit."[13]

Within its own history, the League of Nations' response can be read as an example of the failure of its doctrine of liberal internationalism in the postwar era of economic nationalism.[14] The "liberal internationalism" espoused by the League tended to be shorthand for the unrestricted movement of people, goods, and capital—a shorthand that defined people, goods, and capital as one inseparable mass. Therefore, the passport conferences linked the mobility of people to the movement of goods and capital. Debates about freedom of mobility became debates about free trade. As a general mandate, the League's Organization for Communication and Transit clearly understood that they had "met in order to facilitate travel for the public and also in particular for businessmen."[15] In opening statements at the 1926 conference, delegates acknowledged the public expectation of a return to unfettered mobility, evident in the coverage given in U.S. newspapers and magazines to the conferences as a possible end to the passport nuisance. But delegates also conceded that the requirements of the "present" (usefully defined in the words of one historian as the "problems of demobilization, dislocation, unemployment, fears of Communist subversion, [and] monetary crises"[16]) were so prevalent that the world could not return to the "good old days when optional passports existed."[17] Therefore, the conference legitimated the introduction of the general traveling public into a world of travel documentation that had previously been largely restricted to marginal mobile populations: immigrants and vagrants. However, it did so through a different logic—to facilitate, not control—albeit with the same practical consequences. As recorded in the minutes, conference delegates convinced themselves that the establishment of a passport regime to guarantee freedom of mobility in an *efficient* manner provided the only way to recreate and ensure a sense of the freedom of movement that had characterized prewar travel for nonimmigrants.

Although the Italian delegation complained that the focus on the facilitation of communication and trade ignored the rights of immigrants and foreign laborers, the delegation offered a minority opinion at a conference that illustrated that travelers (commercial and recreational) were intended to be the primary object of the so-called passport regime.[18] These new subjects of the passport regime were clearly differentiated from emigrants who "started their journey from a native village."[19] In a preconference statement, the Canadian representatives invoked a particular history of the passport as a guarantee of privilege to argue for abolishing transit visas on the grounds that "consular officials were after all important officials who could hardly be expected to welcome with open arms the humble peasants who made up the great mass of emigrants."[20] Prioritizing the privileged as the bearers of passports, it was reasoned that the passport regime should offer a limited number of obstacles. To that end, the committee's report encouraged the checking of passports on moving trains prior to border posts, the extension of a passport's standard duration from a single journey to at least two years, and the gradual abolishment of departure and transit visas. Acutely aware that well-to-do travelers now had to use passports, one delegate requested identification techniques be made more appropriate for "people of means." He argued that a photograph should be sufficient identification, for although fingerprints were useful for most immigrants, they "might have some tendency to affect the free movement between countries of the really good class"; an attitude the State Department shared.[21]

In the United States at the end of the 1920s, when the increasingly standardized passport regime began to take shape, the "really good class" of nonimmigrant travelers had been broadened, as a new middle class took over transatlantic steamships from immigrants. While Atlantic steamship companies had struggled to attract tourist business into the early 1920s, they suffered a greater threat to their business through the introduction of immigration quotas in 1921, followed by the stricter enforcement of quotas abroad after 1924. Immigrants had accounted for at least a third of all passengers, but had contributed an even greater percentage to profits because of the minimal care given to them in steerage, and thus the limited money spent accommodating them. In response to changes in immigration law, steamship companies redeveloped steerage as third class cabins in an ultimately successful attempt to remain profitable. Steerage, thanks to tales of immigration to the United States, had long been associated "with hordes of aliens crowded down somewhere in the bowels of a ship, tiers of steel bunks, mattressed [*sic*] with gunny sack, wretched food, no service, and scant opportunity for personal cleanliness or decent privacy."[22] In the mid-1920s it became "a remodeled and uplifted steerage with private staterooms, embroidered bedspreads, clean table cloths, electric lights in every berth, running water and baths," all for a $160 round-trip ticket, or, if you were lucky, a thirty-three day vacation to the United Kingdom and France for $243.[23] These ships generally still carried immigrants, albeit in a separate part of the ship, where it was expected they would remain invisible to tourists.[24] Some companies renovated entire ships into "tourist third."

Magazine and newspapers began to run feature stories on this new form of travel in the summer of 1924, when some shipping lines offered a limited tourist-third service. Although initially college students dominated the public presentation of the new traveler, the "white-collar steerage" tourist increasingly became associated with "the school teacher, the clergyman, the college professor and student, the army veteran who had or hadn't been across, and Mr. and Mrs. Average American with a moderate income and a short vacation period," as described by one journalist;[25] tourist third also became an acceptable way for women, particularly female college students, to travel unaccompanied by men, either alone or in groups.[26]

The increasing number of "average Americans" abroad was to some critics an indication that travel, like other leisure practices, had been commercialized for easy consumption by a mass audience.[27] For these people, tourist third was "the thin edge of the wedge perhaps in transforming foreign travel from a leisure class to a popular avocation."[28] At the end of the 1930s, an embittered travel writer proclaimed that "modern travel [had become] an excursion into a more extended Coney Island."[29] Travel as a relatively fast-paced leisure experience packaged for the middle class allowed people to travel who the writer believed were "not entitled to travel in the first place" because they lacked "the mature knowledge of the historical and psychological conditions which produced them. To the average tourist they are merely a succession of passing objects, a kaleidoscopic profusion, and as such, as destitute of spiritual value as the sights of the American carnival."[30]

Who exactly were these "average tourists"? In 1930 the State Department began to issue an annual breakdown of passport applicants at the request of steamship companies and travel agents. These initial figures, which took over a year to compile, revealed a pattern that remained consistent throughout the 1930s; of the 200,000 applicants in 1929, the largest group did not list an occupation (26,428), closely followed by 23,947 housewives. Other notable groups included: 16,345 laborers, 10,910 clerks, 5,317 bankers, 6,873 merchants, and 630 writers. Almost half the applicants listed travel as the purpose of their trip (94,054), with a third offering family reasons (68,314). Other reasons included: commercial business (15,636), education (12,838), health (3, 033), and professional business (2,324). More than a fifth of applicants gave New York City as residence, with another 13,734 living in other parts of New York State. Pennsylvania provided 18,499 applicants, New Jersey 15,033, Illinois 14,029, Massachusetts 12,479, California 7,877, Nevada 118, and New Mexico 79. Western Europe was the most popular destination (133,479) followed by Eastern Europe, with 10,615. Just over 8,000 people applied for passports for travel to Latin American, the West Indies, and Mexico; 1,201 to Africa; and 670 to Australia and New Zealand.[31]

While the new tourism these U.S. citizens generated may have angered some of their (not so) fellow travelers, the commercialization of travel generated few dissenters within the treasuries of European nations. The annual expenditure of U.S. citizens abroad had been steadily increasing since 1922 when, returning to Europe, they spent $360 million; in the two decades prior to the war, annual expenditure had been $170 million.[32] In 1928 the 430,955 citizens who left the United States spent $860 million abroad. Those who went to Europe spent $525 million, or more than two and a half times what European countries paid to the United States in war debt that year.[33] Despite the economic depression, in 1931 U.S. citizens spent $570 million abroad. However, an English newspaper did note a perceived change in the spending patterns of the Depression-era tourist in Europe:

> The average American tourist this year, particularly the student and teacher type, is seeing Europe at the roc-bottom [*sic*] price. Many are taking their meals in tea-shops and chain restaurants. Even in the fashionable hotels and restaurants, the more affluent Yankees have shown such tightwad tendencies when tipping that the waiters have come to the conclusion that lavish spenders of American nationality are now extinct.[34]

It is not clear to what extent the French government would have noticed this, as U.S. citizens spent almost one-fifth of their money abroad in France, the $110 million equaling five times what the French government paid on its war debt in 1931.[35] Although travelers seemed to spend money abroad eagerly, the passport nuisance referred in part to anger at the need to pay visa fees for each European country, anger fueled through a campaign orchestrated by national business associations.

The passport nuisance was vociferously articulated in newspapers and magazines through complaints about the visas required to travel through the new Europe, which, as one businessman complained, had "been split into a number of small countries" subsequent to the war.[36] The rubber-stamp era became a nuisance when travelers realized they had to pay a $10 visa fee for every country they visited, both the old big ones and the new small ones. European states had increased visa fees for U.S. citizens in retaliation for the United States introducing a $10 visa fee in 1920. The same act also raised the cost of a U.S. passport to $10 from the nominal $1 fee that had been charged since 1888. The attempt to take money from citizens for a document historically considered a courtesy outraged many. In the midst of complaints about the $10 passport fee, one disgruntled citizen complained that, "considering what real protection I could buy from some mutual accident insurance company for that sum I would say that this charge seems to be... both exorbitant and unnecessary."[37] The cost was also challenged by citizens living abroad who, contrary to the wishes of the State Department, continued to use a passport to verify their citizenship. One newspaper calculated that because of the need to begin a passport renewal every eighteen months, it now cost citizens living abroad "2 cents every day, to afford the absolute necessity of an American Passport."[38] In both cases, it forced public recognition that a passport, with its popular association as a claim to official protection, was no longer issued primarily for the benefit of citizens, but had become a document of use by governments not only for security but also for revenue.

However, it was the new $10 visa fee that became a greater concern, because it had a more tangible effect—the retaliatory fee increases raised the cost of travel, especially for budget-conscious travelers in Europe. The $10 U.S. visa fee was arguably the result of a mixture of budgetary and security reasons. Senator Henry Cabot Lodge, the chair of the Senate Immigration Committee, stated simply that visas were required to produce revenue for government departments, but his opponents argued that the restrictionist senator saw the visa system as a way to indirectly limit immigration by making it too expensive to acquire the required visa.[39] However, in contrast to many other countries, which had separate visas for tourists and immigrants, the $10 fee applied to the only visa the State Department issued. Therefore, the fee increase affected not only immigrants, but also tourists traveling to the United States—hence the retaliation of European governments in the form of high visa fees for all U.S. travelers.

The new European visa fees particularly angered businessmen traveling abroad. The New York Merchants Association and the New York Board of Trade instigated a national campaign against the visa fee charged by the U.S. government, on the assumption that a decrease in the U.S. visa cost would result in a reciprocal decrease in the fees other countries charged.[40] Subsequently joined by other local and national merchant and trade organizations, the campaign directed its efforts at newspapers and magazines, the State Department, and congressmen.[41] It found allies within all these targets. The editorial pages of major newspapers offered strong criticism of the passport system, regularly summarizing the campaign's literature. While publicly stating that passport and visa fees were a matter for Congress, privately, State Department and Division of Passport Control officials remained sympathetic to the campaign's position, and occasionally forwarded supporting information to sympathetic congressmen.[42] These congressmen introduced bills to reduce visa and passport fees.[43]

The main argument businessmen had against the visa fee was that it lessened the competitiveness of U.S. businessmen in international trade. In this manner, they presented the businessman abroad as a commercial representative of the nation-state. Business organizations offered numerous comparisons in arguing that the cost of visas put their members at a disadvantage compared to foreign competitors. Individual European countries did not have uniform visa fees for all foreigners. For example, in 1921 a U.S. businessman who traveled from Germany to Czechoslovakia, Austria, and Hungry paid three hundred times more in visa fees than his English equivalent, and one thousand times more than a French businessman.[44] Endorsing one of the main complaints, a newspaper editorial argued that visa fees were "an irritating small check upon that international intercourse and trade which the United States is supposed to be so eager to promote"; or, as a letter writer supporting the editorial stated, the high fee for a U.S. visa was an "indictment of the common sense of those who seek to promote our foreign trade to the best of their ability."[45] In this way, the commercial campaign against visa costs tapped into the pervasive belief that the developing postwar prosperity depended on businessmen having a free reign both at home and abroad.

A second argument presented visa and passport fees as a form of taxation. Through this claim the disgruntled businessmen and merchants actively sought to link themselves to noncommercial travelers, their fellow citizens, on vacation in Europe, who also had to pay the $10 fee. As an example of the negative effect on vacationers, opponents regularly offered the $100 in visa fees U.S. citizens had to pay if they traveled from England to Turkey on the Orient Express.[46] These visa fees, along with the $10 a U.S. citizen paid for a passport, were both referred to as "passport fees," or submerged within complaints about "the passport business" and "passport nuisance"; the majority of letters to newspapers complaining about "passport fees" were in fact about visa fees. This slippage and the successful articulation of European visa fees as retaliatory allowed both sets of fees to be positioned as taxes that were the fault of the U.S. government. For one disgruntled citizen, the fees "put the nation itself in the class of grafters and extortioners [*sic*]."[47] In a 1921 internal memo, the State Department solicitor agreed. He labeled the passport fee "an extraordinary tax, which bears equally upon rich and poor and probably prevents many persons of small means, especially school teachers from traveling abroad."[48] However, publicly the State Department followed a strategy of merely agreeing that the passport system, while necessary, definitely "causes delays and inconveniences."[49] In reply to these public and private criticisms, Senator Lodge did not dispute the labeling of the fees as taxes. He positioned them, along with amusement taxes and the automobile tax, as luxury taxes on activities that were not necessities. For Lodge it was not a question of mobility but travel. While it could be argued that the former was part of a freedom of movement, the latter for him was indisputably an "unnecessary" leisure activity.[50]

In its rhetoric, the campaign against visa fees challenged the association of travel with leisure. Instead, travel was an educational activity to enhance citizenship. Named after the popular guide book, the introduction of so-called Cooks tourists traveling tourist third after 1924 gave complaints about the debilitating cost of visa fees wider currency. The vacation of a less well-off tourist was frequently presented as an unusual, once-in-a-lifetime event that provided the average person with important and necessary knowledge of the world. For such people who planned to travel on a package tour paying $250 or less, it was argued, every dollar had been carefully saved and precisely budgeted. Therefore, an additional $10 passport fee and $50 in visa fees could deny them their dream and its educational benefits.[51] A teacher, with an average salary of $1,500, provided the most potentially sympathetic example of this low-budget tourist. By traveling to benefit "her students," a teacher made explicit the link between the educational benefits of travel and the good of the nation.[52] Although in the mid-1920s the exact number of teachers who traveled abroad remained unknown, the attempt to link travel and education provided the anti–fee campaign with one of its first successes, albeit one that was of little use to businessmen. In 1926 Congress allowed teachers to renew their passports without an additional fee for an extra two-year period beyond the maximum two-year period of validity of the passports of other U.S. citizens; the passport fee remained $10, as did the fee for a U.S. visa.

For most citizens vacationing abroad, the "stupid system by which Americans pay $10 each for passport visas and everyone else pays 30 cents or nothing" continued, such that in 1929 a disgruntled traveler could still write that after he had paid a $100 fare to travel from New York to the United Kingdom, he had to pay $60 in visa fees to travel through Europe.[53] However, by the end of the decade, these fees had begun to drop after Congress gave the president the authority to negotiate reciprocal visa agreements with individual nation-states; thus after several unsuccessful attempts to reduce the visa fee through legislation, the campaign by business groups did see one important success in its attempts to reduce visa fees. Although Congress granted this authority in 1925, the initial agreements were with South American countries and smaller European countries, destinations less favored by the majority of U.S. travelers, business or otherwise; hence travelers still complained in 1929.[54] However, such complaints decreased after an agreement was finally reached with France in 1929, and largely disappeared after Great Britain agreed to reduce its visa fee for nonimmigrants in 1936. In both cases the cost was reduced to $2, the fee the League of Nations had suggested as an international standard.[55] The *New York Times* reported the French decision in a front-page story, which described it as "a development in international relations of considerable importance," especially for the "quarter of a million Americans who visit France annually."[56]

In 1930 national business associations turned their attention to the $10 passport fee and the two-year duration of validity of passports for all citizens except teachers. By the beginning of the 1930s, approximately half of all U.S. citizens going to Europe traveled "tourist third" at a cost of less than $100.[57] Opponents, therefore, continued to present the fee for the passport as a "war tax "and "class taxation." The representation of a passport as a wartime measure attempted to cultivate its contemporary image as a pointless document, "a bit of pasteboard stamped with a red seal," as one opponent put it.[58] A spokesman for the New York Board of Trade commented,

> It seems to take strenuous efforts to convince certain departments of our government that the World War has been over a long time. Although our military and naval branches of the government closed their part of the fight ten years ago the tax department is still functioning splendidly along old lines in many cases. The increased passport fee was a con-

> siderable source of revenue at a time when a national emergency existed, but the need has long since been removed.[59]

The passport fee and an additional $5 departure tax gave rise to the complaint that the middle-American third-class tourist paid an anachronistic and unfair 15% tax to travel abroad.[60] This was cast as "class taxation" in the argument that government departments should be funded from the general tax dollars of all citizens, not particular groups; a response to some State Department officials and members of Congress claiming that those citizens who tended to benefit from the Foreign Service should maintain it through passport and visa fees.

The anti–passport fee campaign was successful enough to cause Congress to hold hearings on the issue. However, comments from congressional participants indicated a healthy skepticism that the need to pay a $10 passport fee every two years had a significant negative impact on the ability of large businesses to function smoothly—the primary reason business groups gave to support their campaign to reduce fees. This caused opponents to place more emphasis on the time-consuming nature of passport and visa applications and requests. These concerns were not new, and had existed alongside complaints about fees from the beginnings of the 1920s. The "irritatingly complex" passport system was "expensive too as regards both time and money," with one traveler in the early 1920s estimating that "passport and visas cost $150 and the loss of approximately $1000 worth of time."[61] In 1924 a congressional opponent of the passport system claimed that many citizens in Europe spent "a fourth of their time in satisfying officials they were what they represented themselves to be and had no dangerous motives against the peace of Europe."[62] In a 1930 hearing before the House Committee on Foreign Affairs, representatives of business groups took up these concerns. They requested an extension of the validity of passports to six years from the "standpoint of economy of time and also very materially from the standpoint of convenience."[63] Business representatives outlined "the nuisance and annoyance which our people at the present time are suffering from": presentation of proof in person, photographs, and birth certificates.[64] The attempt to satisfy these demands could take at least three or four days, and in some instances delayed departure.[65] The fulfillment of these requirements not only cost businessmen valuable time, they also made clear the demand for documents and witnesses was considered disrespectful. As early as 1922, George Brist, chief of the Division of Passport Control, in a memo to the assistant secretary of state, had noted this as a significant source of public problems with the passport application process. He wrote that complaints originated "most often with men at the head of, or high up in some business organization. Among other associates their word is accepted and they feel that government officials should give their statements equal credit."[66]

As Brist's comment indicates, the passport nuisance originated in the perception of a required passport as a challenge not only to the wallet but also to accepted notions of respectability and privacy. The delicate nature of passport applications in a peacetime era of required documentation was an ongoing concern for government officials. A decade after Brist's memo, the secretary of state congratulated then–Passport Division chief Ruth Shipley for the manner in which the division dealt with the public:

> You have had charge of a division which touches the public in a very intimate manner. You have succeeded in maintaining with firmness the principles which underlie the treatment of the subjects with which you have been called upon to deal and, at the same time, applying those principles in a considerate and humane manner. You have made your division an important link in the relation of the Department to the public.[67]

While the secretary of state felt he could celebrate a passport official's considerate and humane manner, the passport nuisance of the previous decade was constituted by complaints that indicated that U.S. citizens felt not intimacy but anxiety as the State Department asked them questions about things they considered private, and then further demanded verification of their responses through documents. This had been a theme from the beginning of peacetime passport requirements. Introducing readers to the postwar world of passports, the pro–immigration restriction journalist Kenneth Roberts reported his frustration with the incessant desire of officials to seek answers "which would be about as valuable on the government records as information as to whether the applicant took two or three lumps of sugar in his coffee, and whether or not he cared for the later works of Henry James."[68] Roberts's frustration with the passport system and his support of immigration restriction show what constituted the "normal circumstances" he and other opponents of the passport longed to return to. Normality was a prewar world of mobility where it was "obvious" and "natural" which people officials could trust and which they had to be concerned about, and, therefore, a world where the lives of "naturally" respectable and trustworthy people were of no interest to the government.

The comments of Mary Greer, who worked at one of the regional passport agencies established in the 1920s, reiterate this implicit definition of a dominant and racialized respectability.[69] In a letter to the Division of Passport Control she expressed discomfort at subjecting "respectable" citizens to identification practices. More precisely, Greer made clear how awkward she found the need to get previously private information from trustworthy citizens in the very public space of the New York Passport Agency, where she worked. There, as in other locations where people applied for passports, applicants stood in a line waiting to be asked questions by a clerk who stood behind a counter. Greer informed the division that she had

> always considered the counter arrangement very bad. If it was possible for each applicant to sit at a desk with the agent who was taking his or her application, it would be so much better and so much more dignified than having to stand in line with the person next listening to every word that is said, or being jammed in with a nervous mother and a crying baby or a hot and unpleasant member of the Jewish race.[70]

These comments speak to a perceived need to accommodate the dignity of those "respectable" citizens recently introduced to official identification practices. Her complaints implicitly position this undisputed citizen as a white, Christian male whose status should not require exposure to such awkward situations. The passport became a nuisance when the requirements of identification documentation were "inappropriately" applied to these people, away from their historic focus on the unstable or marginal populations that governments not only needed to know, but who required their assistance: the untrustworthy (the eavesdropper and the Jew) and those who cannot look after themselves (the nervous mother and her child, and, doing double duty, the unhygienic Jew).

Roberts's and Greer's concerns usefully articulate the passport nuisance to, and through, the cultural conflicts of the 1920s. In this decade, white

Anglo-Saxon "old stock" Protestants struggled to maintain dominance in an "American" society in which their vision of a homogenous world of shared values, local control, and individual autonomy was thought to be under threat; the Red Scare and concerns with immigration restriction were a manifestation of the drive for conformity and homogeneity that many historians argue characterized the 1920s.[71] While at the border the passport played an important role in attempting to police perceived racial threats to national identity, internally the application for a U.S. passport brought out another aspect of the cultural and social uncertainty associated with the 1920s. In her survey of the decade, Lynn Dumenil argues, "The expansion of the corporate national economy eroded local ties and propagated bureaucracy, specialization, and routinization, helping to undermine the individual's sense of community and autonomy. Similarly, urban mass society underlined the individual's fragile status in an anonymous society and compounded a sense of fragmentation."[72] These changes illustrate both modernization and the emergence of modernity, an overused but still useful shorthand to foreground cultural and social responses to new modes of society and experience as rapid technological and social change altered the experience of everyday life—notably captured in Max Weber's arguments about rationalization and the Frankfurt School's analysis of an administered society.[73] The ad hoc development of official identification practices, beginning in the 1840s, offers important insights into the history of such challenges to an individual's sense of community and autonomy prior to the twentieth century. However, in the 1920s the more focused development of identification practices (including fingerprinting) made this more explicit, as the need to know the population was articulated to efforts to create an efficient, systematic, well-behaved, fair, and prosperous society.[74] Opponents of this attempt to "know" citizens through the collection of administrative facts were therefore able to link the extension of identification practices to broader social concerns about the increased power of the state, concerns that centered on questions of individual autonomy and identity.

Throughout the 1920s and into the early 1930s, many applicants were still shocked at the rigorous application of bureaucratic methods they encountered in applying for a passport. Their word, in the form of personal opinion, did not matter; they encountered a world where documents had to verify "facts." This impersonal mode of interaction in what was considered the personal matter of identity constituted much of the "nuisance" associated with the passport outside of the financial costs connected to the document; these interactions failed to recognize respectability. In 1930 an aggrieved son (and lawyer) informed the Passport Division that while his mother was attempting to get a passport, the clerk "was most discourteous and she felt as if he were treating her like a criminal endeavoring to get into the country by unfair means rather than as an American citizen merely asking the courtesy of her own Government."[75] This is an iteration of a frequently invoked framework for the passport nuisance—the association of identification practices with criminals—also seen in concerns over the passport photograph. Because these applicants did not consider themselves criminals, but rather respectable and trustworthy citizens, in forcing them to apply for a passport, and in this manner, their government had seemingly misidentified them as criminals. The demand for documentary proof of identity was a sign of mistrust and a lack of courtesy. Most citizens expected a passport application to be formal and a formality, and certainly not dependent on the forms that a bureaucratically inclined state now considered necessary. One example of this confusion occurred when a woman sought to extend a passport so she could return abroad for health reasons. Although she had been treated courteously on previous visits, this time, her husband wrote, the "treatment received was brusque and offensive, the official not only asking for and making her write and rewrite a detailed account of everything she had done in Europe for the last two years, but also demanding a certificate to prove her contention that she was taking the cure for her ailment."[76]

The requirement that applicants verify their identity through official documents presented practical difficulties that further accentuated the affront some people felt. This frequently arose from the demand that applicants who claimed citizenship through birth in the United States present specific documents to prove that "fact"; the State Department preferred a birth certificate as proof of citizenship. In a series of letters to the State Department in 1927, a resident of Philadelphia, Harvey M. Watts, argued against the "gross bureaucratic absurdity" that required birth certificates.[77] For Watts, the demand for documentary proof of birth was pointless, as in many cases the requirement could only be met through what he labeled "amiable minor perjuries" forced upon a state with limited memory and administrative reach. This was a reference to the alternative documents the State Department accepted in the absence of a birth certificate. Officials were instructed first to ask for a baptismal certificate. However, if the applicant's birth had been undocumented by either church or state, then the department required affidavits from individuals who it considered had to have witnessed the birth (mother, doctor, or midwife). If these individuals were unavailable, the State Department resorted to its prewar technique to verify facts through documents—an affidavit from a citizens known to the applicant whom the department deemed "respectable." In practice, Watts argued, this meant passport clerks "are all busily engaged in accepting any kind of statement" to prove citizenship. He explained to the secretary of state,

> I have been interested, as well as amused in the perfectly frank way in which American citizens cheerfully certify to each others births, wives for husbands, husbands for wives, brothers for sisters, wherein the older members of the families and doctors and all the neighbors have been gathered to their ancestors or moved to distant and inaccessible parts of the country.[78]

However, Watts did not retain his humor for long. He perceived an irritating inconsistency in the way clerks exercised discretion in passport applications. Clerks accepted documented statements verifying citizenship from people who had not witnessed births, but not undocumented statements from respectable citizens; he saw no merit in claims to the primacy of a documented statement over the oral statement of a person's word. Watts offered the example of an "absurd" incident that occurred when he accompanied a "distinguished citizen" to apply for a passport. Although his friend did not have a birth certificate Watts was prepared to verify his citizenship as were two other acquaintances who happened to be there by chance: the provost and vice provost of the University of Pennsylvania. The clerk refused to accept the validity of the statements of either Watts or these two "respectable" gentlemen, especially because the other proscribed alternatives to a birth certificate had not been explored. The applicant was instructed to obtain a sworn statement from his invalid mother that "she knew he was born." The ceding of authority to documents in the official definition of truth and reliability challenged what Watts saw as a more natural and proper understanding of "truth" as manifested in the appearance and status of individuals. He sought a return to what he called the "normal manner" of identification, in which an individual claiming citizenship through birth in the United States in the absence of a birth certificate should be trusted to verify his citizenship, personal identity, and his chosen witness. Before the war this form of identification was only the norm for native-born citizens not naturalized citizens; Watts claimed to have been informed that the postwar requirement for specific documents was in fact targeted at naturalized citizens. His letter made clear that naturalized citizens should indeed be expected to provide a naturalization certificate. Further, the citizens Watts wanted exempt from demands for documents were very particular native born citizens—"Americans who may have come over on the Mayflower and who are indubitably born."[79] The strong implication here was that appearance (a specific recognizable racial and cultural whiteness) would clearly verify the applicant as a distinguished citizen or what Watts labeled the "bona-fide citizen."[80]

In reply to Watts's letter to the secretary of state, the assistant secretary of state argued that documentary proof of citizenship was not "unduly burdensome," particularly as such requirements were necessary to "maintain the prestige of the American passport."[81] That is, such requirements ensured that State Department officials only issued passports to U.S. citizens. Although in his reply he admitted that this created occasions when "it seems superfluous for distinguished American citizens to be required to submit with their applications for passport, documents of [this] nature," this was necessary because minor officials could not be given the discretion to determine citizenship—the discretion that Watts had claimed to observe during his seemingly frequent visits to passport agencies.[82] This official response offers a useful reminder that evidence requirements policed all "local" practices of verification. Documentary requirements were not only used to enforce a specific definition of respectability that took control of the verification of their own identity from citizens, they were also intended to remove the subjective opinions of distant officials. The criteria of bureaucratic objectivity constituted a regime that, at least in theory, policed its own procedures. However, while an official based in Washington, D.C., could outline the documentary regime of verification in its ideal form, Watts's letters indicate that centralized and standardized attempts to produce a constant series of objective decisions did not always guarantee their realization in the actions of minor officials distant from the department.

The response to Watts's letter emphasized the centralizing practices that the State Department had introduced in an attempt to make the U.S. passport an authoritative statement of citizenship, a document that border officials could trust to be in the hands of the right person. A centralization and standardization of the application procedure defined that authority against localized practices of verification, the latter in, contrast, were seen as arbitrary and were therefore "illegible" to an efficient bureaucracy. A controversy over the treatment of a U.S. visa application from Albert Einstein provides a more public example of how the potential administrative reach of the documentary regime of verification could challenge the "local" privilege of social status and reputation in individual identification.

In 1932 Einstein's planned visit to the United States required an appointment with a U.S. consul. While all visitors or immigrants had to go through an interview, this was a first for Einstein; on his previous visits he had been an official representative of the German government and was therefore exempt from this requirement. In the interview the consular official asked Einstein about his relationship to communist organizations. These specific questions were in part a response to a sixteen-page letter the State Department had received from an organization called the Woman's Patriot Corporation that demanded that Einstein not be issued a visa because of his purported membership in communist organizations. The State Department had forwarded this information to Berlin in what it subsequently explained was standard practice so a consul could assess a visa applicant with all available information. Although the consular official determined the accusations to be false and issued Einstein a visa within twenty-four hours of the interview, the exposure of someone of his stature to the "intensive examination" used in the visa process generated dozens of newspaper articles and considerable correspondence to the State Department.[83] In part this was fueled by comments attributed to Einstein after the interview. Having avoided such an encounter in the past, he was described as reluctantly attending the meeting. According to one report, Einstein walked out when questions were raised about his political beliefs, allegedly asking the consul officials, "Gentlemen, are you trying to kid me?"[84] However, a day after the interview it was reported that little of the "clash was left in his mind, which is more accustomed to deal with infinite time and space" (not, it would appear, finite national spaces, and the restrictions on movement they increasingly produced).[85] Einstein later told reporters, "The trouble with hearings of that kind is that you don't realize until some time has passed just where the inquisitor is trying to get under your skin. I suggest in the future consuls put pins in their victims' chairs so they will feel stuck from the beginning."[86]

Newspaper editors, their readers, and letter writers to the State Department generally expressed surprise and regret that someone of Einstein's status had been exposed to such an "inquisition"—according to "Frau Einstein," the couple also received "a deluge of cables" that indicated "Americans of all classes were deeply disturbed over the case."[87] Letters to the State Department were generally critical of the decision to interview Einstein, labeling it "humiliating" and "absurd," and expressing concern that it had made the United States a "laughing stock" around the world. The letters were also critical of the Woman's Patriot Corporation. Numerous other organizations passed resolutions that condemned this group, as well as the State Department's implicit support of it. These organizations included several posts of the American Legion, the United States Veterans Association, Quaker groups, and the Detroit Philosophical Society.[88] The concern over the reputation of the United States was consistent with the belief that Einstein's reputation should have been privileged in this situation. The State Department's standard reply stressed that it had to treat all aliens equally as the law dictated, insisted that Einstein had been treated with "utmost courtesy and consideration," and noted that he had been issued the visa because the consul determined the accusations against him were false. The State Department did not send replies to letters it considered too rude.[89]

The public response indicated that the documentation of identity was still considered secondary to a culture of respectability; if documents were to exist, then prominent people should obtain them without inconvenience and intrusion into their private lives. But the simultaneous acknowledgment that under similar circumstances another person with Einstein's political views might have been denied a visa gently questioned the biases still inherent in the supposedly objective use of documents.[90] However, the attempt to deny Einstein the privilege of his status made explicit that the increasing authority state officials located in the documentary regime of verification had unsettled such undocumented claims to privilege.

The nature of the mistrust applicants could perceive in a passport application is captured in Einstein's characterization of it as an "inquisition." This was a common way for disgruntled citizens to describe the passport application. A letter to the *New York Times* in 1927 headed "The Passport Inquisition" detailed the frustration of such applicants. The writer concluded his letter by stating that "the preliminary modus operandi exacted in applying for passports is today more complicated than ever and one cannot help wondering what reason, if there is any reason, can be back of such silly questions and what their relation to the granting of a passport can possibly be."[91] For some, the answer to such a question was clear—"so long government has meant the browbeating of citizens by the bureaucracy that the purpose of issuing passports to facilitate the needs of the citizen has been lost sight of."[92] From this perspective the government's obsession with bureaucratic procedures generated the mistrust that caused the excess of documents and questions that showed a lack of respect and inappropriate interest into what many considered was a citizen's private life. As noted, in pejoratively using the label "bureaucratic," critics of the passport nuisance sought to tap into this anxiety about lost community and personal autonomy in a rationalized, fragmented, and "modern" society. For critics of state intrusion (but not increased corporate influence) the "b-word" became shorthand for "images of a pervasive and pernicious federal presence that strangled local and individual initiative."[93] Senator William Borah, one of the fiercest critics, argued against "the remorseless urge of centralization" through which the "average citizen becomes the victim of bureaucratic interference—tortured with its persistent leering upon the affairs of his daily life and burdened and exploited by its chronic inefficiency and habitual waste."[94]

Although State Department officials were sensitive to the fact the Passport Division "touches the public in a very intimate manner,"[95] the demand for personal information inherent in the creation of an identification document could easily be turned into a negative critique of the role of the twentieth-century state. When this occurred, the "public" victim of the passport nuisance tended to be a woman. Although, as previous examples indicate, it was the letter of a man that usually made her frustrations known. The use of a woman's experience to expose particular apprehensions regarding the passport acknowledges the complex articulation of anxieties and concerns wrought through the contemporary perception of rapid social and cultural change in the decade following the end of the war. That the rationalism, scientific standards, and objectivity through which some of this change was articulated were in opposition to dominant stereotypes of women (emotional, subjective, irrational, and personal) created one possible context in which it might be assumed that women would experience difficulties negotiating the bureaucratized passport application.[96] However, the regular appearance of women in complaints implicitly illustrated one consequence of the new bureaucratic state; it modeled a new relationship between citizen and state, albeit not what the secretary of state meant when noting that the Passport Division had become "an important link in the relation of the Department to the public."[97] The vulnerability of citizens (represented by women) to the "maw of bureaucracy" lent itself to an implicit critique of the transformation of the passport from a document primarily intended to protect the individual to one that offered the state protection from individuals. Although never explicitly expressed as such, the loss of the protective role of the passport for the individual was in contrast to the men who wrote letters on behalf of annoyed women. As one indignant man complained, "We have a right to apply to the State Department of our own government for aid in such matter and we have a right to know that our wives can go there for aid that is their right without being exposed to insult."[98] In correspondence such as this, men in their role as husband, father, or son exhibited the benevolent, paternal, pastoral protection the state had historically been perceived to offer its citizens through the letter of the passport. However, instead of watching over its citizens, the passport application illustrated for many of these citizens a particular form of the modern nation-state's surveillance of its citizens; a detached accumulation of knowledge, which turned citizens into objects of inquiry.

The passport application as a somewhat public investigation of people was apparent in the counter interview that so angered Mary Greer. The interview at the counter turned the application into a visible and audible public performance of an interaction between state and citizen. The comments of another passport agency official provide a useful example of the perceived unnecessary and awkward nature of this interview, but in a way that genders the issues of respectability and privacy Greer raised. In 1926 the *New York Telegram* published an interview with Beulah Baer, a long-term passport-agency employee, the occasion being the first trip abroad for a woman who had helped so many others travel (figure 11.1). In soliciting Baer's opinions on her job, the article offers an example of how the request for an individual's age annoyed many female applicants, a request that seems to indicate the regular absence of the birth certificate in applications, or its exclusive role as evidence of citizenship, not personal identity. Baer acknowledged that women reluctantly give their age, informing the clerk only because they are impressed with the "seriousness of dealing with the federal government." She clarified that "we do not accept the 'over twenty-one' reply. I think it would be a gracious thing to do, though, because youth is one the greatest of feminine assets, and being as young as we look, it would be less embarrassing for sensitive women not to be compelled to record the difference between appearance and fact."[99] Of course, the emergence of demands for documentary verification, as well as the importance of the accurate identification of an individual, depended on eliminating any difference between appearance and fact. But Baer endorses a practice where the very purpose of identification practices as technologies of verification (to produce an "accurate" connection between appearance and fact) could be negated. This suggests that even in official circles, albeit at the margins occupied by minor officials, there existed a lingering contention that the passport should function less as a document to clarify any doubts as to an individual's identity, and more as a courtesy to allow an individual to travel unhindered.

Baer noted that while women gave their age, many "shade it by a few years," and some women "might whisper their age."[100] The tendency to "whisper" information to a clerk brings into relief the negotiation of public and private that occurred in passport applications. The seriousness of interacting with the federal government did not mitigate a concern with someone else needing to know a fact. The tactic of whispering one's age apparently worked to create a

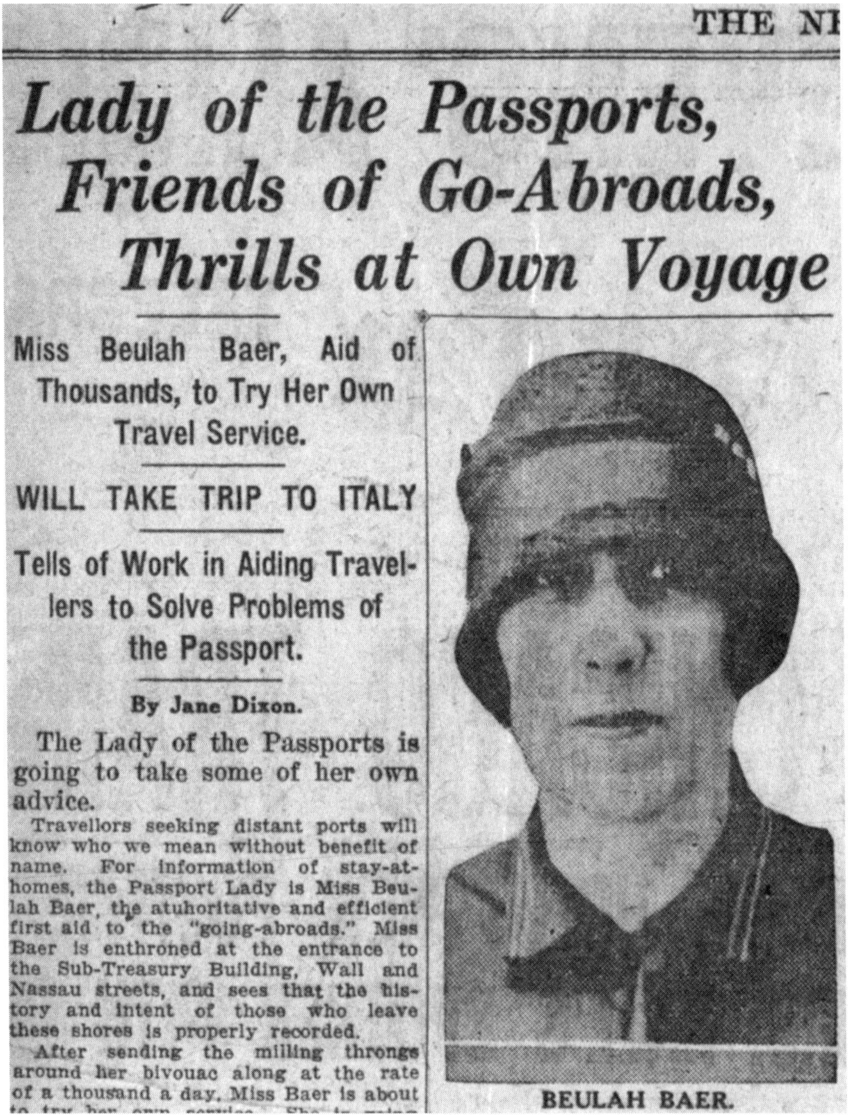

THE N

Lady of the Passports, Friends of Go-Abroads, Thrills at Own Voyage

Miss Beulah Baer, Aid of Thousands, to Try Her Own Travel Service.

WILL TAKE TRIP TO ITALY

Tells of Work in Aiding Travellers to Solve Problems of the Passport.

By Jane Dixon.

The Lady of the Passports is going to take some of her own advice.

Travellors seeking distant ports will know who we mean without benefit of name. For information of stay-at-homes, the Passport Lady is Miss Beulah Baer, the atuhoritative and efficient first aid to the "going-abroads." Miss Baer is enthroned at the entrance to the Sub-Treasury Building, Wall and Nassau streets, and sees that the history and intent of those who leave these shores is properly recorded.

After sending the milling throngs around her bivouac along at the rate of a thousand a day, Miss Baer is about

BEULAH BAER.

Figure 11.1. Newspaper article on New York Passport Agency employee Beulah Baer (National Archives)

space for the applicant that would hopefully be kept private from the strangers in line behind her. However, this private space was created in order to pass on facts that would subsequently appear on a document intended to publicly distribute this information to strangers, albeit "official strangers." To whisper one's age, therefore, functioned as a performance of the uncertainty associated with the passport nuisance: What right did the state have to "intimately" know its citizens? What would happen to such information?

The articulation of age and privacy in the context of these questions appeared again in a series of letters to the *New York Times* in 1934. The letters responded to the suggestion of a "well known authority on travel" that birth dates be excluded from passports on the grounds that age is a personal matter, especially for women, and of no value to the identification of a citizen. For one letter writer (obviously well-traveled both as a child and adult), the inclusion of her age on her passport had been a "life-long source of embarrassment and annoyance."[101] For another woman, it appeared to provide no assistance in "the one thing a passport does... identify the bearer," a possible deference to the equally unflattering passport photograph as the only necessary source of identity.[102] "Forty Plus" argued that

> when one is obviously not an escaped babe from the cradle, what possible difference can one's age make to the law and order of any country? After dropping ten years off of life by an ocean crossing, why must we be rudely reminded? It is bad enough having to carry about with you a little book with the history of your unromantic name and place of birth, not to mention color of eyes, but why that 'when born'?"[103]

However, for one (male) correspondent, the answer to that question was obvious: "the age line on passports facilitates identification" by giving a more precise description of the bearer than a general category like "adult."[104]

By the mid-1930s, the passport nuisance had largely dissipated. Letters to the State Department about the application process were increasingly rare, as were mentions of the passport nuisance in newspapers and magazines. However, the appearance of a debate over age on passports in 1934 indicates that, while not the nuisance it once was, the nature and function of a passport remained unclear, if not unacceptable to some. It was still not accepted that the verification of identity demanded precision in the form of a specific age, not a general category. The disappearance of the passport nuisance did not signal universal acceptance of identification or an understanding of what identification entailed. The less-vocal opposition to the passport seemed to result from the decreasing annoyance people experienced with the application. This change in attitude points toward one possible explanation for the demise of the passport nuisance—if official identification is understood as a skill to be learned by officials and the public, then when people became literate in the practice of documentation, passport applications became less of a nuisance. In a 1928 letter praising a passport official, a company vice-president commented that, "as you are undoubtedly aware, the obtaining of a passport for the *first* time is to the average layman, a somewhat complicated matter... not withstanding the fact [the instructions] are all printed on your form."[105] While officials saw a standardized application as efficient, many members of the public initially encountered it as foreign and unproductive. However, by the 1930s the need to use such forms had rapidly become more pervasive, and "first times" were increasingly a thing of the past. People were becoming subjects of a documentary regime, as documents begat documents—for regular travelers, a passport application had become the simpler task of a renewal, and new applicants were increasingly likely to have a birth certificate or other supporting documents. Thus the disappearance of the anxiety over the demand for documents appears to possibly be a consequence of the fact people had quickly become accustomed to the documentation of individual identity and the general paperization of everyday life. As standardized forms and identification documents (drivers' licenses and social security numbers) became more common, for many people, complying with the request for official identification, and thus with the act of compiling identity through documents, became more of a reflex.

While tracing the passport nuisance in the 1920s and 1930s is a useful way to understand the extension of practices of documentary identification, it is difficult to read this development as a failed opportunity for the power of a centralized and intrusive state to have been seriously challenged. Rather, the passport nuisance, as an almost exclusively 1920s phenomenon, provides a moment from which to try and understand the somewhat rapid acceptance of an enveloping bureaucratic state. Therefore, it can be seen to illustrate irritations that existed within an acceptance of a particular form of rule, but not something that offered strategies to challenge state authority. In this sense, coming to terms with the passport fits within sociologist Anthony Giddens's description of the "bargain with modernity" that individuals make through the nation-state. This is a bargain "governed by specific admixtures of deference and scepticism, comfort and fear."[106] The passport as a document that verified citizenship brought with it the assumed advantages of that legal identity: to enter the United States and to claim the other rights associated with being a certified loyal citizen. However, a passport also carried with it the recognition that the state could depersonalize that relationship as it reduced citizenship to an administrative fact that could only be verified through documents. That the passport was contested through the 1920s illustrates some people did not accept its representation of themselves and the state.

The complicated specifics of the acceptance of the official documentation of identity, and the emergence of official identification in general, is evident in a comparison with the failed campaign for universal fingerprinting that occurred contemporaneously with the demise of the passport nuisance. Both were articulated as modern forms of identification; indeed, for the *New York Times*, which advocated for fingerprinting but was critical of required passports, a "fingerprint was the cheapest kind of passport."[107] However, although originating in a similar set of concerns about making identification more reliable, critical differences emerged in public and official understandings of identification documents and fingerprints. These differences ultimately demarcated the passport as an identification technology with purposes and functions distinct from that of fingerprinting, and hence suggest reasons for its acceptance.

While the call for universal fingerprinting in the United States can be traced back to 1911, such appeals did not take on the form of a campaign until the mid-1920s.[108] At that time, concerns about anarchists and Bolsheviks and the enthusiasm of the newly appointed head of the Bureau of Investigation, J. Edgar Hoover, saw the launch of a two-decades-long crusade that garnered the support of numerous public officials, newspapers, and magazines. President Warren Harding gave his fingerprints in 1921, and throughout the interwar period, various federal departments and agencies, and some private employers, began to fingerprint job applicants.[109] In 1935 John Rockefeller headed a group of prominent businessmen who had their fingerprints taken as the New York police launched a campaign for city residents to voluntarily give their prints; the *New York Times* printed daily totals in the initial weeks of the effort.[110] In 1936 city officials of Berkeley, California, organized an intensive campaign, involving community organizations and businesses, to fingerprint the entire city population.[111] On a smaller scale, advocates introduced the "Thumb-o-graph" and other similar albums to "domesticate" fingerprinting alongside photographs as a way to visually remember friends and family, particularly in their "absence." Though the difficulties fingerprint advocates encountered is captured in the headline—"Rogues Gallery in Every Home"—for a newspaper article about the plan for fingerprint albums. [112] Although universal fingerprinting did not occur, in 1938 the FBI publicly recognized the one millionth person to give fingerprints—a twelve-year-old boy.[113] It cannot have been a coincidence that the FBI bestowed the "honor" on a young boy. The kidnapped child had long been one of the key figures in the argument for universal fingerprinting. After the publicity surrounding the kidnapping of Charles Lindbergh's infant son in 1932, this figure surpassed the amnesiac and the unidentified dead body to become the literal "poster child" in the campaign for universal fingerprinting.

The figures of the kidnapped child, the unidentified dead body, and the amnesiac were invoked to play on the fear of being a stranger that proponents argued the preemptive act of fingerprinting would prevent.[114] In this argument, the possibility of becoming a "stranger" had been increased through the enhanced mobility of modern life, which purportedly took individuals away from small communities and into large cities where people could easily be strangers even in their everyday life. Within the new modern form of anonymous community epitomized by the large city the state needed to have the right and the ability to know its population in order to provide the comfort of familiarity in a developing mass culture. Supporters of a fingerprint-based identification system also argued it would protect honest citizens on vacation or business trips, and even their commercial transactions at home in the city—in fact, one of the earliest attempts to extend fingerprinting to noncriminals involved advocates convincing some banks to use thumbprints in identifications.[115]

Through actions such as these, supporters presented fingerprinting in a discourse of safety both to counter its association with the identification of criminals and to assuage concerns that universal fingerprinting constituted an attempt to institute a comprehensive system of state surveillance.[116] To convince the public that state officials collected fingerprints not out of suspicion but to assist individuals, various officials assured people that their fingerprints would be stored in a separate collection from criminal prints; they would be consulted only when individuals were in situations where they could not identify themselves. The FBI presented the proposed collection of fingerprints as a "depository of protection."[117] Protection and safety became the official rationale for the renegotiation of the public and the private in the form of attempts at the more pervasive collection of information about individuals. The entry on "identification" in the U.S.-published 1932 *Encyclopaedia of the Social Sciences* authorized this discursive move, linking official identification, as a practice within "the growth of modern science," to its development as an "important means of safe-guarding civil rights."[118] The author of the entry offered a list to justify the potential value of identification techniques in "civil life," beginning with the use of passports "containing personal descriptions and photographs" and ending with the frequent footprinting of babies at maternity hospitals. However, he concluded the entry by recognizing that this potential remained largely untapped because of the deep-rooted association between identification practices and the identification of criminals. These practices produced the image of the criminal as an object of inquiry in the public mind, a person whose behavior exhibited dishonesty and a distrust of authority that needed to be investigated; only when those conditions were present did the majority of U.S. citizens believe the state had a right to collect information on individuals.

The association between criminals and fingerprints was even stronger than that between criminals and identification documents. The State Department refused to use fingerprints in passport applications or on the document itself on the grounds that "it is quite certain that the majority of the applicants would look upon this requirement as a hardship and a humiliation."[119] While in its use of supporting documents, the State Department subscribed to the idea of objective reliability associated with the perceived authority of modern practices of identification, in its rejection of fingerprints, the department did not let such claims to accuracy trump the social identities of passport applicants. In the case of fingerprinting, reliability was reevaluated within a web of cultural practices and processes; beyond its association with criminals, the overt use of the body hindered the broader use of fingerprinting as an identification technology. The fact that the body was culturally off-limits produced a greater practical need for, and faith in, the "fact" that identities remain stable, and documents can "verify" that identity. In this context, the department preferred the scientifically less "reliable" but more acceptable combination of the photograph, description, and signature to establish a relationship between the passport and the correct bearer. While in other contexts passport fraud remained an ongoing concern for the State Department, in the correspondence over fingerprinting, officials downplayed the threat of fraud to national security. The Passport Division claimed there was fraud in less than 1% of passports, and, therefore, any excessive attempts to decrease fraud could not be prioritized over the efficient issuance of passports to the majority of citizens who applied in good faith.[120] The rejection of fingerprinting was grounded in the belief that by the mid-1930s, respectable people were no longer appalled by the requirements of passport applications; as noted such demands had ceased to be a hardship, and had become a regular occurrence in the navigation of everyday practices in "modern" society. In comparison fingerprinting remained an irregular occurrence and an exceptional practice.

As the documentary verification of identity became a pervasive practice, and therefore, paradoxically, it was seen less in terms of surveillance. When "average" Americans encountered initial piecemeal forms of state observation such as passport requirements in the early decades of the twentieth century, these were novel and alien. They were comprehended in two ways that linked them to a changing understanding of surveillance: Firstly, identification practices retained the historical associations of intermittent state observation—a marginalization generally invoked rhetorically through images of the criminal or the insane. Secondly, with this as the dominant understanding of the function and role of surveillance, demands for documents in their lives seemed to cause the "better classes" to assume that surveillance had become pervasive through society. The previous absence of state "inquisitions" in their lives in the United States led many citizens to understand the need for passports as evidence of a new form of continuous surveillance orchestrated by a pervasive bureaucratic state. This fueled some of the anxiety over the passport. However, the difficulty of enforcing evidence requirements for the U.S. passport indicates that administrative surveillance remained at best intermittent. It would very quickly become more consistent over the following decades, such that by the end of the 1930s, the need to prove individual identity to a variety of officials and institutions had become a common occurrence.[121] However, by that time knowledge and the skills of how to negotiate modernity in the form of the documentary mediation of people and the world had been acquired, and the giving of information previously considered personal to official strangers had lost much of its annoyingness. Thus the use of documents to mediate interactions with the state and other institutions provoked a decreasing amount of frustration and lessened its association with surveillance. In contrast, fingerprinting remained an occasional and visceral act popularly perceived as surveillance. Therefore, as articles continued for and against universal fingerprinting in the 1930s and the 1940s, the passport nuisance disappeared from the pages of the country's newspapers and magazines.

Conclusion

We have now reached what critic Dieter Hoffmann-Axthelm calls the "paradigmatic scene...of the modern era...the immigration officer examining a passport."[1] It took almost a century for this moment to coalesce into a typical occurrence, but by the end of the 1930s the authority of the passport to identify an individual was, if not universally accepted, at least decreasingly challenged. Based on its history in the United States, immigration officials had come to accept a passport as evidence of identity. Members of the public had seemingly come to tolerate both the general demand for identification, and the passport in particular, as a representation of their identity. This implicitly brought with it the expectation that a person should have an identity that a modern state could recognize, know, and demand to "see." The passport as a seemingly inevitable response to these demands came to represent the naturalization of this state of affairs.

The passport arrived at this paradigmatic moment only after negotiation over its status as proof of identity, and, of the identity the state had come to deem necessary. The arrival of the passport in its modern form critically involved the acceptance of the larger assumption that identity could be documented. The now-apparent naturalness of the passport occurred through a collapsing of identity into identification. However, in questioning this inevitability, the preceding history of the passport is premised on a rejection of the collapsing of identity and identification. To separate identity and identification is to see how the documentation of individual identity depended on a rethinking of identity as the object of identification, and a general acceptance of this new way of thinking about identity. Aspects of the passport nuisance and its scattered forerunners in the nineteenth century indicate a struggle to fully grasp this new relationship between identity and identification. The passport has a history as an identification document precisely because of this struggle to comprehend and accept that identity could be documented. Somewhat anecdotal evidence of the 1930s being the point at which documentation became more pervasive and acceptable can be seen in the Oxford English Dictionary's definition of identification through identity documents; all the examples provided for this usage are dated after 1940.[2]

The need to think critically about the under examined relationship between identity and identification is increasingly urgent, as this unexamined identity has been at the center of contemporary concerns about security and the much-touted solution to these concerns—digital surveillance in the form of biometrics. This identity is not self-awareness or self-knowledge on the part of a person, but identity as an object produced through the investigations of an institution such as the modern nation-state. While today, outside of the so-called "war on terror," the surveillance practices of governments and corporations are frequently ignored or accepted in the name of convenience, their novelty around the turn of the twentieth century made them all too visible and seemingly excessive, particularly for those people not previously exposed to demands to prove their identity. The necessity for travelers to carry a passport made some individuals aware that not only did the government "know" who they were, but also made them conscious of the techniques through which they were known. The demand for standardized forms verified by authorized officials marked for some people an abrupt change from a personal mode of trust to an impersonal mode of trust in official identification. In this manner individuals encountered the rethinking of identification as a problem of record keeping—specifically, the collection, classification, and circulation of information. This archival problematization of identity came to determine the way identity was officially conceived; it provided the parameters within which problems were now understood and solutions offered in a variety of situations. Bertillonage, which emerged from an increasingly bureaucratized and professional French police force in the last quarter of the nineteenth century, embodied the archival elements that would gradually define accurate practices of identification through techniques of cataloguing and retrieval. In the United States, it was not until the first decades of the following century that official identification practices began to be explicitly used to construct a "memory" for the state, albeit in an environment less centralized and possibly less prone to trust the centralization of authority than in France. However, by the 1920s the federal government's need to remember an individual in anticipation of future interactions required the application of archival logics to identification; at that historical moment, documentary technologies and practices came to be seen as a necessity.

As in our current moment, national security concerns brought attention to identification practices. State officials became interested only in those aspects of personal identity that were useful to them. Modern practices of identification such as the passport and fingerprints were useful precisely because they "simplified" identity to only that information necessary for the state, and thus it was thought that accurate identification would be easier to achieve. In this understanding, identity had become something that could be duplicated and filed, and, therefore, potentially more rigorously verified. While these somewhat novel identification technologies produced the stable identity necessary for any ongoing official identification, they did not simply identify people. As this history has shown, these technologies produced a new identity, something made all too explicit to those citizens who felt as if they had become dehumanized objects of inquiry for their government.

The perception by individuals that they were objects of inquiry acknowledges a disconnect between their sense of self and their official recognition, and, therefore, is a recognition of identification as the production of a new identity. In this sense, identification is usefully thought of, and critiqued, as a practice of verification; identification is an act of comparison between a person and his or her official representation. As a technology of verification, the passport performs the function of collapsing reality into representation; it naturalizes the assumption that identity can be documented, as well as the presentation of the passport as an accurate representation of a preexisting identity. The passport did this within a documentary regime of verification.

As an analytical concept, a regime of verification includes the specific ways in which individual identity is defined, the evidence needed to verify that identity, and the authorities who could ultimately determine an individual's (official) identity. Through practices of exclusion, a regime of verification renders a personal and legal identity that is useful to the state. From the second half of the nineteenth century, identification was organized and mediated through documents. These were practices of exclusion in that they legitimated and represented a centralized authority over more local practices. Thinking about the passport within a "regime" locates part of the history of identification documents as a story of how officials and applicants ascertained what sort of ability or what level of knowledge constituted mastery of documentary identification. Fluency had to develop in terms of what constituted an acceptable source and form of evidence. Officials also had to learn how to read identification documents, to recognize in the document both its authenticity and that of the person offering it. Critically, the successful documentary identification of an individual depended on recognition of when and how an identification document depended on an individual's opinion. The reliable documentation of individual identity needed both a stable identity and a clearly defined identity category. While citizenship was increasingly verified through the linkage of documents, as a legal category it was not always so fluently expressed. Nineteenth-century debates over expatriation, the ongoing contested racial underpinnings of citizenship, and changes to the citizenship status of women in the 1920s all revealed dubious citizens. While debates about whiteness and gender caused a rethinking of the definition of citizenship, new definitions of citizenship were also made practicable through the demand that citizenship be verified through documents. In some cases, the application of passport regulations worked to "fix" a problematic aspect of citizenship. In other situations, the passport revealed arguments that challenged how the federal government used citizenship to manage difference.

In contrast to the racialized othering that concerned much of the emergence of the modern documentation of individual identity, the intensified articulation of the need to know someone in the contemporary world occurs within the logics of taste cultures and lifestyle clusters. In the twenty-first century, personal information is entwined in the broader technological transformation of information production. Concerns about identity have become critical to corporations and consumers, as well as corporations and their products. With information a key commodity, the principles of scientific management are now applied to consumption as well as production. A surveillance-based rationalization of consumption has become crucial to advertising and marketing. Individuals, identified as consumers, have increasingly become subject to information collection and identity verification. Loyalty cards and barcodes have resulted in the tracking of products that consumers take home with them, and "cookies" on web browsers automate the collection of personal information to provide data for market research.[3]

While it is important to note this move away from the state as the primary vendor of the collection and verification of individual identity, the problem of identification continues to be thought of as one of objective information. Within the archival problematization of identity, digital practices of verification are now considered a necessary response to the new increased scale of identity demands. This current response is an updated version of the early twentieth-century development of identification into a practice of record keeping. While the novelty of the filing cabinet has long worn off, the contemporary fetishization of the "database" is the filing cabinet expanded to the new scale of contemporary identification practices. The archival problematization of identity defined objectivity as critical to the accurate verification of individual identity. Digital verification has moved the claimed authority of identification closer to that of a "mechanical objectivity," if not a scientific objectivity, as proponents claim that the assessment of individuals is less necessary.[4] This has been achieved as new technologies have been employed to offer a new set of relationships between the body, the archive, and the document.

The so-called "smart cards" of digital identification have the potential to communicate directly with archives in the form of information networks. Such a card, if it works as claimed, would effectively carry the archive in it, rather than point officials in the direction of an absent set of files stored in a faraway government facility, eliminating the need for humans to read documents. The REAL ID Act of 2005, which mandated improved security for drivers' licenses and personal identity cards, also required that digital copies be made of supporting documents such as birth certificates. This digitization renders identity and documents more open to reproduction, distribution, and analysis—elements critical to accuracy as it is defined within the archival problematization of identity as information. The need for more efficient distribution and exchange of identity information has become critical to the increased circulation of information, goods, and people.

Of equal importance is the way in which digital technologies have enabled authorities to use the body in noncriminal identification practices. Historically, the spectacle of using the body remained fixed within the domain of criminal identification and the identification of other marginal populations. However, biometric technology has begun to make the body a more culturally acceptable site for accurate identification. The introduction of digital fingerprinting for all noncitizens entering the United States was championed in just this manner. After its introduction in early 2004, officials proclaimed it a success in that "no one seemed to mind at all."[5] The contrast with the indignity of ink fingerprinting was made apparent when the government of Brazil, which did seem to mind, introduced nondigital fingerprinting for U.S.

citizens in retaliation. Several U.S. citizens were arrested for refusing to comply; in one notable example, an American Airlines pilot "offered" his middle finger to the surveillance camera, not the official inkpad.[6]

Significantly, the introduction of stricter identification via passports and visas did not challenge the assumption that identity can be accurately documented; rather, it produced concerns about the particular way in which it was done. Similar concerns greeted post-9/11 documentation changes that affected U.S. citizens. The nature of the response to these changes is in distinct contrast to the passport nuisance of the 1920s. These differences attest to the acceptance of the documentation of individual identity as a modern necessity, and to the naturalization of the claim that identity can be documented. The extension of passport requirements for U.S. citizens flying home from Mexico, Canada, and the Caribbean in 2007 was presented as an inconvenience, especially when inadequate staffing in the State Department resulted in long delays in issuing passports. Recent unsuccessful attempts by some U.S. states to require voters to present photo identification, along with the less publicized introduction of documentary proof of citizenship for Medicaid recipients, has also led to debates over identification documents. However, opponents of these latter two measures argue that, intentionally or not, these demands discriminate against those who for a variety of reasons do not have the documents or supporting documents necessary to prove their citizenship.[7] Therefore, the campaigns against these changes target the assumption that everyone has documents to prove their identity or status; they do not challenge the authority of documents to prove that identity. In contrast, earlier concerns with identification documents included complaints beyond a mere frustration with bureaucracy and the problems associated with the practice of documentation. The passport nuisance encompassed a questioning of whether identity could be documented, and what identity was documented.

The commonplace need to carry and present identification documents has made the practice of translating individual identity into a document seem somewhat mundane. While the mundane can be annoying, it is outside of most people's concerns whether identity can in fact be successfully documented, or indeed what identity is represented in a document. In our contemporary world, there is general acceptance that identity can be documented, that someone can be known and recognized through a document. However, this book has shown that his "fact," along with the acceptance of the right of a government to know and recognize people through documents and files is less than a hundred years old—a "fact" that came into existence through a contested history of more than fifty years in the United States. The questionable notion that a single sheet of paper twelve inches by eighteen inches, even one labeled a passport, could identify someone is in part what the thwarted journey of the clean-shaven Dane with which this book began speaks to. As the Dane's story reveals, the presentation of a passport created a situation where one could in fact not resemble oneself. It makes apparent that the passport, in the name of the facts collected in a document, actually produced a distinct, if not new, identity. The unease felt by some passport bearers stemmed from the perception that when an official looked at a passport, it was not to establish whether it was an accurate representation of the person presenting it. Rather, the people presenting a passport had to convince the official that they were the document, or more precisely they were the bearers of the identity that the practices of documentation produced. Although in the story of the Dane, this anxiety is represented as a question of physical disconnect, this unease also existed as a concern about the disparity between a personal sense of individuality and identity, and the passport as a collection of "unromantic" facts.[8]

The contested development of the passport shows how concerns about documenting identity reflected debates and doubts about class, race, gender, and national identity from the 1840s to the 1930s. More importantly, it illustrates how this contested ability to document identity has been collapsed into a truth claim. To give the passport a history as an identification document is to argue that this form of identification and the "official identity" it produced in the name of the modern nation-state is not self-evident in either its history or its function.

Appendix
Important Dates in the History of the Regular United States Passport

1782 The Continental Congress gives the Department of Foreign Affairs the responsibility of issuing passports in the name of the United States.

1790 Congress passes a law that provides punishment for the violation of any "safe-conduct or passport duly obtained and issued under the authority of the United States" (1 Stat. 118, sec. 28, Rev Stat. 4602).

1811 First known passport issued by the State Department in Washington to include a description of the bearer. It is presented in paragraph form with blanks after each of the descriptive categories.

1810s A small representation of the U.S. coat of arms becomes the first ornamentation to appear on passports issued in the United States.

1818 The production of all credentials and certificates, including passports, is made the responsibility of a junior clerk. Fewer than one hundred passports are issued annually.

1820s The physical description of the bearer is presented as a list of features on the left side of the passport.

1833 The State Department is restructured according to a series of bureaus. The Translating and Miscellaneous Bureau becomes responsible for issuing passports. Approximately one thousand passports are issued annually.

1835 In *Urtetiqui v. D'Arcy* (34 U.S. [9 Pet.] 692), the Supreme Court rules that a passport only provides prima facie evidence of citizenship.

1838 Responsibility for issuing passports is transferred to the Home Bureau of the State Department.

1845 The State Department issues the first known circular regarding the passport application process.

1846 A second circular clarifies the specific documents a passport applicant has to submit as evidence of personal identity and citizenship.

1847 In an attempt to standardize passport policy, the Secretary of State notes that free African Americans are issued a special certificate, not a regular passport.

1856 Congress passes the first law that clarifies passport policy, specifying that passports can only be issued to citizens and giving the secretary of state the sole authority to issue passports. It also introduces the first passport fee: $1 for passports issued abroad (11 Stat. 60, sec. 23, Rev. Stat. 4075).

1861 From August, the departure and entry of persons at U.S. seaports is subject to a series of regulations that require the presentation of passports. This is a result of the outbreak of the Civil War.
In August a new State Department policy requires applicants to submit additional proof of citizenship in the form of an oath of allegiance. (This remains in force until 1973.)

1862 A passport fee of $3 is introduced (12 Stat. 432, 472).

1863 In March part of the 1856 act is repealed so the State Department can issue passports to noncitizens who are eligible for military service but are leaving the country having paid a bond (12 Stat. 754).

1864 Passport fee increased to $5 (13 Stat. 223, 276).

1865 From June, people entering and leaving the United States no longer have to present passports.

1866 With the end of the Civil War, Congress once again makes it law that passports can only be issued to citizens (14. Stat. 54: Rev. Stat, 4076, 4078).

1869 The State Department issues the first General Instructions for passport applicants.

1870 Oaths, affidavits or affirmations needed in application are required to be made under penalty of perjury (16 Stat. 368–69).
In a State Department reorganization, the Passport Bureau is created.

1871 The $5 passport fee is abolished.

1873 The validity of the passport is extended from one year to two years.
The General Instructions of September 1 make the oath of allegiance a formal requirement. It also includes a new requirement that, in the case of naturalized citizens, the spelling of the applicant's name has to be the same on the application and the naturalization certificate provided as proof of citizenship.
The Passport Bureau is abolished. The Bureau of Archives and Indexes becomes responsible for the issuance of passports.

1874 A $5 fee is reintroduced for the passport.

1886 The Secretary of State clarifies that it is department policy not to issue passports to Mormons who are seeking to make proselytes.

1888 The State Department creates separate application forms for native citizens, naturalized citizens, and persons claiming naturalization through husband or a parent.
The passport fee is reduced to $1.

1892 The phrase "Good for two years from date" is printed on passports.

1896 The "General Instructions for Passport Applicants" is renamed "Rules Governing the Issuance of Passports."

1902 A Passport Bureau is reestablished.
Governors of United States insular possessions are authorized to issue passports (32 Stat. 386).

1903 At the request of immigration officials, U.S passports issued to citizens of Chinese descent include a disclaimer that possession of a passport does not guarantee entry to the United States.

1905 Disclaimer on U.S. passports issued to Chinese is removed. Concern over the stamping of the secretary of state's signature on the passport results in a facsimile signature being engraved on the plate from which passports are printed.

1907 The Passport Bureau is renamed the Bureau of Citizenship. The United States and Japanese governments exchange a series of diplomatic notes into early 1908 that constitute an informal agreement that the United States will not restrict Japanese immigration if the Japanese government agrees not to issue passports to laborers who want to work in the continental United States.
The State Department is given the authority to issue a special passport for immigrants who have declared their intention to become citizens. The same act creates a registration certificate that diplomatic and consular officials can give to U.S. citizens living abroad to satisfy the identification demands of foreign authorities (34 Stat. 1228).

1911 On June 11 a revised version of the Rules Governing Issuing of Passports limits diplomatic and consular authorities to issuing passports only in emergencies.
The United States government abrogates a treaty with Russia over Russian refusal to visa the U.S. passports of Jewish citizens.

1914 Following the outbreak of war in Europe in November the State Department released an announcement stating that all citizens going abroad "should" carry passports.
On November 13 a revised version of the "Rules Governing Issuing of Passports" requires all passport applications to be executed in front of court officials, thereby removing notary publics from the application process.
On December 21 the State Department announced that all U.S. passport applicants have to provide a photograph to be attached to their passport.

1915 An executive order of January 12 reduces the period of validity of a passport from two years to six months.
A subsequent executive order states that the regulations of European countries have made passports a necessity; though the order does not require aliens or citizens to have passports to enter and leave the United States.
Passport applications are changed to include the date and place of departure and the object of visit. "Special identifying

marks" is added as a category in the physical description of the bearer.
It is revealed that German agents have been using U.S. passports to travel. One notable case is that of George Breeckow, who had entered England using a fake U.S. passport copied from a legitimate passport.

1916 The State Department opens a passport agency in New York on January 2.

1917 People making applications outside of their place of residence are required to give contact information for a "reputable professional or business man having his office or place of business in the place where the applicant resides."
After the United States declares war on Germany in April, the State Department requires "proof of necessity" in all passport applications, though it is more strictly enforced for Europe.
The Departments of State and Labor issue a Joint Order on July 26 to diplomatic, consular, and immigration offices. It requires that all aliens who intend to enter U.S. territory have a visa issued by a U.S. consul.
The Bureau of Citizenship is renamed the Division of Passport Control.
At the end of the year, despite the precedent of passport requirements during the Civil War, the attorney general rules that the Executive does not have authority to control the departure of aliens, nor the departure and entry of U.S. citizens.

1918 The Passport Control Act of May 22 (40 Stat. 559) delegates to the president the power to control the travel of citizens and others to and from the United States in wartime; and the authority to give executive departments the power to enforce it.
In an executive order on August 8, President Wilson proclaims rules and regulations governing departure and entry into the United States through passports and visas.
The State Department opens a passport agency in San Francisco.

1919 A Visa Division is created in the State Department.

1920 The fee for passports is increased to $10 ($1 for executing the application and $9 for the passport). The period of validity of passports is increased from six months to two years. The authority to issue passports to immigrants who

have declared their intention to become citizens is repealed (41 Stat. 750).
The fee for a visa is also increased to $10. In response, most countries increase their visa fees to $10 for U.S. citizens.
The League of Nations' Organization for Communication and Transit holds a conference designed to remove or simplify the international passport requirements introduced by individual nations during the war.

1921 In March Congress removes wartime restrictions for citizens entering and leaving country, but retains them for noncitizens (41 Stat. 1217).
An immigration act introduces a national quota system, but the act does not give consuls the authority to issue or refuse visas according to the quotas (42 Stat. 5).
Passport agencies are opened in Chicago, Seattle, and New Orleans.
The secretary of state rules that applicants have to provide a photograph, regardless of religious beliefs.

1924 A new immigration act gives consuls the authority to issue and refuse immigration visas according to the quota system (43 Stat. 153).
Congress approves funding for a border patrol.

1925 The State Department changes its policy to allow a married woman the option of having a passport issued in her maiden name, followed by the phrase "wife of."
The Boston Passport Agency opens.

1926 The League of Nations holds its second passport conference. Among other things, it attempts to establish a standard booklet form for the passport and a $2 fee for visas.
The State Department issues its first passport in the modern booklet form.
The Act of July 3, 1926 (44 Stat. 887) repeals all previous passport laws, while maintaining the language of the 1856 act. It clarifies that the secretary of state has the authority to designate diplomatic and consular officials to issue passports.
The Division of Passport Control is renamed the Passport Division.

1928 As part of a continuing effort to make the passport a more secure document, the State Department starts to use a machine that perforates a legend across the lower part of the photograph after it is attached to a passport.

1929 The U.S. government reaches an agreement with the French government to reduce visa fees to $2.
Infants must now have photographs on passports.

1930 The fee for a passport is reduced from $9 to $5 (the execution fee for an application remains $1). Passports can be renewed for periods of two years, with a final expiration date not more than six years from the original issue date (44 Stat. 887).
The State Department rules that a photograph on a passport can be no older than two years.

1932 The fee for passports is increased from $5 to $9. A passport can be renewed for periods of two years, with a final expiration date not more than four years from the original issue date (47 Stat. 157).

Notes

Introduction

1. *New York Times*, "Grows Mustache to Leave Germany," October 16, 1923; *Washington Post*, "Shave Spoiled His Passport," March 18, 1915; *Washington Post*, "Forgets To Give Passport Shave When He Gets One; Nearly Excluded," November 12, 1916.
2. While several histories of the passport have emerged in recent years, most accept the fact that a passport could document identity. Such histories include Lesley Higgins and Marie-Christine Leps, "'Passport, Please': Legal, Literary, and Cultural Fictions of Identity," *College Literature* 25 (1998): 94–138; Radhika Viyas Mongia, "Race, Nationality, Mobility: A History of the Passport," *Public Culture* 11 (1999): 527–56; John Torpey, *The Invention of the Passport: Surveillance, Citizenship, and the State* (Cambridge, UK: Cambridge University Press, 1999); Martin Lloyd, *The Passport: The History of Man's Most Travelled Document* (Stroud, UK: Sutton, 2003); Mark B. Salter, *Rights of Passage: The Passport in International Relations* (Boulder, CO: Lynne Rienner, 2003); and Jane Doulman and David Lee, *Every Assistance & Protection: A History of the Australian Passport* (Sydney: Federation, 2008). The exceptions that address aspects of the passport as an identification document are Andreas Fahrmeir, "Governments and Forgers: Passports in Nineteenth-Century Europe," in *Documenting Individual Identity: The Development of State Practices in the Modern World*, ed. Jane Caplan and John Torpey (Princeton, NJ: Princeton University Press), 218–34; Valentin Groebner, *Who Are You? Identification, Deception, and Surveillance in Early Modern Europe*, trans. Mark Kyburz and John Peck (Brooklyn, NY: Zone, 2007); and Adam McKeown, *Melancholy Order: Asian Migration and the Globalization of Borders* (New York: Columbia University Press, 2008).

3. Lloyd, *The Passport*; Salter, *Rights of Passage*; N. W. Sibley, "The Passport System," *Journal of the Society of Comparative Legislation* 7 (1906): 26–33; Egidio Reale, "Passport," in *Encyclopaedia of the Social Sciences* (New York: Macmillan, 1934), 12:13–16.
4. Alfred D. Chandler Jr., *The Visible Hand: The Managerial Revolution in American Business* (Cambridge, MA: Belknap, 1977); Richard Franklin Bensel, *Yankee Leviathan: The Origins of Central State Authority in America, 1859–1877* (Cambridge, UK: Cambridge University Press, 1990); Morton Keller, *Affairs of State: Public Life in Late Nineteenth Century America* (Cambridge: Belknap Press of Harvard University, 1977); Stephen Skowronek, *Building a New American State: The Expansion of National Administrative Capacities, 1870–1920* (Cambridge, UK: Cambridge University Press, 1982); Leonard D. White, *The Republican Era: A Study in Administrative History, 1869–1901* (New York: MacMillan, 1958).
5. James W. Carey, "The Internet and the End of the National Communication System: Uncertain Predictions of an Uncertain Future," *Journalism and Mass Communication Quarterly* 75 (1998): 28– 33. These developments, along with the passport, provide examples of "logistical media" that arrange people and property into time and space. On this see John Durham Peters, "Calendar, Clock, Tower" (lecture, Media in Transition 6 conference, Massachusetts Institute of Technology, Cambridge, MA, April 25, 2009).
6. Matthew G. Hannah, *Governmentality and the Mastery of Territory in Nineteenth-Century America* (Cambridge, UK: Cambridge University Press, 2000); Margo J. Anderson, *The American Census: A Social History* (New Haven, CT: Yale University Press, 1988).
7. Charles Dickens, *The Pickwick Papers* (Oxford: Oxford University Press, 1998), 512. For a brief discussion of this scene see Erving Goffman, *Stigma: Notes on the Management of Spoiled Identity* (Englewoods Cliff, NJ: Prentice-Hall, 1963), 70.
8. For an analysis of this change in record-keeping practices in prisons in the United States see Pamela Sankar, "State Power and Record-Keeping: The History of Individualized Surveillance in the United States, 1790–1935" (PhD diss., University of Pennsylvania, 1992).
9. Keller, *Affairs of State*, 316.
10. S. Shapiro, "Development of Birth Registration and Birth Statistics in the United States," *Population Studies* 4 (1950), 87–8, 92–3.
11. Sankar, "State Power and Record-Keeping," 24.
12. Bruce Curtis offers a useful list of possible sources of local knowledge in the mid-nineteenth century: "kinship, neighborliness, mutual economic dependence, community school and community church, parish institutions and exchange networks." (Bruce Curtis, "Administrative Infrastructure and Social Enquiry: Finding the Facts about Agriculture in Quebec, 1853–4," *Journal of Social History* 32 [1998]: 312.)
13. Jennifer L. Mnookin, "Scripting Expertise: The History of Handwriting Identification Evidence and the Judicial Construction of Expertise," *Virginia Law Review* 87 (2001), 1763; Sankar, "State Power and Record-Keeping," 164.

14. Josh Lauer, "From Rumor to Written Record: Credit Reporting and the Invention of Financial Identity in Nineteenth-Century America," *Technology and Culture* 49 (2008): 301–24.
15. Richard Bensel, "The American Ballot Box: Law, Identity, and the Polling Place in the Mid-Nineteenth Century," *Studies in American Political Development* 17, no. 1 (Spring 2003): 1–27.
16. Mnookin, "Scripting Expertise."
17. These are adapted from the questions that Mary Poovey argues could structure a history of numeracy (Mary Poovey, *A History of the Modern Fact: Problems of Knowledge in the Sciences of Wealth and Society* [Chicago: University of Chicago Press, 1998], 5).
18. This book focuses on the "regular passport" issued to citizens. Over the course of its history the United States has issued other types of passports; these include "special passports" to people going abroad to represent the country in some way and diplomatic or service passports to official representatives of the State Department. Courier passports have also been issued to people going abroad as bearers of official dispatches. The State Department issued a specific identification document to seamen. In specific circumstances the U.S. government has also issued distinct travel documents. See Green Haywood Hackworth, *Digest of International Law* (Washington, DC: GPO, 1942): 3:442–62; U.S. Passport Office, *The United States Passport: Past, Present, Future* (Washington, DC: GPO, 1976), 89–116.
19. Jane Caplan also argues that identification is more usefully understood as a history of "categories and indicators" (Jane Caplan, " 'This or That Particular Person': Protocols of Identification in Nineteenth-Century Europe," in *Documenting Individual Identity: The Development of State Practices in the Modern World*, ed. Jane Caplan and John Torpey [Princeton, NJ: Princeton University Press, 2001], 51).
20. Christopher Dandeker, *Surveillance, Power, and Modernity: Bureaucracy and Discipline from 1700 To The Present Day* (New York: St. Martin's, 1990).
21. Lynn Dumenil, *The Modern Temper: American Culture and Society in the 1920s* (New York: Hill and Wang, 1995); Warren I. Susman, *Culture as History: The Transformation of American Society in the Twentieth Century* (New York: Pantheon, 1984); Miles Orvell, *The Real Thing: Imitation and Authenticity in American Culture, 1880–1940* (Chapel Hill: University of North Carolina Press, 1989); Roland Marchand, *Advertising the American Dream: Making Way for Modernity, 1920–1940* (Berkeley: University of California Press, 1985).
22. It is in this sense that the passport needs to be understood as an "identification document," not an "identity document." The use of the former is intended to place explicit emphasis on the practice of identifying. This is done to make the argument that a document does not merely represent an "identity;" rather it produces a specific new identity unique to the logics and procedures of identification as a practice. For a discussion of the importance of distinguishing identity

and identification see David Lyon, *Identifying Citizens: ID Cards as Surveillance* (Cambridge, UK: Polity, 2009), 10–15.

23. Craig Robertson, "A Documentary Regime of Verification: The Emergence of the US Passport and the Archival Problematization of Identity," *Cultural Studies* 23 (2009): 329–54.
24. This borrows from Michel Foucault's idea of a regime. See Michel Foucault, "Truth and Power" in *Power/Knowledge: Selected Interviews and Other Writings, 1972–1977*, ed. and trans. Colin Gordon (New York: Pantheon, 1980), 133; Michel Foucault, "Questions of Method," in *The Foucault Effect: Studies in Governmentality*, ed. Graham Burchell, Colin Gordon, and Peter Miller (Chicago: University of Chicago Press, 1991), 79.
25. Torpey, *The Invention of the Passport*, 21–56.
26. Groebner, *Who Are You?* Although I only encountered Groebner's landmark research as I finished writing this book, our overlapping interest in how documents identify people has resulted at a general level in a series of similar arguments about the translation of identity onto paper. Most notable are two arguments: that identification is the production of a distinct identity, and therefore, there is a loss of individual control over their official identification; and that official identification provides a potential basis for an all-knowing state. But despite this overlap his oft-repeated claim for the medieval origin of modern passports demands some important clarification.
27. See Andreas Fahrmeir, *Citizens and Aliens: Foreigners and the Law in Britain and the German States, 1789–1870* (New York: Berghahn, 2000), 100–151; Fahrmeir, "Governments and Forgers"; Lloyd, *The Passport*, 74–89, 115–18; Torpey, *Invention of the Passport*, 57–92; Susan Buck-Morss, "Passports," *Documents* 1 (1993): 66–77; Leo Lucassen, "A Many Headed-Monster: The Evolution of the Passport System in the Netherlands and Germany in the Long Nineteenth Century," in *Documenting Individual Identity: The Development of State Practices in the Modern World*, ed. Jane Caplan and John Torpey (Princeton, NJ: Princeton University Press, 2001), 235–255.
28. Fahrmeir, *Citizens and Aliens*, 129.
29. Groebner, *Who Are You?*, 234.
30. James W. Carey, *Communication as Culture: Essays on Media and Society* (Boston: Unwin Hyman, 1989).
31. Prior to the formation of the United States some of the British colonies required people to have a pass issued by the governor before leaving the colony; this was to ensure people did not leave owing money. However, these passes made no attempt to identify the bearer beyond their name. For the example of Virginia see U.S. Passport Office, *United States Passport*, 8–13.
32. Dorothy Williams Potter, *Passports of Southeastern Pioneers, 1770–1823: Indian, Spanish and other Land Passports for Tennessee, Kentucky, Georgia, Mississippi, Virginia, North and South Carolina* (Baltimore: Gateway 1982).
33. Elizabeth Pryor argues that the slave pass system was more standardized and systematic in its implementation and therefore important in identifying Black

people as "anti-citizens." (Elizabeth Pryor, "'Jim Crow' Cars, Passport Denials and Atlantic Crossings: African-American Travel, Protest and Citizenship at Home and Abroad, 1827–1865" [Ph.D diss., University of California, Santa Barbara, 2008], 88–100.) See also Sally E. Hadden, *Slave Patrols: Law and Violence in Virginia and the Carolinas* (Cambridge, MA: Harvard University Press, 2001). Runaway notices provided an informal print-based system for the identification of slaves. These notices were either advertisements in newspapers or handbills that had basic descriptions of runaway slaves. Daniel Meaders, "South Carolina Fugitives as Viewed through Local Colonial Newspapers with Emphasis on Runaway Notices 1732–1801," *Journal of Negro History* 60 (1975): 288–319; Rachel Hall, *Wanted: The Outlaw in American Visual Culture* (Charlottesville: University of Virginia Press 2009), 42–50.

34. Douglas L. Stein, "Passports and Sea Letters: Protection Documents for American Ships, ca. 1789–1860," *The Log of Mystic Seaport* 44 (1992): 18–20.
35. U.S. Passport Office, *United States Passport*, 220.
36. Alan Rogers, "Passports and Politics: The Courts and the Cold War," *Historian* 47 (1985): 497–511; Ken Lawless, "'Continental Imprisonment': Rockwell Kent and the Passport Controversy," *Antioch Review* 38 (1980), 304–11; Wen-chu Torrey Sun, "Regulation of the Foreign Travel of U.S. Citizens" (PhD diss., Claremont Graduate University, 1993).
37. Robertson, "Documentary Regime." For a discussion of problematization, see Michel Foucault, "Problematics" in *Foucault Live (Interviews 1961–1984)*, ed. Sylvère Lotringer (New York: Semiotext[e], 1996): 416–22; Chris Russill, "For a Pragmatist Theory of Publics: Advancing Carey's Cultural Studies through John Dewey…and Michel Foucault?!" in *Thinking with James Carey: Essays on Communications, Transportation, History*, ed. Jeremy Packer and Craig Robertson (New York: Peter Lang, 2006): 57–78.
38. Kelly Gates, "The U.S. Real ID Act and the Securitization of Identity," in *Playing the Identity Card: Surveillance, Security and Identification in Global Perspective*, ed. Colin J. Bennett and David Lyon (London: Routledge, 2008): 218–32.

Chapter 1

1. Naomi W. Cohen, "The Abrogation of the Russo-American Treaty of 1832," *Jewish Social Studies* 25 (1963): 3–41.
2. House Committee on Foreign Affairs, *Termination of the Treaty Between the United States and Russia: Hearings*, 62nd Cong., 2nd sess., December 11, 1911, 6.
3. Josh Lauer, "Money as Mass Communication: U.S. Paper Currency and the Iconography of Nationalism," *Communication Review* 11 (2008): 115.
4. Ibid.
5. For the origins of letters of introduction see Valentin Groebner, *Who Are You? Identification, Deception, and Surveillance in Early Modern Europe*, trans. Mark Kyburz and John Peck (Brooklyn, NY: Zone, 2007), 157–64.

6. Shipley to Consul [Edinburgh], February 8, 1934, RG 59 138/3256, National Archives.
7. James Blanchard, "Passport Troubles," *New York Times*, August 26, 1931.
8. Seward to Asboth, March 27 1867, No. 27, RG 59 MS. Inst. Argentine Repub. XV 275, National Archives.
9. Flournoy to Walsh, February 21, 1920, RG 59 138/1233, National Archives.
10. Dorothy Williams Potter, *Passports of Southeastern Pioneers, 1770–1823: Indian, Spanish and other Land Passports for Tennessee, Kentucky, Georgia, Mississippi, Virginia, North and South Carolina* (Baltimore: Gateway 1982).
11. 1 Stat. 118: Rev. State 4062.
12. It is frequently noted that the first U.S. passport was issued to Francis Maria Barrere on July 8, 1796. This is the oldest known extant passport. As Barrere sent it in for renewal, it is clearly not the first issued document. For a description of this passport see Gaillard Hunt, *The American Passport: Its History and a Digest of Laws, Rulings and Regulations Governing its Issuance by the Department of State* (Washington, DC: GPO, 1898), 77.
13. U.S. Passport Office, *The United States Passport: Past, Present, Future* (Washington, DC: GPO, 1976), 35.
14. Circular to Diplomatic and Consular Officials, July 13, 1931, RG 59 138/2976a, National Archives.
15. Baynard to Straus, May 10, 1887, quoted in John Bassett Moore, *A Digest of International Law* (Washington, DC: GPO, 1906), 3:1004.
16. Brist to Flournoy, January 5, 1923, RG 59 138/1740 Box 598, National Archives. See also Batum to Secretary of State, April 27, 1912, RG 59 138/2 Box 590, National Archives; Everett to Ingersoll, December 7, 1852, RG 59 Diplomatic Instructions, Great Britain XVI 178, National Archives. For a discussion of a similar concern about mid-nineteenth-century European passports see Andreas Fahrmier, "Governments and Forgers: Passports in Nineteenth-Century Europe," in *Documenting Individual Identity: The Development of State Practices in the Modern World*, ed. Jane Caplan and John Torpey (Princeton, NJ: Princeton University Press), 232–3.
17. Consular Bureau to Hengetler, November 6, 1923, RG 59 138.8/38, National Archives. Also see Ayme to Bryan, August 8, 1908, RG 59 Numerical File 15265 M862/R922, National Archives.
18. *Outlook*, "Why Passports," September 22, 1926, 105.
19. Isabel Hapgood, "Passports, Police and Post-Office in Russia," *Atlantic Monthly* 72, 43. The deliberate production of a passport issued to immigrants who had declared their intention to become U.S. citizens as a document smaller than a regular passport indicates an official belief in the importance of size to the perceived authority of the U.S. passport. The State Department issued this passport from 1907 to 1920 to aliens who had declared their intention to be U.S. citizens but had not yet fulfilled the residential requirements for naturalization. See Scott to Hunt, March 7, 1907, RG 59 Numerical File 5630, M862/R461, National Archives.

20. Vox Populi, "Passports," *New York Times*, July 31, 1874.
21. *New York Times*, "The Value of Passports," December 3, 1882, 5.
22. Act of Sept. 15, 1789, ch. 14, 1 Stat. L. 68.
23. Marc Shell, *Money, Language, and Thought: Literary and Philosophical Economies from the Medieval to the Modern Era* (Berkeley: University of California Press, 1982), 5.
24. David M. Henkin, *City Reading: Written Words and Public Spaces in Antebellum New York* (New York: Columbia University Press, 1998), 7, 14–16.
25. Viviana A. Zelizer, *The Social Meaning of Money: Pin Money, Pay Checks, Poor Relief, and Other Currencies* (Princeton, NJ: Princeton University Press, 1994), 13.
26. David R. Johnson, *Illegal Tender: Counterfeiting and the Secret Service in Nineteenth-Century America* (Washington, DC: Smithsonian Institution Press, 1995), 37.
27. Henkin, *City Reading*, 147–160.
28. Zelizer, *Social Uses of Money*, 13.
29. Johnson, *Illegal Tender*.
30. Ibid., 176.
31. Eric Helleiner, "National Currencies and National Identities," *American Behavioral Scientist* 41(1998), 1409–36.
32. Lauer, "Money as Mass Communication."
33. This will be discussed in chapter 10.
34. "McC." to Brist, June 27, 1925, RG 59, 138/1976L, National Archives.
35. State Department to Consuls [Europe], May 12, 1918, RG 59, 811.111/22705a, National Archives; *New York Times*, "Forge Passports for Foreign Reds," December 16, 1919; *New York Times*, German Red Agent Caught in Chicago," August 6, 1920; *New York Times*, "Forging of Passports to America Revealed," December 24, 1920; T. R. Ybarra, "Seize Reds' Store of False Passports," *New York Times*, October 19, 1924; *New York Times*, "Passport Swindlers Seized in Berlin," January 4, 1928; *New York Times*, "Belgians Drop Charge of Anti-Fascist Plot," February 23, 1930; *New York Times*, "'Mill' for American Passports Discovered by Italian Police," October 4, 1932.
36. "History of Shipside Inspection of American Passports," January 25, 1935, RG 59 138.81/408, National Archives; "Violation of the Passport Laws Committed for the Purpose of Effecting the Illegal Entry of Aliens into the United States," August 7, 1933, RG 59 138.81/366 Box 645, National Archives, 52–56.
37. *New York Times*, "New Type of Paper Adopted to Balk Passport Forgeries," November 8, 1930.
38. "Forged Passports and Altered Naturalization Certificates of Giuseppe Gemmiti and Giuspppe Palmieri," October 20, 1937, RG 59 138.81/338a, National Archives; "Concerning Passport Fraud," July 19, 1932, RG 59 138.81/338a, National Archives.
39. Olds to Consul General [London], February 7, 1927, RG 59 138/2181a, National Archives.

40. Olds to Min. in Panama, March 18, 1926, RG 59 138/2082, National Archives.
41. "DFN," January 31, 1938, RG 59 138.81/524 Box 645, National Archives; Shipley to Hamilton, April 20, 1939, RG 59 138.81/588, National Archives.
42. Shipley to Breed, August 25, 1937, RG 59 138.8/216, National Archives; Bannerman to Shipley, June 14, 1929, RG 59 138/2583, National Archives.
43. Report to Bannerman, September 19, 1933, RG 59 138.8/170, National Archives; Scanlan to Shipley, April 3, 1934, RG 59 138.8/178, National Archives.
44. Report to Bannerman, September 19, 1933, RG 59 138.8/170, National Archives.
45. "Re *News-Week* use of 'Passport,'" October, 1933, RG 59 138.8/170–72, National Archives.
46. Ibid.
47. Scanlan to Shipley, April 3, 1934, RG 59 138.8.178, National Archives.

Chapter 2

1. One cause of misspelling could also be the inability to read someone's handwriting. For example I remain unsure of the exact spellings that Mr. Zimmerman offered for his client's name. Zimmerman to Benedict, September 23, 1885, RG 59 Entry 509, Box 80, National Archives.
2. Gaillard Hunt, *The American Passport: Its History and a Digest of Laws, Rulings and Regulations Governing its Issuance by the Department of State* (Washington, DC: GPO, 1898), 56.
3. Except where noted otherwise, the following brief history is drawn from Jane Caplan, "'This or That Particular Person': Protocols of Identification in Nineteenth-Century Europe," in *Documenting Individual Identity: The Development of State Practices in the Modern World*, ed. Jane Caplan and John Torpey (Princeton, NJ: Princeton University Press, 2001), 54–65. For a more detailed history of naming practices in Western Europe and the United States see Stephen Wilson, *The Means of Naming: A Social and Cultural History of Personal Naming in Western Europe* (London: University College London Press, 1998).
4. Caplan, "This or That Particular Person," 55.
5. Valentin Groebner, *Who Are You? Identification, Deception, and Surveillance in Early Modern Europe*, trans. Mark Kyburz and John Peck (Brooklyn, NY: Zone, 2007), 68–71.
6. Howard Barker, quoted in H. L. Mencken, *The American Language: An Inquiry into the Development of English in the United States: Supplement 2* (New York, Alfred Knopf, 1948), 441. See also H. L. Mencken, *The American Language: An Inquiry into the Development of English in the United States*, 4th ed. (New York, Alfred Knopf, 1977), 610.
7. Estelle T. Lau, *Paper Families: Identity, Immigration Administration, and Chinese Exclusion* (Durham, NC: Duke University Press, 2006), 44.
8. Ibid., 107–9.

9. Kantowitz to Secretary of State, October 18, 1884, RG 59, Entry 509, Box 79, National Archives; Russell to Passport Bureau, March 14, 1885, RG 59, Entry 509, Box 79, National Archives.
10. *New York Times*, "Let's Have One Rule for Everybody," November 12, 1917.
11. Jacqueline Stevens, *Reproducing the State* (Princeton, NJ: Princeton University Press, 1999).
12. Howard F. Barker, "How We Got Our Surnames," *American Speech* 4 (October, 1928): 53; Wilson, *The Means of Naming*, 303–4. For a detailed summary of the name-changing patterns of immigrant groups in the United States through the 1930s see Mencken, *The American Language: Supplement* 2, 396–525.
13. *New York Times*, "Let's Have One Rule for Everybody."
14. Greshamto Raine, June 4, 1894, RG 59, Domestic Letters, 197:245, National Archives; "Note re Name, Passport number 49849," May 27, 1876, RG 59 Entry 510, Box 9, National Archives.
15. Wharton to Osiel, July 8, 1889, RG 59, Domestic Letters, 173:547, National Archives.
16. George Kennan, "T. B. Aldrich's Adventure with Russian Police," *New York Times*, June 25, 1911.
17. *New York Times*, "Ruth Hale or Mrs. Broun?" February 18, 1921. Interestingly, her passport was issued in the form very similar to that by which the State Department would resolve this problem four years later: "Mrs Heywood Broun, otherwise known as Ruth Hale."
18. Una Stannard, "Manners Make Laws: Married Women's Names in the United States," *Names* 32, no. 3 (1984): 114–18, 123; Susan Kupper, *Surnames for Women: A Decision-making Guide*, (Jefferson, NC: McFarland, 1990), 16.
19. Assistant-Secretary of State to Secretary of State, April 15, 1925, RG 59 138/1952a, National Archives.
20. Matthews to Kellogg, April 27, 1925, RG 59 138/1952a, National Archives; "Memo," 'RLF' Department of State Solicitor, May 16, 1925, RG 59 138/3455, National Archives.
21. Margaret Whitmore, to Kellogg, April 15, 1925, RG 59 138/1952a, National Archives.
22. "Brief of the National Woman's Party Against the Rule" in Matthews to Kellogg, April 27, 1925, RG 59 138/1934, National Archives.
23. *New York Times*, "Why Content with Father's Name?" May 8, 1925.
24. "Memo," "RLF"; "RLF" to MacMurray, May 4, 1925, RG 59 138/3455, National Archives.
25. "Memo," "RLF."
26. Miss Elizabeth Achelis to Kellogg, May 6, 1925, RG 59, 138/1942, National Archives.
27. "RLF" to MacMurray.
28. Memo, "RLF."
29. "RLF" to MacMurray.
30. Ibid.

31. "A-2 (McM)" to Secretary of State, Memo, April 16, 1925, RG 59 138/3455, National Archives.
32. Ibid.
33. Memo, "RLF."
34. *Equal Rights*, "A Preliminary Victory," April 25, 1925.
35. Shipley to English/Hackworth, October 20, 1937, RG 59 138/3837A, National Archives.
36. Hoyt to Shipley, May 21, 1938, RG 59 138/3857, National Archives; Shipley to Hoyt, May 27, 1938, RG 59 138/3857, National Archives.

CHAPTER 3

1. Department of State to Consul General at Naples, February 13, 1933. Quoted in Green Haywood Hackworth, *Digest of International Law* (Washington, DC: GPO, 1942), 3:481.
2. Roy Harris, *Rethinking Writing* (Bloomington: Indiana University Press, 2000), 182.
3. Consul [Southampton, England] to Secretary of State, September 19, 1921, RG 59 138/1536, Box 597, National Archives.
4. Gaillard Hunt, *The American Passport: Its History and a Digest of Laws, Rulings and Regulations Governing its Issuance by the Department of State* (Washington, DC: GPO, 1898), 61.
5. Seward to Irving, December 14, 1861, RG 59 Domestic Letters, 56: 46, National Archives. For the signature to function as an attempt to prevent fraud officials had to assume that the person who had originally signed the passport was the person named in the application and supporting documents. Issuance procedure meant that no official actually witnessed the signing of the passport by an applicant.
6. It is important to note the U.S. law does not share this cultural understanding of the form of the signature. In the absence of any specific statute "the law requires nothing of a signature other than that it be a documentary mark intended by the signer to be (and be accepted as) a signature." Therefore, what is important is the intention of the signers that these mark be their signatures and that they are intended to authenticate the documents to which they are appended. See Michael Hancher, "The Law of Signatures," in *Law and Aesthetics*, ed. Roberta Kevelson (New York: Peter Lang, 1992): 234.
7. Roy Harris, *Signs of Writing* (London: Routledge, 1995), 82; Harris, *Rethinking Writing*, 181. Harris also points out that as a result of the demand for an idiosyncratic signature many people produce a signature that in fact is not written in their usual hand (Harris, *Signs of Writing*, 83).
8. Jennifer L. Mnookin, "Scripting Expertise: The History of Handwriting Identification Evidence and the Judicial Construction of Expertise," *Virginia Law Review* 87 (2001), 1760–64.
9. Quoted in Tamara Plakins Thornton, *Handwriting in America: A Cultural History* (New Haven, CT: Yale University Press, 1996), 91.
10. Quoted in ibid., 90.

11. Randall McGowan, "Knowing the Hand: Forgery and the Proof of Writing in Eighteenth-Century England," *Historical Reflections* 24 (1998): 385–414; Mnookin, "Scripting Expertise," 1762.
12. Mnookin, 'Scripting Expertise,' 1756, 1763.
13. Carlo Ginzburg, "Morelli, Freud and Sherlock Holmes: Clues and Scientific Method," *History Workshop* 9 (Spring, 1980): 5–36.
14. Mnookin, "Scripting Expertise," 1789.
15. Thornton, *Handwriting in America*, 92–105; P. G. Baxter, "The Distinction between 'Graphology' and 'Questioned Document Examination,' *Medicine, Science and the Law* 6 (1966): 75–86. Thornton argues that graphology was more of a mass phenomenon in the United States, while it achieved more recognition as a science in Europe, particularly Germany (Thornton, *Handwriting in America*, 132).
16. Thornton, *Handwriting in America.*
17. Harris, *Rethinking Writing*, 175.
18. *New York Sun/Herald*, "The Unsigned Passports," March 17, 1920. See also *New York Sun/Herald*, "U.S. Can Issue No Passports," March 16, 1920.
19. Thornton, *Handwriting in America*; Michael Warner, *The Letters of the Republic: Publication and the Public Sphere in Eighteenth-Century America* (Cambridge, MA: Harvard University Press, 1990).
20. Thornton, *Handwriting in America*, 31.
21. David M. Henkin, *City Reading: Written Words and Public Spaces in Antebellum New York* (New York: Columbia University Press, 1998), 157.
22. Samuel J. Barrows and Isabel C. Barrows, "Personal Reminiscences of William H. Seward," *Atlantic Monthly*, March 1889, 382. It should be noted that in the sample of Seward's signatures I have seen, there are clearly discernible letters between the S and D.
23. Ibid.
24. Ibid. The State Department issued 40,683 passports during Seward's eight years as secretary of state, averaging fourteen passports a day for him to sign. However, many of those were issued in his first three years, when passports were required for leaving the United States during the Civil War. U.S. See U.S. Passport Office, *The United States Passport: Past, Present, Future* (Washington, DC: GPO, 1976), 220.
25. I am indebted to Henkin's insightful argument in *City Reading* about the importance of a paradoxical relationship between replication and singularity in the development of printed documents.
26. Sherman to Storer, September 18, 1897, quoted in U.S. State Department, *Papers Relating to the Foreign Relations of the United States* (Washington, DC: GPO, 1897), 27–28. This dispatch lists Seward as one of the secretaries whose signature was stamped on the passport.
27. U.S. Passport Office, *The United States Passport*, 220.
28. Gaillard Hunt, *The Department of State of the United States: Its History and Functions* (New Haven, CT: Yale University Press, 1914), 380.
29. The culturally specific value attached to the signing of a name by hand is apparent when it is contrasted with the practice of using a seal. The distinct cultural

origin of these practices was evident when the League of Nations sought to establish what should count as a signature. In summarizing Beatrice Fraenkel's research on this, Harris argues that Western delegates did not regard the "Oriental" practice of using a seal as adequately constituting a genuine signature. From a Western perspective, "the seal placed too much emphasis on the replication as a guarantee of authenticity." From a non-Western perspective, "the insistence on the signature as a direct manual trace placed too much emphasis on the specifics of each signing" (Harris, *Signs of Writing*, 82).

30. Frances Robertson, "The Aesthetics of Authenticity: Printed Banknotes as Industrial Currency," *Technology and Culture* 46 (2005), 47.
31. Ibid.

CHAPTER 4

1. R. C. Lehman "The Passport," *Living Age*, April 3, 1915, 49–50.
2. U.S. Passport Office, *The United States Passport: Past, Present, Future* (Washington, DC: GPO, 1976), 29–30, 40; Gaillard Hunt, *The American Passport: Its History and a Digest of Laws, Rulings and Regulations Governing its Issuance by the Department of State* (Washington, DC: GPO, 1898), 82–85.
3. John Torpey, *The Invention of the Passport: Surveillance, Citizenship, and the State* (Cambridge, UK: Cambridge University Press, 1999).
4. Andrea Geselle, "Domenica Saba Takes to the Road: Origins and Development of a Modern Passport System in Lombardy-Veneto," in *Documenting Individual Identity: The Development of State Practices in the Modern World*, ed. Jane Caplan and John Torpey (Princeton, NJ: Princeton University Press, 2001), 204.
5. Andreas Fahrmeir, *Citizens and Aliens: Foreigners and the Law in Britain and the German States, 1789–1870* (New York: Berghahn, 2000), 103.
6. Hunt, *The American Passport*, 78, 79; U.S. Passport Office, *The United States Passport*, 61, 62.
7. George Kennan, "T. B. Aldrich's Adventure with Russian Police," *New York Times*, June 25, 1911.
8. In contrast the actions of some European states indicate a greater concern with passport fraud. See Andreas Fahrmeir, "Governments and Forgers: Passports in Nineteenth-Century Europe," in *Documenting Individual Identity: The Development of State Practices in the Modern World*, ed. Jane Caplan and John Torpey (Princeton, NJ: Princeton University Press), 225.
9. Ibid., 228.
10. *New York Times*, "The Value of Passports," December 3, 1882.
11. A similar development occurred in the format of prisoners' files in U.S. jails in this period. See Pamela Sankar, "State Power and Record-Keeping: The History of Individualized Surveillance in the United States, 1790–1935" (PhD diss., University of Pennsylvania, 1992), 76.
12. Paul Fussell, *Abroad: British Literary Traveling Between the Wars* (New York: Oxford University Press, 1980), 25.
13. *Harper's New Monthly Magazine*, "Noses," August 1858, 378.

14. Tooker to Secretary of State, June 8, 1885, RG 59 Entry 509, Box 80, National Archives; Bailey to Bayard, November 7, 1888, RG 59 MLR 509, Box 86, National Archives.
15. John Miller to Department of State, June 27, 1896, RG 59 MLR 509, Box 95, National Archives.
16. Martine Kaluszynski, "Republican Identity: Bertillonage as Government Technique," in Caplan and Torpey, eds., *Documenting Individual Identity*, 123–38.
17. Peter Becker, "The Standardized Gaze: The Standardization of the Search Warrant in Nineteenth-Century Germany," in Caplan and Torpey, eds., *Documenting Individual Identity*, 140.
18. Simon A. Cole, *Suspect Identities: A History of Fingerprinting and Criminal Identification* (Cambridge, MA: Harvard University Press, 2001), 34–43.
19. Becker, "The Standardized Gaze," 150.
20. Allan Sekula, "The Body and the Archive," *October* 39, no. 3 (1986): 28; Cole, *Suspect Identities*, 45.
21. Jane Caplan, " 'Speaking Scars': The Tattoo in Popular Practice and Medico-Legal Debate in Nineteenth-Century Europe," *History Workshop Journal* 44 (1997), 127–28.
22. Shawn Michelle Smith, *American Archives: Gender, Race, and Class in Visual Culture* (Princeton, NJ: Princeton University Press, 1999).
23. Sekula, "The Body and the Archive," 11.
24. For an example of the popular application of this see Cara A Finnegan, "Recognizing Lincoln: Image Vernaculars in Nineteenth-Century Visual Culture," *Rhetoric and Public Affairs* 8:1 (2005), 31–58.
25. Lawrence M. Friedman, *Crime and Punishment in American History* (New York: Basic Books, 1993), 12–13, 193–210.
26. John F. Kasson, *Rudeness and Civility: Manners in Nineteenth-Century Urban America* (New York: Hill and Wang, 1990), 109. See also Karen Halttunen, *Confidence Men and Painted Women: A Study of Middle-Class Culture in America, 1830–1870* (New Haven, CT: Yale University Press, 1982).
27. Kasson, *Rudeness and Civility*, 116.
28. Rachel Hall, *Wanted: The Outlaw in American Visual Culture* (Charlottesville: University of Virginia, 2009), 65–69; Tom Gunning, "Tracing the Individual Body: Photography, Detectives, and Early Cinema," in *Cinema and the Invention of Modern Life*, ed. Leo Charney and Vanessa R. Schwartz (Berkeley: University of California Press, 1995), 24.
29. Richard Franklin Bensel, *The American Ballot Box in the Mid-Nineteenth Century* (Cambridge, UK: Cambridge University Press, 2004), 134–35, 140.
30. Estelle T. Lau, *Paper Families: Identity, Immigration Administration, and Chinese Exclusion* (Durham, NC: Duke University Press, 2006), 99.
31. For the emergence of the category of "distinguishing marks" on identification papers from the fifteenth century, see Valentin Groebner, *Who Are You? Identification, Deception, and Surveillance in Early Modern Europe*, trans. Mark Kyburz and John Peck (Brooklyn, NY: Zone, 2007), 95–116.

32. Hunt, *American Passport*, 78; U.S. Passport Office, *The United States Passport*, 61.
33. U.S. Passport Office, *The United States Passport*, 80. The category of "occupation remained on passports until 1961.

CHAPTER 5

1. President Woodrow Wilson issued an executive order outlining the requirements in more detail on February 1, 1915 (U.S. Passport Office, *The United States Passport: Past, Present, Future* [Washington, DC: GPO, 1976], 80).
2. For a discussion of the wartime addition of photographs to Australian passports that parallels the U.S. history see Jane Doulman and David Lee, *Every Assistance & Protection: A History of the Australian Passport* (Sydney: Federation, 2008), 55–57.
3. *New York Times*, "Hint Official Here is in Passport Plot," January 6, 1915; Carr to Consul General, Cairo, February 12, 1915, RG 59 138/68, National Archives.
4. U.S. Passport Office, *The United States Passport: Past, Present, Future* (Washington, DC: GPO, 1976), 85.
5. Ibid., 80.
6. *New York Times*, "Must Have Passport Photo Despite Religious Scruples," May 26, 1921.
7. U.S. Passport Office, *The United States Passport*, 80.
8. Diplomatic & Consular Circular, March 7, 1924, RG 59 138/1857a, National Archives; Shipley to Consul General, Bucharest, August 4, 1928, RG 59 138/2422 Box 600, National Archives.
9. *New York Times*, "No Respecter of Persons," September 19, 1930.
10. Ibid.
11. John Tagg, *The Burden of Representation: Essays on Photographies and Histories* (Amherst: University of Massachusetts Press, 1988), 42–43.
12. See the seminal works of John Tagg and Allan Sekula: Tagg, *The Burden of Representation*; Allan Sekula, "The Body and the Archive," *October* 39, no. 3 (1986), 3–64.
13. Shawn Michelle Smith, *American Archives: Gender, Race, and Class in Visual Culture* (Princeton, NJ: Princeton University Press, 1999), 56–61.
14. Ibid.
15. Alan Trachtenberg, "Likeness as Identity: Reflections on the Daguerrean Mystique," in *The Portrait in Photography*, ed. Graham Clarke (London: Reaktion Books, 1992), 187.
16. Suren Lalvani, "Photography, Epistemology and the Body," *Cultural Studies* 7 (1998): 448. See also Sekula, "The Body and the Archive," 8–9.
17. Smith, *American Archives*, 165.
18. Tom Gunning, "Tracing the Individual Body: Photography, Detectives, and Early Cinema," in *Cinema and the Invention of Modern Life*, ed. Leo Charney and Vanessa R. Schwartz (Berkeley: University of California Press, 1995), 24.

19. Sekula, "The Body and the Archive," 5–7.
20. Lalvani, "Photography, Epistemology and the Body," 449.
21. Sekula, "The Body and the Archive," 40–55.
22. Tagg, *The Burden of Representation*, 11.
23. This paragraph draws from Daston and Galison's insightful and provocative article (Lorraine Daston and Peter Galison, "The Image of Objectivity," *Representations* 40 [1992]: 81–128).
24. This discussion is based on Jennifer Mnookin's arguments about the emergence of the photograph as legal evidence (Jennifer L. Mnookin, "The Image of Truth: Photographic Evidence and the Power of Analogy," *Yale Journal of Law and the Humanities* 10 [1998]: 1–74).
25. Quoted in ibid., 16.
26. Ibid., 50.
27. Anna Pegler-Gordon, "In Sight of America: Photography and U.S. Immigration Policy, 1880–1930" (PhD diss., University of Michigan, 2002), 5. Pegler-Gordon's innovative research on this subject adds an important new dimension to arguments about the contestation involved in photographic representation. See also Anna Pegler-Gordon, "Chinese Exclusion, Photography, and the Development of U.S. Immigration Policy," *American Quarterly* 58 (2006): 51–77.
28. Pegler-Gordon, "In Sight of America," 117.
29. Ibid., 86.
30. Ibid., 90–91.
31. Ibid., 120.
32. *Outlook*, "Why Passports?," September 22, 1926, 105.
33. *New York Times*, "No Respecter of Persons," September 19, 1930.
34. Ibid.
35. U.S. Passport Office, *The United States Passport*, 64.
36. Gunning, "Tracing the Individual Body," 29–30.
37. Diplomatic and Consular Memo, March 7, 1924, RG 59 138/1857a, National Archives.
38. W. Castle Jr to Diplomatic and Consular Service, October 24, 1930, RG 59 138/2905a, National Archives.
39. Shipley to American Consul, Curaco, Netherland West Indies, June 19, 1935, RG 59 138/3403 Box 602, National Archives.
40. *New York Times*, "Curb Photo Trickery," January 7, 1932; *New York Times*, "Costly Passport Photographs," June 23, 1930.
41. W. Castle Jr to Diplomatic and Consular Service, October 24, 1930, RG 59 138/2905a, National Archives.
42. Menken to Stimson, July 23, 1930, RG 59 111.28 NY/63, Box 225, National Archives.
43. Consul General, London, to Secretary of State, January 13, 1934, RG 59 138.81 London/6, National Archives.
44. Trachtenberg, "Likeness as Identity," 178.

45. The idea of state rule and "simplification" is from James Scott, *Seeing Like a State: How Certain Schemes to Improve the Human Condition Have Failed* (New Haven, CT: Yale University Press, 1998), 3, 80.
46. Carson Hathaway, "Woman to Head Passport Bureau," *New York Times*, May 20, 1928.

CHAPTER 6

1. John Bassett Moore, *A Digest of International Law* (Washington, DC: GPO, 1906), 3:899–901.
2. U.S. Passport Office, *The United States Passport: Past, Present, Future* (Washington, DC: Department of State, 1976), 141; Gaillard Hunt, *The American Passport: Its History And A Digest Of Laws, Rulings, And Regulations Governing Its Issuance By The Department Of State* (Washington, DC: GPO, 1898), 45.
3. McKenzie to Department of State, July 18, 1897, RG 59 MLR 509, Box 99, National Archives.
4. As a woman not born in the U.S. her citizenship status remained contingent on her father or husband. Virginia Sapiro, "Women, Citizenship, and Nationality: Immigration and Naturalization Policies in the United States," *Politics and Society* 13 (1984): 8. Nancy F. Cott, "Marriage and Women's Citizenship in the United States, 1830–1934," *American Historical Review* 103 (1988): 1456–61.
5. McKenzie to Department of State, July 18, 1897, RG 59 MLR 509, Box 99, National Archives.
6. Moore, *A Digest of International Law*, 3:918–19.
7. For examples of discussion of the passport fee, see *New York Times*, [no title] December 19, 1873, 4; Evarts to Christiancy, July 22, 1880, RG 59 Department of State, Diplomatic Instructions, Peru M77 R131: 456, National Archives; [Passport Clerk] to Shipley, March 21, 1885, RG59, Entry 509 Box 79, National Archives.
8. Pamela Sankar, "State Power and Record-Keeping: The History of Individualized Surveillance in the United States, 1790–1935" (PhD diss., University of Pennsylvania, 1992), 5, 22. As noted, Sankar's groundbreaking work remains the definitive statement on the development of federal record keeping in the United States.
9. Documents emerged as part of voting with the arrival of absentee ballots during the Civil War, to enable soldiers to vote. The gradual acceptance of absentee ballots brought into focus the new form of impersonal interaction that emerged within the changing scalar dynamics of the nineteenth-century state. It depersonalized the understanding and comprehension of "the public" that lay at the heart of democracy. For the largely Democratic opponents of absentee voting, public trust constituted the act of voting; the community became the primary grantor. The right to vote only emerged in the presence of the community–it had to be witnessed; in this sense it was not a permanent attribute of an individual. The predominantly Republican supporters argued that because the right to vote was inherent in the individual, it could be successfully preserved in its written record. In this argument the act of voting was located in the counting of the vote, not

the physical gesture of voting, that required a witness. See Jennifer Horner, "The 1864 Union Soldier Vote: Historical-critical perspectives on Public Space and the Public Sphere" (paper, annual meeting of the International Communication Association, San Francisco, May 24, 2007).

10. Richard Franklin Bensel, *The American Ballot Box in the Mid-Nineteenth Century* (Cambridge, UK: Cambridge University Press, 2004), 20, 90–92.
11. Richard Bensel, "The American Ballot Box: Law, Identity, and the Polling Place in the Mid-Nineteenth Century," *Studies in American Political Development* 17, no. 1 (Spring 2003), 10 n. 31.
12. Matt K. Matsuda, *The Memory of the Modern* (New York: Oxford University Press, 1996), 133.
13. For an insightful discussion of the tension between centralized administration and local respectability (albeit outside of the U.S.), see Bruce Curtis, "Administrative Infrastructure and Social Enquiry: Finding the Facts about Agriculture in Quebec, 1853–4," *Journal of Social History* 32 (1998): 324–25.
14. Hunt, *The American Passport*, 46–48.
15. Ibid., 49.
16. The oath required from 1861 to 1888 was borrowed from one introduced during the Civil War for civil service employees: "I, ___, do solemnly swear that I will support, protect, and defend the Constitution and Government of the United States against all enemies, whether domestic or foreign; and that I will bear true faith, allegiance, and loyalty to the same, any ordinance, resolution, or law of any State, convention or legislature to the contrary notwithstanding; and further, that I do this with a full determination, pledge, and purpose, without any mental reservation or evasion whatever; and, further, that I will well and faithfully perform all the duties which may be required of me by law. So help me God." In 1888 this oath was changed to reflect the new oath passed in 1884 for civil servants: "Further, I do solemnly swear that I will support and defend the Constitution of the United States against all enemies, foreign and domestic; that I will bear true faith and allegiance to the same; and that I take this obligation freely, without any mental reservation or purpose of evasion. So help me God." Quoted in ibid., 69–70. The requirement for an oath of allegiance remained in force until 1973 (U.S. Passport Office, *The United States Passport*, 169).
17. Harold M. Hyman, *To Try Men's Souls: Loyalty Tests in American History* (Berkeley: University of California Press, 1959), viii.
18. Rogers M. Smith, *Civic Ideals: Conflicting Visions of Citizenship in U.S. History* (New Haven, CT: Yale University Press, 1997), 245.
19. Different oaths usually came from citizens whose religious beliefs prevented them from swearing allegiance to the Constitution. These were accepted by some secretaries but rejected by others. In an example of the gradual attempt to make passport policy consistent, a departmental letter from 1897 authorized an alternative oath that substituted "government" for "constitution"; this became the only alternative oath the department would accept. Moore, *A Digest of International Law*, 3:916; Hunt, *The American Passport*, 70.

20. Flournoy to Johnson, December 24, 1914, RG 59 138.28/1, Box 66, National Archives.
21. By the end of the 1920s there were passport agencies in New York, Boston, Chicago, Seattle, San Francisco, and New Orleans; in other cities and towns people continued to apply to a state or federal court clerk. All applications were still forwarded to the State Department in Washington, D.C.
22. *New York Times*, "Avoid Rush for Passports, Official Warns Tourists," March 31, 1924; American Consul General [London] to Secretary of State, January 14, 1921, RG 59 138/1408, Box 596, National Archives.
23. Burhman to Bannerman, May 14, 1927, RG 59 138/2248, National Archives; Shipley to Collins, October 19, 1932, RG 59 138.81.541, National Archives.
24. Carr to Murphy, March 30, 1915, RG 59 138.7/17 Box 638, National Archives.
25. Olds to South, July 19, 1926, RG 59 138.1/14, Box 631, National Archives.
26. Hunt, *The American Passport*, 59.
27. Baynard to McLane, July 20, 1888. U.S. State Department, *Papers Relating to the Foreign Relations of the United States* (Washington, DC: GPO, 1888), 1:552.
28. Cressy L. Wilbur, *The Federal Registration Service of the United States: Its Development, Problems, and Defects* (Washington, DC: GPO, 1916), 47.
29. Ibid., 42.
30. S. Shapiro, "Development of Birth Registration and Birth Statistics in the United States," *Population Studies* 4 (1950), 92–3.
31. House Committee on the Census, *Authorizing the Director of the Census to Issue Birth Certificates: Hearing before the Committee on the Census*, 77th Cong., 2nd Sess., June 4, 9, 10, 1942, 27.
32. Shapiro, "Development of Birth Registration," 98–103.
33. Consul (Prague) to Secretary of State, March 26, 1924 RG 59 138.81/95; Report, May 1, 1924, RG 59 138.81/75, National Archives.
34. Olds to Secretary of Interior, February 20, 1926, RG 59 138.25/13, National Archives.
35. Memo to Scanlan, January 13, 1926, RG 59 138.25/13, National Archives.
36. Bayard to McLane, August 10, 1888, U.S. Department of State, *Foreign Relations*, 1888, 1:555. See also Moore, *A Digest of International Law*, 3:907–8. It should be noted that this particular applicant also presented expired U.S. passports, but Bayard's memo strongly implies that personal knowledge was all that was required.
37. An affidavit would be accepted if (a) the prior existence of the certificate was shown, (b) it could be proved the certificate had been destroyed by fire or in other circumstances, (c) in the case of a lost certificate, evidence of diligent search could be provided, and (d) it could be proved that the original record or certificate is unobtainable (Moore, *A Digest of International Law*, 3:905–6).
38. Ibid., 3:907; Green Haywood Hackworth, *Digest of International Law* (Washington, DC: GPO, 1942), 3:492.

CHAPTER 7

1. The following narrative is compiled from Graham H. Stuart, *The Department of State: A History of its Organization, Procedure, and Personnel* (New York: MacMillan, 1949); Gaillard Hunt, *The Department of State of the United States: Its History and Functions* (New Haven, CT: Yale University Press, 1914); and Gaillard Hunt, *The American Passport: Its History and a Digest of Laws, Rulings and Regulations Governing its Issuance by the Department of State* (Washington, DC: GPO, 1898).
2. Stuart, *The Department of State*, 219.
3. James R. Beniger, *The Control Revolution: Technological and Economic Origins of the Information Society* (Cambridge, MA: Harvard University Press, 1986), 15.
4. Christopher Dandeker, *Surveillance, Power, and Modernity: Bureaucracy and Discipline from 1700 To The Present Day* (New York: St. Martin's, 1990); David Beetham, *Bureaucracy* (Minneapolis: University of Minnesota Press, 1996); Morton Keller, *Affairs of State: Public Life in Late Nineteenth Century America* (Cambridge: Belknap Press of Harvard University, 1977), 195–210; Stephen Skowronek, *Building a New American State: The Expansion of National Administrative Capacities, 1870–1920* (Cambridge, UK: Cambridge University Press, 1982).
5. Beniger, *The Control Revolution*, 279–80.
6. I have borrowed this insight from Ian McNeely's work on scribes in German states in the early decades of the nineteenth century (Ian F. McNeely, *The Emancipation of Writing: German Civil Society in the Making, 1790s–1820s* [Berkeley: University of California Press, 2003], 165).
7. Beniger, *The Control Revolution*, 14.
8. Cindy Sondik Aron, *Ladies and Gentlemen of the Civil Service: Middle-Class Workers in Victorian America* (New York: Oxford University Press, 1987), 7, 94, 119, 130, 132–33.
9. Keller, *Affairs of State*, 316.
10. Aron, *Ladies and Gentlemen*; Keller, *Affairs of State*, 195–210.
11. Aron, *Ladies and Gentlemen*, 78–81, 95.
12. Stuart, *The Department of State*, 205; Peter Bridges, "Some Men Named William Hunter," *Diplomacy & Statecraft* 16 (2005): 255.
13. Stuart, *The Department of State*, 130.
14. Ibid., 143.
15. Peter Bridges, "An Appreciation of Alvey Adee," *Diplomacy & Statecraft* 10 (1999): 47.
16. Stuart, *The Department of State*, 273, 275.
17. A rough parallel to this is evident in the broader cultural move away from "men of affairs" and the "best men" to the "bureaucratic technician" and "scientist-official" as authoritative sources of knowledge. On this see Matthew G. Hannah, *Governmentality and the Mastery of Territory in Nineteenth-Century America* (Cambridge, UK: Cambridge University Press, 2000), 55–56, 61–76.

18. An earlier example of the attempt to extract relevant material from State Department correspondence is the series entitled *Papers Relating to the Foreign Relations of the United States*. Begun in 1861, it was an annual compilation of U.S. diplomatic documents and other materials. In the 1850s the State Department also issued its first book-length set of instructions for consuls. See Stuart, *The Department of State*, 122.
19. The first attempt to excerpt passport policy from correspondence occurred as part of the publication of the U.S. government's multivolume *Digest of International Law* (Francis Wharton, *A Digest of International Law of the United States* [Washington, DC: GPO, 1886], 2:456–81). However, Hunt's work represented the first attempt to provide a specific, detailed history of the State Department's passport policy.
20. Stuart describes this as a harsh picture of the department, but Root's comments appear to endorse it (Stuart, *The Department of State*, 194).
21. Keller, *Affairs of State*, 318.
22. Hunt, *Department of State*, 416–18.
23. Milton O. Gustafson, "State Department Records in the National Archives: A Profile," *Prologue* 2 (1970): 179.
24. For a detailed summary of the 1909 categories see Hunt, *Department of State*, 418–23.
25. Matt K. Matsuda, *The Memory of the Modern* (New York: Oxford University Press, 1996).
26. Edward Higgs, *The Information State in England: The Centralized Collection of Information on Citizens since 1500* (Houndmills, UK: Palgrave Macmilllan, 2004), 54.
27. "A press book [also called a copy book] is a bound book containing three hundred to five hundred sheets of tissue paper. Letters were written or (later) typed with copying ink and when they were ready to be sent out they were placed between the dampened sheets of tissue in the book. Then a letter press was used to compress the book, causing impressions of the letters to remain in the tissue paper sheets." JoAnne Yates, "From Press Book and Pigeonhole to Vertical Filing: Revolution in Storage and Access Systems for Correspondence," *Journal of Business Communication* 19 (1982): 9.
28. JoAnne Yates, "Business Use of Information and Technology During the Industrial Age," in *A Nation Transformed By Information: How Information Has Shaped the United States from Colonial Times to the Present*, ed. Alfred D. Chandler Jr. and James W. Corteda (Oxford: Oxford University Press, 2000), 118; Joanne Yates, *Control Through Communication: The Rise of System in American Management* (Baltimore: Johns Hopkins University Press, 1989), 62.
29. This discussion of the enforcement of the Chinese Exclusion Act draws heavily from Adam McKeown, *Melancholy Order: Asian Migration and the Globalization of Borders* (New York: Columbia University Press, 2008), 218–91.
30. Ibid., 240–41.

31. For an example of this argument see Miles Ogborn, *Indian Ink: Script and Print in the Making of the English East India Company* (Chicago, University of Chicago, 2007).
32. For an example of this from the 1920s see Karen W. Tice, *Tales of Wayward Girls and Immoral Women: Case Records and the Professionalization of Social Work* (Urbana: University of Illinois Press, 1998). The idea of "simplification" comes from James C. Scott, *Seeing Like a State: How Certain Schemes to Improve the Human Condition Have Failed* (New Haven, CT: Yale University Press, 1998).
33. The previous two sentences are adapted from a summary of Suzanne Briet's definition of a document (Michael K. Buckland, "What is a 'Document'?" *Journal of the American Society for Information Science* 48 [1997]: 804–9). Briet was a mid-twentieth-century French documentalist. The documentalists developed "documentation" as a set of techniques to manage information starting in the late nineteenth century. This is a further example of the broader context of the developing information management practices that enabled modern identification documents to function as a technology within the archival problematization of identity. Also see Ronald E. Day *The Modern Invention of Information: Discourse, History, and Power* (Carbondale: Southern Illinois University Press, 2001), 7–37.

Chapter 8

1. *Urtetiqui v. D'Arcy*, 34 U.S. 698 (1835). For the background of the case see Stephen Krueger, *Krueger on United States Passport Law* (Hong Kong: Crossbow, 1996), 7–14.
2. John Bassett Moore, *A Digest of International Law* (Washington, DC: GPO, 1906), 3:862.
3. 1 Stats at Large USA 103 (March 26, 1790); 1 Stats at Large of USA 414 (January 29, 1795).
4. Quoted in Andor Klay, *Daring Diplomacy: The Case of the First American Ultimatum* (Minneapolis: University of Minnesota Press, 1957), 165–66.
5. Brent to Glazer, June 7, 1823, RG 59 Notes to Foreign Legations, III, 137, National Archives.
6. Buchanan to Huren, August 20, 1846, RG 59 Domestic Letters 36: 73, National Archives.
7. Gerald L. Neuman, " 'We Are the People': Alien Suffrage in German and American Perspective," *Michigan Journal of International Law* 13 (1991–92): 297–99.
8. Marsh to Marcy, August 4, 1853, RG 59 Dispatches Min. Turkey, No, 48, National Archives; Moore, *A Digest of International Law*, 3:870.
9. Gaillard Hunt, *The American Passport: Its History and a Digest of Laws, Rulings and Regulations Governing its Issuance by the Department of State* (Washington, DC: GPO, 1898), 85.
10. Everett to Ingersoll, December 21, 1852, RG 59 Diplomatic Instructions, Gt. Britain XVI: 180, National Archives.

11. "The verification which should be placed upon the back of the certificates might be in these words: 'Legation of the United States at . . . I hereby certify that according to the best of my knowledge and belief, the within document is genuine. [Seal of Legation] Signature.' " Marcy to James Peden, April 10, 1856, RG 59 Diplomatic Instructions, Argentina XV91, National Archives. See also Marcy to Buchanan, April 13, 1854, RG 59 Manuscript Instructions Gr. Brit XVI 285; Marcy to Siebels, May 27, 1854, RG 59 Manuscript Instructions Belgium I 82.
12. Marcy to Clay, December 28, 1854, RG 59 Diplomatic Instructions Peru M77 R130:150, National Archives.
13. H. G. Dwight, "American Political Workers Abroad: The Consular Service," *Bookman*, May 1906, 276. A U.S. passport had limited use in satisfying foreign passport requirements. The laws that underwrote the demand for passports usually referred to a document issued by that government or countersigned by it. In the case of the former the precise role of a U.S. passport was not always clear. Buchanan to Davis, March 8, 1847 in John Bassett Moore (ed.) *The Works of James Buchanan, Comprising his Speeches, State Papers and Private Correspondence* (Philadelphia: James B Lippincott, 1909), 7: 236–7.
14. Rogers M. Smith, *Civic Ideals: Conflicting Visions of Citizenship in U.S. History* (New Haven, CT: Yale University Press, 1997).
15. Leon F. Litwack, "The Federal Government and the Free Negro, 1790–1860," *Journal of Negro History* 43 (1958): 271–73.
16. Kelly S. Drake, "The Seaman's Protection Certificate as Proof of American Citizenship for Black Sailors," *Log of the Mystic Seaport* 50 (Summer 1998): 11–12.
17. Litwack, "Federal Government and the Free Negro," 271.
18. *National Era*, "Passports for Colored People," September 27, 1849.
19. *New York Evening Post*, "Secretary Clayton's Law of Passports" reprinted in the *North Star*, August 24, 1849; *National Era*, "Official Injustice—No Protection for Colored Men," July 5, 1849.
20. *National Era*, "Passports for Colored People."
21. *National Era*, "Official Injustice—No Protection for Colored Men."
22. *North Star*, "From a letter from Wm. Wells Brown to Wm. L. Garrison," November 30, 1849.
23. *North Star*, "Letter from William W. Brown," December 14, 1849.
24. Clayton to Clarke, August 8, 1849, RG 59 Domestic Letters 37:269, National Archives.
25. Elizabeth Pryor, " 'Jim Crow' Cars, Passport Denials and Atlantic Crossings: African-American Travel, Protest and Citizenship at Home and Abroad, 1827–1865" (Ph.D diss., University of California, Santa Barbara, 2008), 112–126.
26. *North Star*, "Passports to People of Color." For more on the Purvis application see Pryor " 'Jim Crow' Cars, Passport Denials and Atlantic Crossings," 119–122.
27. *North Star*, "Passports to People of Color."
28. *Emancipator and Republican*, October 31, 1850.

29. Buchanan to Jones in John Bassett Moore (ed.) *The Works of James Buchanan, Comprising his Speeches, State Papers and Private Correspondence Volume 6* (Philadelphia: James B Lippincott, 1909), 356.
30. Pryor, " 'Jim Crow' Cars, Passport Denials and Atlantic Crossings," 89–100.
31. Sabine Freitag, " 'The Begging Bowl of Revolution': The Fund-Raising Tours of German and Hungarian Exiles to North America, 1851–1852," in *Exiles from European Revolutions: Refugees in Mid-Victorian England*, ed. Sabine Freitag (New York: Berghahn, 2003), 169–76.
32. Peter Bridges, "Some Men Named William Hunter," *Diplomacy & Statecraft* 16 (2005), 254; *New York Daily Times*, "The Koszta Correspondence," September 30, 1853.
33. *New York Daily Times*, "The Koszta Correspondence."
34. Moore, *A Digest of International Law*, 3:824–35, 3:835–54. See also Edwin M. Bouchard, *The Diplomatic Protection of Citizens Abroad; or, The Law of International Claims* (New York: Banks Law, 1915), 570–74.
35. Brown to Marcy, July 5, 1853, quoted in *New York Daily Times*, "The Case of Koszta," March 10, 1854.
36. Marsh to Marcy, July 7, 1853, quoted in Klay, *Daring Diplomacy*, 33.
37. Brown to Marcy, July 5, 1853, quoted in *New York Daily Times*, "The Case of Koszta," March 10, 1854.
38. Hulsemann to Marcy, August 29, 1853, quoted in *New York Daily Times*, "The Koszta Correspondence," September 30, 1853.
39. John E. Findling, *Dictionary of American Diplomatic History* (Westport, CT: Greenwood, 1980), 72.
40. "By this public instrument be it known to all whom the same doth or may in anywise concern, that I, JOSEPH B. NONES, a public notary in and for the state of New-York by letters patent under the great seal of the State duly commissioned and sworn dwelling in the City of New-York, do hereby certify that the persons named in the annexed paper appear before me, and being duly sworn according to law each subscribed the declaration made by him, respectively, which I deem sufficient proof of the affiliated citizenship of the said ___, and I certify the annexed description of his person to be correct. I also certify the annexed affiliation paper of the State of New-York to be genuine, and the said ___ having forever renounced all allegiance, except to the United States of America, and having conformed to the requirements of the several acts of Congress, in such case made and provided, and having received his affiliation certificate, is entitled to all the benefits and protection of an affiliated citizen of the United States of America, and I hereby request all whom it may concern to permit safely and freely to pass the said ___, and in case of need to give him all lawful aid and protection.

    In testimony whereof, I have subscribed my name and caused my national seal of office to be hereunto affixed."Quoted in *New York Daily Times*, "The Case of Koszta," March 10, 1854, 2.
41. Brown to Marcy, July 5, 1853, RG 59 Dispatches from U.S. Min. to Turkey, Dispatch No. 42, National Archives.

42. Buchanan to Marcy, March 24, 1854, RG 59 Dispatches from U.S. Min. to GB., National Archives; Marcy to Nones, April 11, 1854, RG 59 Domestic Letters, 42:354, National Archives.
43. Nones to Marcy, April 12, 1854, RG 59 Manuscript Letters, National Archives.
44. Marcy to Nones, April 14 1854, RG 59 Domestic Letters, 42:363.
45. Kennedy to Seward, November 20,1861, RG 59 MLR 509 Box 2, National Archives; Nones to Seward, October 11, 1861, RG 59 MLR 509 Box 3, National Archives; Irving to Seward, October 14, 1861, RG 59 MLR 509 Box 3, National Archives.
46. Hunter to Rowan, September 6, 1869, RG 59 Domestic Letters, 82:39, National Archives.
47. Moore, *A Digest of International Law*, 3:864.
48. Sherman to Storer, November 8, 1897, U.S. State Department, *Papers Relating to the Foreign Relations of the United States* (Washington, DC: GPO, 1897), 29.
49. "Circular," August 19, 1861, RG 59, Entry 731, National Archives; Seward to Robbins, August 29, 1861, RG 59 Domestic Letters, 54:563, National Archives; Seward, March17, 1862, RG 59 Entry 731, National Archives; Seward, "Circular to the Diplomatic and Consular Officers of the U.S. in Foreign Countries No. 18," August 8, 1862, RG 59 Diplomatic Instructions, The Netherlands M77 R123: 261, National Archives; Seward, "Circular No. 56," March 15, 1865, Circs to Consuls RG 59 MLR 731, National Archives.
50. Act of March 3, 1863, Secretary 23 (12 U.S. Stats 754). This was repealed by the act approved May 30, 1866 (14 U.S. Stats 54). Bayard to Colema, July 10, 1888, U.S. Department of State, *Foreign Relations*, 1888, 1:646–47.
51. Dorothy B. Porter, "Sarah Parker Remond, Abolitionist and Physician," *Journal of Negro History* 20 (1935): 287–93. Her father, John Remond, had been issued a passport in 1854 (Litwack, "Federal Government and the Free Negro," 271).
52. *New York Times*, "Colored Persons and Passports," January 24, 1860, 4.
53. Min to Secretary of State, December 15, 1859, RG 59 Dispatches from U.S. Min to Gt. Britain, Dispatch no, 228: M30 R70, National Archives.
54. Marcy to Min. London, June 16, 1856, RG 59 Diplomatic Instructions, Gt. Britain, M77 R75, National Archives.
55. Min to Secretary of State, December 15, 1859.
56. Ibid. Letter attached. Underlining in original.
57. Ibid; Sarah Remond, September 8, 1858, RG 59 Entry 508, Passport Applications, National Archives.
58. Sarah Remond, September 8, 1858.
59. *New York Times*, "Colored Persons and Passports," 4.
60. *Liberator*, November 28, 1856.
61. Thomas to Rice, November 4, 1856, RG 59 Domestic Letters 28: 397, National Archives.
62. U.S. Department of Justice, *Official Opinions of the Attorneys-General of the United States* (Washington, DC: GPO, 1862), 10:405.

63. Ibid., 10:383.
64. 60 U.S. (19 How.) 393 (1857).
65. *New York Times*, "Passports to Men of Color," April 12, 1858.
66. Saidiya V. Hartman, *Scenes of Subjection: Terror, Slavery, and Self-Making in Nineteenth-Century America* (New York: Oxford University Press, 1997), 164–206.
67. *Liberator*, December 30, 1864.
68. Litwick, "Federal Government and the Free Negro," 273.
69. Somewhat regularly before World War 1, and occasionally even as late as the 1930s, the State Department sent out firm but polite reprimands to officials who issued "passports" or documents in the "nature of passports." Fish to Coke March 23, 1875, RG 59 Domestic Letters, 107:229, National Archives; Hill to Mayor, New Orleans, December 5, 1899, RG 59 Domestic Letters, 241:429, National Archives; Consul General, [Budapest, Hungary] to Secretary of State, July 25, 1910, RG 59 138.8/9 Box 642, National Archives; "DFN," December 22, 1932, RG 59 138.8/166 Box 642, National Archives.
70. Grant to Blaine, December 6, 1889, U.S. Department of State, *Foreign Relations*, 1890, 333.
71. Merriam to Blaine, April 11, 1890, U.S. Department of State, *Foreign Relations*, 1890, 335.
72. The main text of the document stated: "The bearer hereof, John Jagger, is a worthy and respected citizen of this State, a resident of St. Paul, county of Ramsey, State of Minnesota, United States of America. He is now about leaving his home to travel in Europe, and I cordially bespeak for him the kind of attention of all to whom these presents may come." Grant to Blaine, December 6, 1889, U.S. Department of State, *Foreign Relations*, 1890, 333.
73. Andreas Fahrmeir, *Citizens and Aliens: Foreigners and the Law in Britain and the German States, 1789–1870* (New York: Berghahn, 2000), 138.
74. Ibid., 138–41.
75. Ibid., 140; *New York Times*, "Passports," August 7, 1875.
76. George Barr Baker, "The American Diplomatic Service," *Bookman* 44 (September, 1916): 89.
77. Adee to Conger, August 24, 1899, U.S. Department of State, *Foreign Relations*, 1899, 185–87.
78. Foster to Newberry, July 21, 1892, RG 59 Diplomatic Instructions, Turkey M77 R.166: 369–71, National Archives; Bayard [Secretary of State], "No. 700: To diplomatic officers abroad," February 23, 1887, U.S. Department of State, *Foreign Relations*, 1887, 1034.
79. Adee to Conger, August 24, 1899, U.S. Department of State, *Foreign Relations*, 1899, 185–87.
80. Before 1873 a passport was valid for a maximum of one year, though those who chose to carry one were encouraged to get a new passport for every journey abroad. Moore, *A Digest of International Law*, 3:977–83.
81. Hunt, *American Passport*, 134.

82. 15 Stat. L. 233; I-Mien Tsiang, "The Question of Expatriation in America Prior to 1907," (PhD diss., Johns Hopkins University, 1941), 86–88, 95–100; Richard W. Flournoy Jr., "Naturalization and Expatriation," *Yale Law Journal* 31 (1922): 714; Gaillard Hunt, "The New Citizenship Law," *North American Review* 185 (1907): 536; U.S. Department of Justice, *Official Opinions of the Attorneys-General of the United States* (Washington, DC: GPO, 1875), 14:295–96.
83. Fish to Grant, August 15, 1873. Reprinted in Hunt, *American Passport*, 130, 134.
84. Lincoln to Sherman, February 14, 1890, U.S. Department of State, *Foreign Relations*, 1890, 324.
85. Hunt, *American Passport*, 143.
86. Huntington Wilson, "The American Foreign Service," *Outlook*, March 3, 1906, 501.
87. Dwight, "American Political Workers Abroad"; Lawrence E. Gelfand, "Towards a Merit System for the American Diplomatic Service 1900–1930," *Irish Studies in International Affairs* 2, no. 4 (1988): 49–63.
88. H. C. Chatfield-Taylor, "American Diplomats in Europe," *North American Review*, July 1896, 125–28; Waldo H. Heinrichs Jr. "Bureaucracy and Professionalism in the Development of American Career Diplomacy," in *Twentieth-Century American Foreign Policy*, ed. John Braeman, Robert H Bremner, and David Brody (Columbus: Ohio State University Press, 1971), 119–206.
89. Winchester to Bayard, August 26, 1885, U.S. Department of State, *Foreign Relations*, 1885, 809–10.
90. Frelinguysen to Sargent, July 26, 1883, RG 59 Diplomatic Instructions, Germany, XVII 293–95, National Archives.
91. Winchester to Bayard, September 26, 1887, U.S. Department of State, *Foreign Relations*, 1887, 1072.
92. Wharton to Phelps, July 22, 1891, U.S. Department of State, *Foreign Relations*, 1891, 515.
93. Sherman to Hitchcock, December 22, 1897, RG 59 Diplomatic Instructions, Russia M77 R139: 656, National Archives.
94. Ibid.
95. Hay to White, February 23, 1899, RG 59 Diplomatic Instructions, Great Britain XXXIII: 97, National Archives.
96. Bayard to McLane, October 29, 1888, U.S. Department of State, *Foreign Relations*, 1888, 1:561.
97. Hay to Hardy, June 7, 1901, RG 59 Diplomatic Instructions, Switzerland III 263, National Archives.
98. Ibid.; Hay to Fletcher, February 4, 1901, RG 59 Domestic Letters 250:528, National Archives; Olney to Townsend, October 31, 1895, U.S. Department of State, *Foreign Relations*, 1895, 24.
99. Hunt, *American Passport*, 135; Blaine to Ryan, April 9, 1892, RG 59 Diplomatic Instructions Mexico M77 R119, 207, National Archives.

100. Hay to Hardy, June 7, 1901, RG 59 Diplomatic Instructions, Switzerland III 263, National Archives.
101. For a summary of nineteenth-century passport policy towards missionaries, particularly with regards to missionaries resident in China, see Moore, *A Digest of International Law*, 3:971–75.
102. Blaine to Grant, March 25, 1890, U.S. Department of State, *Foreign Relations*, 1890, 12; Wharton to Thayer, March 22, 1892, RG 59 Diplomatic Instructions, Netherlands M77 R125: 118, National Archives.
103. Matthew Frye Jacobson, *Barbarian Virtues: The United States Encounters Foreign Peoples at Home and Abroad, 1876– 1917* (New York: Hill and Wang, 2000), 21, 28.
104. Bayard to Winchester, October 12, 1887, U.S. Department of State, *Foreign Relations*, 1887, 1074.
105. Fish to Washburne, June 28 1873, U.S. Department of State, *Foreign Relations*, 1873, 1:260.
106. Blaine to Hirsch, June 18, 1890, RG 59 Diplomatic Instructions, Turkey M77 R166, 134–36, National Archives.
107. Ibid.
108. Fish to Davis, November 4, 1876, RG 59 Diplomatic Instructions Germany XVI, 252–55, National Archives.
109. Blaine to Hirsch, June 18, 1890, RG 59 Diplomatic Instructions Turkey M77 R166, 134–36, National Archives.
110. Ibid.
111. Bayard to Winchester, June 9, 1886, U.S. Department of State, *Foreign Relations*, 1886, 847.
112. Adee to Conger, August 24, 1899, U.S. Department of State, *Foreign Relations*, 1899, 186–87.
113. Wilson to Iddings, January 31, 1907, U.S. Department of State, *Foreign Relations*, 1907, 1082. See also Wilson to Beaupre, April 27, 1907, U.S. Department of State, *Foreign Relations*, 1907, 1088.
114. Moore, *A Digest of International Law*, 3:921.
115. Bayard to Walker, March 29, 1888, U.S. Department of State, *Foreign Relations*, 1888, 1:420.
116. Adee to Conger, August 24, 1899, U.S. Department of State, *Foreign Relations*, 1899, 186.
117. [Author unknown] to Bacon, February 14, 1907, RG 59 Numerical File, 3752/43, National Archives.
118. Fahrmeir, *Citizens and Aliens*, 138.
119. *Report on the Subject of the Citizenship of the United States, Expatriation and Protection Abroad*, 59th Cong. 2nd sess., H.R. Doc. 326; 34 Stat. L. 1228 (March 2, 1907).
120. *Citizenship of the United States, Expatriation and Protection Abroad*, 14.
121. Green Haywood Hackworth, *Digest of International Law* (Washington, DC: GPO, 1942), 3:538.

CHAPTER 9

1. E. P. Hutchinson, *Legislative History of American Immigration Policy, 1798–1965* (Philadelphia: University of Pennsylvania Press, 1981).
2. 22 Stat. 214; 26 Stat. 1084.
3. Ian F. Haney-López, *White By Law: The Legal Construction of Race* (New York: New York University Press 1996), 100.
4. Mae M. Ngai, *Impossible Subjects: Illegal Aliens and the Making of Modern America* (Princeton, NJ: Princeton University Press, 2004), 44.
5. United States v. Thind, 261 U.S. 209, 211, (1923); Matthew Frye Jacobson, *Whiteness of a Different Color: European Immigrants and the Alchemy of Race* (Cambridge, MA: Harvard University Press, 1998), 236, 222–23.
6. Lucy E. Salyer, *Laws Harsh as Tigers: Chinese Immigrants and the Shaping of Modern Immigration Law* (Chapel Hill: University of North Carolina Press, 1995).
7. Ibid., 201; Elizabeth Yew, "Medical Inspection of Immigrants at Ellis Island, 1891–1924," *Bulletin of the New York Academy of Medicine* 56 (1980): 494–95.
8. Nayan Shah, *Contagious Divides: Epidemics and Race in San Francisco's Chinatown* (Berkeley: University of California Press, 2001), 186; Yew, "Medical Inspection of Immigrants," 492.
9. Amy L. Fairchild, *Science at the Borders: Immigrant Medical Inspection and the Shaping of the Modern Industrial Labor Force* (Baltimore: Johns Hopkins University Press, 2003), 109, 115.
10. Yew, "Medical Inspection of Immigrants," 495.
11. Fairchild, *Science at the Borders*, 125.
12. Alfred C. Reed, "The Medical Side of Immigration," *Popular Science Monthly*, April 1912, 384–85.
13. Jacobson, *Whiteness of a Different Color*, 72–73, 75.
14. Estelle T. Lau, *Paper Families: Identity, Immigration Administration, and Chinese Exclusion* (Durham, NC: Duke University Press, 2006), 67.
15. Although it affected U.S. border control in general, this decision was in a response to a case originating in the enforcement of the Chinese Exclusion Act (Chae Chan Ping v. United States, 130 U.S. . 601–10 [1889]); Salyer, *Laws Harsh as Tigers*, 23).
16. U.S. Bureau of Immigration, *Annual Report of the Commissioner General of Immigration to the Secretary of Commerce and Labor* (Washington, DC: GPO, 1913), 182.
17. For a detailed description of onboard inspection, see "Organization of the U.S. Emigrant Station at Ellis Island, New York, Together with a Brief Description of the Work Done in Each of its Divisions, October 23, 1903" in *Ellis Island, Statue of Liberty National Monument, New York-New* Jersey, ed. Harlan D. Unrau, (Washington, DC: U.S. Department of the Interior, National Park Service, 1984), 2:312–53; and "Rules for the U.S. Immigrant Station at Ellis Island, February 1912," in Unrau, *Ellis Island*, 434–46.
18. Howe to Cmr.-Gen. Immigration, September 24, 1915, RG. 85, 53438/15, National Archives.

19. Ibid.; Gelett Burgess, "The Steerage Revisited," *Colliers*, April 16, 1910, 17–18; Shah, *Contagious Divides*, 184.
20. Sargent to Hunt, June 16, 1908, RG 85 51831/106, National Archives. See also Fairchild, *Science at the Borders*, 125.
21. Fairchild, *Science at the Borders*, 123. See also Thomas M. Pitkin, *Keepers of the Gate: A History of Ellis Island* (New York: New York University Press, 1975), 44, 64.
22. Mary B. Sayles, "The Keepers of the Gate," *Outlook*, December 28, 1907, 918.
23. For discussions and analysis of immigration inspection at Ellis Island see Allan McLaughlin, "How Immigrants are Inspected," *Popular Science Monthly*, February 1905, 357–61; Victor Safford, *Immigration Problems: Personal Experiences of an Official* (New York: Dodd Mead, 1925); Sayles, "The Keepers of the Gate"; Edith Abbott, *Immigration: Select Documents and Case Records* (Chicago: University of Chicago Press, 1924), 244–51; Yew, "Medical Inspection of Immigrants"; Fairchild, *Science at the Borders*, 86–98.
24. Alfred C. Reed, "Going Through Ellis Island," *Popular Science Monthly*, January 1913, 6.
25. E. K. Sprague, "Medical Inspection of Immigrants," *Survey* 30 (April–September 1913), 420–22.
26. Edward A. Steiner, *On the Trail of the Immigrant* (New York: F. H. Revell, 1906), 67.
27. Reed, "Medical Side of Immigration," 386–87. For a similarly detailed outline of the medical inspection performed along the U.S./Mexican border, see John W. Tappen, "The Medical Inspection of Immigrants with Special Reference to the Texas-Mexican Border," *Texas State Journal of Medicine* 15 (July 1919): 120–24.
28. Yew, "Medical Inspection of Immigrants," 501.
29. Reed, "Medical Side of Immigration," 387; H. D. Geddings "Report to Surgeon-General, November 16, 1906," in Unrau, *Ellis Island*, 671; Fairchild, *Science at the Borders*, 98.
30. The subsequent description of the immigrant inspection comes from the following: Robert Watchorn, "The Gateway of the Nation," *Outlook*, December 28, 1907, 897–911; Sayles, "Keepers of the Gate"; Pitkin, *Keepers of the Gate*, 67–72; Steiner, *On The Trail of the Immigrant*, 64–77; "Report from Inspectors of the Boarding Division," January 22, 1914, RG 85 53438/15, National Archives.
31. William Williams, "Annual Report, 1909," Box 5, William Williams Papers, New York Public Library (NYPL).
32. Salyer, *Laws Harsh as Tigers*, 147.
33. Clothing, however, did offer the possibility of fraud. If officials suspected this, an immigrant could be asked to disrobe to reveal the "reliable" evidence of a disease or deformity a body was presumed to offer. On at least one occasion officials demanded disrobing to see if a person's sex matched the sex suggested by their clothing (Erica Rand, *The Ellis Island Snow Globe* [Durham, NC: Duke University Press, 2005], 76).

34. William Williams, "Confidential Memo on Report," Box 5, William Williams Papers, NYPL.
35. Joseph H. Senner, "How We Restrict Immigration," *North American Review* 158 (1894): 498.
36. "Ellis Island Scrapbook" (dated December 3, 1902), 22, William Williams Papers, NYPL.
37. Williams to Cmr.-Gen. of Immigration, August 29, 1903, William Williams Papers, Box 1, NYPL.
38. William Williams to Messers Vernon H Brown and Co., May 5, 1903, William Williams Papers, Box 1, NYPL.
39. Williams, "To The Owners of Steamships," August 23, 1902, RG 85 53438/15, National Archives.
40. "Ellis Island Scrapbook," 8, William Williams Papers, NYPL.
41. U.S. Bureau of Immigration, *Annual Report of the Commissioner General of Immigration to the Secretary of Commerce and Labor* (Washington, DC: GPO, 1913), 181.
42. Williams, "As to Manifests and Cabin Inspection," October 20, 1902, RG 85 53438/15, National Archives.
43. Ibid.; "Ellis Island Scrapbook," 19, William Williams Papers, NYPL.
44. William Williams, "Ellis Island, Its Organization and Some of Its Work," 40, December 1912, William Williams Papers, Box 5, NYPL.
45. "Rules for the U.S. Immigrant Station at Ellis Island, February 1912" in Unrau, *Ellis Island*, 475.
46. Benjamin Friedman to William Williams, May 9, 1910, William Williams Papers, Box 2, NYPL.
47. Andrew Gyory, *Closing the Gate: Race, Politics, and the Chinese Exclusion Act* (Chapel Hill: University of North Carolina Press, 1998); Salyer, *Laws Harsh As Tigers*, 6–17.
48. Mary Roberts Coolidge, *Chinese Immigration* (New York: H. Holt, 1909), 169.
49. Adam McKeown, *Melancholy Order: Asian Migration and the Globalization of Borders* (New York: Columbia University Press, 2008), 144–48.
50. Erika Lee, *At America's Gates: Chinese Immigration During the Exclusion Era, 1882–1943* (Chapel Hill: University of North Carolina Press, 2003); McKeown, *Melancholy Order*.
51. Lau, *Paper Families*, 95.
52. Amendment to Exclusion Act, 1884, quoted. in Kitty Calavita, "The Paradoxes of Race, Class, Identity, and 'Passing': Enforcing the Chinese Exclusion Acts, 1882–1910," *Law and Social Inquiry* 25 (2000): 21.
53. Lee, *At America's Gates*, 79–80.
54. Lau, *Paper Families*, 96.
55. Lee, *At America's Gates*, 84–85; McKee, *Chinese Exclusion*, 123.
56. Calavita, "Paradoxes of Race," 24.

57. Ibid., 23.
58. Ibid., 25. While Calavita's examples are from the turn of the century, Lee cites two examples of the privileging of the body over documents from 1912 and 1917 (Lee, *At America's Gates*, 89–90).
59. McKeown, *Melancholy Order*, 145; *In re Low Yam Chow*, 13 F. 609, 612–15 (1882); *In re Cheen Heong* 21 F. 793 (1884); *In re Tung Yeong* 19 F. 184–90 (1884).
60. Lee, *At America's Gates*, 175.
61. Ibid., 162.
62. Department of Commerce and Labor, *Annual Report of the Commissioner-General of Immigration, 1905*, (Washington D.C: Government Printing Office), 95.
63. Lee, *At America's Gates*, 79–80.
64. The commissioner of immigration for San Francisco, quoted in Calavita, "Paradoxes of Race," 14–15.
65. Lau, *Paper Families*, 105.
66. Ibid., 36–41, 67, 71, 93, 99–100, 115–30.
67. Ibid., 99–100.
68. McKeown, *Melancholy Order*; Lau, *Paper Families*.
69. Raymond A. Esthus, *Theodore Roosevelt and Japan* (Seattle: University of Washington Press, 1966), 129, 161.
70. Esthus, *Theodore Roosevelt and Japan*, 146. For further discussion of events leading up to the Gentlemen's Agreement, see Roger Daniels, *Asian America: Chinese and Japanese in the United States since 1850* (Seattle: University of Washington Press, 1988), 116–123; and Roger Daniels, *The Politics of Prejudice, the Anti-Japanese Movement in California, and the Struggle for Japanese Exclusion* (Gloucester, MA: Peter Smith, 1966), 37.
71. Daniels, *Asian America*, 126; Eithne Luibhéid, *Entry Denied: Controlling Sexuality at the Border* (Minneapolis: University of Minnesota Press, 2002), 55–76.
72. Daniels, *Asian America*, 130–31; Luibhéid, *Entry Denied*, 73–75.
73. For a discussion of the status of Chinese as U.S. citizens, see Salyer, *Laws Harsh as Tigers*, 94–116.
74. Metcalf to Root, October 25, 1905, RG 85 52088/64, National Archives. See also letters of July 18, 1903 and July 22, 1903, RG 85 52088/64, National Archives.
75. Root to Metcalf, October 7, 1905, RG 85 52088/64, National Archives.
76. Metcalf to Root, October 23, 1905, RG 85 52088/64, National Archives; Memo. re issuance of passports to Chinese persons, October 10, 1905, RG 85 52088/64, National Archives.
77. Metcalf to Root, October 25, 1905, RG 85 52088/64, National Archives.
78. Lee, *At America's Gates*, 107.
79. "Notice Concerning Manifesting of United States Citizens And Inspection of Cabin Passengers," April 11, 1912, RG 85 98524/88, National Archives.

80. Ibid.; Williams to Keefe, December 30, 1912, RG 85 98524/88, National Archives; Keefe to Williams, January 3, 1913, RG 85 98524/88, National Archives; Williams to Nth. German Lloyd Steamship Co., July 8. 1912, RG 85 98524/88, National Archives.
81. Root to Metcalf, November 15, 1905, RG 85 52088/64, National Archives; Circular "Passports for Persons of the Chinese Race Born in the United States," November 20, 1905, RG 85 52088/64, National Archives.
82. Straus to Bacon, February 19, 1909, RG 85, 52088/64, National Archives.
83. Ibid.; Bacon to Straus, May 1, 1909, RG 85, 52088/64, National Archives.
84. *New York Times*, "Keeping Tab on Immigrants," March 29, 1909; *New York Times*, "For Aliens' Finger Prints," October 25, 1913.
85. C. F. Goodrich, "Brand Alien Felons," *New York Times*, March 5, 1913; C. F. Goodrich, "Foreign Convicts," *New York Times*, October 3, 1913.
86. "Inspector in Charge" to "Commissioner of Immigration," January 22, 1914, RG 85 5438/15, National Archives.

CHAPTER 10

1. *New York Sun*, "W. K. Vanderbilt Tries To Identify Himself," October 20, 1915.
2. *New York Sun*, "First Passport Issued President," November 28, 1918.
3. Flournoy to Johnson, December 24, 1914, RG 59 138.28/1 Box 66, National Archives.
4. John Torpey, *The Invention of the Passport: Surveillance, Citizenship, and the State* (Cambridge, UK: Cambridge University Press, 1999), 155.
5. Executive Order No. 2285, December 15, 1915.
6. Flournoy to Phillips, March 1, 1917, RG 59 138/417, National Archives.
7. *New York Times*, "Lack of Passports Holds Up Americans," June 25, 1915; *New York Times*, "Seventeen Americans Held," June 26, 1915.
8. *Washington Post*, "Hard To Get U.S. Passports," March 5, 1916.
9. *New York Times*, "Americans Ignore British Passport Rules," June 24, 1915.
10. Secretary of Commerce to Gen.-Manager, Holland-America Line, June 5, 1917, RG 59 138/609, National Archives; Secretary of Commerce to Secretary of State, August 31, 1917. RG 59 138/609, National Archives.
11. House Committee on Foreign Affairs, *Control of Travel From and Into the United States: Hearings before the Committee on Foreign Affairs*, 65th Cong., 2nd sess., February 18, 1918, 5, 6.
12. Gregory to Lansing, August 18, 1917, RG 59 811.111/583, National Archives.
13. Lansing to Gregory, September 19, 1917, RG 59 811.111/583, National Archives.
14. House Committee on Foreign Affairs, *Control of Travel*, 36.
15. Ibid., 26.
16. Ibid., 3.

17. Secretary of War to Secretary of State, October 22, 1917, RG 59 811.111/871, National Archives.
18. House Committee on Foreign Affairs, *Control of Travel*, 27.
19. *Washington Post*, "Takes His Passports," September 10, 1915; *Washington Post*, "Her Passports Suspected," January 17, 1915.
20. House Committee on Foreign Affairs, *Fees Charged for Passports and for Viséing Foreign Passports: Hearings before the Committee on Foreign Affairs*, 66th Cong., 2nd sess., February 3, 4, 7, 1920, 24.
21. Lansing to Secretary of Treasury, March 25, 1918, RG 59 811.111/4687a Box 13, National Archives.
22. Flournoy to Secretary of State, October12, 1917, RG 59 811.111/927, National Archives.
23. Secretary of Treasury to Secretary of State, February 19, 1917, RG 59 138/415, National Archives; Secretary of Treasury to Secretary of State, March 17, 1917, RG 59 138/426, National Archives.
24. In one case the suspicions of fellow passengers ensured that an interrogation of some supposed citizens occurred when the ship arrived in New York. Post to Secretary of State, May 1, 1917, RG 59 138/483, National Archives; Post to Secretary of State, May 7, 1917, RG 59 138/490, National Archives.
25. For problems at the Madrid consul see RG 59 811.111/1879, National Archives.
26. *New York Times*, "Tourists in Paris are in War Panic," August 1, 1914.
27. *New York Times*, "Not American Passports," October 30, 1914.
28. *Washington Post*, "Posing as Americans," September 9, 1914.
29. Berlin Legation to Secretary of State, August 25, 1915, RG 59 138.28/13 Box 636, National Archives.
30. Secretary of State to U.S. Ambassador [London], November 25, 1914, RG 59 138/37 Box 590, National Archives.
31. Secretary of State to U.S. Ambassador [Paris], February 15, 1915, RG 59 138/77 Box 590, National Archives.
32. Daniel C. Turack, "Freedom of Movement and the International Regime of Passports," *Osgoode Hall Law Journal* 6 (1968): 249.
33. Ellen Adair, "War Time Traveling in France is Beset With Trials, Especially for One who Can Speak German," *Washington Post*, August 29, 1915.
34. *Washington Post*, "More Passports to Archibald Will Be Denied," September 9, 1915; *Washington Post*, "All Americans in England Must Now Show Passport," August 8, 1915.
35. *Washington Post*, "Threaten Suits to Obtain Passports," November 4, 1915.
36. In contrast, a U.S. official visaed an alien's passport with the word "seen" (Carr to Murphy [Consul-Gen., Cape Town], March 30, 1915, RG 59 138.7/17 Box 638, National Archives).
37. *Washington Post*, "Asks For Unused Passports," January 13, 1916; Assist. Secretary of Treasury to Secretary of State, March 29, 1916, RG 59, 138.81/18,

National Archives; Secretary of State to Secretary of Labor, October 28, 1916 RG 85, MLR#9, 54410/331c, National Archives.

38. Flournoy to Johnson, December 24, 1914, RG 59 138.28/1 Box 66, National Archives.
39. *Washington Post*, "New Passport Ruling," April 19, 1916.
40. *New York Sun*, "Passport Rules Strict," June 19, 1917.
41. *New York Sun*, "Branch Office Opens Here," January 4, 1916. The State Department had employed individual passport agents in New York City and Boston during the Civil War.
42. *Washington Post*, "Tighten Rules on Passports," February 2, 1917.
43. *Washington Post*, "Hard To Get U.S. Passports," March 5, 1916.
44. Ibid.
45. Ibid.
46. *Washington Post*, "No Missionary Passports," October 10, 1915; *Washington Post*, "No Student Passports," September 18, 1915; *Washington Post*, "New Passport Policy," October 26, 1915.
47. *Washington Post*, "Passports Held Back," April 8, 1915; *Washington Post*, "Kaiser Puts Americans into Army When their Passports Expire," October 8, 1917.
48. *Washington Post*, "Limits Passport Issuance," April 24, 1915.
49. *New York Sun*, "Adolph Dietzel Arrested at Aberdeen," April 1, 1915.
50. *New York Times*, "Baron Zwiedinek Sent Suggestion to Buy Passports," December 11, 1915; *New York Times*, "Bryan Admits Spies Get our Passports," November 14, 1914; *New York Times*, "Exposure Balks Officer," January 6, 1915.
51. *New York Sun*, "Stiegler Arrested New German Plot," February 25, 1915.
52. *New York Tribune* article (stamped August 29, 1915) attached to Page to Secretary of State, June 18, 1915, RG 59 138.8/55, National Archives.
53. Page to Secretary of State, June 16, 1915, RG 59 138.8/53, National Archives.
54. Ibid.; Page to Secretary of State, June 28, 1915, RG 59 138.8/64, National Archives.
55. "RWF" to Lansing, June 18, 1915, RG 59 138.8/78, National Archives; "RWF" to Woolsey, July 14, 1915, RG 59 138.8/78, National Archives.
56. Page to Secretary of State, November 11, 1915, RG 59 138.8/87, National Archives.
57. Aristide R. Zolberg, "The Great Wall Against China: Responses to the First Immigration Crisis, 1855–1925," in *Migration, Migration History, History: Old Paradigms and New Perspectives*, ed. Jan Lucassen and Leo Lucassen (Bern, Switzerland: Peter Lang, 1997), 308.
58. Clifford Alan Perkins, *Border Patrol: With the U.S. Immigration Service on the Mexican Boundary, 1910–54* (El Paso: Texas Western Press, University of Texas at El Paso, 1978), 73.
59. Assistant Secretary of Treasury to Secretary of State, April 18, 1918, RG 59 811.111/4681, National Archives.
60. Totten, "Report on Conditions on the Mexican Border," January 20, 1918, RG 59 811.111/3253, National Archives, 7.

61. American Consul [Sonara] to Secretary of State, May 6, 1921, RG 59 13/1459, National Archives.
62. U.S. Bureau of Immigration, *Annual Report of the Commissioner General of Immigration to the Secretary of Commerce and Labor* (Washington, DC: GPO, 1918), 11, 321.
63. Berkshire to Adee, March 4, 1920, RG 59 811.111/28903, National Archives; Berkshire to Chief, Division of Passport Control, May 15, 1921, RG 59 811.111/21691, National Archives; *New York Times*, "Criticizes Ruling on Mexico Passport," September 14, 1920; *New York Times*, "Hard Drinking Oasis Before the Cabinet," October 22, 1921.
64. David M. Kennedy, *Over Here: The First World War and American Society* (New York: Oxford University Press, 1980), 98.
65. Alfred D. Chandler Jr., *The Visible Hand: The Managerial Revolution in American Business* (Cambridge, MA: Belknap, 1977); Stephen Skowronek, *Building a New American State: The Expansion of National Administrative Capacities, 1870–1920* (Cambridge, UK: Cambridge University Press, 1982), 200. For debates about the changes this brought to social priorities in the United States, see Ellis W. Hawley, *The Great War and the Search for a Modern Order: A History of the American People and their Institutions, 1917–1933* (New York: St. Martin's, 1992); Paul L. Murphy, *World War I and the Origin of Civil Liberties in the United States* (New York: Norton, 1979); Kennedy, *Over Here*.
66. Kennedy, *Over Here*.
67. Charles H. McCormick, *Seeing Reds: Federal Surveillance of Radicals in the Pittsburgh Mill District, 1917–1921* (Pittsburgh, PA: University of Pittsburgh Press, 1997), 4.
68. Ibid., 29; Kennedy, *Over Here*, 67–68.
69. Christopher Capozzola, *Uncle Sam Wants You: World War I and the Making of the Modern American Citizen* (New York: Oxford University Press, 2008), 23.
70. U.S. Department of Justice, *Annual Report of the Attorney General of the United States, 1918* (Washington, DC: GPO, 1918), 15; Kennedy, *Over Here*, 82.
71. Capozzola, *Uncle Sam Wants You*, 37, 22–53.
72. Department of Justice, *Annual Report, 1918*, 29–31, 686–727; Pamela Sankar, "State Power and Record-Keeping: The History of Individualized Surveillance in the United States, 1790–1935" (PhD diss., University of Pennsylvania, 1992), 261–63.
73. Capozzola, *Uncle Sam Wants You*, 174.
74. *New York Times*, "President Urges Longer Alien Ban," August 26, 1919.
75. *New York Times*, "Barring Undesirables," October 19, 1919.
76. House Committee on Foreign Affairs, *Fees Charged for Passports*, 25.
77. House Committee on Foreign Affairs, *Extension of Passport Control: Hearings*, 66th Cong., 1st sess., October 7, 8, 10, 1919, 29, 9.

78. House Committee on Foreign Affairs, *Extension of Passport Control*; House Committee on Foreign Affairs, *Fees Charged for Passports*; McCormick, *Seeing Red; Washington Post*, "Alien Order Is Modified," July 2, 1920, 6; Polk to Atty.-Gen., February 12, 1920, RG 59 138.8/119.
79. *New York Herald*, "Test May Be Made In Passport Mixup," April 3, 1921; *New York Times*, "Need Passports No Longer," April 5, 1921.
80. House Committee on Foreign Affairs, *Further Regulating*, 32.
81. Adee to Otter Manufacturing Co., September 5, 1922, RG 59 811.111/38008, National Archives.
82. Flournoy to Carr, Oct 15, 1919, RG 59 811.111/27192a, National Archives.
83. House Committee on Foreign Affairs, *Fees Charged for Passports*, 36.
84. Assistant Secretary of Labor to Secretary of State, November 12, 1921, RG 59 811.111/34894, National Archives; 2nd Assistant Secretary of Labor to Secretary of State, November 8, 1922, RG 59 811.111/38504, National Archives; Secretary of State to Consular Officers, November 19, 1923 RG 59 811.111/42198a, National Archives.
85. *Washington Post*, "Germans Coming To U.S.," March 7, 1920; *Washington Post,* "State Department Power On Alien Passports Final," January 20, 1921.
86. For example, a 1923 *New York Times* editorial argued that the Departments of Labor and State should work together so that quota numbers determined the issuance of visas, an argument that incorrectly assumed an already existing role for visas in immigration regulations (*New York Times*, "Controlling Immigration at the Source," August 3, 1923). See House Committee on Foreign Affairs, *Fees Charged*, 30–31.
87. 42 Stat 5 (May 19, 1921).
88. Mae Ngai traces the principle behind this change back to the 1917 Act, which introduced a literacy test (Mae M. Ngai, *Impossible Subjects: Illegal Aliens and the Making of Modern America* [Princeton, NJ: Princeton University Press, 2004], 19).
89. RG 59 811.111/41008, National Archives; *New York Times*, "Controlling Immigration at the Source," August 3, 1923.
90. *New York Times* "Controlling Immigration at the Source."
91. *New York Times*, "Aliens on Four Ships Too Soon to Enter," September 2, 1923.
92. *New York Times*, "Fines Ships $600,000 for Surplus Aliens," September 6, 1923.
93. Department of Labor, *Annual Report 1924*, 1.
94. Perhaps not surprisingly, some immigration officials still considered the face-to-face expertise of immigration inspectors more effective than a system of excessive documentation ("Taking the Queue out of Quota: An Interview with W. W. Husband, Commissioner-General of Immigration," *Survey*, March 15, 1924, 667–69.)
95. I did not find any discussion of how the issuance of visas abroad was coordinated with visas issued in Canada or Mexico to ensure that the monthly and

annual quotas were not oversubscribed. But neither did I find any complaints, so the system appears to have worked more effectively than under the 1921 act.

96. Thomas M. Pitkin, *Keepers of the Gate: A History of Ellis Island* (New York: New York University Press, 1975), 155–57; William C. White, "Ellis Island Altered by Immigration Trend," *New York Times*, October 8, 1933, 12.
97. U.S. Department of State, *The Immigration Work of the Department of State and its Consular Officers* (Washington, DC: GPO, 1932), 6.
98. By 1932 medical inspections had been implemented in the United Kingdom, the Irish Free State, Belgium, Netherlands, Germany, Norway, Denmark, Sweden, Poland, Italy, Czechoslovakia, and Austria (U.S. Department of State, *Immigration Work*, 2). For the initial English experiment, see Amy L. Fairchild, *Science at the Borders: Immigrant Medical Inspection and the Shaping of the Modern Industrial Labor Force* (Baltimore: Johns Hopkins University Press, 2003), 259–76; *New York Times*, "Examine Britons Before Coming Here," August 2, 1925; *New York Times*, "Examining Immigrants Abroad," August 7, 1925; *New York Times*, "Examining Immigrants Abroad," May 31, 1926.
99. *New York Times*, "Held in Poland for Visa Forgeries," February 28, 1930; *New York Times*, "Nine Indicted Here as Fake Visa Ring," March 5, 1930.
100. *New York Times*, "False Passport Plot Nipped in Hungary," November 2, 1925, 25; Nathan to Secretary of State, July 24, 1924; RG 59 138.28/52, National Archives.
101. Carr to White, April 7, 1930, RG 59 138/2673, National Archives.
102. Consul-Gen. (Budapest) to Secretary of State, Nov 14, 1925, RG 59 138.28/67, Box 636, National Archives; "American Passport Fraud Detection in Italy," June 11, 1934, RG 59 138.81/388, National Archives; Consul-Gen. (Naples) to Secretary of State, November 3, 1931, RG 59 138.81/238, National Archives.
103. House Committee on Immigration and Naturalization, *Review of the Action of Consular Officers in Refusing Immigration Visas: Hearings*, 72nd Cong., 1st sess., March 16, 1932; House Committee on Immigration and Naturalization, *Review of Refusal of Visas by Consular Officers: Hearings*, 73rd Cong., 1st sess., May 18, 23, 1933.
104. Donald H. Avery, "Canadian Workers and American Immigration Restriction: A Case Study of the Windsor Commuters, 1924–1931," *Mid-America* 80 (1998): 235–63.
105. For a detailed description of the bathing process, see John W. Tappen, "The Medical Inspection of Immigrants with Special Reference to the Texas-Mexican Border," *Texas State Journal of Medicine* 15 (July 1919), 122. On the continuation of this practice in the 1920s, see Mae M. Ngai "Illegal Aliens and Alien Citizens: United States Immigration Policy and Racial Formation, 1924–1945" (PhD diss., Columbia University, 1998), 165–66.
106. Ngai, *Impossible Subjects*, 7, 54–55, 67–71.
107. Lawrence A. Cordoso, *Mexican Emigration to the United States, 1897–1931: Socio-economic Patterns* (Tucson: University of Arizona Press, 1980), 130.

108. Leon A. Dickinson, "New England Offers 'Ideal' Mountain Trip," *New York Times*, July 14, 1929.
109. *New York Times*, "Answers Criticism by Border Tourists," July 17, 1929, 26.
110. Senate Committee on Commerce, *Border Patrol Part 1–3: Hearings before the Committee on Commerce*, 71st Cong., 2nd sess., December 18, 1930, January 15, 1931, 60.
111. Remsen Crawford, "Halt! Who's There!" *Saturday Evening Post*, January 7, 1928, 202.
112. Ibid., 197.
113. *New York Times*, "Boundary Line Bars Owner From House," October 23, 1932.
114. For a detailed discussion of this see Craig Robertson, "Locating the Border," *Social Identities* 14 (2008): 447–56.
115. House Committee on the Judiciary, *To Establish a Border Patrol: Hearings before the Committee on the Judiciary*, 69th Cong., 1st sess., April 12, 19, 1926, 17.
116. U.S. Statutes at Large 43 (1925): 1049; Memorandums: August 21, 1924, August 30, 1924, September 2, 1924, RG 85, 53108/22, National Archives; Wilmuth to Comm.-Gen. of Immigration, April 24, 1930, RG 85 E9. 55688/876, National Archives; House Committee on the Judiciary, *To Establish a Border Patrol*; House Committee on Immigration and Naturalization, *Immigration Border Patrol: Hearings*, 70th Cong., 1st sess., March 5, 1928; House Committee on Interstate and Foreign Commerce, *Border Patrol: Hearings*, 71st Cong., 2nd sess., April 24, 25, 1930; Senate Committee on Commerce, *Border Patrol*.
117. White to Secretary of State, August 25, 1924, RG 59 811.111/4322.
118. White, "Ellis Island Altered."
119. For very-long-term residents, it often proved impossible to locate records of entry from the prewar period. In these situations an alien resident had to locate two witnesses who could swear to their long-term residence, and then pay $20 to get a certificate of arrival (*New York Times*, "Re-Entry Delay Defended," May 30, 1932).
120. Day to Comm.-Gen. of Immigration, March 15, 1930, RG 85 55630/4A, National Archives.
121. *New York Times*, "Wheeler Assails Alien Registration," February 17, 1930; *New York Times*, "Alien Registration Scored as Czaristic," January 10, 1926.
122. *New York Times*, "Davis for Listing Aliens," March 3, 1922; *New York Times*, "Plans Annual Fees By Resident Aliens," March 12, 1922; James J. Davis, "Who Are the American People?" *The Saturday Evening Post*, December 8, 1923, 29.
123. *The Saturday Evening Post*, "Why Not Register Them?" March 22, 1930, 24.

CHAPTER 11

1. Irving E. Dooe, "A Passport Abroad," *New York Sun*, November 28, 1919.

2. *Washington Post*, "The Passport System," July 31, 1920.
3. U.S. Passport Office, *The United States Passport: Past, Present, Future* (Washington, DC: GPO, 1976), 220–21.
4. Pamela Sankar, "State Power and Record-Keeping: The History of Individualized Surveillance in the United States, 1790–1935" (PhD diss., University of Pennsylvania, 1992), 24.
5. Alexander S. Banks, "Who is Respectable?" *New York Times*, April 27, 1924.
6. *Literary Digest*, "Red Tape Worse Than Barbed-Wire Entanglements in Central Europe," January 22, 1921, 48.
7. *Living Age*, "Passport Adventures," June 26, 1920, 788.
8. *New York Times*, "Outlook for Touring in Europe Next Autumn," May 18, 1919.
9. T. R. Ybarra, "Passport Worries in Europe," *New York Times*, February 6, 1921.
10. *New York Times*, "Passport Levies Hit Travel, He Says," November 26, 1922. See also *New York Times*, "Swiss Are Demanding Easier Passport Law," April 17, 1921.
11. Ybarra, "Passport Worries," 10.
12. *New York Evening Post*, "Passports and Postage," October 4, 1920, 8; League of Nations, Organization for Communication and Transit, *Passport Conference Held at Geneva from May 12th to 18th, 1926* (Geneva, Switzerland: The League of Nations, 1926).
13. League of Nations, *Passport Conference*, 70.
14. F. P. Walters, *A History of the League of Nations* (London: Oxford University Press, 1952); F .S. Northedge, *The League of Nations: Its Life and Times, 1920–1946* (Leicester, UK: Leicester University Press, 1986); United Nations Library, *The League of Nations in Retrospect: Proceedings of the Symposium* (New York: Walter de Gruyter, 1983).
15. League of Nations, *Passport Conference*, 57.
16. Michael R. Marrus, *The Unwanted: European Refugees in the Twentieth Century* (New York: Oxford University Press, 1985), 93.
17. League of Nations, *Passport Conference*, 42.
18. Ibid., 28.
19. Ibid., 81.
20. Ibid., 36.
21. Ibid., 81.
22. Helen Woodbury, "A New Era in Travel," *Independent*, October 3, 1925, 391.
23. James Collins, "The Steerage Puts On a White Collar," *Saturday Evening Post*, September 27, 1924, 16.
24. The Bureau of Immigration also contributed to the ongoing separation of immigrants when it loosened its requirement that all third-class passengers be inspected on shore at an immigration station. Inspectors were given permission to inspect "third class passengers who are apparently non-immigrants" on board

(*New York Times*, "Third Class Tourists To Escape Detention," November 14, 1925).

25. Collins, "Steerage,"17.
26. Bunice Fuller Barnard, "The Swelling Tide of Foreign Travel," *New York Times*, May 6 1928.
27. In 1928 430,955 citizens left the United States, though it is unknown how many of those people were travelers. The percentage of citizens who left the United States was consistently around 0.3% from 1900–1930. See *Literary Digest*, "Our Tourists a Large Factor in World Finance," June 8, 1929, 68. See also Christopher Endy, "Travel and World Power: Americans in Europe, 1890–1917," *Diplomatic History* 22 (1998): 567.
28. *Literary Digest*, "Our Tourists," 68.
29. Thomas Craven, "New Innocents Abroad," *Forum*, April 1930, 239–44.
30. Ibid.
31. *New York Times*, "Why Our Citizens Go Abroad," March 9, 1930.
32. The prewar figure refers to the net expenditure—that is, the amount of money foreign tourists spent in the United States subtracted from the total spent abroad by U.S. citizens. The equivalent figure for 1922 was $300 million (*Literary Digest*, "Our Tourists," 68).
33. Ibid.; *New York Times*, "England Plans World Publicity Campaign to Attract Larger Share of Tourists' Millions," January 19, 1930.
34. *Literary Digest*, "Our Tourists Turning Tightwad," September 13, 1930, 54–55.
35. *New York Times*, " 'Invisible Exports' a Billion Says Klein," July 18, 1932.
36. *New York Times*, "Americans Pay High Passport Charges," January 16, 1921; see also *New York Times*, "Passport Prices Mount," September 14, 1920.
37. Herbert Kahn, "Passports and Visas," *New York Times*, May 21, 1929.
38. *Washington Post*, "Raise In Passport Fees For Americans Who Live Abroad," August 15, 1920.
39. House Committee on Foreign Affairs, *Fees Charged for Passports and for Viséing Foreign Passports: Hearings before the Committee on Foreign Affairs*, 66th Cong., 2nd sess., February 3, 4, 7, 1920, 44.
40. Farrell to Hanna, May 10, 1922, RG 59 138.101/272, Box 634, National Archives.
41. Mead to Sen. Calder, April 12, 1921, RG 59 138.101/225, National Archives; Boston Chamber of Commerce to Secretary of State, April 20, 1922, RG 59 138.101/272, National Archives; Secretary, National Foreign Trade Council to Secretary of State, January 23, 1924, RG 59 138.101/312, National Archives; "Resolution: Chamber of Commerce of New York," February 7, 1924, RG 59138.101/313, National Archives; *New York Times*, "Wants Passports Ended," October 27, 1924; *New York Times*, "Want Cheaper Passports," December 22, 1924; *New York Times*, "Would Speed Canal Funds," January 15, 1925; *New York Herald*, "Businessmen Want Passport Abolished," October 7, 1922.
42. Brist to Adee, January 13, 1922, RG 59 138.101/266, National Archives; RG 59 138.101/266, National Archives.

43. *New York Times*, "Asks Visa Fee Cut to $2," May 6, 1922; *New York Times*, "Porter for Easing Passport Trouble," August 3, 1923.
44. Snow to Secretary of State, December 22, 1921, RG 59 138.101/250, National Archives.
45. *New York Times*, "What Do We Care For Abroad?" February 17, 1921; Herbert A. Sillco, "Passport Fees Too High," *New York Times*, February 23, 1921.
46. *New York Times*, "Americans Abroad to Pay Higher Fees," December 13, 1921; *Washington Post*, "Cost of Passports Nearly as Great as Fare Over Atlantic," August 19, 1923.
47. E. F. Strickland, "Would Abolish Passports," *New York Times*, November 9, 1924.
48. "RLF" to Nielsen, October 22, 1921, RG 59 138.101/266, National Archives.
49. "RLF" to Brist, October 16, 1920, RG 59 811.111/29834, National Archives.
50. Lodge to Merchants Assoc. of New York, October 21, 1921, RG 59 138.101/249, National Archives. Also see Lodge to Merchants Assoc. of New York, June 30, 1921, RG 59 138.101/249, National Archives.
51. *Outlook*, "The Question of Passports," April 7, 1926, 512.
52. House Committee on Foreign Affairs, *Validity of Passports: Hearing before the Committee on Foreign Affairs*, 69th Cong., 1st sess., May 12, 1926, 10, 17, 18.
53. Edwin L. James, "Protest on Visas Expected in Paris," *New York Times*, October 30, 1927; A. Victim, "Passport Difficulties," *New York Times*, March 17, 1929.
54. By 1928 the U.S. government had signed agreements with thirty countries, twenty-two of which waived the need for U.S. citizens to acquire visas (*New York Times*, "Travelers Now Save on Passport Visas," April 28, 1929).
55. In 1936 the most expensive visas for U.S. citizens were for Russia ($17.37) and Greece ($14.60); Carlisle McDonald, "Visa Fee Cut to $2 By France and U.S.," *New York Times*, May 14, 1929; *New York Times*, "Britain To Agree on Visa Fee Cut," December 1, 1936; Helen Dallas, "Cost of Visas is Declining," *New York Times*, December 6, 1936.
56. McDonald, "Visa Fee Cut."
57. *New York Times*, "Reveals Passport Survey," March 28, 1930; *New York Times*, "Passport Fee Sought By Ship Man," February 27, 1932; *Literary Digest*, "Nation Spends Millions on Travel," September 30, 1933, 38.
58. *World's Work*, "Passports for Summer Travel," June 1930, 22.
59. *New York Times*, "Business Men Ask Cut in Passport Fee," January 3, 1930.
60. *World's Work*, "Passports for Summer Travel," 22.
61. *New York Times*, "Passports Are Too Expensive," March 19, 1921; Kenneth Roberts, "Trial by Travel," *Saturday Evening Post*, September 4, 1920.
62. *New York Times*, "American Travelers Tired of Passports," September 21, 1924.
63. House Committee on Foreign Affairs. *Passport Renewals: Hearing before the Committee on Foreign Affairs*, 71st Cong., 2nd sess., April 15–16, 1930, 8.
64. Ibid., 9.

65. Ibid., 20. In 1930 the cost of the issuance of a passport was reduced to $6, and renewals were extended to all citizens at a cost of $2. In 1932 the cost of a passport was again raised to $10.
66. Brist to Adee, January 13, 1922, RG 59 138.101/266 Box 634, National Archives.
67. Stimson to Shipley, March 3, 1933, RG 59, 111.28/232A, Box 224, National Archives.
68. Roberts, "Trial by Travel," 67.
69. By the end of the 1920s, there were passport agencies in New York, Boston, Chicago, Seattle, San Francisco, and New Orleans. In other cities and towns, people had to apply to a state or federal court clerk. All applications were still forwarded to the State Department in Washington, D.C.
70. Greer to Phillips, July 3, 1923, RG 59 111.28 NY, National Archives.
71. Lynn Dumenil, *The Modern Temper: American Culture and Society in the 1920s* (New York: Hill and Wang, 1995); Warren I. Susman, *Culture as History: The Transformation of American Society in the Twentieth Century* (New York: Pantheon, 1984); Miles Orvell, *The Real Thing: Imitation and Authenticity in American Culture, 1880–1940* (Chapel Hill: University of North Carolina Press, 1989); Roland Marchand, *Advertising the American Dream: Making Way for Modernity, 1920–1940* (Berkeley: University of California Press, 1985).
72. Dumenil, *Modern Temper*, 86.
73. Max Weber, *From Max Weber: Essays in Sociology* (New York: Oxford University Press, 1946.); David Held, *Introduction to Critical Theory: Horkheimer to Habermas* (Berkeley: University of California Press, 1980).
74. Simon A. Cole, *Suspect Identities: A History of Fingerprinting and Criminal Identification* (Cambridge, MA: Harvard University Press, 2001), 165.
75. Menken to Stimson, July 23, 1930, RG 59 111.28 NY/63 Box 225, National Archives.
76. "DFN," April 20, 1931, RG 59 111.28 N.Y/67, National Archives.
77. Watts to Kellogg, May 13, 1927, RG 59 138/2223, National Archives. For another example of frustration with the need for birth certificates see Sophie Kerr, "You Must Tell All," *Saturday Evening Post*, April 18, 1931, 22.
78. Watts to Kellogg, May 13, 1927.
79. Watts to Olds, May 26, 1927, RG 59 138/2223, National Archives.
80. Ibid.
81. Olds to Watts, May 25, 1927, RG 59 138/2223, National Archives.
82. Ibid.
83. For a sample of newspaper articles see clippings attached to Hogdon to Carr, December 5, 1932, RG 59, 811.111, Einstein, Albert, National Archives.
84. *New York Times*, "Einstein Ultimatum Brings a Quick Visa," December 6, 1932.
85. *New York Times*, "Einstein Resumes Packing for Voyage," December 7, 1932.
86. *New York Times*, "Einstein Embarks; Jests About Quiz," December 11, 1932.

87. *Washington Post*, "Visa Dispute Cleared Up, Einstein Sails Saturday," December 7, 1932.
88. RG 59, 811.111, Einstein, Albert, National Archives.
89. Memo, Hogdon, Visa Division, December 17, 1933, RG 59, 811.111, Einstein, Albert, National Archives.
90. *New York Times*, "The Alien Entering America Must Answer Many Questions," December 11, 1932; Alexander H. Kuhnel, "The Einstein Episode," *New York Times*, December 8, 1932.
91. Charles F. Ault, "The Passport Inquisition," *New York Times*, July 21, 1927.
92. Hilton Burnside Sonneborn, "Easing Passport Difficulties," *New York Times*, March 5, 1929.
93. Lynn Dumenil, " 'The Insatiable Maw of Bureaucracy': Antistatism and Education Reform in the 1920s," *Journal of American History* 77 (1990): 518.
94. *World's Work*, "Borah on Local Self-Government," June 1925, 127–28; Dumenil, "Insatiable Maw," 518.
95. Stimson to Shipley, March 3, 1933, RG 59 111.28/232A, Box 224, National Archives.
96. Nancy F. Cott, *The Grounding of Modern Feminism* (New Haven, CT: Yale University Press, 1987), 216. For an analysis of the masculinized enforcement model J. Edgar Hoover introduced in the 1920s see Rachel Hall, *Wanted: The Outlaw in American Visual Culture* (Charlottesville: University of Virginia Press), 95–106.
97. Stimson to Shipley, March 3, 1933, RG 59, 111.28/232A, Box 224, National Archives.
98. Peaslee to Kellogg, August 24, 1925, RG 59 111.28/New York 15, National Archives.
99. *New York Telegram*, September 3, 1926, RG 59 111.28/NY 32, National Archives.
100. Ibid.
101. Progressive, [untitled letter], *New York Times*, June 5, 1934.
102. Femina, "Passport Information," *New York Times*, May 30, 1934.
103. Forty Plus, "Passport Age Data," *New York Times*, June 5, 1934.
104. Charles S. Taylor, "Passport Data," *New York Times*, June 1, 1934.
105. Highham to Shipley, August 28, 1928, RG 59 111.28 Boston/29, National Archives (emphasis added).
106. Anthony Giddens, *The Consequences of Modernity* (Stanford, CA: Stanford University Press, 1990), 90.
107. *New York Times*, "Why Object to Finger-Prints?" February 7, 1928.
108. Sankar, "State Power and Record-Keeping," 245.
109. Ibid., 246, 254; *New York Times*, "Wider Use of Fingerprinting," May 3, 1931.
110. By the end of the month, eighteen thousand people had been voluntarily fingerprinted. See *New York Times*, "Rockefeller Files his Fingerprint," February 8, 1935. *New York Times*, "18,000 Are Fingerprinted at Invitation of Police," February 28, 1935.

111. Donald C. Dilworth, ed., *Identification Wanted: Development of the American Criminal Identification System, 1893–1943* (Gaithersburg, MD: International Association of Chiefs of Police, 1977), 218–22.
112. *New York Times*, "Buffalo Police Head Suggests Rogues Gallery in Every Home," September 18, 1932; Sankar, "State Power and Record-Keeping," 296.
113. *New York Times*, "Millionth to File Fingerprints," November 22, 1938.
114. *Literary Digest*, "To Fingerprint us All," October 24, 1925, 21–22.
115. *Literary Digest*, "Finger-print Identification in Banks," August 24, 1912, 297.
116. For a detailed example of the importance of "safety" to modern practices of governing in the United States, see Jeremy Packer, *Mobility without Mayhem: Safety, Cars, and Citizenship* (Durham, NC: Duke University Press, 2008).
117. Courtney Ryley Cooper, "Hold for Identification: Twenty-Five Hundred Fingerprints A Day," *The Saturday Evening Post*, January 12, 1935, 66; American Civil Liberties Union, *Thumbs Down! The Fingerprint Menace to Civil Liberties* (New York: American Civil Liberties Union, 1938), 6.
118. Thorsten Sellin, "Identification," in *Encyclopaedia of the Social Sciences* (New York: Macmillan, 1932), 7:573–74.
119. Hull to Watts, September 27, 1934, RG 59 138/3333, National Archives.
120. Ruth Shipley, "Memo," September 15, 1934, RG 59 138/3333, National Archives. In a subsequent memo, Shipley clarified that she was not opposed to fingerprinting ("Memo," November 1, 1934, RG 59 138/3333, National Archives).
121. A similar claim can be made about the United Kingdom in this period. See Edward Higgs, "The Rise of the Information State: The Development of Central State Surveillance of the Citizen in England, 1500–2000," *Journal of Historical Sociology* 14 (2001): 190. As well as proving their identity people encountered an increased demand to answer detailed questions about things previously considered private. This included job interviews. See, Kerr, "You Must Tell All."

CONCLUSION

1. Dieter Hoffmann-Axthelm, "Identity and Reality: The End of the Philosophical Immigration Officer," in *Modernity and Identity*, ed. Scott Lash and Jonathan Friedman, (Oxford: Blackwell, 1991).
2. *Oxford English Dictionary*, 2d ed.
3. Dan Schiller, *How to Think About Information* (Urbana: University of Illinois Press, 2007); Mark Andrejevic, *iSpy: Surveillance and Power in the Interactive Era* (Lawrence: University of Kansas Press, 2007).
4. Lorraine Daston and Peter Galison, "The Image of Objectivity," *Representations* 40 (1992): 81–128.
5. Fred Barbash and Sara Kehaulani Goo, "U.S. Begins Tracking Foreign Arrivals," *Washington Post*, January 5, 2004.
6. Washington Post, "U.S. Pilot Fined for Obscene Gesture in Brazil," *Washington Post*, January 15, 2004; Elaine Sciolino, "World Opinion is Fragmented on Tighter Security for Visitors," *New York Times*, January 7, 2004.

7. Shelley de Alth, "ID at the Polls: Assessing the Impact of Recent State Voter ID Laws on Voter Turnout," *Harvard Law and Policy Review* 3 (2009), 187–189; Robert Pear, "Citizens Who Lack Papers Lose Medicaid," *New York Times*, March 12, 2007.
8. Forty Plus, "Passport Age Data," *New York Times*, June 5, 1934.

Bibliography

Archival Sources

National Archives Branch Depository, College Park, MD, and Washington, D.C. Records of the Immigration and Naturalization Service. RG 85.
———. Records of the U.S. State Department. RG 59.
A. 1789–1906.
Diplomatic Correspondence; Consular Correspondence; Miscellaneous Correspondence (Domestic Letters and Miscellaneous Letters).
B. 1906–1910.
Numerical File.
C. 1910–1963.
Decimal File: 130–138.
D. Inventory 15.
Records of the Passport Division, 1790–1917.
Records of the Passport Division, 1906–1925.
Numerical series: indexed by subject.
New York Public Library: William Williams Papers.

Other Sources

Abbott, Edith. *Immigration: Select Documents and Case Records*. Chicago: University of Chicago Press, 1924.

Adair, Ellen. "War Time Traveling in France is Beset With Trials, Especially for One who Can Speak German." *Washington Post*, August 29, 1915.

American Civil Liberties Union. *Thumbs Down! The Fingerprint Menace to Civil Liberties*. New York: American Civil Liberties Union, 1938.

Anderson, Margo J. *The American Census: A Social History*. New Haven, CT: Yale University Press, 1988.

Andrejevic, Mark. *iSpy: Surveillance and Power in the Interactive Era*. Lawrence: University of Kansas Press, 2007.

Aron, Cindy Sondik. *Ladies and Gentlemen of the Civil Service: Middle-Class Workers in Victorian America*. New York: Oxford University Press, 1987.

Ault, Charles F. "The Passport Inquisition." *New York Times*, July 21, 1927.

Avery, Donald H. "Canadian Workers and American Immigration Restriction: A Case Study of the Windsor Commuters, 1924–1931." *Mid-America* 80 (1998): 235–63.

Banks, Alexander S. "Who is Respectable?" *New York Times*, April 27, 1924.

Barbash, Fred, and Sara Kehaulani Goo. "U.S. Begins Tracking Foreign Arrivals." *Washington Post*, January 5, 2004.

Barker, Howard F. "How We Got Our Surnames." *American Speech* 4 (October 1928): 48–53.

Barrows, Samuel J., and Isabel C. Barrows. "Personal Reminiscences of William H. Seward." *Atlantic Monthly*, March 1889, 379–97.

Baxter, P. G. "The Distinction between 'Graphology' and 'Questioned Document Examination.' *Medicine, Science and the Law* 6 (1966): 75–86.

Becker, Peter. "The Standardized Gaze: The Standardization of the Search Warrant in Nineteenth-Century Germany." In *Documenting Individual Identity: The Development of State Practices in the Modern World*, edited by Jane Caplan and John Torpey, 139–63. Princeton, NJ: Princeton University Press, 2001.

Beetham, David. *Bureaucracy*. 2nd ed. Minneapolis: University of Minnesota Press, 1996.

Beniger, James R. *The Control Revolution: Technological and Economic Origins of the Information Society*. Cambridge, MA: Harvard University Press, 1986.

Bensel, Richard Franklin. "The American Ballot Box: Law, Identity, and the Polling Place in the Mid-Nineteenth Century." *Studies in American Political Development* 17, no. 1 (Spring 2003):1–27.

———. *The American Ballot Box in the Mid-Nineteenth Century*. Cambridge, UK: Cambridge University Press, 2004.

———. *Yankee Leviathan: The Origins of Central State Authority in America, 1859–1877*. Cambridge, UK: Cambridge University Press, 1990.

Blanchard, James. "Passport Troubles." *New York Times*, August 26, 1931.

Bouchard, Edwin M. *The Diplomatic Protection of Citizens Abroad; or, The Law of International Claims*. New York: Banks Law, 1915.

Bridges, Peter. "An Appreciation of Alvey Adee." *Diplomacy & Statecraft* 10 (1999): 31–49.

———. "Some Men Named William Hunter." *Diplomacy & Statecraft* 16 (2005): 251–57.

Bright, John Irwin. "The Passport." *Atlantic Monthly*, November 1920, 666–68.

Buck-Morss, Susan. "Passports." *Documents* 1 (Summer 1993): 66–77.

Buckland, Michael K. "What is a 'Document'?" *Journal of the American Society for Information Science* 48 (1997): 804–9.

Burgess, Gelett. "The Steerage Revisited." *Colliers*, April 16, 1910, 17–18.

Butler Judith. *Precarious Life: The Powers of Mourning and Violence*. New York: Verso, 2004.

Calavita, Kitty. "The Paradoxes of Race, Class, Identity, and 'Passing': Enforcing the Chinese Exclusion Acts, 1882–1910." *Law and Social Inquiry* 25 (2000): 1–40.

Caplan, Jane. " 'Educating the Eye': The Tattooed Prostitute." In *Sexology in Culture: Labelling Bodies and Desires*, edited by Lucy Bland and Laura Doan, 100–115. Chicago: University of Chicago Press, 1999.

———. "'Speaking Scars': The Tattoo in Popular Practice and Medico-Legal Debate in Nineteenth-Century Europe." *History Workshop Journal* 44 (1997): 107–42.

———. "'This or That Particular Person': Protocols of Identification in Nineteenth-Century Europe." In *Documenting Individual Identity: The Development of State Practices in the Modern World*, edited by Jane Caplan and John Torpey, 49–66. Princeton, NJ: Princeton University Press, 2001.

Caplan, Jane, and John Torpey, eds. *Documenting Individual Identity: The Development of State Practices in the Modern World.* Princeton, NJ: Princeton University Press, 2001.

———. "Introduction." In *Documenting Individual Identity: The Development of State Practices in the Modern World*, edited by Jane Caplan and John Torpey, 1–12. Princeton, NJ: Princeton University Press, 2001.

Capozzola, Christopher. *Uncle Sam Wants You: World War I and the Making of the Modern American Citizen.* New York: Oxford University Press, 2008.

Cardoso, Lawrence A. *Mexican Emigration to the United States, 1897–1931: Socio-economic Patterns.* Tucson: University of Arizona Press, 1980.

Carey, James W. *Communication as Culture: Essays on Media and Society.* Boston: Unwin Hyman, 1989.

———. "The Internet and the End of the National Communication System: Uncertain Predictions of an Uncertain Future." *Journalism and Mass Communication Quarterly* 75 (1998): 28–34.

Carr, Wilbur J. "The American Consular Service." *American Journal of International Law* 1 (1907): 891–913.

Chandler, Alfred D., Jr. *The Visible Hand: The Managerial Revolution in American Business.* Cambridge, MA: Belknap, 1977.

Chatfield-Taylor, H. C. "American Diplomats in Europe." *North American Review*, July 1896, 125–28.

Clanchy, M T. *From Memory to Written Record, England 1066–1307.* 2d ed. Oxford: Blackwell, 1993.

Cohen, Naomi W. "The Abrogation of the Russo-American Treaty of 1832." *Jewish Social Studies* 25 (1963): 3–41.

Cohen, Patricia Cline. *A Calculating People: The Spread of Numeracy in Early America.* Chicago: University of Chicago Press, 1982.

Cole, Simon A. *Suspect Identities: A History of Fingerprinting and Criminal Identification.* Cambridge, MA: Harvard University Press, 2001.

Collins, James H. "The Steerage Puts On a White Collar." *Saturday Evening Post*, September 27, 1924, 17.

Coolidge, Mary Roberts. *Chinese Immigration.* New York: H. Holt, 1909.

Cooper, Courtney Ryley. "Hold for Identification: Twenty-Five Hundred Fingerprints A Day." *Saturday Evening Post*, January 12, 1935, 64–69.

Cott, Nancy F. *The Grounding of Modern Feminism.* New Haven, CT: Yale University Press, 1987.

———. "Marriage and Women's Citizenship in the United States, 1830–1934." *American Historical Review* 93 (1988): 1440–74.

Craven, Thomas. "New Innocents Abroad." *Forum*, April 1930, 239–44.

Crawford, Remsen. "Halt! Who's There!" *Saturday Evening Post*, January 7, 1928, 201–11.

Curran, Henry H. "Smuggling Aliens." *Saturday Evening Post*, January 31, 1925, 12.

Curtis, Bruce. "Administrative Infrastructure and Social Enquiry: Finding the Facts about Agriculture in Quebec, 1853–4." *Journal of Social History* 32 (1998): 309–327.

———. "Foucault on Governmentality and Population: The Impossible Discovery." *The Canadian Journal of Sociology* 27 (2002): 505–33.

———. "Official Documentary Systems and Colonial Government: From Imperial Sovereignty to Colonial Autonomy in the Canadas, 1841–1867." *Journal of Historical Sociology* 10 (1997): 389–417.

———. *The Politics of Population: State Formation, Statistics, and the Census of Canada, 1840–1875*. Toronto: University of Toronto Press, 2001.

Dallas, Helen. "Cost of Visas is Declining." *New York Times*, December 6, 1936.

Dandeker, Christopher. *Surveillance, Power, and Modernity: Bureaucracy and Discipline From 1700 To The Present Day*. New York: St. Martin's, 1990.

Daniels, Roger. *Asian America: Chinese and Japanese in the United States since 1850*. Seattle: University of Washington Press, 1988.

———. *The Politics of Prejudice, the Anti-Japanese Movement in California, and the Struggle for Japanese Exclusion*. Gloucester, Mass: Peter Smith, 1966.

Daston, Lorraine, and Peter Galison. "The Image of Objectivity." *Representations* 40 (1992): 81–128.

Davis, James J. "Who Are the American People?" *Saturday Evening Post*, December 8, 1923, 29.

Day, Ronald E. *The Modern Invention of Information: Discourse, History, and Power*. Carbondale: Southern Illinois University Press, 2001.

De Alth, Shelley. "ID at the Polls: Assessing the Impact of Recent State Voter ID Laws on Voter Turnout." *Harvard Law and Policy Review* 3 (2009): 185-202.

Dickens, Charles. *The Pickwick Papers*. Oxford: Oxford University Press, 1998.

Dickinson, Leon A. "New England Offers 'Ideal' Mountain Trip." *New York Times*, July 14, 1929.

Dilworth, Donald C., ed. *Identification Wanted: Development of the American Criminal Identification System, 1893–1943*. Gaithersburg, MD: International Association of Chiefs of Police, 1977.

Dooe, Irving E. "A Passport Abroad." *New York Sun*, November 28, 1919.

Doulman, Jane, and David Lee. *Every Assistance & Protection: A History of the Australian Passport*. Sydney: Federation, 2008.

Drake, Kelly S. "The Seaman's Protection Certificate as Proof of American Citizenship for Black Sailors." *Log of the Mystic Seaport* 50 (Summer 1998): 11–14.

Dumenil, Lynn. "'The Insatiable Maw of Bureaucracy': Antistatism and Education Reform in the 1920s." *Journal of American History* 77 (1990): 499–518.

———. *The Modern Temper: American Culture and Society in the 1920s*. New York: Hill and Wang, 1995.

Dwight, H. G. "American Political Workers Abroad: The Consular Service." *Bookman*, May 1906, 263–80.

Endy, Christopher. "Travel and World Power: Americans in Europe, 1890–1917." *Diplomatic History* 22 (1998): 565–94.

Esthus, Raymond A. *Theodore Roosevelt and Japan*. Seattle: University of Washington Press, 1966.

Fahrmeir, Andreas. *Citizens and Aliens: Foreigners and the Law in Britain and the German States, 1789–1870*. New York: Berghahn, 2000.

———. "Governments and Forgers: Passports in Nineteenth-Century Europe." In *Documenting Individual Identity: The Development of State Practices in the Modern World*, edited by Jane Caplan and John Torpey, 218–34. Princeton, NJ: Princeton University Press, 2001.

Fairchild, Amy L. *Science at the Borders: Immigrant Medical Inspection and the Shaping of the Modern Industrial Labor Force*. Baltimore: Johns Hopkins University Press, 2003.

Femina [pseudo.]. "Passport Information." *New York Times*, May 30, 1934.

Findling, John E. *Dictionary of American Diplomatic History*. Westport, CT: Greenwood, 1980.

Finnegan, Cara A. "Recognizing Lincoln: Image Vernaculars in Nineteenth-Century Visual Culture." *Rhetoric and Public Affairs* 8 (2005): 31–58.

Flournoy, Richard W., Jr. "Naturalization and Expatriation." *Yale Law Journal* 31 (1922): 702–19.

Foucault, Michel. "Problematics." In *Foucault Live (Interviews 1961–1984)*, edited by Sylvère Lotringer, translated by Lysa Hoxroth and John Johnston, 416–22. New York: Semiotext(e), 1996.

———. "Questions of Method." In *The Foucault Effect: Studies in Governmentality*, edited by Graham Burchell, Colin Gordon, and Peter Miller, 73–86. Chicago: University of Chicago Press, 1991.

———. "Truth and Power." In *Power/Knowledge: Selected Interviews and Other Writings, 1972–1977*, edited by Colin Gordon, 109–33. New York: Pantheon, 1980.

Fraccaroli, Arnoldo. "Crossing Frontiers." *Living Age*, October 9, 1920, 89–92.

Forty Plus [pseudo.]. "Passport Age Data." *New York Times*, June 5, 1934.

Friedman, Lawrence M. *Crime and Punishment in American History*. New York: Basic Books, 1993.

Freitag, Sabine. "'The Begging Bowl of Revolution': The Fund-Raising Tours of German and Hungarian Exiles to North America, 1851–1852." In *Exiles from European Revolutions: Refugees in Mid-Victorian England*, edited by Sabine Freitag, 164–86 (New York: Berghahn, 2003).

Fussell, Paul. *Abroad: British Literary Traveling Between the Wars*. New York: Oxford University Press, 1980.

Gates, Kelly. "The U.S. Real ID Act and the Securitization of Identity." In *Playing the Identity Card: Surveillance, Security and Identification in Global Perspective*, edited by Colin J. Bennett and David Lyon, 218–32. London: Routledge, 2008.

Gelfand, Lawrence E. "Towards a Merit System for the American Diplomatic Service 1900–1930." *Irish Studies in International Affairs* 2, no. 4 (1988): 49–63.

Geselle, Andrea. "Domenica Saba Takes to the Road: Origins and Development of a Modern Passport System in Lombardy-Veneto." In *Documenting Individual Identity: The Development of State Practices in the Modern World*, edited by Jane Caplan and John Torpey, 199–217. Princeton, NJ: Princeton University Press, 2001.

Giddens, Anthony. *The Consequences of Modernity*. Stanford, CA: Stanford University Press, 1990.

Goffman, Erving. *Stigma: Notes on the Management of Spoiled Identity*. Englewood Cliffs, NJ: Prentice-Hall, 1963.

Goodrich, C. F. "Brand Alien Felons." *New York Times*, March 5, 1913.

———. "Foreign Convicts." *New York Times*, October 3, 1913.

Groebner, Valentin. *Who Are You? Identification, Deception, and Surveillance in Early Modern Europe*. Translated by Mark Kyburz and John Peck. Brooklyn, NY: Zone, 2007.

Gunning, Tom. "Tracing the Individual Body: Photography, Detectives, and Early Cinema." In *Cinema and the Invention of Modern Life*, edited by Leo Charney and Vanessa R. Schwartz, 15–45. Berkeley: University of California Press, 1995.

Gustafson, Milton O. "State Department Records in the National Archives: A Profile." *Prologue* 2 (1970): 175–184.

Gyory, Andrew. *Closing the Gate: Race, Politics, and the Chinese Exclusion Act*. Chapel Hill: University of North Carolina Press, 1998.

Hackworth, Green Haywood. *Digest of International Law*, vol. 3. Washington, DC: Government Printing Office, 1942.

Hadden, Sally E. *Slave Patrols: Law and Violence in Virginia and the Carolinas*. Cambridge, MA: Harvard University Press, 2001.

Hall, Rachel. *Wanted: The Outlaw in American Visual Culture*. Charlottesville: University of Virginia Press, 2009.

Halttunen, Karen. *Confidence Men and Painted Women: A Study of Middle-Class Culture in America, 1830–1870*. New Haven, CT: Yale University Press, 1982.

Hancher, Michael "The Law of Signatures." In *Law and Aesthetics*, edited by Roberta Kevelson, 227–43. New York: Peter Lang, 1992.

Haney-López, Ian F. *White By Law: The Legal Construction of Race*. New York: New York University Press, 1996.

Hannah, Matthew G. *Governmentality and the Mastery of Territory in Nineteenth-Century America*. Cambridge, UK: Cambridge University Press, 2000.

Hapgood, Isabel. "Passports, Police and Post-Office in Russia." *Atlantic Monthly* 72, 42–49.

Harper's New Monthly Magazine. "Noses." August 1858, 377–81.

Harris, Roy. *Rethinking Writing*. Bloomington: Indiana University Press, 2000.

———. *Signs of Writing*. London: Routledge, 1995.

Hartman, Saidiya V. *Scenes of Subjection: Terror, Slavery, and Self-Making in Nineteenth-Century America*. New York: Oxford University Press, 1997.

Hathaway, Carson. "Woman to Head Passport Bureau." *New York Times*, May 20, 1928.

Hawley, Ellis W. *The Great War and the Search for a Modern Order: A History of the American People and their Institutions, 1917–1933*. New York: St. Martin's, 1992.

Heinrichs, Waldo H., Jr. "Bureaucracy and Professionalism in the Development of American Career Diplomacy." In *Twentieth-Century American Foreign Policy*, edited by John Braeman, Robert H Bremner, and David Brody, 119–206. Columbus: Ohio State University Press, 1971.

Held, David. *Introduction to Critical Theory: Horkheimer to Habermas*. Berkeley: University of California Press, 1980.

Helleiner, Eric. "National Currencies and National Identities." *American Behavioral Scientist* 41 (1998): 1409–1436.

Henkin, David M. *City Reading: Written Words and Public Spaces in Antebellum New York*. New York: Columbia University Press, 1998.

Higgins, Lesley, and Marie-Christine Leps. "'Passport, Please': Legal, Literary, and Cultural Fictions of Identity." *College Literature* 25 (1998): 94–138.

Higgs, Edward. *The Information State in England: The Centralized Collection of Information on Citizens since 1500*. Houndmills, UK: Palgrave Macmilllan, 2004.

———. "The Rise of the Information State: The Development of Central State Surveillance of the Citizen in England, 1500–2000." *Journal of Historical Sociology* 14 (2001): 175–97.

Hoffmann-Axthelm, Dieter. "Identity and Reality: The End of the Philosophical Immigration Officer." In *Modernity and Identity*, edited by Scott Lash and Jonathan Friedman, 196–217. Oxford: Blackwell, 1991.

Horner, Jennifer. "The 1864 Union Soldier Vote: Historical-critical Perspectives on Public Space and the Public Sphere." Paper, annual meeting of the International Communication Association, San Francisco, May 24, 2007.

Hunt, Gaillard. *The American Passport: Its History and a Digest of Laws, Rulings and Regulations Governing its Issuance by the Department of State*. Washington, DC: Government Printing Office, 1898.

———. *The Department of State of the United States: Its History and Functions*. New Haven, CT: Yale University Press, 1914.

———. "The New Citizenship Law." *North American Review* 185 (1907): 530–39.

Hunt, Michael H. *Ideology and U.S. Foreign Policy*. New Haven, CT: Yale University Press, 1988.

Hutchinson, E. P. *Legislative History of American Immigration Policy, 1798–1965*. Philadelphia: University of Pennsylvania Press, 1981.

Hyman, Harold M. *Era of the Oath: Northern Loyalty Tests during the Civil War and Reconstruction*. Philadelphia: University of Pennsylvania Press, 1954.

———. *To Try Men's Souls: Loyalty Tests in American History*. Berkeley: University of California Press, 1959.

Jacobson, Matthew Frye. *Barbarian Virtues: The United States Encounters Foreign Peoples at Home and Abroad, 1876–1917*. New York: Hill and Wang, 2000.

———. *Whiteness of a Different Color: European Immigrants and the Alchemy of Race*. Cambridge, MA: Harvard University Press, 1998.

James, Edwin L. "Protest on Visas Expected in Paris." *New York Times*, October 30, 1927.

Johnson, David R. *Illegal Tender: Counterfeiting and the Secret Service in Nineteenth-Century America*. Washington, DC: Smithsonian Institution Press, 1995.

Kahn, Herbert. "Passports and Visas." *New York Times*, May 21, 1929.

Kaluszynski, Martine. "Republican Identity: Bertillonage as Government Technique." In *Documenting Individual Identity: The Development of State Practice in the Modern World*, edited by Jane Caplan and John Torpey, 123–38. Princeton, NJ: Princeton University Press, 2001.

Kasson, John F. *Rudeness and Civility: Manners in Nineteenth-Century Urban America*. New York: Hill and Wang, 1990.

Keller, Morton. *Affairs of State: Public Life in Late Nineteenth Century America*. Cambridge, MA: Belknap Press of Harvard University, 1977.

Kennedy, David M. *Over Here: The First World War and American Society*. New York: Oxford University Press, 1980.

Kennen, George. "T. B. Aldrich's Adventure with Russian Police." *New York Times*, June 25, 1911.

Kerber, Linda K. "The Meanings of Citizenship." *Journal of American History* 84 (1997): 833–54.

Kerr, Sophie. "You Must Tell All." *Saturday Evening Post*, April 18, 1931, 22.

Klay, Andor. *Daring Diplomacy: The Case of the First American Ultimatum*. Minneapolis: University of Minnesota Press, 1957.

Krueger, Stephen. *Krueger on United States Passport Law*. Hong Kong: Crossbow, 1996.

Kuhnel, Alexander H. "The Einstein Episode." *New York Times*, December 8, 1932.

Kupper, Susan. *Surnames for Women: A Decision-making Guide*. Jefferson, NC: McFarland, 1990.

Lalvani, Suren. "Photography, Epistemology and the Body." *Cultural Studies* 7 (1998): 442–65.

———. *Photography, Vision, and the Production of Modern Bodies*. Albany: State University of New York Press, 1996.

Lau, Estelle T. *Paper Families: Identity, Immigration Administration, and Chinese Exclusion*. Durham, NC: Duke University Press, 2006.

Lauer, Josh. "From Rumor to Written Record: Credit Reporting and the Invention of Financial Identity in Nineteenth-Century America." *Technology and Culture* 49 (2008) 301–24.

———. "Money as Mass Communication: U.S. Paper Currency and the Iconography of Nationalism." *Communication Review* 11 (2008): 109–32.

Lawless, Ken. "'Continental Imprisonment': Rockwell Kent and the Passport Controversy. *Antioch Review* 38 (1980): 304–11.

League of Nations. Organization for Communication and Transit. *Passport Conference Held at Geneva from May 12th to 18th, 1926*. Geneva, Switzerland: The League of Nations, 1926.

Lears, T. J. Jackson. *No Place of Grace: Antimodernism and the Transformation of American Culture, 1880–1920*. New York: Pantheon, 1981.

Lee, Erika. *At America's Gates: Chinese Immigration During the Exclusion Era, 1882–1943*. Chapel Hill: University of North Carolina Press, 2003.

Lehman, R. C. "The Passport." *Living Age*, April 3, 1915, 49–50.

Leuchtenburg, William E. *The Perils of Prosperity, 1914–1932*. 2d ed. Chicago: University of Chicago Press, 1993.

Literary Digest. "Finger-print Identification in Banks." August 24, 1912, 297.

———. "Nation Spends Millions on Travel." September 30, 1933, 38.

———. "Our Tourists a Large Factor in World Finance." June 8, 1929, 68.

———. "Red Tape Worse Than Barbed-Wire Entanglements in Central Europe." January 22, 1921, 48–49.

———. "To Fingerprint us All." October 24, 1925, 21–22.

Litwack, Leon F. "The Federal Government and the Free Negro, 1790–1860." *Journal of Negro History* 43 (1958): 261–78.

Living Age. "Passport Adventures." June 26, 1920, 787–89.

Lloyd, Martin. *The Passport: The History of Man's Most Travelled Document*. Stroud, UK: Sutton, 2003.

Lucassen, Leo. "A Many Headed-Monster: The Evolution of the Passport System in the Netherlands and Germany in the Long Nineteenth Century." In *Documenting*

Individual Identity: The Development of State Practices in the Modern World, edited by Jane Caplan and John Torpey, 235–255. Princeton, NJ: Princeton University Press, 2001.

Luibhéid, Eithne. *Entry Denied: Controlling Sexuality at the Border*. Minneapolis: University of Minnesota Press, 2002.

Lyon, David. *Identifying Citizens: ID Cards as Surveillance*. Cambridge, UK: Polity, 2009.

Marchand, Roland. *Advertising the American Dream: Making Way for Modernity, 1920–1940*. Berkeley: University of California Press, 1985.

Marrus, Michael R. *The Unwanted: European Refugees in the Twentieth Century*. New York: Oxford University Press, 1985.

Matsuda, Matt K. *The Memory of the Modern*. New York: Oxford University Press, 1996.

McCormick, Charles H. *Seeing Reds: Federal Surveillance of Radicals in the Pittsburgh Mill District, 1917–1921*. Pittsburgh: University of Pittsburgh Press, 1997.

McDonald, Carlisle. "Visa Fee Cut to $2 By France and U.S." *New York Times*, May 14, 1929.

McDonnell, Eleanor. "Plain Tales from the Tourists." *Saturday Evening Post*, April 19, 1930, 10.

McGowen, Randall. "Knowing the Hand: Forgery and the Proof of Writing in Eighteenth-Century England." *Historical Reflections* 24 (1998): 385–414.

McKee, Delber L. *Chinese Exclusion versus the Open Door Policy, 1900–1906: Clashes over China Policy in the Roosevelt Era*. Detroit: Wayne State University Press, 1977.

McKeown, Adam. *Melancholy Order: Asian Migration and the Globalization of Borders*. New York: Columbia University Press, 2008.

McLaughlin, Allan. "How Immigrants are Inspected." *Popular Science Monthly*, February 1905, 357–61.

McNeely, Ian F. *The Emancipation of Writing: German Civil Society in the Making, 1790s–1820s*. Berkeley: University of California Press, 2003.

Meaders, Daniel. "South Carolina Fugitives as Viewed through Local Colonial Newspapers with Emphasis on Runaway Notices 1732-1801." *Journal of Negro History* 60 (1975): 288–319.

Mencken, H. L. *The American Language: An Inquiry into the Development of English in the United States*. 4th ed. New York, Alfred Knopf, 1977.

———. *The American Language: An Inquiry into the Development of English in the United States: Supplement 2*. New York: Alfred Knopf, 1948.

Miller, Toby. *The Well-Tempered Self: Citizenship, Culture, and the Postmodern Subject*. Baltimore: Johns Hopkins University Press, 1993.

Mnookin, Jennifer L. "The Image of Truth: Photographic Evidence and the Power of Analogy." *Yale Journal of Law and the Humanities* 10 (1998): 1–74.

———. "Scripting Expertise: The History of Handwriting Identification Evidence And The Judicial Construction of Reliability." *Virginia Law Review* 87 (2001): 1723–1845.

Mongia, Radhika Viyas. "Race, Nationality, Mobility: A History of the Passport." *Public Culture* 11 (1999): 527–56.

Moore, John Bassett. *A Digest of International Law*, vol. 3. Washington, DC: Government Printing Office, 1906.

———. *The Works of James Buchanan, Comprising his Speeches, State Papers and Private Correspondence, Volumes 1-11*. Philadelphia: James B Lippincott, 1909.

Murphy, Paul L. *World War I and the Origin of Civil Liberties in the United States*. New York: Norton, 1979.

Neuman, Gerald L. " 'We Are the People': Alien Suffrage in German and American Perspective." *Michigan Journal of International Law* 13 (1991–92): 259–335.

Ngai, Mae M. "Illegal Aliens and Alien Citizens: United States Immigration Policy and Racial Formation, 1924–1945." PhD diss., Columbia University, 1998.

———. *Impossible Subjects: Illegal Aliens and the Making of Modern America*. Princeton, NJ: Princeton University Press, 2004.

Noiriel, Gérard. *The French Melting Pot: Immigration, Citizenship, and National Identity*. Translated by Geoffroy de Laforcade. Minneapolis: University of Minnesota Press, 1996.

Northedge, F. S. *The League of Nations: Its Life and Times, 1920–1946*. Leicester, UK: Leicester University Press, 1986.

Ogborn, Miles. *Indian Ink: Script and Print in the Making of the English East India Company*. Chicago, University of Chicago, 2007.

Orvell, Miles. *The Real Thing: Imitation and Authenticity in American Culture*. Chapel Hill: University of North Carolina Press, 1989.

Outlook. "The Question of Passports." April 7, 1926, 512.

———. "Why Passports?" September 22, 1926, 105.

Packer, Jeremy. *Mobility without Mayhem: Safety, Cars, and Citizenship*. Durham, NC: Duke University Press, 2008.

Peabody, Francis. "Americans Abroad." *North American Review* 201 (1915): 366–71.

Pear, Robert. "Citizens Who Lack Papers Lose Medicaid." *New York Times*, March 12, 2007.

Pegler-Gordon, Anna. "Chinese Exclusion, Photography, and the Development of U.S. Immigration Policy." *American Quarterly* 58 (2006): 51–77.

———. "In Sight of America: Photography and U.S. Immigration Policy, 1880–1930." Ph.D. diss., University of Michigan, 2002.

Perkins, Clifford Alan. *Border Patrol: With the U.S. Immigration Service on the Mexican Boundary, 1910–54*. El Paso: Texas Western Press, University of Texas at El Paso, 1978.

Peters, John Durham."Calendar, Clock, Tower." Paper, Media in Transition 6 conference, Cambridge, MA, April 25, 2009.

Pitkin, Thomas M. *Keepers of the Gate: A History of Ellis Island*. New York: New York University Press, 1975.

Poovey, Mary. *A History of the Modern Fact: Problems of Knowledge in the Sciences of Wealth and Society*. Chicago: University of Chicago Press, 1998.

Porter, Dorothy B. "Sarah Parker Remond, Abolitionist and Physician." *Journal of Negro History* 20 (1935): 287–93.

Potter, Dorothy Williams. *Passports of Southeastern Pioneers, 1770–1823: Indian, Spanish and other Land Passports for Tennessee, Kentucky, Georgia, Mississippi, Virginia, North and South Carolina*. Baltimore: Gateway, 1982.

Pryor, Elizabeth. " 'Jim Crow' Cars, Passport Denials and Atlantic Crossings: African-American Travel, Protest and Citizenship at Home and Abroad, 1827-1865." Ph.D diss., University of California, Santa Barbara, 2008.

Ramirez, Bruno. *Crossing the 49th Parallel: Migration from Canada to the United States, 1900–1930*. Ithaca, NY: Cornell University Press, 2001.
Rand, Erica. *The Ellis Island Snow Globe*. Durham, NC: Duke University Press, 2005.
Reale, Egidio. "Passport." In *Encyclopaedia of the Social Sciences*, vol. 12, 13–16. New York: Macmillan, 1934.
Reed, Alfred C. "Going Through Ellis Island." *Popular Science Monthly*, January 1913, 5–18.
———. "The Medical Side of Immigration." *Popular Science Monthly*, April 1912, 383–92.
Roberts, Kenneth. "Trial By Travel." *Saturday Evening Post*, September 4, 1920, 67–73.
Robertson, Craig. "A Documentary Regime of Verification: The Emergence of the US Passport and the Archival Problematization of Identity." *Cultural Studies* 23 (2009): 329–54.
———. "Locating the Border." *Social Identities* 14 (2008): 447–56.
Robertson, Frances. "The Aesthetics of Authenticity: Printed Banknotes as Industrial Currency." *Technology and Culture* 46 (2005): 31–50.
Rogers, Alan. "Passports and Politics: The Courts and the Cold War." *Historian* 47 (1985): 497–511.
Root, Elihu. "The Basis of Protection to Citizens Residing Abroad." *American Journal of International Law* 4 (1910): 517–28.
Russill, Chris. "For a Pragmatist Theory of Publics: Advancing Carey's Cultural Studies through John Dewey . . . and Michel Foucault?!" In *Thinking with James Carey: Essays on Communications, Transportation, History*, edited by Jeremy Packer and Craig Robertson, 57–78. New York: Peter Lang, 2006.
Safford, Victor. *Immigration Problems: Personal Experiences of an Official*. New York: Dodd Mead, 1925.
Salter, Mark B. *Rights of Passage: The Passport in International Relations*. Boulder, CO: Lynne Rienner, 2003.
Salyer, Lucy E. *Laws Harsh as Tigers: Chinese Immigrants and the Shaping of Modern Immigration Law*. Chapel Hill: University of North Carolina Press, 1995.
Sankar, Pamela. "State Power and Record-Keeping: The History of Individualized Surveillance in the United States, 1790–1935." PhD diss., University of Pennsylvania, 1992.
Sapiro, Virginia. "Women, Citizenship, and Nationality: Immigration and Naturalization Policies in the United States." *Politics and Society* 13 (1984): 1–26.
Sayles, Mary B. "The Keepers of the Gate." *Outlook*, December 28, 1907, 913–23.
Schiller, Dan. *How to Think About Information*. Urbana: University of Illinois Press, 2007.
Sciolino, Elaine. "World Opinion is Fragmented on Tighter Security for Visitors." *New York Times*, January 7, 2004.
Scott, James C. *Seeing Like a State: How Certain Schemes to Improve the Human Condition Have Failed*. New Haven, CT: Yale University Press, 1998.
Sekula, Allan. "The Body and the Archive." *October* 39, no. 3 (1986), 3–64.
Sellin, Thorsten. "Identification." In *Encyclopaedia of the Social Sciences*, vol. 7, 573–74. New York: Macmillan, 1932.

Senner, Joseph H. "How We Restrict Immigration." *North American Review* 158 (1894): 494–99.

Shah, Nayan. *Contagious Divides: Epidemics and Race in San Francisco's Chinatown.* Berkeley: University of California Press, 2001.

Shapiro, S. "Development of Birth Registration and Birth Statistics in the United States." *Population Studies* 4 (1950): 86–111.

Shell, Marc. *Money, Language, and Thought: Literary and Philosophical Economies from the Medieval to the Modern Era.* Berkeley: University of California Press, 1982.

Sherwood, Herbert. "The Silent Keeper of the Gate." *Outlook*, June 6, 1908, 289–96.

Sibley, N. W. "The Passport System." *Journal of the Society of Comparative Legislation* 7 (1906): 26–33.

Sillco, Herbert A. "Passport Fees Too High." *New York Times*, February 23, 1921.

Skowronek, Stephen. *Building a New American State: The Expansion of National Administrative Capacities, 1870–1920.* Cambridge, UK: Cambridge University Press, 1982.

Smith, Rogers M. *Civic Ideals: Conflicting Visions of Citizenship in U.S. History.* New Haven, CT: Yale University Press, 1997.

Smith, Shawn Michelle. *American Archives: Gender, Race, and Class in Visual Culture.* Princeton, NJ: Princeton University Press, 1999.

Sonneborn, Hilton Burnside. "Easing Passport Difficulties." *New York Times*, March 5, 1929.

Sprague, E. K. "Medical Inspection of Immigrants." *Survey* 30 (April–September 1913): 420–22.

Stannard, Una. "Manners Make Laws: Married Women's Names in the United States." *Names* 32, no. 3 (1984): 114–18.

Stein, Douglas L. "Passports and Sea Letters: Protection Documents for American Ships, ca. 1789–1860." *The Log of Mystic Seaport* 44 (1992): 18–20.

Steiner Edward A. *On The Trail of the Immigrant.* New York: F. H. Revell, 1906.

Stevens, Jacqueline. *Reproducing the State.* Princeton, NJ: Princeton University Press, 1999.

Strickland, E. F. "Would Abolish Passports." *New York Times*, November 9, 1924.

Stuart, Graham H. *The Department of State: A History of its Organization, Procedure, and Personnel.* New York: Macmillan, 1949.

Sun, Wen-chu Torrey. "Regulation of the Foreign Travel of U.S. Citizens." PhD diss., Claremont Graduate University, 1993.

Survey. "Taking the Queue out of Quota: an Interview with W. W. Husband, Commissioner-General of Immigration." March 15, 1924, 667–69.

Susman, Warren I. *Culture as History: The Transformation of American Society in the Twentieth Century.* New York: Pantheon, 1984.

Tagg, John. *The Burden of Representation: Essays on Photographies and Histories.* Amherst: University of Massachusetts Press, 1988.

Tappen, John W. "The Medical Inspection of Immigrants with Special Reference to the Texas-Mexican Border." *Texas State Journal of Medicine* 15 (July 1919): 120–24.

Taylor, Charles S. "Passport Data." *New York Times*, June 1, 1934.

Thornton, Tamara Plakins. *Handwriting in America: A Cultural History.* New Haven, CT: Yale University Press, 1996.

Tice, Karen W. *Tales of Wayward Girls and Immoral Women: Case Records and the Professionalization of Social Work*. Urbana: University of Illinois Press, 1998.

Torpey, John. "The Great War and the Birth of the Modern Passport System." In *Documenting Individual Identity: The Development of State Practices in the Modern World*, edited by Jane Caplan and John Torpey, 256–70. Princeton, NJ: Princeton University Press, 2001.

———. *The Invention of the Passport: Surveillance, Citizenship, and the State*. Cambridge, UK: Cambridge University Press, 1999.

Trachtenberg, Alan. "Likeness as Identity: Reflections on the Daguerrean Mystique." In *The Portrait in Photography*, edited by Graham Clarke, 173–221. London: Reaktion Books, 1992.

Tsiang, I-Mien. "The Question of Expatriation in America Prior to 1907." PhD diss., Johns Hopkins University, 1941.

Turack, Daniel C. "Freedom of Movement and the International Regime of Passports." *Osgoode Hall Law Journal* 6 (1968): 230–51.

United Nations Library. *The League of Nations in Retrospect: Proceedings of the Symposium*. New York: Walter de Gruyter, 1983.

Unrau, Harlan D. *Ellis Island, Statue of Liberty National Monument, New York-New Jersey*. Vol. 2. Washington, DC: U.S. Department. of the Interior, National Park Service, 1984.

U.S. Bureau of Immigration. *Annual Report of the Commissioner General of Immigration to the Secretary of Commerce and Labor*. Washington, DC: Government Printing Office, 1911–30.

U.S. Congress. House. Committee on the Census. *Authorizing the Director of the Census to Issue Birth Certificates: Hearing before the Committee on the Census*. 77th Cong., 2nd sess., June 4, 9, 10, 1942.

U.S. Congress. House. Committee on Foreign Affairs. *Termination of the Treaty Between the United States and Russia: Hearings*. 62nd Cong., 2nd sess., December 11, 1911.

———. *Control of Travel From and Into the United States: Hearings*. 65th Cong., 2nd sess., February 18, 1918.

———. *Extension of Passport Control: Hearings*. 66th Cong., 1st sess., October 7, 8, 10, 1919.

———. *Fees Charged for Passports and for Viséing Foreign Passports: Hearings*. 66th Cong., 2nd sess., February 3, 4, 7, 1920.

———. *Further Regulating the Granting of Visas By Diplomatic and Consular Officers: Hearings*. 66th Cong., 3rd sess., January 5, 22, 24, 28, 31, 1921.

———. *Modification of Vise Requirements: Hearings*. 68th Cong., 2nd sess., January 26, 28, 1925.

———. *Restricting Passport Visas in Certain Cases: Hearings*. 69th Cong. 1st sess. March 23, 1926.

———. *Validity of Passports: Hearings*. 69th Cong.,1st sess., May 12, 1926.

———. *Passport Renewals: Hearings*. 71st Cong., 2nd sess., April 15, 16, 1930.

U.S. Congress. House. Committee on Immigration and Naturalization. *Registration of Aliens: Hearings*. 64th Cong. 2nd sess., February 28, 1917.

———. *Conditions at Ellis Island: Hearings*. 66th Cong. 1st sess., November 24, 26, 28, 1919.

———. *Admission of Aliens in Excess of Percentage Quotas for June: Hearings.* 67th Cong. 2nd sess., June 10, 1921.

———. *Immigration Border Patrol: Hearings.* 70th Cong., 1st sess., March 5, 1928.

———. *Immigration Border Patrol: Hearings.* 71st Cong., 2nd sess., January 15, 1930.

———. *Review of the Action of Consular Offices in Refusing Immigration Visas: Hearings.* 72nd Cong., 1st sess., March 16, 1932.

———. *Review of Refusal of Visas by Consular Officers: Hearings.* 73rd Cong., 1st sess., May 18, 23, 1933.

U.S. Congress. House. Committee on Interstate and Foreign Commerce. *Border Patrol: Hearings.* 71st Cong., 2nd sess., April 24, 25, 1930.

U.S. Congress. House. Committee of the Judiciary. *To Create a National Police Bureau, to Create a Bureau of Criminal Identification: Hearings.* 68th Cong. 1st sess., April 17, 24, 1924.

———. *To Establish a Border Patrol: Hearings.* 69th Cong., 1st sess., April 12, 19, 1926.

U.S. Department of Commerce and Labor. *Annual Report of the Commissioner General of Immigration.* Washington, DC: Government Printing Office, 1905.

U.S. Department of Justice. *Annual Report of the Attorney General of the United States, 1918.* Washington, DC: Government Printing Office, 1918.

———. *Official Opinions of the Attorneys-General of the United States*, vol. 10. Washington, DC: Government Printing Office, 1862.

———. *Official Opinions of the Attorneys-General of the United States*, vol. 14. Washington, DC: Government Printing Office, 1875.

U.S. Department of State. *Compilation of Certain Departmental Circulars Relating to Citizenship, Registration of American Citizens, Issuance of Passports, etc.* Washington, DC: Government Printing Office, 1925.

———. *The Immigration Work of the Department of State and its Consular Officers.* Washington, DC: Government Printing Office, 1932.

———. *Papers Relating to the Foreign Relations of the United States.* Washington: Government Printing Office, 1870–1930.

U.S. Passport Office. *The United States Passport: Past, Present, Future.* Washington, DC: Government Printing Office, 1976.

U.S. Senate. Committee on Commerce. *Border Patrol Part 1–3: Hearings.* 71st Cong., 2nd sess., December 18, 1930, January 15, 1931.

Victim, A. [pseudo.]. Passport Difficulties." *New York Times*, March 17, 1929.

Vox Populi [pseudo.]. "Passports." *New York* Times, July 31 1874.

Walters, F. P. *A History of the League of Nations.* London: Oxford University Press, 1952.

Warner, Michael. *The Letters of the Republic: Publication and the Public Sphere in Eighteenth-Century America.* Cambridge, MA: Harvard University Press, 1990.

Watchorn, Robert. "The Gateway of the Nation." *Outlook*, December 28, 1907, 897–911.

Weber, Max. "Bureaucracy." In *From Max Weber: Essays in Sociology*, edited by H. H. Gerth and C. Wright Mills, 96–244. New York: Oxford University Press, 1946.

———. *From Max Weber: Essays in Sociology.* Edited by H. H. Gerth and C. Wright Mills. New York: Oxford University Press, 1946.

Wharton, Francis. *A Digest of International Law of the United States*, vol. 2. Washington, DC: Government Printing Office, 1886.

White, Leonard D. *The Republican Era: A Study in Administrative History, 1869–1901*. With the assistance of Jean Schneider. New York: Macmillan, 1958.

White, William C. "Ellis Island Altered by Immigration Trend." *New York Times*, October 8, 1933.

Wilbur, Cressy L. *The Federal Registration Service of the United States: Its Development, Problems, and Defects*. Washington, DC: Government Printing Office, 1916.

Wilson, Huntington. "The American Foreign Service." *Outlook*, March 3, 1906, 499–504.

Wilson, Stephen. *The Means of Naming: A Social and Cultural History of Personal Naming in Western Europe*. London: University College London Press, 1998.

Woodbury, Helen. "A New Era in Travel." *Independent*, October 3, 1925, 391.

World's Work. "Borah on Local Self-Government." June 1925, 127–28.

———. "Passports for Summer Travel." June 1930, 22.

Yates, JoAnne. "Business Use of Information and Technology During the Industrial Age." In *A Nation Transformed By Information: How Information Has Shaped the United States from Colonial Times to the Present*, edited by Alfred D. Chandler Jr. and James W. Corteda, 107–36. Oxford: Oxford University Press, 2000.

———. *Control Through Communication: The Rise of System in American Management*. Baltimore: Johns Hopkins University Press, 1989.

———. "From Press Book and Pigeonhole to Vertical Filing: Revolution in Storage and Access Systems for Correspondence." *Journal of Business Communication* 19, no. 3 (1982): 5–26.

Ybarra, T. R. "Passport Worries in Europe." *New York Times*, February 6, 1921.

———. "Seize Reds' Store of False Passports." *New York Times*, October 19, 1924.

Yew, Elizabeth. "Medical Inspection of Immigrants at Ellis Island, 1891–1924." *Bulletin of the New York Academy of Medicine* 56 (1980): 488–510.

Zelizer, Viviana A. *The Social Meaning of Money: Pin Money, Pay Checks, Poor Relief, and Other Currencies*. Princeton, NJ: Princeton University Press, 1994.

Zolberg, Aristide R. "The Great Wall Against China: Responses to the First Immigration Crisis, 1855–1925." In *Migration, Migration History, History: Old Paradigms and New Perspectives*, edited by Jan Lucassen and Leo Lucassen, 291–316. Bern, Switzerland: Peter Lang, 1997.

Index